A Literary Chronicle: 1920–1950

Edmund Wilson

A LITERARY
CHRONICLE:
1920–1950

Doubleday Anchor Books
Doubleday & Company, Inc.
Garden City, New York, 1956

Edmund Wilson was born on May 8, 1895, in Red Bank, New Jersey, and was educated at Princeton. He is the author of a novel, *I Thought of Daisy* (1929); two volumes of poetry; an historical study, *To the Finland Station* (1940); short stories, *Memoirs of Hecate County* (1946); and several plays. He is perhaps best known for his works of criticism, among them *Axel's Castle* (1931), *The Triple Thinkers* (1938), *The Wound and the Bow* (1941), and for his journalism, collected in *Classics and Commercials* (1950) and *The Shores of Light* (1952), from which the present volume is derived. Mr. Wilson's most recent book is *The Scrolls from the Dead Sea* (1955).

The Shores of Light and *Classics and Commercials* are published in hardbound editions by Farrar, Straus and Cudahy, Inc.

Cover and typography by Edward Gorey

CONTENTS

Prologue, 1952: Christian Gauss as a Teacher of
    Literature   9
F. Scott Fitzgerald   30
Ring Lardner's American Characters   37
Emergence of Ernest Hemingway   41
Gilbert Seldes and the Popular Arts   49
Poe at Home and Abroad   65
The All-Star Literary Vaudeville   76
Mencken's Democratic Man   92
The Sportsman's Tragedy   96
Thornton Wilder   102
The Death of Elinor Wylie   109
Signs of Life: *Lady Chatterley's Lover*   113
Dostoevsky Abroad   117
Citizen of the Union   123
Dos Passos and the Social Revolution   128
T. S. Eliot and the Church of England   133
Dahlberg, Dos Passos and Wilder   138
Notes on Babbitt and More   146
The Nietzschean Line   161
Lytton Strachey   166
André Malraux   171
The Literary Worker's Polonius   178
Letter to the Russians about Hemingway   194
It's Terrible! It's Ghastly! It Stinks!   206
Twilight of the Expatriates   211
The Boys in the Back Room   216
Alexander Woollcott of the Phalanx   249
Mr. Joseph E. Davies as a Stylist   254

CONTENTS

The Life and Times of John Barrymore   259

"Never Apologize, Never Explain": The Art of Evelyn Waugh   265

What Became of Louis Bromfield   271

J. Dover Wilson on Falstaff   278

A Toast and a Tear for Dorothy Parker   284

A Treatise on Tales of Horror   287

A Guide to *Finnegans Wake*   295

A Long Talk about Jane Austen   302

"You Can't Do This to Me!" Shrilled Celia   309

Katherine Anne Porter   313

A Picture to Hang in the Library: Brooks's Age of Irving   317

Why Do People Read Detective Stories?   323

Reëxamining Dr. Johnson   328

Leonid Leonov: The Sophistication of a Formula   333

Who Cares Who Killed Roger Ackroyd?   338

"Mr. Holmes, They Were the Footprints of a Gigantic Hound!"   346

Splendors and Miseries of Evelyn Waugh   353

George Saintsbury's Centenary   359

Ambushing a Best-Seller   363

Oscar Wilde: "One Must Always Seek What Is Most Tragic"   369

Books of Etiquette and Emily Post   380

A Dissenting Opinion on Kafka   389

Jean-Paul Sartre: The Novelist and the Existentialist   398

The Musical Glasses of Peacock   407

The Original of Tolstoy's Natasha   413

William Faulkner's Reply to the Civil-Rights Program   422

Index   432

Christian Gauss as a Teacher of Literature

WHEN Christian Gauss of Princeton died on November 3, 1951, I was asked by the Princeton *Alumni Weekly* to write something for a set of tributes that were to appear in the issue of December 7. I sent the editor, who wanted a column, only part of what I had written in response to this request, and even this was much cut before it was printed. I have now further elaborated my original memoir, and I am including it here to serve as a sort of prologue, for it indicates to some extent the point of view from which I started off in my criticism of the twenties.

I have been asked to write about Christian Gauss as an influence on my generation at Princeton. Since we knew him as a teacher of literature only—I was in the class of 1916, and he did not become dean of the college till 1925—I shall speak mainly of this side of his activity.

As a professor of French and Italian, then, one of the qualities that distinguished Gauss was the unusual fluidity of mind that he preserved through his whole career. A teacher like Irving Babbitt was a dogmatist who either imposed his dogma or provoked a strong opposition. Christian Gauss was a teacher of a different kind—the kind who starts trains of thought that he does not himself guide to conclusions but leaves in the hands of his students to be carried on by themselves. The student might develop, extend them, transpose them into different terms, build out of them constructions of his own. Gauss never imposed, he suggested; and his own ideas on any subject were always taking new turns: the light in which he saw it would be shifted, it would range itself in some new context. It bored him, in his course on French Romanticism, to teach the same texts year after year; and with the writers that he could not get away from, he would vary the works read. With the less indispensable ones, he would change the repertory altogether. If Alfred de Vigny, for example, had been featured in the course when you took it, you might come back a few years later and find that he had been pushed into the background by Stendhal. Christian would have been reading up Stendhal, and his interest in him would seem almost as fresh as if he had never read him before. He would have some new insights about him, and he would pass these on to you when you came to see him, as he was doing to his students in class. I know from my own experience how the lightly dropped seeds from his lectures could take root and unfold in another's mind; and, while occupied in writing this memoir, I have happened to find striking evidence of the persistence of this vital gift in the testimony of a student of Romance languages who sat under Gauss twenty years later, and who has told me that, in preparing his doctor's thesis, he had at first been exhilarated by an illusion of developing original ideas, only to find the whole thing in germ in his old notes on Gauss's lectures. But though his influence on his students was so penetrating, Gauss founded no school of teaching—not even, I suppose, an academic tradition—because, as one of his colleagues pointed out to me, he had no communicable body of doctrine and no pedagogical method that other teachers could learn to apply. If one went back to Princeton to see him, as I more or less regularly did, after one had got out of college, one's memory of his old preceptorials (relatively informal discussions with groups of five or six students) would seem prolonged, without interruptions, into one's more recent conversations, as if it had all been a long conversation that had extended, off and on, through the years: a commentary that, on Christian's part, never seemed to be trying to prove anything in any overwhelming way, a voyage of speculation that aimed rather to survey the world than to fix a convincing vision. In his role of the least didactic of sages, the most accessible of talkers, he seemed a part of that good eighteenth-century Princeton which has always managed to flourish between the pressures of a narrow Presbyterianism and a rich man's suburbanism. It is probable that Christian was at home in Princeton as he would not have been anywhere else. He was delightful in the days of his deanship, in the solid and compact and ample yellow-and-white Joseph Henry house, built in 1837, where there was always, during the weekends, a constant going and coming of visitors, who could pick up with him any topic, literary, historical or collegiate, and pursue it till someone else came and the thread was left suspended. Though by this time so important a local figure, he seemed always, also, international. He had been born of German parents in Michigan, and German had been his first language. In his youth he had spent a good deal of time in France. He had no foreign accent in English, and, so far as I was able to judge, spoke all his languages correctly and fluently; but French, Italian and English, at any rate, with a deliberate articulation, never running the words together, as if they were not native to him. One did not learn a bad accent from him, but one did not learn to speak the Romance languages as they are spoken in their own countries. On the other hand, the very uniformity of his candid tone, his unhurried pace and his scrupulous precision, with his slightly drawling intonations, made a kind of neutral medium in which everything in the world seemed soluble. I have never known anyone like him in any academic community. He gave the impression of keeping in touch, without the slightest effort—he must have examined all the printed matter that came into the university library—with everything that was going on everywhere, as well as everything that had ever gone on. It used to amuse me sometimes to try him out on unlikely subjects. If one asked him a question about the Middle Ages, one absolutely got the impression that he had lived in Europe then and knew it at firsthand.

This extreme flexibility and enormous range were, of course, a feature of his lectures. He was able to explain and

appreciate almost any kind of work of literature from almost
any period. He would show you what the author was aiming at and the methods he had adopted to achieve his ends.
He was wonderful at comparative literature, for his reading
had covered the whole of the West, ancient, medieval and
modern, and his memory was truly Macaulayan (an ad-
jective sometimes assigned too cheaply). He seemed to be
able to summon almost anything he wanted in prose or
verse, as if he were taking down the book from the shelf.
(He told me once that, in his younger days, he had set
out to write something about Rabelais and had presently
begun to grow suspicious of what he saw coming out. On
looking up Taine's essay on Rabelais, he found that he had
been transcribing whole paragraphs from it, his unconscious doing the work of translation.) He was brilliant at
revealing the assumptions, social, aesthetic and moral, implicit in, say, a scene from a romantic play as contrasted
with a scene from a Greek tragedy, or in the significance of
a character in Dante as distinguished from the significance
of a character in Shakespeare. I remember his later quoting
with approval A. N. Whitehead's statement, in *Science and
the Modern World,* that, "when you are criticizing the
philosophy of an epoch," you should "not chiefly direct your
attention to those intellectual positions which its exponents
feel it necessary explicitly to defend. There will be some
fundamental assumptions which adherents of all the variant
systems within the epoch unconsciously presuppose. Such
assumptions appear so obvious that people do not know
what they are assuming because no other way of putting
things has ever occurred to them." Gauss had always had
a special sense of this. But he was interested also in individuals and liked to bring out the traits of a literary personality. His commentary on a poem of Victor Hugo's—*Le
Mendiant* from *Les Contemplations*—would run along something like this: "A poor man is passing in the frost and rain,
and Victor Hugo asks him in. He opens the door *'d'une
façon civile'*—he is always democratic, of course. *'Entrez,
brave homme,'* he says, and he tells the man to warm him-

self and has a bowl of milk brought him—as anybody, of course, would do. He makes him take off his cloak—'*tout mangé des vers, et jadis bleu*'—and he hangs it on a nail, where the fire shines through its holes, so that it looks like a night illumined by stars.

> Et, pendant qu'il séchait ce haillon désolé
> D'où ruisselaient le pluie et l'eau des fondrières,
> Je songeais que cet homme était plein de prières.
> Et je regardais, sourd à ce que nous disions,
> Sa bure où je voyais des constellations.

"This sounds impressive, but what does it mean? Not a thing. We have not been told anything that would indicate that the old man is full of prayers. It is a gratuitous assumption on the part of Hugo. That the cloak with its holes reminded him of a heaven with constellations has no moral significance whatever. Yet with his mastery of verse and his rhetoric, Victor Hugo manages to carry it off.—I don't mean," he would add, "that he was insincere. Rather than live under Louis Napoleon, he went into voluntary exile—at considerable personal inconvenience—for almost twenty years. He lived up to his democratic principles, but he was always a bit theatrical, and he was not very profound."

I include such reminiscences of the classroom in the hope that they may be of interest in putting on record Gauss's methods as a teacher, for the work of a great teacher who is not, as Gauss was not, a great writer is almost as likely to be irrecoverable as the work of a great actor. Not that Christian was ever in the least histrionic, as some of the popular professors of the time were. On the contrary, for all the friendliness of one's relations with him outside class when one eventually got to know him, his tone was sober and quiet, his attitude detached and impersonal. This was partly due to shyness, no doubt; but the impression he made was formidable. He would come into the classroom without looking at us, and immediately begin to lecture, with his eyes dropped to his notes, presenting a mask that was almost Dantesque and levelling on us only occasionally the clear gaze that came through his eyeglasses. When he made us recite in Dante, he would sometimes pace to and fro between the desk and the window, with his hands behind his back, rarely consulting the text, which he apparently knew by heart. In the case of some appalling error, he would turn with a stare of ironic amazement and remonstrate in a tone of mock grief: "You thought that barretry was the same as banditry? O-o-oh, Mr. X, that's too-oo ba-a-ad!" This last exclamation, drawled out, was his only way of indicating disapproval. His voice was always low and even, except at those moments when he became aware that the class was falling asleep, when he would turn on another voice, loud, nasal, declamatory and pitilessly distinct, which would be likely to begin in the middle of a sentence for the sake of the shock-value, I think, and in order to dissociate this special effect from whatever he happened to be saying—which might be something no more blood-curdling than a statement that André Chénier had brought to the classical forms a nuance of romantic feeling. When this voice would be heard in the class next door—for it penetrated the partition like a fire-siren—it always made people laugh; but for the students in Gauss's own room, it seemed to saw right through the base of the spine and made them sit forward intently. When it had had this effect, it would cease. He was never sarcastic and never bullied; but the discipline he maintained was perfect. Any signs of disorder were silenced by one straight and stern look.

Nevertheless, though Christian's methods were nondramatic, he had a knack of fixing in one's mind key passages and key facts. His handling of Rousseau, for example, was most effective in building up the importance of a writer whom we might otherwise find boring. (In this case, he *has* left something that can be used by his successors in his volume of *Selections* from Rousseau, published by the Princeton University Press—though, as usual with Gauss's writing, the introduction and notes have little of the peculiar effectiveness of his lecture-room presentation.) He would start off by planting, as it were, in our vision of the panorama of history that critical moment of Rousseau's life which, since he did not include it in the *Confessions*, having already described it in the first of his letters to M. de Malesherbes, is likely to be overlooked or insufficiently emphasized (compare Saintsbury's slurring-over of this incident and its consequences for Western thought, in his *Encyclopaedia Britannica* article): the moment, almost as momentous as that of Paul's conversion on the road to Damascus, when Jean-Jacques, then thirty-seven, was walking from Paris to Vincennes, where he was going to see Diderot in prison, and happened to read the announcement that the Academy of Dijon was offering a prize for the best essay on the question, "Has the progress of the arts and sciences contributed to corrupt or to purify society?" Such an incident Gauss made memorable, invested with reverberating significance, by a series of incisive strokes that involved no embroidery or dramatics. It was, in fact, as if the glamor of legend, the grandeur of history, had evaporated and left him exposed to our passing gaze, the dusty and sunstruck Jean-Jacques—the clockmaker's son of Geneva, the ill-used apprentice, the thieving lackey, the vagabond of the roads—sinking down under a tree and dazzled by the revelation that all the shames and misfortunes of his life had been the fault of the society that had bred him—that "man is naturally good and that it is only through institutions that men have become wicked." In the same way, he made us feel the pathos and the psychological importance of the moment when the sixteen-year-old apprentice, returning from a walk in the country, found for the third time the gates of Geneva locked against him, and decided that he would never go back.

Christian admired the romantics and expounded them with the liveliest appreciation; but the romantic ideal in literature was not his own ideal. In spite of his imaginative gift for entering into other people's points of view, he was devoted to a certain conception of art that inevitably asserted itself and that had a tremendous influence on the students with literary interests who were exposed to Gauss's teaching. Let me try to define this ideal. Christian had first known Europe at firsthand as a foreign correspondent in the Paris of the late nineties, and he had always kept a certain loyalty to the "aestheticism" of the end of the century. There was a legend that seemed almost incredible of a young Christian Gauss with long yellow hair—in our time he was almost completely bald—who had worn a green velvet jacket;* and he would surprise you from time to time by telling you of some conversation he had had with Oscar Wilde or describing some such bohemian character as Bibi-La-Purée. It was rumored—though I never dared ask him about this—that he had once set out to experiment one by one with all the drugs mentioned in Baudelaire's *Les Paradis Artificiels*. He rather admired Wilde, with whom he had talked in cafés, where the latter was sitting alone and running up high piles of saucers. He had given Christian copies of his books, inscribed; and Christian used to tell me, with evident respect, that Wilde in his last days had kept only three volumes: a copy of Walter Pater's *The Renaissance* that had been given him by Pater, Flaubert's *La Tentation de Saint Antoine* and Swinburne's *Atalanta in Calydon*. And it was always Gauss's great advantage over the school of Babbitt and More that he understood the artist's morality as something that expressed itself in different terms than the churchgoer's or the citizen's morality; the fidelity to a kind of truth that is rendered by the discipline of aesthetic form, as distinct from that of the professional moralist: the explicit communication of a "message." But there was nothing in his attitude of the truculent pose, the defiance of the bourgeoisie, that had been characteristic of the fin de siècle and that that other professor of the Romance languages, Gauss's near-contemporary, Ezra Pound, was to sustain through his whole career. How fundamental to his point of view, how much a thing to be taken for granted, this attitude had become,

---

* I learn from Mrs. Gauss, who has shown me a photograph, that the realities behind this legend were a head of blond bushy hair and a jacket which, though green, was not velvet.

was shown clearly in a conversation I had with him, on some occasion when I had come back after college, when, in reply to some antinomian attitude of mine, or one that he imputed to me, he said, "But you were saying just now that you would have to rewrite something before it could be published. That implies a moral obligation." And his sense of the world and the scope of art was, of course, something very much bigger than was common among the aesthetes and the symbolists.

Partly perhaps as a heritage from the age of Wilde but, more deeply, as a logical consequence of his continental origin and culture, he showed a pronounced though discreet parti pris against the literature of the Anglo-Saxon countries. In our time, he carried on a continual feud—partly humorous, yet basically serious—with the canons of the English department. I remember his telling me, with sly satisfaction, about a visiting French professor, who had asked, when it was explained to him that someone was an authority on Chaucer, "Il est intelligent tout de même?" Certain classical English writers he patronized—in some cases, rightly, I think. Robert Browning, in particular, he abominated. The author of Pippa Passes was one of the very few writers about whom I thought his opinions intemperate. "That Philistine beef-eating Englishman," he would bait his colleagues in English, "—what did he know about art? He writes lines like 'Irks care the crop-full bird? Frets doubt the maw-crammed beast?'" When I tried to find out once why Browning moved Christian to such special indignation, he told me, a little darkly, that he had greatly admired him in boyhood and had learned from him "a lot of bad doctrine." He said that the irregular love affairs in Browning were made to seem too jolly and simple, and insisted that the situation of the self-frustrated lovers of The Statue and the Bust had never been faced by Browning: If "the end in sight was a vice," the poet should not have wanted to have them get together; if he wanted them to get together, he ought not to have described it as a vice, but, on the other hand, he ought to have foreseen a mess. "He is one of the most immoral poets because he makes moral problems seem easy. He tells you that the good is sure to triumph." He would suggest to you an embarrassing picture of a Browning offensively hearty—"not robust," he would say slily, "but robustious"—bouncing and booming in Italy, while the shades of Leopardi and Dante looked on, as Boccaccio said of the latter, *con isdegnoso occhio.* The kind of thing he especially hated was such a poem as the one, in *James Lee's Wife,* that begins, "O good gigantic smile o' the brown old earth." . . . Of Byron— though Byron's writing was certainly more careless than Browning's—he had a much better opinion, because, no doubt, of Byron's fondness for the Continent as well as his freer intelligence and his experience of the ills of the world. He accepted Byron's love affairs—he had nothing of the prig or the Puritan—because Byron knew what he was doing and was not misleading about it. As for Shakespeare, though Christian was, of course, very far from the point of view of Voltaire, there was always just a suggestion of something of the kind in the background. He knew Shakespeare well and quoted him often, but Shakespeare was not one of the authors whom Christian had lived in or on; and he always made us feel that that sort of thing could never come up to literature that was polished and carefully planned and that knew how to make its points and the meaning of the points it was making. He was certainly unfair to Shakespeare in insisting that the Shakespearean characters all talk the same language, whereas Dante's all express themselves differently. For Christian, the great poet was Dante, and he gradually convinced you of this in his remarkable Dante course. He made us see the objectivity of Dante and the significance of his every stroke, so that even the geographical references have a moral and emotional force (the Po that finds peace with its tributaries in the Paolo and Francesca episode, the mountain in the Ugolino canto that prevents the Pisans from seeing their neighbors of Lucca); the vividness of the scenes and the characters (he liked to point out how Farinata's arrogant poise was thrown into dramatic relief by the passionate interruption of Cavalcanti); and the tremendous intellectual power by which all sorts of men and women exhibiting all sorts of passions have been organized in an orderly vision that implies, also, a reasoned morality. No Englishman, he made us feel, could ever have achieved this; it would never have occurred to Shakespeare. Nor could any English novelist have even attempted what Gustave Flaubert had achieved—a personal conception of the world, put together, without a visible seam, from apparently impersonal descriptions, in which, as in Dante, not a stroke was wasted. He admired the Russians, also, for their sober art of implication. I remember his calling our attention to one of the church scenes in Tolstoy's *Resurrection*, in which, as he pointed out, Tolstoy made no overt comment, yet caused you to loathe the whole thing by describing the ceremony step by step. This non-English, this classical and Latin ideal, became indissolubly associated in our minds with the summits of literature. We got from Gauss a good many things, but the most important things we got were probably Flaubert and Dante. John Peale Bishop, who came to Princeton intoxicated with Swinburne and Shelley, was concentrating, by the time he graduated, on hard images and pregnant phrases. Ezra Pound and the imagists, to be sure, had a good deal to do with this, but Gauss's courses were important, too, and such an early poem of Bishop's as *Losses*, which contrasts Verlaine with Dante, was directly inspired by them. Less directly, perhaps, but no less certainly, the development of F. Scott Fitzgerald from *This Side of Paradise* to *The Great Gatsby*, from a loose and subjective conception of the novel to an organized impersonal one, was also due to Christian's influence. He made us all want to write something in which every word, every cadence, every detail, should perform a definite function in producing an intense effect.

Gauss's special understanding of the techniques of art was combined, as is not always the case, with a highly developed sense of history, as well as a sense of morality (he admirably prepared us for Joyce and Proust). If he played down—as I shall show in a moment—the Thomist side of Dante to make us see him as a great artist, he brought out in Flaubert the moralist and the bitter critic of history. And so much, at that period, was all his thought pervaded by the *Divine Comedy* that even his own version of history had at moments a Dantesque touch. It would not have been difficult, for example, to transpose such a presentation as the one of Rousseau that I have mentioned above into the sharp concise self-description of a character in the *Divina Commedia:* "I am the clockmaker's son of Geneva who said that man has made man perverse. When for the third time the cruel captain closed the gates, I made the sky my roof, and found in Annecy the love Geneva had denied" . . .

With this sense of history of Christian's was involved another strain in his nature that had nothing to do with the aestheticism of the nineties and yet that lived in his mind with it quite comfortably. His father, who came from Baden—he was a relative of the physicist Karl Friedrich Gauss—had taken part in the unsuccessful German revolution of 1848 and come to the United States with the emigration that followed it. The spirit of '48 was still alive in Christian, and at the time of the first World War an hereditary hatred of the Prussians roused him to a passionate championship of the anti-German cause even before the United States declared war. Later on, when Prohibition was imposed on the nation, the elder Gauss, as Christian told me, was so much infuriated by what he regarded as an interference nothing short of Prussian with the rights of a free people that he could not talk calmly about it, and, even when dean of the college and obliged to uphold the law, the American-born Christian continued in public to advocate its repeal, which required a certain courage in Presbyterian Princeton. It was this old-fashioned devotion to liberty that led him to admire Hugo for his refusal to live under the Second Empire, and Byron for his willingness to fight for Italian and Greek liberation. "Everywhere he goes in Europe," Christian would say of Byron, "it is the places, such as the prison of Chillon, where men have been oppressed, that arouse him." When he lectured on Anatole France, he would point out the stimulating contrast between the early France of *Sylvestre Bonnard,* who always wrote, as he said, like a kindly and bookish old man, and the France who defended Dreyfus, made a tour of the provinces to speak for him and remained for the rest of his life a social satirist and a radical publicist. In the years when I was first at Princeton, Gauss called himself, I believe, a socialist; and during the years of depression in the thirties, he gravitated again toward the Left and, in *A Primer for Tomorrow* (1934), he made some serious attempt to criticize the financial-industrial system. In an inscription in the copy he sent me, he said that my stimulation had counted for something in his writing the book. But I was never able to persuade him to read Marx and Engels at firsthand: he read Werner Sombart instead; and I noted this, like the similar reluctance of Maynard Keynes to look into Marx, as a curious confirmation of the theory of the Marxists that the "bourgeois intellectuals" instinctively shy away from Marxist thought to the extent of even refusing to find out what it really is. Yet Christian had read Spengler with excitement—it was from him that I first heard of *The Decline of the West*—immediately after the war; and he never, in these later years, hesitated, in conversation, to indulge the boldest speculations as to the destiny of contemporary society.

He was a member of the National Committee of the American Civil Liberties Union, and he made a point, after the second war, of speaking to Negro audiences in the South. On my last visit to Princeton when I saw him, in the spring of 1951, he talked to me at length about his adventures in the color-discrimination states—how the representatives of some Negro organization under whose auspices he had been speaking had been unable to come to see him in his white hotel, and how, as he told me with pride, he had succeeded, for the first time in the history of Richmond, in assembling—in a white church, to which, however, he found the Negroes were only admitted on condition of their sitting in the back pews—a mixed black and white audience. As he grew older, he became more internationalist. He foresaw, and he often insisted, at the end of the first World War, that nothing but trouble could come of creating more small European states, and, at the end of the second war, he was bitterly opposed to what he regarded as the development of American nationalism. He complained much, in this connection, of the intensive cultivation, in the colleges, of American literature, which had been carried on since sometime in the middle thirties with a zeal that he thought more and more menacing to sound international values. I did not, on the whole, agree with him in disapproving of the growth of American studies; but I could see that, with his relative indifference to English literature, he must have conceived, at the end of the century, an extremely low opinion of American. He took no interest in Henry James and not very much in Walt Whitman. He told me once that Henry Ford had said, "Cut your own wood and it will warm you twice," not knowing that Ford had been quoting Thoreau. For Christian, the level of American writing was more or less represented by William Dean Howells, the presiding spirit of the years of his youth, for whom he felt hardly the barest respect. It was absolutely incredible to him—and in this I did agree with him—that *The Rise of Silas Lapham* should ever have been thought an important novel. "It wasn't much of a rise," he would say. Yet the "renaissance" of the twenties—unlike Paul Elmer More—he followed with sympathetic, if critical, interest.

Christian Gauss was a complex personality as well as a subtle mind, and one finds it in some ways difficult to sort out one's impressions of him. I want to try to deal now with the moral qualities which, combined with his unusual intellectual powers, gave him something of the stature of greatness. In some sense, he was a moral teacher as well as a literary one; but his teaching, in the same way as his criticism, was conveyed by throwing out suggestions and dropping incidental comments. In this connection, I want to quote here the tribute of Mr. Harold R. Medina, the distinguished federal judge, from the symposium in the *Alumni Weekly*. It expresses a good deal better than anything I was able to write myself, when I drafted this memoir for the first time, the penetrating quality of Gauss's power, and it is interesting to me in describing an experience that closely parallels my own on the part of an alumnus of an earlier class—1909—who was to work in a different field yet who had known Christian Gauss, as I had, not as dean of the college, but as teacher of literature.

"Of all the men whom I have met," Mr. Medina writes, "only four have significantly influenced my life. Dean Gauss was the second of these; the first, my father. From freshman year on I had many courses and precepts with Dean Gauss and during my senior year I was with him almost daily. He attracted me as he did everyone else; and I sensed that he had something to impart which was of infinitely greater importance than the mere content of the courses in French Literature. It was many years after I left Princeton before I realized that it was he who first taught me how to think. How strange it is that so many people have the notion that they are thinking when they are merely repeating the thoughts of others. He dealt in ideas without seeming to do so; he led and guided with so gentle a touch that one began to think almost despite oneself. The process once started, he continued in such fashion as to instil into my very soul the determination to be a seeker after truth, the elusive, perhaps never to be attained, complete and utter truth, no matter where it led or whom it hurt. How he did it I shall never know; but that it was he I have not the slightest doubt. His own intellectual integrity was a constant example for me to follow. And to this precious element he added another. He gave me the vision of language and literature as something representing the continuous and never-ending flow of man's struggle to think the thoughts which, when put into action, constitute in the aggregate the advance of civilization. Whatever I may be today or may ever hope to be is largely the result of the germination of the seeds he planted. The phenomena of cause and effect are not to be denied. With Dean Gauss there were so many hundreds of persons, like myself, whom he influenced and whose innate talents he developed that the ripples he started in motion were multiplied again and again. In critical times I always wondered whether he approved or would approve of things I said and did. And this went on for over forty years."

"To instil into my very soul the determination to be a seeker after truth . . . no matter where it led or whom it hurt." I remember my own thrilled response when, in taking us through the seventeenth canto of the *Paradiso*, Christian read without special emphasis yet in a way that brought out their conviction some lines that remained from that moment engraved, as they say, on my mind:

> E s'io al vero son timido amico,
> Temo di perder viver tra coloro
> Che questo tempo chiameranno antico.

—"If to the truth I prove a timid friend, I fear to lose my life [to fail of survival] among those who will call this time ancient." The truth about which Dante is speaking is his opinion of certain powerful persons, who will, as he has just been forewarned in Heaven, retaliate by sending him into exile—a truth which, as Heaven approves, he will not be deterred from uttering. Another moment in the classroom comes back to me from one of Christian's preceptorials. He had put up to us the issue created by the self-assertive type of romantic, who followed his own impulse in defiance of conventional morality and with indifference to social consequences; and he called upon me to supply him with an instance of moral conflict between social or personal duty and the duty of self-realization. I gave him the case of a problem with which I had had lately to deal as editor of the *Nassau Lit*, when I had not been able to bring myself to tell a friend who had set his heart upon contributing that the manuscripts he brought me were hopeless. "That's not an impulse," said Christian, "to do a humane thing: it's a temptation to do a weak thing." I was struck also by what seemed to me the unusual line that he took one day in class when one of his students complained that he hadn't been able to find out the meaning of a word. "What did you call it?" asked Christian. "Didn't you call it something?" The boy confessed that he hadn't. "That's bad intellectual form," said Christian. "Like going out in the morning with your face unwashed. In reading a foreign language, you must never leave a gap or a blur. If you can't find out what something means, make the best supposition you can. If it's wrong, the chances are that the context will show it in a moment or that you'll see, when the word occurs again, that it couldn't have meant that." This made such an impression on me that—just as Mr. Medina says he has been asking himself all his life whether Christian would approve of his actions—I still make an effort to live up to it.

I love to remember, too, how Christian began one of his lectures as follows: "There are several fundamental philosophies that one can bring to one's life in the world—or rather, there are several ways of taking life. One of these ways of taking the world is not to have any philosophy at all—that is the way that most people take it. Another is to regard the world as unreal and God as the only reality; Buddhism is an example of this. Another may be summed up in the words *Sic transit gloria mundi*—that is the point of view you find in Shakespeare." He then went on to an explanation of the eighteenth-century philosophy which assumed that the world was real and that we ourselves may find some sense in it and make ourselves happy in it. On another occasion, in preceptorial, Christian asked me, "Where do you think our ideals come from—justice, righteousness, beauty and so on?" I replied, "Out of the imaginations of men"; and he surprised me by answering, "That is correct." This made an impression on me, because he usually confined himself to a purely Socratic questioning, in which he did not often allow himself to express his own opinions. I felt that I had caught him off guard: what he had evidently been expecting to elicit was either Platonic idealism or Christian revelation.

It was only outside class and at secondhand that I learned that he said of himself at this time that his only religion was Dante; yet it could not escape us in the long run that the Dante we were studying was a secular Dante—or rather, perhaps, a Dante of the Reformation—the validity of whose art and morality did not in the least depend on one's acceptance or non-acceptance of the faith of the Catholic Church. Christian would remind us from time to time of Dante's statement, in his letter to Can Grande, that his poem, though it purported to describe a journey to the other world, really dealt with men's life in this, and we were shown that the conditions of the souls in Hell, Purgatory and Heaven were metaphors for our moral situation here. The principle of salvation that we learned from Dante was not the Catholic surrender to Jesus—who plays in the *Divine Comedy* so significantly small a role—but the vigilant cultivation of "*il ben del intelletto.*"

Some of those who had known Christian Gauss in his great days as a teacher of literature were sorry, after the war, to see him becoming involved in the administrative side of the University. I remember his saying to me one day, in the early stages of this, "I've just sent off a lot of letters, and I said to myself as I mailed them, 'There are seventeen letters to people who don't interest me in the least.'" But the job of the Dean's office did interest him—though it seemed to us that it did not take a Gauss to rule on remiss or refractory students. He had never liked repeating routine, and I suppose that his department was coming to bore him. He made, by all accounts, a remarkable dean—for his card-catalogue memory kept all names and faces on file even for decades after the students had left, and the sensitive feeling for character that had been hidden behind his classroom mask must have equipped him with a special tact in dealing with the difficult cases. His genius for moral values had also a new field now in which it could exercise itself in an immediate and practical way, and the responsibilities of his office—especially in the years just after the war, when students were committing suicide and getting into all sorts of messes—sometimes put upon him an obvious strain. Looking back since his death, it has seemed to me that the Gauss who was dean of Princeton must have differed almost as much from the Gauss with whom I read French and Italian as this austere teacher had done from the young correspondent in Paris, who had paid for Oscar Wilde's drinks. The Gauss I had known in my student days, with his pale cheeks and shuttered gaze, his old raincoat and soft flat hat, and a shabby mongrel dog named Baudelaire which had been left with him by the Jesse Lynch Williamses and which sometimes accompanied him into class—the Gauss who would pass one on the campus without speaking, unless you attracted his attention, in an abstraction like that of Dante in Hell and who seemed to meet the academic world with a slightly constrained self-consciousness at not having much in common with it—this figure warmed up and filled out, became recognizably Princetonian in his neckties and shirts and a touch of that tone that combines a country-club self-assurance with a boyish country-town homeliness. He now met the college world, unscreened, with his humorous and lucid green eyes. He wore golf stockings and even played golf. He interested himself in the football team and made speeches at alumni banquets. Though I know that his influence as dean was exerted in favor of scholarships, higher admission requirements and the salvaging of the Humanities—I cannot do justice here to this whole important phase of his career—the only moments of our long friendship when I was ever at all out of sympathy with him occurred during these years of officialdom; for I felt that he had picked up a little the conventional local prejudices when I would find him protesting against the advent in Princeton of the Institute for Advanced Study or, on one occasion, censoring the *Lit* for publishing a "blasphemous" story. One was always impressed, however, by the way in which he seemed to have absorbed the whole business of the University.

We used to hope that he would eventually be president; but, with the domination of business in the boards of trustees of the larger American colleges, it was almost as improbable that Christian would be asked to be president of Princeton as it would have been that Santayana should be asked to be president of Harvard. Not, of course, that it would ever have occurred to anyone to propose such a post for Santayana, but it was somehow characteristic of Christian's career that the idea should have entered the minds of his friends and that nothing should ever have come of it. There appeared in the whole line of Christian's life a certain diversion of purpose, an unpredictable ambiguity of aim, that corresponded to the fluid indeterminate element in his teaching and conversation. He had originally been a newspaper correspondent and a writer of reviews for the literary journals, who hoped to become a poet. He was later a college professor who had developed into a brilliant critic—by far the best, so far as I know, in our academic world of that period—and who still looked forward to writing books; I once found him, in one of his rare moments of leisure, beginning an historical novel. Then, as dean, in the late twenties and thirties, he came to occupy a position of intercollegiate distinction rather incongruous with that usually prosaic office. Was he a "power" in American education? I do not believe he was. That kind of role is possible only for a theorist like John Dewey or an administrator like Charles W. Eliot. Though he was offered the presidency of another college, he continued at Princeton as dean and simply awaited the age of retirement. When that came, he seemed at first depressed, but later readjusted himself. I enjoyed him in these post-official years. He was no longer overworked and he no longer had to worry about the alumni. He returned to literature and started an autobiography, with which, however, he said he was unsatisfied. In October of 1951, he had been writing an introduction for a new edition of Machiavelli's *Prince,* and he was pleased with it when he had finished. He took Mrs. Gauss for a drive in the car, and they talked about a trip to Florida. He had seemed in good spirits and health, though he had complained the Saturday before, after going to the Cornell game, where he had climbed to one of the top tiers of seats, that he was feeling the effects of age—he was now seventy-three. The day after finishing his introduction, he took the manuscript to his publisher in New York and attended there a memorial service for the Austrian novelist Hermann Broch, whom he had known when the latter lived in Princeton. While waiting outside the gates for the train to take him back to Princeton, with the evening paper in his pocket, his heart failed and he suddenly fell dead.

One had always still expected something further from Christian, had hoped that his character and talents would arrive at some final fruition. But—what seems to one still incredible—one's long conversation with him was simply forever suspended. And one sees now that the career was complete, the achievement is all there. He has left no solid body of writing; he did not remake Princeton (as Woodrow Wilson in some sense was able to do); he was not really a public man. He was a spiritual and intellectual force—one does not know how else to put it—of a kind that it may be possible for a man to do any of those other things without in the least becoming. His great work in his generation was unorganized and unobtrusive; and *Who's Who* will tell you nothing about it; but his influence was vital for those who felt it.

> Chè in la mente m'è fitta, ed or m'accora,
> La cara e buona imagine paterna
> Di voi, quando nel mondo ad ora ad ora
> M'insegnavate come l'uom s'eterna. . . .

F. Scott Fitzgerald

IT HAS BEEN SAID by a celebrated person* that to meet F. Scott Fitzgerald is to think of a stupid old woman with whom someone has left a diamond; she is extremely proud of the diamond and shows it to everyone who comes by, and everyone is surprised that such an ignorant old woman should possess so valuable a jewel; for in nothing does she appear so inept as in the remarks she makes about the diamond.

The person who invented this simile did not know Fitzgerald very well and can only have seen him, I think, in his more diffident or uninspired moods. The reader must not suppose that there is any literal truth in the image. Scott Fitzgerald is, in fact, no old woman, but a very good-looking young man, nor is he in the least stupid, but, on the contrary, exhilaratingly clever. Yet there *is* a symbolic truth in the description quoted above: it is true that Fitzgerald has been left with a jewel which he doesn't know quite what to do with. For he has been given imagination without intellectual control of it; he has been given the desire for beauty without an aesthetic ideal; and he has been given a gift for expression without very many ideas to express.

Consider, for example, the novel—*This Side of Paradise* —with which he founded his reputation. It has almost every fault and deficiency that a novel can possibly have. It is not only highly imitative but it imitates an inferior model. Fitzgerald, when he wrote the book, was drunk with Compton Mackenzie, and it sounds like an American attempt to rewrite *Sinister Street*. Now, Mackenzie, in spite of his gift for picturesque and comic invention and the capacity for

* This was Edna St. Vincent Millay, who met Scott Fitzgerald in Paris in the spring of 1921.

pretty writing that he says he learned from Keats, lacks both the intellectual force and the emotional imagination to give body and outline to the material which he secretes in such enormous abundance. With the seeds he took from Keats's garden, one of the best-arranged gardens in England, he exfloreated so profusely that he blotted out the path of his own. Michael Fane, the hero of *Sinister Street*, was swamped in the forest of description; he was smothered by creepers and columbine. From the time he went up to Oxford, his personality began to grow dimmer, and, when he last turned up (in Belgrade) he seemed quite to have lost his identity. As a consequence, Amory Blaine, the hero of *This Side of Paradise*, had a very poor chance of coherence: Fitzgerald did endow him, to be sure, with a certain emotional life which the phantom Michael Fane lacks; but he was quite as much a wavering quantity in a phantasmagoria of incident that had no dominating intention to endow it with unity and force. In short, one of the chief weaknesses of *This Side of Paradise* is that it is really not *about* anything: its intellectual and moral content amounts to little more than a gesture—a gesture of indefinite revolt. The story itself, furthermore, is very immaturely imagined: it is always just verging on the ludicrous. And, finally, *This Side of Paradise* is one of the most illiterate books of any merit ever published (a fault which the publisher's proofreader seems to have made no effort to remedy). Not only is it ornamented with bogus ideas and faked literary references, but it is full of literary words tossed about with the most reckless inaccuracy.

I have said that *This Side of Paradise* commits almost every sin that a novel can possibly commit: but it does not commit the unpardonable sin: it does not fail to live. The whole preposterous farrago is animated with life. It is rather a fluttering and mercurial life: its emotions do not move you profoundly; its drama does not make you hold your breath; but its gaiety and color and movement did make it come as something exciting after the realistic heaviness and dinginess of so much serious American fiction. If one recalls the sort of flavorless fodder of which Ernest Poole's *The Harbor* was an example, one can understand the wild enthusiasm with which *This Side of Paradise* was hailed. The novel was also well-written—well-written in spite of its illiteracies. It is true, as I have said above, that Fitzgerald mishandles words; his works are full of malapropisms of the most disconcerting kind. You will find: "Whatever your flare [sic] proves to be—religion, architecture, literature"; "the Juvenalia of my collected editions"; "There were nice things in it [the room] . . . offsprings of a vicarious [vagarious] impatient taste"; "a mind like his, lucrative in intelligence, intuition and lightning decision"; etc., etc. It reminds one rather of:

> Agib, who could readily, at sight,
> Strum a march upon the loud Theodolite.
> He would diligently play
> On the Zoetrope all day,
> And blow the gay Pantechnicon all night.

It is true that Scott Fitzgerald plays the language entirely by ear. But his instrument, for all that, is no mean one. He has an instinct for graceful and vivid prose that some of his more pretentious fellows might envy.

In regard to the man himself, there are perhaps two things worth knowing, for the influence they have had on his work. In the first place, he comes from the Middle West —from St. Paul, Minnesota. Fitzgerald is as much of the Middle West of large cities and country clubs as Sinclair Lewis is of the Middle West of the prairies and little towns. What we find in him is much what we find in the more prosperous strata of these cities: sensitivity and eagerness for life without a sound base of culture and taste; a structure of millionaire residences, brilliant expensive hotels and exhilarating social activities built not on the eighteenth century but simply on the flat Western land. And it seems to me rather a pity that he has not written more of the West: it is perhaps the only milieu that he thoroughly understands. When Fitzgerald approaches the East, he brings to it the standards of the wealthy West—the preoccupation with display, the appetite for visible magnificence and audible jamboree, the vigorous social atmosphere of amiable flappers and youths comparatively untainted as yet by the snobbery of the East. In *The Beautiful and Damned,* for example, we feel that he is moving in a vacuum; the characters have no real connection with the background to which they have been assigned; they are not part of the organism of New York as the characters, in, say, the short story *Bernice Bobs Her Hair* are a part of the organism of St. Paul. Surely F. Scott Fitzgerald should some day do for Summit Avenue what Lewis has done for Main Street.

But you are not to suppose from all this that the author of *This Side of Paradise* is merely a typical well-to-do Middle Westerner, with correct clothes and clear skin, who has been sent to the East for college. The second thing one should know about him is that Fitzgerald is partly Irish and that he brings both to life and to fiction certain qualities that are not Anglo-Saxon. For, like the Irish, Fitzgerald is romantic, but also cynical about romance; he is bitter as well as ecstatic; astringent as well as lyrical. He casts himself in the role of playboy, yet at the playboy he incessantly mocks. He is vain, a little malicious, of quick intelligence and wit, and has an Irish gift for turning language into something iridescent and surprising. He often reminds one, in fact, of the description that a great Irishman, Bernard Shaw, has written of the Irish: "An Irishman's imagination never lets him alone, never convinces him, never satisfies him; but it makes him that he can't face reality nor deal with it nor handle it nor conquer it: he can only sneer at them that do . . . and imagination's such a torture that you can't bear it without whisky. . . . And all the while there goes on a horrible, senseless, mischievous laughter."

For the rest, F. Scott Fitzgerald is a rather childlike fellow, very much wrapped up in his dream of himself and his projection of it on paper. For a person of his mental agility, he is extraordinarily little occupied with the general affairs of the world: like a woman, he is not much given to abstract or impersonal thought. Conversations about politics or general ideas have a way of snapping back to Fitzgerald. But this seldom becomes annoying; he is never pretentious or boring. He is quite devoid of affectation and takes the curse off his relentless egoism by his readiness to laugh at himself and his boyish uncertainty of his talent. And he exhibits, in his personality as well as in his writings, a quality rare today among even the youngest American writers: he is almost the only one among them who is capable of lighthearted high spirits. Where a satirist like Sinclair Lewis would stew "the Problem of Salesmanship" in acrid rancorous fumes, Fitzgerald, in *The Beautiful and Damned*, has made of it hilarious farce. His characters—and he—are actors in an elfin harlequinade; they are as nimble, as gay and as lovely—and as hardhearted—as fairies: Columbine elopes with Harlequin on a rope ladder dropped from the Ritz and both go morris-dancing amuck on a case of bootleg liquor; Pantaloon is pinked with an epigram that withers him up like a leaf; the Policeman is tripped by Harlequin and falls into the Pulitzer Fountain. Just before the curtain falls, Harlequin puts on false whiskers and pretends to be Bernard Shaw; he gives reporters an elaborate interview on politics, religion and history; a hundred thousand readers see it and are more or less impressed; Columbine nearly dies laughing; Harlequin sends out for a case of gin.

Let me quote a characteristic incident in connection with *The Beautiful and Damned*. Since writing *This Side of Paradise*—on the inspiration of Wells and Mackenzie—Fitzgerald has become acquainted with a different school of fiction: the ironical-pessimistic. In college, he had supposed that the thing to do was to write biographical novels with a burst of ideas toward the close; since his advent in the literary world, he has discovered that another genre has recently come into favor: the kind which makes much of the tragedy and what Mencken has called "the meaninglessness of life." Fitzgerald had imagined, hitherto, that the thing to do in a novel was to bring out a meaning in life;

but he now set bravely about it to contrive a shattering tragedy that should be, also, a hundred-percent meaningless. As a result of this determination, the first version of *The Beautiful and Damned* culminated in an orgy of horror for which the reader was imperfectly prepared. Fitzgerald destroyed his characters with a succession of catastrophes so arbitrary that, beside them, the perversities of Hardy seemed the working of natural laws. The heroine was to lose her beauty at a prematurely early age, and her character was to go to pieces with it; Richard Carmel, a writer of promise, was to lose his artistic ideals and prostitute himself to the popular taste; and the wealthy Anthony Patch was not only to lose his money but, finding himself unable to make a living, abjectly to succumb to drink and eventually to go insane. But the bitterest moment of the story was to come at the very end, when Anthony was to be wandering the streets of New York in an attempt to borrow some money. After several humiliating failures, he finally approaches an old friend whom he sees with an elegant lady just getting into a cab. This is the brilliant Maury Noble, a cynic, an intellectual and a man of genuine parts. Maury cuts Anthony dead and drives away in the taxi. "But," the author explains, "he really had not seen Anthony. For Maury had indulged his appetite for alcoholic beverage once too often: he was now stone-blind!" But the point of my story is this: though Fitzgerald had been perfectly serious in writing this bathetic passage, he did not hesitate, when he heard people laugh at it, to laugh about it himself, and with as much surprise and delight as if he had just come across it in Max Beerbohm. He at once improvised a burlesque: "It seemed to Anthony that Maury's eyes had a fixed glassy stare; his legs moved stiffly as he walked and when he spoke his voice was lifeless. When Anthony came nearer, he saw that Maury was dead."

To conclude, it would be quite unfair to subject Scott Fitzgerald, who is still in his twenties and has presumably most of his work before him, to a rigorous overhauling. His restless imagination may yet produce something durable.

For the present, however, this imagination is certainly not seen to the best advantage: it suffers badly from lack of discipline and poverty of aesthetic ideas. Fitzgerald is a dazzling extemporizer, but his stories have a way of petering out: he seems never to have planned them completely or to have thought out his themes from the beginning. This is true even of some of his most successful fantasies, such as *The Diamond as Big as the Ritz* or his comedy, *The Vegetable*. On the other hand, *The Beautiful and Damned*, imperfect though it is, marks an advance over *This Side of Paradise:* the style is more nearly mature and the subject more solidly unified, and there are scenes that are more convincing than any in his previous fiction.

But, in any case, even the work that Fitzgerald has done up to date has a certain moral importance. In his very expression of the anarchy by which he finds himself bewildered, of his revolt which cannot fix on an object, he is typical of the war generation—the generation so memorably described on the last page of *This Side of Paradise* as "grown up to find all gods dead, all wars fought, all faiths in men shaken." There is a moral in *The Beautiful and Damned* that the author did not perhaps intend to point. The hero and the heroine of this giddy book are creatures without method or purpose: they give themselves up to wild debaucheries and do not, from beginning to end, perform a single serious act; yet somehow you get the impression that, in spite of their fantastic behavior, Anthony and Gloria Patch are the most rational people in the book. Wherever they come in contact with institutions, with the serious life of their time, these are made to appear ridiculous, they are subjects for scorn or mirth. We see the army, finance and business successively and casually exposed as completely without point or dignity. The inference we are led to draw is that, in such a civilization as this, the sanest and most honorable course is to escape from organized society and live for the excitement of the moment. It cannot be merely a special reaction to a personal situation which gives rise to the paradoxes of such a book. It may be that we cannot demand too high a degree of moral balance from young men, however able or brilliant, who write books in the year 1921: we must remember that they have had to grow up in, that they have had to derive their chief stimulus from the wars, the society and the commerce of the Age of Confusion itself.

March, 1922

Ring Lardner's American Characters

MR. RING LARDNER is a popular journalist who writes for the New York *American* and who also provides the text for a syndicated comic strip. It has therefore been thought appropriate to present his new collection of short stories as if it were a volume of popular humor. There are a preface in the vein of Bill Nye and a jocose introduction to every story, and the title page is brightened by a humorous cut that is evidently by John Held. The book itself, from its burlesque preface, is called *How to Write Short Stories,* instead of, as it ought to be, *Champion and Other Stories.*

Is all this an idea of the publishers, who do not want to forfeit the prestige of Mr. Lardner's reputation as a humorist, or is it due to Mr. Lardner, who is timid about coming forward in the role of serious writer? The fact is that this new book of his, instead of belonging to the gruesome department of, say, Irvin Cobb's *Speaking of Operations,* contains some of the most interesting work that Ring Lardner has yet produced. These stories he observes in his preface, "will illustrate in a half-hearted way what I am trying to get at." But the stories are not half-hearted: it is the jokes that he intrudes among them. The nonsense of his introductions is so far below his usual level that one suspects him of a guilty conscience at attempting to disguise his talent for social observation and satire. For, aside from a very few things, such as *The Facts,* that seem a little magazine-made, what one finds in *How to Write Short Stories* is a series of studies of American types almost equal in importance to those of Sherwood Anderson and Sinclair Lewis.

It may, indeed, be said of Ring Lardner that, if we compare him with these other two writers, he shows a certain specific advantage over each of them. In those of Mr. Lardner's stories in which he attempts something rather similar to Sherwood Anderson's *The Egg* or *I'm a Fool*, he shows a firmer grasp both of the Western vernacular and of the external realities with which he is dealing. In a sense, he is closer to life. It is curious to speculate what would have happened to some of the stories in this collection if they had been written by Sherwood Anderson. Two of Lardner's baseball players—Alibi Ike and a scout who is willing to risk ruining his team for the sake of a perfect quartet—may almost be called neurotics; and a third—the demon batter in *My Roomy*—is evidently quite insane. What startling preoccupations might not have been revealed to the reader if Anderson had X-rayed their deepest insides! Is not the mysterious Elliot, who insists upon shaving in the middle of the night and cannot sleep unless the water in the bathtub is running, a brother to John Webster of *Many Marriages*, who appeared before his daughter naked, and to the girl in *Out of Nowhere Into Nothing*, who used to listen to the water-pail slopping over? With Anderson, you are sometimes so far submerged in the spiritual sensations of these characters that you lose sight of them as actual people in an actual Western community; with Lardner's queer cases, however, you are never taken inside them; you see them only in their relations with other people. And when Lardner comes closest to Lewis, as in the story called *The Golden Honeymoon*, he is less likely than Lewis to caricature, and hence to falsify, because he is primarily interested in studying a kind of person rather than in drawing up an indictment.

But Mr. Lardner has, of course, not as yet attained the stature of either of these men. Anderson has a poet's sensi-

bility; Lewis, a satirist's fury. But what Lardner may have
to match these he has never yet fully revealed. For all his
saturnine tone, his apparent scorn of vulgar values, he seems
committed to popular journalism. He does not even care to
admit that he has tried to do work on a higher level—hence
the clownish presentation of these stories. Yet he would
seem to come closer than anyone else among living American writers to possessing the combination of qualities that
made *Huckleberry Finn* a masterpiece. For one thing, he
has ready invention—which most American realists have
not; and for another—what is even rarer—an unmistakable
personal accent which represents a special way of looking
at things. Even such important examples of recent American realism as Sinclair Lewis's *Main Street* and *Babbitt*
have been put together largely out of literary materials that
the author found ready to hand—the pre-war English novel
of Bennett and Wells. But Ring Lardner seems to have
imitated nobody, and nobody else could reproduce his
essence. You have to read the whole of a novel of Lewis
to find out that there is anything remarkable about it; but
there is scarcely a paragraph of Lardner's which, in its irony
both fresh and morose, does not convey somehow the sense
of a distinguished aloof intelligence. And he has shown an
unexcelled, a perhaps unrivalled, mastery of what since the
publication of Mencken's book, has come to be known as
the American language. Mark Twain, in his foreword to
Huckleberry Finn, explained that he had taken great care
to differentiate between "the Missouri Negro dialect; the
extremist form of the backwoods Southwestern dialect; the
ordinary 'Pike County' dialect; and four modified varieties
of this last." So Lardner has marked the distinction between
the baseball player's and the prize-fighter's slang, can speak
the language of the Chicago song-writer of *Some Like
Them Cold,* who has come to New York to make his fortune, and has equally at his command the whole vocabulary of adolescent clichés of the young girl who writes to
the song-writer, and of the quite different set of clichés of
the middle-aged man from New Jersey who goes to Florida

for his golden honeymoon. And he understands the difference between the spoken language of these semi-literate types and the language they will use when they write. Finally, what is most important, he writes the vernacular like an artist and not merely like a clever journalist—as George Ade or O. Henry did. There is nothing artificial or forced about the use of slang in these stories; it is as natural as it is apt. Lardner's language is the product of a philologist's ear and a born writer's relish for words.

Will Ring Lardner, then, go on to his *Huckleberry Finn* or has he already told all he knows? It may be that the mechanical repetition of a trick that one finds in such a story as *Horseshoes* and the melodramatic exaggeration of *Champion* indicate limitations. But you never know: here is a man who has had the freedom of the modern West no less than Mark Twain did of the old one, who approaches it, as Mark Twain did, with a perceptive interest in human beings instead of with the naturalist's formula—a man who lives at a time when, if one be not sold irredeemably into bondage to the *Saturday Evening Post,* it is far easier for a serious writer to get published and find a hearing than it was in Mark Twain's day. If Ring Lardner has anything more to give us, the time has now come to deliver it. He has not even popular glory to gain by pursuing any other course. His popular vein is about worked out; and he has always been too much of an artist to make the biggest kind of success as a clown; his books have never sold so well as Stephen Leacock's or Irvin Cobb's. When Lewis himself, in his earlier phase a humorist for the *Saturday Evening Post,* took a chance and composed in *Main Street* his satire upon its readers, he received unexpected support. It turned out that there were thousands of people who were ready to hear what he wanted to say. What bell might not Lardner ring if he set out to give us the works?

July, 1924

Emergence of Ernest Hemingway

ON OCTOBER 21, 1923, the following note appeared in Burton Rascoe's *A Bookman's Daybook,* a feature of the Sunday edition of the New York *Tribune,* of which Rascoe was at that time literary editor:

Called upon Mary and Edmund Wilson late in the afternoon, and Wilson called my attention to some amusing stuff by Ernest Hemingway in the new issue of the *Little Review.** [Lewis] Galantière sent me a copy of Hemingway's *Three Stories and Ten Poems,* which was published in Paris, and said that I would find it interesting, but I have not yet got around to reading it. Wilson was ill with a cold and complained that the difficulty with New York is that it is hard to keep feeling well here, that it ties one up nervously and residents of Manhattan are always having colds.

I presently had the following letter from Hemingway, who was then working on a newspaper in Canada:

November 11, 1923

Dear Mr. Wilson:

In Burton Rascoe's Social and Literary Notes I saw you had drawn his attention to some writing of mine in the *Little Review.*

I am sending you *Three Stories and Ten Poems.* As far as I know it has not yet been reviewed in the States. Gertrude Stein writes me she has done a review but I don't know whether she has gotten it published yet.

---

* These contributions were *In Our Time,* comprising six of the little vignettes that afterward appeared in the two books of that title, and a satirical prose poem called *They All Made Peace— What Is Peace?*

You don't know anything in Canada.

I would like to send out some for review but do not know whether to put a dedication, as compulsory in France, or what. Being an unknown name and the books unimposing they would probably be received as by Mr. Rascoe who has not yet had time, after three months, to read the copy Galantière sent him. (He could read it all in an hour and a half.)

The Contact Publishing Co. is McAlmon. It has published Wm. Carlos Williams, Mina Loy, Marsden Hartley and McAlmon.

I hope you like the book. If you are interested could you send me the names of four or five people to send it to to get it reviewed? It would be terribly good of you. This address will be good until January when we go back to Paris.

Thanking you very much whether you have the time to do it or not.

Yours sincerely,
Ernest Hemingway

1599 Bathurst Street
Toronto, Canada

I acknowledged the book when I got it, mentioning that I might do a note on it in the *Dial*, and had from him the following reply:

November 25
1599 Bathurst Street
Toronto

Dear Mr. Wilson:

Thank you ever so much for the letter. It was awfully good of you.

The book is a silly size. McAlmon wanted to get out a series of small books with Mina Loy, W. C. Williams, etc. and wanted me in it. I gave him the stories and poems. I am glad to have it out and once it is published it is back of you.

I am very glad you liked some of it. As far as I can think at the minute yours is the only critical opinion in the

States I have any respect for. Mary Colum is sometimes sound. Rascoe was intelligent about Eliot. There are probably good ones that I don't know.

No I don't think *My Old Man* derives from Anderson. It is about a boy and his father and race-horses. Sherwood has written about boys and horses. But very differently. It derives from boys and horses. Anderson derives from boys and horses. I don't think they're anything alike. I know I wasn't inspired by him.

I know him pretty well but have not seen him for several years. His work seems to have gone to hell, perhaps from people in New York telling him too much how good he was. Functions of criticism. I am very fond of him. He has written good stories.

Would it perhaps be better to postpone the "Briefer Mentions" in the *Dial* until *In Our Time* comes out sometime next month and I will send it to you. You can get from it what I am trying to get at and the two of them together could make one review.

I am awfully glad you liked the *In Our Time* stuff in the *Little Review* and it is where I think I have gotten hold of it.

There is no use trying to explain it without the book.

It is very sporting of you to offer to help me get a book before the publishers. I don't know any of them.

Edward O'Brien wrote me the other day asking formal permission to reprint *My Old Man* in his *Best Short Stories of 1923* and asking if he could dedicate the book to me. As the book isn't out that is confidential. He prints bum ones and good ones. He asked me if I had enough stories for a Boni and Liveright book. I don't know whether that means he could get them to publish it. I will write and ask you about it when the time comes if you don't mind.

E. E. Cummings' *Enormous Room* was the best book published last year that I read. Somebody told me it was a flop. Then look at *One of Ours*. Prize, big sale, people taking it seriously. You were in the war weren't you? Wasn't that last scene in the lines wonderful? Do you know where it came from? The battle scene in *Birth of a Nation*. I identified episode after episode, Catherized. Poor woman she had to get her war experience somewhere.

The thing in the *L.R.* was a joke.* I wrote it in the wagon-restaurant going back to Lausanne, had been at a very fine lunch at Gertrude Stein's and talked there all afternoon and read a lot of her new stuff and then drank a big bottle of Beaune myself in the dining car. Facing opening the wire again in the morning I tried to analyse the conference.

Her method is invaluable for analysing anything or making notes on a person or a place. She has a wonderful head. I would like to write a review of an old book of hers sometime. She is where Mencken and Mary Colum fall down and skin their noses.

Please excuse this very long letter and thanks again ever so much for your letter and the good advice. I would like to see you very much when we go through N. Y.

Very sincerely,
Ernest Hemingway

He looked me up on his next visit to New York and sent me the first *In Our Time* (lower-cased *in our time*), which was published in the spring of 1924 in an edition of a hundred and seventy copies by the Three Mountains Press in Paris. This contained only eleven of the fifteen stories that appeared in the Boni and Liveright edition of 1925.

I wrote a review of *in our time* and *Three Stories and Ten Poems*, which appeared in the *Dial* of October, 1924. Though it is not of much interest in itself, I am proud of it because it is, so far as I know, the first criticism of Hemingway that appeared in print. (It is not, however, listed by Louis Henry Cohn in his *Bibliography of the Works of Ernest Hemingway*. The first article noted by him is of November, 1925: a review by Burton Rascoe of the expanded *In Our Time*.)

* *They All Made Peace—What Is Peace?*

MR. HEMINGWAY'S DRY-POINTS

Three Stories and Ten Poems. By Ernest Hemingway. 12mo. 58 pages. Contact Publishing Company. Paris. $1.50.

In Our Time. By Ernest Hemingway. 12mo. 30 pages. The Three Mountains Press. Paris. $2.

Mr. Hemingway's poems are not particularly important, but his prose is of the first distinction. He must be counted as the only American writer but one—Mr. Sherwood Anderson—who has felt the genius of Gertrude Stein's *Three Lives* and has evidently been influenced by it. Indeed, Miss Stein, Mr. Anderson and Mr. Hemingway may now be said to form a school by themselves. The characteristic of this school is a naïveté of language, often passing into the colloquialism of the character dealt with, which serves actually to convey profound emotions and complex states of mind. It is a distinctively American development in prose —as opposed to more or less successful American achievements in the traditional style of English prose—which has artistically justified itself at its best as a limpid shaft into deep waters.

Not, however, that Mr. Hemingway is imitative. On the contrary, he is rather strikingly original, and in the dry compressed little vignettes of *In Our Time*, has almost invented a form of his own:

"They shot the six cabinet ministers at half-past six in the morning against the wall of a hospital. There were pools of water in the courtyard. There were dead leaves on the paving of the courtyard. It rained hard. All the shutters of the hospital were nailed shut. One of the ministers was sick with typhoid. Two soldiers carried him downstairs and out into the rain. They tried to hold him up against the wall but he sat down in a puddle of water. The other five stood very quietly against the wall. Finally the officer told the soldiers it was no good trying to make him stand up. When they fired the first volley he was sitting down in the water with his head on his knees."

Mr. Hemingway is remarkably successful in suggesting moral values by a series of simple statements of this sort. His more important book is called *In Our Time*, and, behind its cool objective manner, it constitutes a harrowing record of the barbarities of the period in which we live: you have not only political executions, but hangings of criminals, bull-fights, assassinations by the police and the cruelties and horrors of the war. Mr. Hemingway is unperturbed as he tells us about these things: he is not a propagandist even for humanity. His bull-fight sketches have the dry sharpness and elegance of the bull-fight lithographs of Goya. And, like Goya, he is concerned first of all with making a fine picture. Too proud an artist to simplify in the interests of conventional pretenses, he is showing you what life is like. And I am inclined to think that his little book has more artistic dignity than anything else about the period of the war that has as yet been written by an American.

Not perhaps the most vivid book, but the soundest. Mr. Hemingway, who can make you feel the poignancy of the Italian soldier deciding in his death agony that he will "make a separate peace," has no anti-militarist parti pris which will lead him to suppress from his record the exhilaration of the men who had "jammed an absolutely perfect barricade across the bridge" and who were "frightfully put out when we heard the flank had gone, and we had to fall back." It is only in the paleness, the thinness of some of his effects that Mr. Hemingway sometimes fails. I am thinking especially of the story called *Up in Michigan*, which should have been a masterpiece, but has the curious defect of dealing with rude and primitive people yet leaving them rather shadowy.

In Our Time has a pretty and very amusing cover designed from scrambled newspaper clippings. The only objection I have to its appearance is that the titles are printed throughout without capitals—thus: "in our time by ernest hemingway—paris." This device, which had a certain effectiveness when the modernists used it first to call attention to the newness of what they were offering, is now becoming a bore. The American advertisers have taken it over as one of their stock tricks. And it is so unsightly in itself that one does not like to see it become—as in the case of Mr. Hemingway's book and Mr. Hueffer's* *transatlantic review*—a kind of badge for all that is freshest and most interesting in contemporary writing.

October, 1924

In connection with this review, Hemingway wrote me the following letter:

113 Rue Notre Dame des Champs
Paris VII
October 18, 1924

Dear Wilson:

Thank you so much for writing the review in the October *Dial*. I liked it very much. You are very right about the lack of capital letters—which seemed very silly and affected to me—but Bird had put them in and as he was printing the *In Our Time* himself and that was all the fun he was getting out of it I thought he could go ahead and be a damn fool in his own way if it pleased him. So long as he did not fool with the text.

I'm awfully glad you liked it.

How are you anyway? and did you ever get Chaplin for your ballet?

We have lived very quietly, working hard, except for a trip to Spain, Pamplona, where we had a fine time and I learned a lot about bull fighting, the inside the ring scene. We had a lot of minor adventures.

I've worked like hell most of the time and think the stuff gets better. Finished the book of 14 stories with a chapter on *In Our Time* between each story—that is the way they were meant to go—to give the picture of the whole

* Ford Madox Ford, who changed his family name from Hueffer.

between examining it in detail. Like looking with your eyes at something, say a passing coast line, and then looking at it with 15X binoculars. Or rather, maybe, looking at it and then going in and living in it—and then coming out and looking at it again.

I sent the book to Don Stewart* at the Yale Club about three weeks ago. When he was here he offered to try and sell it for me. I think you would like it, it has a pretty good unity. In some of the stories since the *In Our Time* I've gotten across both the people and the scene. It makes you feel good when you can do it. It feels now as though I had gotten on top of it.

Will you get over here this winter do you think? We will probably be in Paris all winter. Not enough money to get out. The baby is very well and husky. Hadley is working on the piano.

She sends her best regards to you and Mrs. Wilson.

Hope everything is going well with you and that you have a good winter. I would like to hear from you and I did appreciate the review. It was cool and clear minded and decent and impersonal and sympathetic. Christ how I hate this terrible personal stuff. Do you remember my writing from Toronto wanting some reviews and publicity? and then got some and it turned me sick.

I think there's nothing more discouraging than unintelligent appreciation. Not really discouraging; but just driving something back inside of you. Some bright guy said *In Our Time* was a series of thumbnail sketches showing a great deal of talent but obviously under the influence of Ring Lardner. Yeah! That kind of stuff is fine. It doesn't bother. But these wordy, sentimental bastards. You are the only man writing criticism who or whom I can read when the book being criticized is one I've read or know something about. I can read almost anybody when they write on things I don't know about. Intelligence is so damn rare and the people who have it often have such a bad

* Donald Ogden Stewart.

time with it that they get bitter or propagandistic and then it's not much use.

With best wishes to you and to your wife,

Very sincerely,

Ernest Hemingway

Is this *What Price Glory?* really a good play. I don't mean a good *play*—it sounds fine over here.

I have learned, since the above was written, that my review of *In Our Time* was not the first. An earlier one, signed M. R., had appeared in Paris in the April, 1924, issue of *the transatlantic review*.   1953

Gilbert Seldes and the Popular Arts

I. *The Seven Lively Arts* (1924)

MR. SELDES HAS WRITTEN a valuable and enormously entertaining book on the vulgar arts of vaudeville, jazz music, newspaper satire, the movies, the revue, the circus, and the comic strip. He has tried to do for the field of popular entertainment very much what Mr. Mencken has done for philology in his treatise on the American language; and everybody interested in American culture should pay attention to the results of his researches.

Unfortunately, Mr. Seldes has not to the same degree as Mencken the gift of lucid presentation. He does not seem to realize that the function of his book is primarily one of exposition—the conveying of information, the unfolding of novel ideas—and that in order to do this successfully, you must cultivate patience and order. Mr. Seldes proceeds obliquely by means of metaphysical discussions of theory and elliptical literary allusions, jokes, curses, cries of ecstasy and hysterical revelations—the whole rather bewilderingly distributed among chapters of the normal kind, open letters and imaginary dialogues, which are supplemented by footnotes, appendices and parenthetical interpolations. You have a feeling that the quicksilver ideas are escaping through the interstices of the ill-woven sentences. There are passages in *The Seven Lively Arts* that I cannot understand at all, and others that I should not understand unless I happened, in the particular case, to possess some independent knowledge of what the author is trying to tell me about. I cite, for example, the footnote on page 336: "I haven't seen The Covered Wagon. Its theme returns to the legendary history of America. There is no reason why it should not have been highly imaginative. But I wonder whether the thousands of prairie schooners one hears about are the film or the image. In the latter case there is no objection." Now what does he mean by this? On the opposite page I find: "By corrupting the action [of novels and plays which were being turned into movies] the producers changed the idea; bad enough in itself, they failed to understand what they were doing and supplied nothing to take the place of what they had destroyed." I can see that a possible sense might be given to this passage by interchanging the semicolon and the comma, but there are so many other passages like it that it is impossible to tell whether this particular one has been misprinted or not. Again: "You [the 'movie magnates'] gave us Marguerite Clark in films no better than the 'whimsy-me' school of stage plays." Now I know what Mr. Seldes means when he refers to the "whimsy-me" school of drama, because I happened to be present on the single night when the Algonquin group of humorists put on the entertainment called *The No-Siree,* and saw their burlesque of A. A. Milne in which an old gentleman said, "Ah, whimsy me!"; but if I had not, I should barely have been able to guess what Mr. Seldes meant by this passage.

Mr. Seldes does succeed, none the less, for all his tendency toward woolly writing, in disengaging some judicious observations. The chapter from which I have just quoted, for example, contains admirable criticism of the movies; and the discussion of the technique of vaudeville is, it seems to me, equally sound. And, though his bons mots do not always come off, he strikes at times—as in his passage on Christopher Morley—a debonair vein of wit that has the air of unexpectedly igniting when he is not trying for it especially. But where he seems to me most successful is in simply reporting the things that he has seen. It is then that he writes his best prose and produces his most persuasive effects. The descriptions of the Chaplin films, the Krazy Kat comic strip and the antics of the Fratellini clowns really bring them most vividly before us: we laugh with delight as we read. Mr. Seldes, I suppose, is surest here because he is closest to his object. As soon as he stops looking at his object, he has a way of becoming bedazzled by strange intellectual fancies, and is almost as likely to come out with something wildly inappropriate as with something penetrating and true. How, for example, did he arrive at the following: "It was odd that in *Vanity Fair's* notorious 'rankings,' Krazy tied with Doctor Johnson, to whom he owes much of his vocabulary." In what way does Krazy Kat's vocabulary resemble Doctor Johnson's? The romantic passages quoted certainly fail to convince one of this. Mr. Seldes describes Krazy Kat, also, as "a creature more like Pan than any other creation of our time"—though it is difficult to see how Krazy Kat is much more like Pan than he is like Doctor Johnson. And on what evidence does he prophesy that Ring Lardner is capable of becoming a second Mr. Dooley? Ring Lardner, so far as I know, has never shown a taste for political satire; his recent tendencies have been, on the one hand, toward sheer nonsense and, on the other, in such short stories as *The Golden Honeymoon*, toward a sort of realistic fiction. Nor is it possible to understand what the passage about the kittens that Mr. Seldes quotes from Lardner has to do with the "Black Beauty-Beautiful Joe style of writing," of which Mr. Seldes says it is a parody. "It may shock Mr. Lardner," says Mr. Seldes, "to know that he has here done in little what Mr.

Joyce has done on the grand scale in *Ulysses*." It is not only
Mr. Lardner who is likely to be surprised by this statement;
and he will not be more surprised than the composers of
I Wonder Who's Kissing Her Now when they learn from
Mr. Seldes's book that they have "skillfully built up a senti-
mental situation in order to tear it down with two words."
These shots go too far or miss, but Mr. Seldes often does
hit the mark—as when he says that Mr. Dooley, in respect
to the Dreyfus case, was performing the same service for
Americans that Anatole France performed for the French.
The difference was, as he notes, that a different sort of
audience required a different vehicle of satire. What Mr.
Dooley had to say was essentially no more genial than what
Anatole France had to say, but it was only his good humor
and his dialect that made it possible for him to say it at all.
So, in our generation, when manners have passed from
back-slapping to brutality, we have Mencken using a
bludgeon on a society that understands nothing but bludg-
eons. We have never yet reached the stage when an Anatole
France could be influential.

Much of the clouding of Mr. Seldes's judgment in individual cases arises, I fancy, from his feverish approach
to his subject as a whole. In his most ecstatic moments, he
is given to making extravagant claims—as when he asserts
that Charlie Chaplin and George Herriman, the inventor of
Krazy Kat, are the only two "great artists" in America, and
that Krazy Kat is our "most satisfactory work of art"; then,
apparently in reaction from such excesses, he will protest
for whole chapters at a time that he is not really trying to
compare Herriman with Picasso and Irving Berlin with
Stravinsky, but merely backing them against the "faux
bon," the "bogus" imitations of the fine arts—thus creating,
with an immense amount of pother, what is, so far as I can
see, very largely an artificial issue, and one that lands Mr.
Seldes in a foolish and inaccurate disparagement of opera
and the drama. Why shouldn't it be possible for him simply
to go ahead and write a book about the popular arts, without all these protestations? They have been written about

before—by Anatole France, for example, who did not think it necessary to denigrate the theater in order to justify the café chantant. Well, there is a real reason, no doubt, why the popular arts should present a slightly more difficult problem in America than they do in a country like France. The French have a culture which diffuses itself more or less through all their social classes and their various fields of activity. The same thing which you find at its highest pitch of purity and intensity in a comedy of Molière appears also in a farce by Guitry, a topical revue by Rip, an illustrated joke in *Le Rire* or even in a conversation between strangers in a railway coach. But in America we have no such homogeneous culture penetrating our whole society. Today a whole race of Americans goes to school and arrives at maturity without more than the sketchiest acquaintance with the classic Anglo-American culture that has been so far our only heritage; and it is inevitable that, among this race, individuals should sometimes appear who, working in some department of popular slapstick humor and with no other language than the common slang, should achieve distinction or brilliance. Such a popular humorist as this may not only go unrecognized as an artist; he may not know that he is one himself. Herriman, I suppose, is such a man; so, perhaps, is Ring Lardner. And Mr. Seldes, in *The Seven Lively Arts,* has performed a feat of some daring in bringing them within the field of criticism. He has overdone it a little, and his case may suffer in consequence; but if he had not been capable of overdoing it, he might never have done it at all.

One thing which, I suspect, has had much to do with making Mr. Seldes self-conscious in his relation to the popular arts is the fact that, unlike most Americans, he has not been brought up on them from boyhood, that he has not learned to take them for granted. He tells us that he had scarcely in his youth ever been either to a circus or to a vaudeville show; and his failure to discuss either the early work of Opper (save for a bare mention of Happy

Hooligan) or the burlesque of Weber and Fields, suggests that he may never have known them. This lack of familiarity has the advantage of putting Mr. Seldes in a position to see in the vulgar arts certain qualities of style and imagination which are likely to be missed by people who do not expect anything of them, because they have left them behind with childhood, but it also has the disadvantage of allowing Mr. Seldes to approach them with a sensibility so sophisticated, that, not, for example, having been entertained by a given vaudeville act at the mental age for which it was intended—that is, at the age that Mr. Seldes was about twenty years ago and that the average vaudeville audience is forever—he tends either to reject it angrily as an unsuccessful attempt to do something artistically dignified or to read into it all sorts of profundities that do not have any actual existence.

As a result of this deficient background, we find Mr. Seldes neglecting an interesting aspect of his subject which I should very much like to see discussed: I mean, the revolution in humor that seems to be taking place in New York. In the old days of Weber and Fields, the latter would look down from his bullying height at the former's flowered vest and say, "Aha, now I know vere de lounge vent!" Nowadays, Joe Cook asks "the Senator," his stooge, "How's your uncle?"—and the Senator answers, "I haven't got an uncle." "Fine," says Cook. "How is he?" The difference is that the Weber and Fields joke is a "gag": it is fantastic but it makes sense; whereas Cook's is simply idiotic: you laugh at it, if you do, because it is perfectly pointless.

I should like to bring to the notice of Mr. Seldes two of the older vaudeville comedians who seem to have been transition figures in this change from the smart to the silly: Charlie Case and James J. Morton. Charlie Case was a black-face monologist with a Chaplinesque overtone of pathos who used to sing curious unrhymed songs to a monotonous dirge-like accompaniment. He had developed a vein of his own which was refreshingly unconventional, since it did not depend on gagging, and his death is said to have been hastened by disappointment at his failure to establish himself with anything like the public he deserved. If he had been launched only eight or ten years ago, he would probably now have a show of his own—like Frank Tinney who is, to my mind, a much less gifted performer than Case. As it was, Charlie Case was the object of a cult on the part of a few fans like F.P.A., who printed Case's songs in his column at the time of the latter's death. James J. Morton, the other of these comics, was a large solemn middle-aged man in an ill-fitting frock-coat, who gave a schoolboy recitation that began, "Hark, mother! I hear the sound of footsteps in the village street," to the accompaniment of deafening off-stage noises, and told interminable pointless stories rather in the manner of Ed Wynn. Neither Case nor Morton had much in common with the typical comedians of that era: the Jimmy Powerses, the Nat M. Willses, the McIntyres and Heaths. They were more subtle, more intellectual, more like the comedians in vogue today. One can see in them the first faint foreshadowings of the Algonquin school of humor—the cult of the flat joke, the irrelevant remark, the sophisticated naïveté.

That this cult has some meaning as a sign of the times and is not merely a local fashion would seem to be indicated by its kinship with the European movement called dadaism. It has always been natural for the people of the English-speaking countries to amuse themselves with what they call nonsense, and, though the nonsense of Joe Cook and Robert Benchley is distinct from that of Carroll and Lear, it is not in itself a phenomenon that has anything abnormal or surprising about it. But that our cultivation of nonsense of this special kind should have been paralleled in France by the development of a similar school of nonsense suggests a common cause. For the French have never been given to nonsense; they have scarcely even understood it. French jokes, unlike English jokes, are usually funny, not because they are silly, but because they reveal some truth. The French, since the war, however, have suddenly discovered nonsense. Jean Cocteau's *Le Potomok* and *Les*

Mariés de la Tour Eiffel came close to Carroll and Lear, and the dadaists have gone all the way in the direction of a deliberate lunacy. Though the French have made an issue of their nonsense, an occasion for polemics and riots, as Benchley or Lardner would never do, the non sequiturs and the practical jokes of the French and the American humorists (though the dadaists pretend to grim seriousness) seem the product of similar situations: in France, the collapse of Europe and the intellectual chaos that accompanied it; in America—what is perhaps another aspect of a general crisis: the bewildering confusion of the modern city and the enfeeblement of the faculty of attention. It relieves some anxiety for people to watch acts or listen to stories that are completely inconsecutive and pointless, because that is the way the world is beginning to seem, the way their own minds are beginning to work. They have to think about too many things and the relation between all these things is not in the least clear. It is comforting to hear Joe Cook when he is genially incoherent: our laughter both confesses and dismisses our fears.

In any case, *The Seven Lively Arts* is a genuine contribution to America's new orientation in respect to her artistic life which was inaugurated in 1915 by Brooks's *America's Coming of Age* and two years later more violently promoted by Mencken's *A Book of Prefaces*. Mr. Seldes's view of the arts has perhaps been a little confused by his evidently quite recent discovery that it is possible to appreciate, not only Krazy Kat at the same time as James Joyce, but both Krazy Kat and Joyce at the same time as "the *Medea* of Euripides"; but his book contains a brilliant chronicle of the high spots in our popular entertainment. If not all these forms of entertainment have really quite reached the dignity of arts, Mr. Seldes has succeeded in inventing them as such: it is he who is the artist here. He has precipitated pure crystals of irony from the cheap adulterated compounds in which it is usually sold; he has caught the enchanting echoes of our popular gaiety and melody as they drift in the city air. To read his book is to live again the last ten years of vaudeville and revue, newspapers and moving pictures, but in a purified and concentrated form—tasting nothing but the magic tune, the racy flash of characterization, the moment of mad laughter. As for the trained dogs, the melodramatic playlet and the sentimental soloist, they, too, become entertaining through the wit of our guide's comments. If he were only a little less fanatical about magnifying the importance of the whole affair, he would make the perfect companion.

September, 1924

II. *The Great Audience* (1950)

In 1924, Mr. Gilbert Seldes published a book called *The Seven Lively Arts,* the object of which was to show that the popular arts in America were remarkable for vitality and imagination and that the best they had produced was to be preferred to the "faux bon" of our respectable arts. There were chapters on vaudeville, movies, revues, newspaper humor, the comic strip, ragtime and jazz music, and Mr. Seldes's heroes were Joe Cook, Charlie Chaplin, Florenz Ziegfeld, Ring Lardner, Krazy Kat, Al Jolson and Irving Berlin. That was the epoch, in the United States, of the liquidation of genteel culture, and Mr. Seldes's audacious book marked one of the steps in this process. He had at that time just resigned from the managing editorship of the *Dial,* a literary and artistic monthly that maintained very close relations with everything that was newest in Europe, and *The Seven Lively Arts* had its connections with the more general movement of which the jazz rhythms of Stravinsky and Edith Sitwell, the ballets of Jean Cocteau and the premeditated delirium of the dadaists were among the manifestations. Gilbert Seldes had at that time, in common with these, a touch of that upsidedown snobbery of the café chantant and the music hall that probably stemmed from Toulouse-Lautrec. The Fratellini clowns of the Cirque Médrano figured among his favorites, along with Ed Wynn and Joe Jackson.

During the twenty-six years that have elapsed since the appearance of this early book, Mr. Seldes has been up to his neck in the seven lively arts, as well as in a couple of new ones that had not yet arrived at that time. He has not only continued, as a critic, to follow and comment on the various phases of popular entertainment; he has served on the production end of several of them and got to know them from the inside. Between 1937 and 1945, he was head of the Television Program Department of C.B.S., functioning also as producer, director, writer and M.C., and he has also been associated with the radio side of C.B.S. and has intermittently written radio scripts and delivered series of broadcasts. He has collaborated on movie documentaries and he has sweated out his term in Hollywood on the writing staff of Paramount. Through all this, he has steadily worked—as a check on his activities shows—to realize the best possibilities, aesthetic and educational, of these new techniques of mass amusement; and he has now written a large-scale study of television, radio and movies, with a section on comic books, summing up his conclusions about them.

Mr. Seldes's new book, *The Great Audience,* is quite different from *The Seven Lively Arts,* but it is a logical sequel to it, which makes, also, a dramatic contrast. The early book was a series of essays celebrating distinguished artists. The new one has little to say about individual writers and performers; it uses them only as illustrations. It is a solid and sober report, authoritatively documented, of the industries with which it deals: a history of their development, an analysis of their economic and technical problems, a survey of their present condition and an estimate of their probable future. It is also a critical essay, the most comprehensive and searching I know, on mass entertainment in the United States—an essay which draws conclusions that could never have been foreseen by the early Seldes or by anybody else at that stage. These analyses, predictions and conclusions will undoubtedly provoke objection, but they cannot fail to carry weight. This is the first time, so far as I know, that a man of intelligence and taste, with a sound enough education to give him cultural and historical perspective, who has at the same time a practical grasp of the technical and financial aspects of the entertainment business, has set out to attack the whole subject: to describe it, to explain it, to assess it, to assign it to its place in society; and before one goes on to discuss the special questions that Mr. Seldes raises, it should be said that *The Great Audience* seems one of those "definitive" works that, taking advantage of a crucial moment, sum up and deliver judgment on some phase of human activity; that make us understand what has happened, that establish enduring assumptions and that remain indispensable landmarks.

It is not possible to summarize briefly the contents of Mr. Seldes's book, but its main conclusions are these:

The movies, he says, have been losing their public. Between 1947 and 1950, a thirty-percent drop has taken place, and the movie-theater audience is mainly made up of teen-agers; after twenty, people go less often, and after thirty, almost not at all. The films are mostly aimed at the young and, in consequence, have become, at the present time, repetitions of stereotyped myths that have no roots whatever in reality. Mr. Seldes is at his most brilliant in his descriptions of the imaginary worlds presented by the mass entertainments. He shows that the contemporary world of the films is one in which men and women are never allowed to have sexual relations. Extramarital liaisons are barred, and even when people get married, the consummation is infinitely delayed by a series of unfortunate accidents. Later on, when the wives have acquired children by some parthenogenic process, the marriage may be threatened by a bad woman whose badness consists of an interest in sex; but Providence will always arrange that the couple shall be brought together by the injury or illness of a child. In the meantime, the hiatus left by the exclusion of sensual passion that is imposed by the censorship is filled by a strangely uncensored sadistic indulgence in violence. A woman may not be desired but she may be indecently spanked or given a sock in the jaw. And the hero and heroine never work; it is enough for the young man that he should marry the boss's daughter, or, in the case of a composer, that he should write "a great song or symphony in a single blinding flash of inspiration." Only the milkman and such people work, and these workers are invariably good-natured and respectful toward the more fortunate class they serve. The married couples remain immature till the children begin to grow up, whereupon they revert to the springtime of youth and are saved from amorous follies only through the intervention of their bright adolescent children. No one, says Mr. Seldes, ever really grows up in the movies, and that is the reason they do not interest adults.

While the movies, in the thirties and forties, were petrifying into these formulas, the radio had been developing two new kinds of formularized commodity: the news broadcast and the daytime serial. The problems of free speech and good taste that arise in connection with news commentators and the commercial announcements of sponsors have been decided in different instances, the most important of which are recorded by Mr. Seldes, in a variety of different ways; but, with the recent decline in radio, in proportion as television has been taking its place, the barriers against propaganda and the plugging of obnoxious products have been largely broken down. You can now buy time for almost anything: a laxative that is advertised at mealtime or a bigoted religious program. As for the daytime serial, it is a dreary and inspired story that is made to creep on from day to day in such a way that as little as possible will happen in any given instalment and that that little will take as long as possible. The typical situation here is one in which a decisive and self-dependent woman intervenes in the lives of others. She must never meet another character who is vigorous and determined also, because that would precipitate action. Her husband is invariably unready and hesitant; he probably suffers from impotence. She herself is probably frigid. A check on radio audiences has shown that the listeners to these serials are housewives with impoverished lives, themselves lacking competence and resolution. The continual small anxieties created by the situations in the serials correspond to their own anxieties and afford the humble satisfaction of hearing them vicariously resolved. But it is probable, Mr. Seldes believes, that this interminable purveying of anxieties has the effect of keeping up artificially the state of mind it appears to soothe, just as the playing down to immaturity, in the case of the young movie audience, has become perhaps the principal influence that induces it to remain immature.

What, then, about television, with which Mr. Seldes has been involved almost since its commercial inception and to which, though he does not say so, he has contributed his own best efforts with a view to directing its development toward a respectable art of its own? He admits that, at its present stage, TV has produced nothing really new, but he believes that since it has the advantage of letting you both see and hear its performers while their performance is going on, it should encourage a more natural relation between the performer and his audience than either radio or movie does, and he hopes that, in its handling of drama, it will approximate to the regular stage in allowing us to see characters in the round. Unfortunately, the only examples that Mr. Seldes is able at this time to invoke in order to persuade us of these possibilities are such features as Milton Berle and the puppets Kukla, Fran and Ollie, about whose quality he makes it plain that he is not enthusiastic, and he has already chilled the reader's blood by introducing his section on this subject with the heading *Pandora's Box*.

Mr. Seldes has tried to be as hopeful as the conditions will possibly permit; he does not want to accept dead ends. Television, if it only will, can, he says, give us real theater in the living room. The movies can retrieve their slipping public by appealing to an untouched audience—that of mature men and women. He preaches to the public as a whole the need for non-official protests on the part of groups of citizens—though he has noted the discouraging apathy of the people who patronize these mass media. To those who don't listen to radio, who don't look at television, and who rarely go to the movies, he insists that this will not save them. They must live in a common society conditioned by the effect of these things. Might not a man who had never turned on the radio find himself being trampled to death by a panic-stricken mob driven frantic by some such broadcast as Orson Welles's *War of the Worlds?* On the other hand, the remedy proposed for minimizing this kind of hazard seems a heavy price to pay for escape from even such a fate as this. In order to keep informed as to what is going on in these departments, the non-lover of television and radio will be obliged, Mr. Seldes suggests, to "suspend whatever he is doing and look for an hour or two at the best that is now offered." But "if a nation cannot survive half slave and half free, a democracy cannot endure if the forces making for free minds are apathetic and the forces of invincible ignorance are aggressive and brilliantly managed and irresponsible. If it is already inconvenient to attack them, it will be dangerous in five years, and it will be impossible in ten." If no pressure is brought by the public to have the level of these media raised, the result may be simply that the movies will be superseded by television, and that radio will go bankrupt in the attempt to finance its successor before television has had the chance to outgrow its rudimentary stages. This would greatly facilitate the step that is Mr. Seldes's principal bug-bear, as it may well be anyone's: the taking over of the mass media by the government and the use of them, not for more or less legitimate informative and cultural purposes, as the B.B.C. has used them, but for unscrupulous total control of a spineless depersonalized public. The exploiters of mass entertainment, in aiming, for steady and sure returns, at the lowest common denominator, have in some departments been losing their audience, but they have also been stultifying those who share in this lowest common denominator and artificially extending its realm.

We are almost as far here from the Seldes who delighted in the *Ziegfeld Follies* and the vaudeville turns at the Palace as we are from the Toulouse-Lautrec who frequented the Nouveau Cirque or, for that matter, from Toulouse-Lautrec's predecessor, the seventeenth-century Jacques Callot, who amused himself in Italy at the *commedia dell' arte*. This book is about the audience, not about the artists. Mr. Seldes says he cannot take time to pay his compliments to the shows and the actors that have given him particular pleasure, but, after all, the films as we have them could hardly produce a new Chaplin. Mr. Seldes has told briefly here the story of Walt Disney's capitulation, in competition with the comic books and under pressure to pay off his financing, by turning out long features in quantity. He might have added that of Jimmy Durante, surely the greatest comic that has appeared since Mr. Seldes's first book, who has been compelled to descend from the wild poetry of the Parody Club to the routine personality gags of his work on the screen and air. Mr. Seldes mentions in passing that Li'l Abner may perhaps "to a degree" take the place of Krazy Kat; but he is occupied chiefly with the problem of curing the degenerate tendencies of the seven hundred million comic books that are now printed every year.

Mr. Seldes, since he left the *Dial*, has been cultivating certain conceptions that sometimes land him in a false position. He asserts that the more serious American writers have always been contemptuous of "the average man," that they have vilified American life and made no effort to understand America. He even goes to the length of implying that Walt Whitman was deficient in sympathy for ordinary American humanity and indifferent to the Civil War. It is a pity that Mr. Seldes should so long ago have taken up a position that has prevented him from becoming as

well-acquainted with the history of American thought as
he is with that of our popular arts. Since this question, in
his latest book, is raised only incidentally, one need not go
into it here any further than to make the point that the
better American writers have given expression to a variety
of points of view and that these points of view themselves
have varied in response to varying epochs. Mr. Seldes's
own point of view seems rather to belong to the category
of what Frank Moore Colby meant when he called one
of his books *Constrained Attitudes*. This attitude is contra-
dicted on almost every page of Mr. Seldes's book by what
he thinks and says and is. Such occasional pokes as he takes
at his antagonist, the straw-man "intellectual," who is supposed to disdain the popular arts, are quite inconsistent
with the bitter complaints of "anti-intellectualism" that he
brings against the radio and movies for their habit of representing schoolteachers as invariably either "angular spin-
sters" or "absent-minded professors," who are treated "the
former without sympathy, the latter without respect," and
their convention that all studious young people are absurd
little prigs and bores.

The truth is, of course, that Mr. Seldes is nothing if not
an intellectual himself, and, as *The Great Audience* proves,
an exceptionally able one. He has come out of his twenty
years of wrestling professionally with the lively arts even
less well-disposed toward mediocrity, toward the facile, the
false and the trashy, than he was at the time when he was
editing the *Dial* and when the floods of that rubbish were
not threatening to swamp us. Mr. Seldes's whole appeal to
the public is based on the hope—I believe quite justified—
that there are still a great many Americans who are also
intellectuals, to the degree, at least, of not being satisfied
with the goods that the mass media are putting out. His
"intellectual" and his "average man" are in reality dema-
gogic devices, taken over from the very agencies against
which he now protests; they have never been anything
other than masks to mislead the simple. Mr. Seldes shows
them up at once when he comes to grips with his subject, as

in his section called *Nine P. M. Tuesday,* in which he tells us that "the average man lives at many emotional and intellectual levels," and when he declares, in *The Menace of the Years,* that "the people desperately need arts that are serious." Intellectual that he is, he cannot help expressing a doubt whether, at this point, the people are "capable of accepting" them; and no critic of our post-Civil War period or of the Mencken and Lewis era has ever taken a gloomier view of the results of American commercialism or issued a grimmer warning. The radio and movies, Mr. Seldes says, "are the great engines of democratic entertainment and culture," yet, through their imposition of uniformity, "they are committed to the destruction of democracy."

October 28, 1950

Poe at Home and Abroad

I

THE RECENT REVIVAL of interest in Poe has brought to light a good deal of new information and supplied us for the first time with a serious interpretation of his personal career, but it has so far entirely neglected to explain why we should still want to read him. In respect to such figures as Poe, we Americans are still perhaps almost as provincial as those of their contemporaries who now seem to us ridiculous for having failed to recognize their genius. Today, we take their eminence for granted, but we still cannot help regarding them, not from the point of view of their real contributions to western culture, but primarily as fellow-Americans, whose activities we feel the necessity of explaining in terms of America and the circumstances of whose personal lives we are, as neighbors, in a position to investigate. Thus, at a date when "Edgar Poe" has figured in Europe for the last three-quarters of a century as a writer of the first importance, we in America are still preoccupied—though no longer in moral indignation—with his bad reputation as a citizen. Thus, Dr. J. W. Robertson, who perhaps started off the recent researches, five years ago published a book to show that Poe was a typical alcoholic. Thus, last year we saw the publication of Poe's correspondence with his foster-father. Thus, we are promised the early revelation of Poe's plagiarism of his plots from a hitherto unknown German source (as James Huneker has pointed out that Poe's later and most celebrated poems must certainly have owed a good deal to an obscure American poet named Thomas Holley Chivers). Thus, a Miss Mary E. Phillips has just published an enormous biography running to sixteen hundred and eighty-five pages—*Edgar Allan Poe, the Man*—a monument of uncritical devotion which it must have taken a lifetime to compile, stuffed with illustrations that include not only photographs of the little Scotch town from which Poe's foster-father came, of the librarian of the University of Virginia at the time when Poe was a student there and of the clock on the mantelpiece of Poe's cottage at Fordham, but also maps of New York, Richmond and Baltimore at the time when Poe lived in those cities; and containing embedded in its pudding-stone prose perhaps more miscellaneous facts about him than have ever before been assembled.

The ablest and the most important of recent American books on Poe, is, however, without any doubt, Mr. Joseph Wood Krutch's *Edgar Allan Poe: A Study in Genius*. Mr. Krutch has made an attempt to go beyond Doctor Robertson in diagnosing Poe's nervous malady, and his conclusions are by this time well known: he believes that Poe was driven in the first instance into seeking a position of literary eminence by a desire to compensate himself for the loss of social position of which his foster-father had deprived him; that, in consequence, perhaps of a "fixation" on his mother, he became sexually impotent and was forced, as a result of his inability to play a part in the normal world, to invent an abnormal world full of horror, repining and doom (the universally recognized concomitants, according to Mr.

Krutch, of sexual repression of this sort) in which he could take refuge; that his very intellectual activity, his love of working out cryptograms and crimes, had been primarily stimulated by the desire to prove himself logical when he felt he was going insane; and, finally, that his critical theory was merely a justification of his peculiar artistic practice, which was itself thus, in turn, a symptom of his disease. It must be said, in fairness to Mr. Krutch, that he does not fail to draw, at the end of his book, the conclusions about artists in general which follow from his particular conclusions. Mr. Krutch fully admits that, if what he says about Poe is true, it must also be true of "all imaginative works," which, in that case, should be regarded as the products of "unfulfilled desires" springing from "either idiosyncratic or universally human maladjustments to life." This does not, however, prevent Mr. Krutch from misunderstanding Poe's writings and seriously undervaluing them, nor even from complacently caricaturing them—as the modern school of social-psychological biography, of which Mr. Krutch is a typical representative, seems inevitably to tend to caricature the personalities of its subjects. We are nowadays being edified by the spectacle of some of the principal ornaments of the human race exhibited exclusively in terms of their most ridiculous manias, their most disquieting neuroses and their most humiliating failures. Mr. Krutch has chosen for the frontispiece of what he calls a "study in genius" a daguerreotype of Poe taken in 1849, shortly before his death: it shows a pasty and dilapidated personage with untrimmed untidy hair, an uneven toothbrush mustache and large pouches under the eyes; the eyes themselves have a sad unfocussed stare; one eyelid is drooping; one hand is thrust into the coat-front with an air of feeble pretentiousness. The dignified solemnity of the figure is as ludicrous as a bad old-fashioned actor attempting to play *Hamlet*, and its visible disintegration unpleasantly suggests an alcoholic patient recently admitted to a cure. And something like this is the final impression left by Mr. Krutch's book. Mr. Krutch quotes with disapproval the statement of President Hadley of Yale in explaining the refusal of the Hall of Fame to accept Poe among its immortals: "Poe wrote like a drunkard and a man who is not accustomed to pay his debts"; and yet Mr. Krutch himself, so interesting as a psychologist, is almost as unperceptive when he tells us, in effect, that Poe wrote like a dispossessed Southern gentleman and a man with a fixation on his mother.

For the rest, Mr. H. L. Mencken has written with admiration of Poe's destructive reviewing—that is, he has paid a tribute to an earlier practitioner of an art of his own; Mr. Van Wyck Brooks has examined Poe's work for evidences of the harshness and the sterility of a Puritan-pioneer society, and found it unsatisfactory as literature; and Mr. Lewis Mumford, in *The Golden Day*, seems to have taken his cue from Mr. Brooks when he finds in the hardness of Poe's effects the steel of the industrial age. It may, I believe, be said that no recent American critic, with the exception of Mr. Waldo Frank in his article on the Poe-Allan letters, has written with any real appreciation of Poe's absolute artistic importance.

II

One of the most striking features of all this American criticism of Poe is its tendency to regard him as a freak, having his existence somehow apart not merely from contemporary life but even from contemporary literature. "That his life happened to fall," writes Mr. Krutch, "between the years 1809 and 1849 is merely an accident, and he has no more in common with Whittier, Lowell, Longfellow or Emerson than he has with either the eighteenth or nineteenth centuries in England. . . . His works bear no conceivable relation, either external or internal, to the life of any people, and it is impossible to account for them on the basis of any social or intellectual tendencies or as the expression of the spirit of any age." Worse than this, we are always being told that Poe has no connection with "reality," that he writes exclusively of a "dream world" which has no point of contact with our own. The error of this second assertion immediately becomes apparent when we consider the falsity of the first. So far from having nothing in common with the spirit of the first half of the nineteenth century, Poe is certainly one of its most typical figures; that is to say, he is a thorough romantic, closely akin to his European contemporaries. Thus, his nightmarish vein of fantasy is very much like that of Coleridge; his poetry in its earlier phase derives from Shelley and Keats; his "dream fugues" resemble De Quincey's and his "prose poems," Maurice de Guérin's. His themes—which, as Baudelaire says, are concerned with "the exception in the moral order" —are in the tradition of Chateaubriand and Byron, and of the romantic movement generally. It is, then, in terms of romanticism that we must look for reality in Poe. It shows a lack of historical sense to expect of him the same sort of treatment of life that we find in Dreiser or Sinclair Lewis and the recent preoccupation with which seems so to have misled our critics. From this modern sociological point of view, the European writers whom I have named above had no more connection with their respective countries than had Poe with the United States. Their settings and their dramatis personae, the images by which they rendered their ideas, were as different as those of Poe from the images of modern naturalism, and they used them for a different kind of story-telling which conveyed a different kind of moral.

What, then, are the morals of Poe, the realities he tried to express? The key is to be found in Baudelaire's phrase about "the exception in the moral order." The exception in the moral order was the predominant theme of the romantic movement. It is absurd to complain, as our critics do, of Poe's indifference to the claims of society, as if this indifference were something abnormal: one of the principal features of romanticism was, not merely an indifference to the claims of society, but an exalted revolt against them. The favorite figure of the romantic writers was the sympathetic individual considered from the point of view of his non-amenability to law or convention. And in this, Poe runs absolutely true to type: his heroes are the brothers of Rolla and René; of Childe Harold, Manfred and Cain. Like these latter, they are superior individuals who pursue extravagant fancies, plumb abysses of dissipation or yield to forbidden passions (Poe made one or two experiments with the common romantic theme of incest; but his specialties were a frigid sadism and a curious form of adultery which never took place till the woman whom the hero betrayed was dead). And, as in the case of the other romantic heroes, their drama is the conflict of their impulses with human or divine law. This impulse of the individual does not, however, in Poe, take often, as it does with the other romantics, the form of a too generous passion overflowing the canals of the world; but assumes rather the sinister character of what Poe called the "Imp of the Perverse." Yet this very perversity of Poe, the kind of dizzy terror it engenders, due to whatever nervous instability and whatever unlucky circumstances, have their poetry and their deep pathos—from those lines in one of the finest of his poems in which he tells how the doom of his later life appeared to him even in childhood as he gazed on "the cloud that took the form (When the rest of Heaven was blue) Of a demon in my view," to that terrible picture of the condemned man, "sick —sick unto death with that long agony," when "first [the candles] wore the aspect of charity, and seemed white slender angels who would save me; but then, all at once, there came a most deadly nausea over my spirit, and I felt every fibre in my frame thrill as if I had touched the wire of a galvanic battery, while the angel forms became meaningless specters, with heads of flame, and I saw that from them there would be no help. And then there stole into my fancy, like a rich musical note, the thought of what sweet rest there must be in the grave." And it is the lifelong "agony" of his moral experience that gives to Poe's *William Wilson* its superior sincerity and intensity over Stevenson's *Doctor Jekyll and Mr. Hyde.* In Stevenson, it is the virtuous half of the dual personality that destroys the divided man by exorcising the evil; but, in Poe, it is the evil half that does away with the good and that is even made to tell the whole story from its own point of view. Yet does not *William Wilson* bring home to us the horror of the moral transmutation more convincingly than the melodramatic fable of Doctor Jekyll and Mr. Hyde?

There is one special tragic theme of Poe's which deserves to be noted in this connection. Mr. Krutch says that Poe was impotent, and that, for this reason, though perhaps unconsciously, he chose to marry a girl of thirteen with whom it would be impossible for him to have regular conjugal relations. Mr. Krutch does not offer any proof of this, but we do not have to assume it to be true in order to agree with Mr. Krutch that Poe's marriage with Virginia Clemm was somehow unsatisfactory, and that it plays a strange role in his work. Virginia was Poe's first cousin, and it may be that, on this account, he had scruples about consummating the marriage. In any case, she became tubercular, and, twelve years after their marriage, died; while Poe himself grew neurotic, irritable and at last unbalanced. He was obsessed by desperate fantasies and seems, after her death, to have been almost insane. It is possible to follow Mr. Krutch in admitting that the atrocious sadism of many of Poe's later tales must have been due to some emotional repression. Though he undoubtedly adored Virginia, he seems at the same time to have wished her dead. He is always imagining, in his tales, long before her actual death, that a woman like Virginia has died and that her lover is free to love other women. But even here, the dead woman intervenes: in *Ligeia,* she reincarnates herself in the corpse of her successor, who has also died; in *Morella,* in her own daughter. And it is evidently this conflict of Poe's emotions which inspires, not merely these bizarre fancies, but also the unexplained feelings of remorse that so often haunt his heroes. After Virginia has actually died, the situation he has foreseen in the stories seems to be realized. He conducts flirtations with other women; but they are accompanied by "a wild inexplicable sentiment that resembles nothing so

nearly as a consciousness of guilt." "I was never really insane," he writes to Mrs. Clemm just before his miserable
death, "except on occasions when my heart was touched.
I have been taken to prison once since I came here for
getting drunk; but then I was not. It was about Virginia."
The story of Poe and Virginia is a painful and rather unpleasant one; but it is perhaps worth discussing to this
extent, for we recognize in it the actual relation which,
viewed in the light of a romantic problem and transposed
into romantic terms, fills Poe's writings with the ominous
sense of a deadlock between the rebellious spirit, the individual will, on the one hand, and both its very romantic
idealisms and its human bonds, on the other. "The whole
realm of moral ideals," says Mr. Krutch, "is excluded [from
Poe's work], not merely as morality *per se*, but also as
artistic material used for the creation of conflicts and situations." What, then, does he suppose such stories as
Eleanora and *Ligeia* are about? He goes on to say that
horror is the only emotion which is "genuinely Poe's own"
and that this "deliberately invents causes for itself," that
"it is always a pure emotion without any rational founda-
tion." How, he would no doubt ask, can anything describ-
able as moral interest be found in the *Descent into the
Maelström* or the *Case of M. Valdemar?* This question I
propose to discuss in a moment.

III

Poe was, then, a typical romantic. But he was also something more. He contained the germs of a further development. By 1847, Baudelaire had begun to read Poe and
had "experienced a strange commotion": when he had
looked up the rest of Poe's writings in the files of American
magazines, he found among them stories and poems which
he had "thought vaguely and confusedly" of writing himself, and Poe became an obsession with him. He published
in 1856 a volume of translations of Poe's tales; and from

then on, the influence of Poe became one of the most important in French literature. M. Louis Seylaz has recently traced this influence in a book called *Edgar Poe et les Premiers Symbolistes Français*, in which he discusses the indebtedness to Poe of the French symbolist movement, from Baudelaire, through Verlaine, Rimbaud, Mallarmé (who translated Poe's poems), Villiers de L'Isle-Adam and Huysmans, to Paul Valéry in our own day (who has just written some interesting pages on Poe in a preface to a new edition of Baudelaire's *Les Fleurs du Mal*).

Let us inquire as to precisely in what this influence of Poe consisted that was felt so profoundly by the French through a whole half-century of their literature, yet which has so completely failed to impress itself upon the literature of Poe's own country that it is still possible for Americans to talk about him as if his principal claim to distinction were his title to be described as the "father of the short story." In the first place, says M. Valéry, Poe brought to the romanticism of the later nineteenth century a new aesthetic discipline. Perhaps more than any other writer, French or English, of the first half of the century, he had thought seriously and written clearly about the methods and aims of literature. He had formulated a critical theory, and he had supplied brilliant specimens of its practice. Even in poetry, by the time that Poe's influence had begun to be felt in France, it had been the ideals of naturalism that the post-romantic generation had tried to bring into play against the extravagance and the looseness of romanticism running to seed. But the American was now to provide them with a new and logical program that would aim to lop the overgrowths of romanticism and yet to achieve effects that can only be called romantic. What *were* these ultra-romantic effects which had first been described by Poe, and by what means did he propose to attain them?

"I *know*," writes Poe, "that indefiniteness is an element of the true music [of poetry]—I mean of the true musical expression . . . a suggestive indefiniteness of meaning with a view of bringing about a definiteness of vague and therefore of spiritual *effect*." This is already the doctrine of symbolism. Poe had exemplified it in his own poems. Poe's poetry is rarely quite successful; but it is, none the less, of first-rate importance. He tells us rather pathetically, in his preface to his poems, apologizing for their imperfections, that "events not to be controlled" have prevented him "from making, at any time, any serious effort in what, under happier circumstances, would have been the field of my choice." The immaturity of his early verse, where he is imitating Shelley and Coleridge, is certainly not redeemed by the deliberate tricks of his later, which he seems to have borrowed from Chivers and which are always a little trashy. Yet all of Poe's poetry is interesting, because more than that of any other romantic (except perhaps Coleridge in *Kubla Khan*), it does approach the indefiniteness of music—that supreme goal of the symbolists. That is to say that, from the ordinary point of view, Poe's poetry is more nonsensical than that of any of the other romantics—and nonsensical in much the same way as, to the ordinary point of view, much of our best modern poetry appears. To note but a single instance: one of the characteristic traits of modern symbolism is a sort of psychological confusion between the impressions of the different senses. This confusion distinctly appears in Poe: thus we find him, in one of his poems, *hearing* the approach of the darkness; and, in the marvellous description in one of his tales of the fusing sensations that follow death, we read that "night arrived; and with its shadows a heavy discomfort. It oppressed my limbs with the oppression of some dull weight, and was palpable. There was also a moaning sound, not unlike the distant reverberation of surf, but more continuous, which, beginning with the first twilight, had grown in strength with the darkness. Suddenly lights were brought into the room . . . and issuing from the flame of each lamp, there flowed unbrokenly into my ears a strain of melodious monotone."

Poe's theory of short-story writing was similar to his theory of verse. "A skilful artist," he writes, "has constructed a tale. If wise, he has not fashioned his thought to accommodate his incidents; but having conceived, with deliberate care, a certain unique or single *effect* to be wrought out, he then invents such incidents—he then combines such events as may best aid him in establishing this preconceived effect." So the real significance of Poe's short stories does not lie in what they purport to relate. Many are confessedly dreams; and, as with dreams, though they seem absurd, their effect on our emotions is serious. And even those that pretend to the logic and the exactitude of actual narratives are, nevertheless, also dreams. The happenings in them differ from the mere macabre surprises and the astonishing adventures and voyages of such imitators of Poe as Conan Doyle. The descent into the maelström is a metaphor for the horror of the moral whirlpool into which, with some justification, Poe had, as we know from more explicit stories, a giddy apprehension of going down; the precariously delayed dissolution of M. Valdemar stands for that horror of living death that figures also in *Premature Burial*, which, arising from whatever blight, haunted Poe through all his later life. No one understood better than Poe that, in fiction and in poetry both, it is not what you say that counts, but what you make the reader feel (he always italicizes the word "effect"); no one understood better than Poe that the deepest psychological truth may be rendered through phantasmagoria. Even the realistic stories of Poe are, in fact, only phantasmagoria of a more circumstantial kind. Any realism of any age which does not convey some such truth is, of course, bound to be unsatisfactory. And today when a revolt is in progress against the literalness and the superficialty of the naturalistic movement that has come between Poe's time and ours, he ought to be of special interest.

"Poe's mentality was a rare synthesis," writes Mr. Padraic Colum. "He had elements in him that corresponded with the indefiniteness of music and the exactitude of mathematics." Is not this what modern literature is tending toward? It was Poe who sent out the bridge from the romanticism of the early nineteenth century to the symbolism of the later; and symbolism, as M. Seylaz points out, though scarcely any of its original exponents survive, now permeates literature. We must not, however, expect that Poe should be admired or understood in his capacity of suspension across this chasm by critics who are hardly aware that either of its banks exists.

December 8, 1926

The All-Star Literary Vaudeville

THE WRITER of this article is a journalist whose professional activities have been chiefly concerned with the American literary movement of the last fifteen years.[*] He has written reviews of the productions of that movement and worked on magazines which were identified with it; he has lived constantly in its atmosphere. And he feels a certain human sympathy with all of its manifestations, even with those of which, artistically, he disapproves. It is to him a source of deep gratification that literature has been "sold" to the American public, and, on principle, in the face of alien attack, he will stand by even the least intelligent, the least disinterested, of its salesmen: he has served in that army himself. But it has recently occurred to him that, when he comes to take stock and is perfectly honest with himself, he must admit to feeling only the mildest interest in most of the contemporary literary goods which now find so wide a market, and that he is disaffected to the point of disgust with the publicity service which has grown up in connection with them. He has to take account of the fact that it is scarcely possible nowadays to tell the reviews from the advertising: both tend to convey the impression that masterpieces are being manufactured as regularly as new models of motor-cars. In the early days of the present era, the

[*] This essay first appeared anonymously.

reviews of H. L. Mencken, Francis Hackett, Floyd Dell and Louis Untermeyer set an example of honesty and boldness. Today these journalist critics, having got the kind of literature they want, are apparently quite content; and most of the reviews are now written by people who do not try to go beyond them. The present writers on American literature all have interests in one phase or another of it: either the authors know one another personally or they owe one another debts of gratitude or they are bound together by their loyalty to some stimulating common cause. And almost all forget critical standards in their devotion to the great common causes: the cause of an American national literature in independence of English literature, and the cause of contemporary American ideas as against the ideas of the last generation. Even Stuart P. Sherman, once so savage in the opposite camp, has become as benevolent as Carl Van Doren and now occupies what has perhaps become, from the popular point of view, the central desk of authority, to which each of the performers in the all-star circus, from Ben Hecht to Ring Lardner, steps up to receive his endorsement. The present writer has, therefore, for his own satisfaction, for the appeasement of his own conscience, made an attempt to draw up a balance-sheet of his opinions in regard to his contemporaries, not merely in disparagement of those whom he considers rather overrated but in justice to those he admires. If he succeeds in disturbing one editor or reviewer, in an atmosphere where now for some time politeness and complacency have reigned, he will feel that he has not written in vain.

To begin with the contemporary American novel—which is commonly assumed to be our principal glory—I must confess that I have difficulty in reading our novelists. We compare our fiction with English fiction and conclude that we have been brilliantly successful in this field; but the truth is merely that the English novel is just now at a particularly low ebb. We have no novelist of the first importance, of the importance of James, Joyce or Proust; or of that of Balzac or Dostoevsky. Dreiser commands our respect; but the truth is he writes so badly that it is almost impossible to read him, and, for this reason, I find it hard to believe in his literary permanence. To follow the moral disintegration of Hurstwood in *Sister Carrie* is to suffer all the agonies of being out of work without being rewarded by the aesthetic pleasure which art is supposed to supply. Sinclair Lewis, with a vigorous satiric humor, has brought against certain aspects of American civilization an indictment that has its local importance, but, when one has been through *Main Street* and *Babbitt*, amusing though they certainly are, one is not left with any appetite to read further novels by Lewis: they have beauty neither of style nor of form and they tell us nothing new about life. Joseph Hergesheimer, though he knows how to tell a story, writes nearly as badly in a fancy way as Dreiser does in a crude one: the judgment of him that I most agree with is the remark attributed to Max Beerbohm: "Poor Mr. Hergesheimer, he wants so much to be an artist." Cabell, though a man of real parts, is, at his worst, a case of the same kind: *Beyond Life* I regard as one of the most obnoxiously written books I have ever read. *Jurgen* certainly had its merits: it was well-planned and curiously successful in the artificial evocation of the atmosphere of primitive folklore. But, except at Cabell's moments of highest imaginative intensity, which are neither very frequent nor very intense, he is likely to be simply insipid. His genealogies and maps of Poictesme bore me beyond description, and the whole Poictesme business strikes me as the sort of thing with which ingenious literary schoolboys sometimes amuse themselves. I dislike also Cabell's Southern sentimentality, which leaves him soft when he thinks he is most cynical. One cannot help feeling that, in the impression he gives of living and working in a vacuum, he furnishes a depressing illustration of the decay of the South since the Civil War. Willa Cather is a good craftsman, but she is usually rather dull. In spite of a few distinguished stories, she suffers from an anemia of the imagination and, like that other rather distinguished novelist, Zona Gale, is given to terrible lapses into feminine melodrama. As for Waldo Frank, he writes in a style—to me, never quite satisfactory—that combines James Joyce with the Hebrew prophets. At his best, he touches tragedy and, at his worst, embraces melodrama. He possesses a real poetic sensibility and is refreshing in so far as his vision is different from that of any one else; but, in his novels, where we hope to see him stage a drama, he is usually content to invoke an apocalypse. I consider Jean Toomer's *Cane* rather better in literary quality than Frank's somewhat similar *Holiday*. I feel more interest in John Dos Passos and F. Scott Fitzgerald than in any of the writers mentioned above: they are younger than the others, and one does not feel as yet that one knows exactly what to expect of them. Dos Passos is ridden by adolescent resentments and seems given to documenting life from the outside rather than knowing it by intimate experience; but, though, like Lewis, that other documentator, he is far too much addicted to making out cases against society, he is a better artist than Lewis and has steadily progressed in his art. Scott Fitzgerald, possessing from the first, not merely cleverness, but something of inspired imagination and poetic literary brilliance, has not until recently given the impression of precisely knowing what he was about; but with *The Great Gatsby* and some of his recent short stories, he seems to be entering upon a development in the course of which he may come to equal in mastery of his material those novelists whom he began by surpassing by vividness in investing it with glamor. Besides these, there are the other fabricators of fantasy and the realists, satiric and plain; but the former, so far as I have read them, are either tawdry, like Ben Hecht, or awfully mild, like Carl Van Vechten; and the latter, though both in novel and drama they have learned to apply the formulas of naturalism to almost every phase of American life and have, therefore, a certain interest in the history of American culture, are otherwise especially uninteresting at a time when naturalism has run its course and everywhere except in America is either being transformed or discarded. And we have also had the Wellsian social novel, at various levels of mediocrity.

Sherwood Anderson is a different matter. In his novels, despite excellent pages, I invariably become exasperated, before I have got to the end of them, by the vagueness of the characters and the constant repetitiousness of the form. But his short stories and his symbolist prose-poems have a kind of artistic authenticity that neither Lewis's richer resources nor Miss Cather's technical efforts have been able to win for those writers. Without ever having learned the tricks of his trade, Sherwood Anderson, in the best of his stories, has shown an almost perfect instinct that fashions, from what seems a more intimate stratum of feeling and imagination than our novelists usually explore, visions at once fresh and naïve and of a slightly discomfiting strangeness. He could stand to learn something, however, from the methods both of Miss Cather and of Lewis: too much of his material has evaporated in his hands from his not knowing how to deal with it. It can probably be said that, in general, the newer American writers have so far been distinguishing themselves in the short story rather than the novel. The short stories of Sherwood Anderson, Ernest Hemingway's *In Our Time* and Gertrude Stein's early *Three Lives,* to which should be added the best of Ring Lardner, constitute an impressive group and one quite free from the outworn conventions and the suggestion of second-rate imitation that make many of the novels unsatisfactory. It is interesting to note that all four of these writers have certain characteristics in common, that they may almost be said to form a school, and that, remote though they may seem from one another, there is a fairly close relationship between them. Thus, Anderson has read Gertrude Stein and seems to have been influenced by *Three Lives;* and Hemingway has evidently read and been influenced by all three of the others. Each of these four writers has developed what seems only a special branch of the same simple colloquial language, based directly on the vocabulary and rhythm of ordinary American speech; and, if there can be said to be an American school of writing, aside from American journalese or from the use of American slang in otherwise conventional English prose, these writers would seem to represent it. It is a genre that has already produced one masterpiece in Mark Twain's *Huckleberry Finn,* a work to which Anderson, Hemingway and Lardner are probably all indebted.

As for the dramatists, there is still only O'Neill, who, for all his efforts to break away from naturalism, remains a typical naturalistic dramatist of something under the very first rank. He is a writer of the same school as Hauptmann, with much the same kind of merits; but, where Hauptmann is as steady as Shakespeare, O'Neill is hysterically embittered. He forces his tragic catastrophes and, at the same time, fails to prepare them; and, despite the magnificent eloquence of which he is sometimes capable, especially when handling some form of the vernacular, he has grave deficiencies of literary taste which allow him to leave great areas of his dialogue either banal or bald. John H. Lawson has a wit and a fancy which have found their proper vehicle in the theater; but, even more than his ally, Dos Passos, he is given to adolescent grievances and adolescent enthusiasms.

We come now to literary criticism. In my opinion, H. L. Mencken (who is perhaps a prophet rather than a critic) is ordinarily underrated as a writer of English prose. Belonging himself to the line of Butler and Swift rather than to that of Pater and De Quincey, he cherishes a rustic reverence for the more "aesthetic" branch and is never tired of celebrating the elegances of such provincial fops as Lord Dunsany, Hergesheimer and Cabell, who have announced—it is, I think, Mr. Cabell's phrase—that they aim to "write beautifully about beautiful things." But although it is true that Mencken's style lends itself to excesses and vulgarities, especially in the hands of his imitators, who have taken over the Master's jargon without possessing his admirable literary sense, I believe that his prose is more successful in its way than that of these devotees of beauty usually is in theirs. The ideas themselves behind Mencken's writing are neither many nor subtle and, even in his most serious productions, even in *The American Language,* he overindulges an appetite for paradox. But some strain of the musician and poet has made it possible for Mencken to turn these ideas into literature: it is precisely through the color and rhythm of a highly personal prose that Mencken's opinions have become so infectious. He has now been repeating these opinions with the same pugnacious emphasis for fifteen or twenty years, and one has become rather tired of hearing them; yet he sustains a certain distinction and affords a certain satisfaction. Consider, for example, the leaflet he recently circulated on the adventures of the *American Mercury* with the Boston Watch and Ward Society: his statement, of no literary pretensions, in which he appears without war-paint or feathers, displays most attractive eighteenth-century qualities of lucidity, order and force, for lack of which the youngest of the younger literary generation, who have thrown Mencken overboard, have proved so far rather ineffective.

Paul Rosenfeld is another critic very unpopular with this youngest generation who seems to me an excellent writer. Though he, too, has his faults of style, which include a confusing weakness for writing French and German locutions in English, his command of a rich English vocabulary is one of the things that make him exceptional among recent American writers—who are not infrequently handicapped by not having at their disposal a large enough variety of English words, or, if they have them, by not knowing what they mean. Mr. Rosenfeld, at his worst, is given to overwriting: receiving in his soul the seed of a work by some such writer as Sherwood Anderson, himself one of the tenderer plants, he will cause it to shoot up and exfloreate into an enormous and rather rank "Mystic Cabbage-Rose." On these occasions, his prose seems sometimes rather coarse in quality and his colors a little muddy;

but, at his best, Mr. Rosenfeld's writing is certainly among
our soundest and his colors are both brilliant and true. He
is sensitive, intelligent, well-educated and incorruptibly
serious; and he is perhaps the only American critic of the
generation since that of James Huneker who has written
anything of any real value on the current artistic life of
Europe. Van Wyck Brooks, who also writes excellent prose,
though of quite a different sort, I propose to discuss in
another connection.

George Jean Nathan is a wonderful humorous writer
and a better critic of the theater than A. B. Walkley, in a
recent article, gave him credit for being; but his writing,
which superficially resembles Mencken's, is usually lacking
in the qualities that give Mencken's its durable texture.
Willard Huntington Wright, some years ago, gave the
impression of being some one important; and Lewis Mumford now gives the impression of some one perhaps about
to be. Gilbert Seldes, through his activities as an editor of
the *Dial* and his cultivation of the popular arts, has filled a
role of considerable importance; but his principal literary
quality is a kind of undisciplined wit which figures too
often in his writings at the expense of lucidity and taste.
He has lately become addicted to aesthetic editorial writing, a department for which his alert and vivid but glancing
and volatile mind, is perhaps not very well adapted. In my
opinion, he is seen at his best in passages of straight description of some movie or vaudeville act which has aroused
his imagination. Burton Rascoe has performed the astonishing and probably unprecedented feat of making literature
into news. A master of all the tricks of newspaper journalism,
which he has introduced into the Sacred Grove to the
horror of some of its high priests, his career has yet been
singularly honorable in its disregard of popular values; and
the cause of letters has profited more from his activities
than the proprietors of popular newspapers who have inevitably discovered in the long run that they would feel
more comfortable with a literary editor who did not find
books so exciting. Mr. Rascoe has always written respect-

ably and, at his best, with much ease and point. Most of the younger generation of critics either are badly educated or have never learned to write, and many suffer from both disabilities. At best, we have produced no literary critic of the full European stature. The much-abused Paul Elmer More still figures as our only professional critic whose learning is really considerable and whose efforts are ambitious and serious. His prose is quite graceless and charmless, but always precise and clear; his point of view, though the Puritan rationalism of which it is a late product has imposed on it some rigid limitations, has the force of a deep conviction and the advantage of a definite formulation. Mr. More, although hopelessly inhibited in the exercise of his aesthetic sensibility, has become, in so far as is possible without the free range of this, a real master of ideas.

The new post-war method of biography, based on Strachey and psychoanalysis, has had many practitioners in America: Katherine Anthony, Van Wyck Brooks, Thomas Beer, M. R. Werner and others; but, though it has turned out a number of agreeable books, I have not seen any except Brooks's *Mark Twain* that seemed of first-rate importance. In the special departments of scholarly and expository writing, the general inferiority of the level of our culture to that of Great Britain or France becomes inescapably plain. There are not many of our college professors who can command the attention of the reading public. Professor John Dewey writes much and his influence has been considerable, but he has not inherited with pragmatism William James's literary gift. Professor Morris Cohen, who does possess a literary gift, has so far published nothing but reviews, and not very many of them. In the classics, Professor Tenney Frank seems the only representative of a new generation; but Professor Frank, although competent in a literary way and bold in interpretation, appears to be rather indifferent to the literary interest of the classics. Professor Paul Shorey of Chicago is perhaps the only other scholar who writes readable books in this field. We have, in short, no university professor with a literary reputation equal to that of Garrod, of Gilbert Murray, of Mackail, of A. E. Housman, or of Whitehead or Bertrand Russell or Lowes Dickinson. I can remember no recent book by an American professor which has been widely read on its literary merits, except Professor Warner Fite's *Moral Philosophy* and Professor Samuel Morison's *Maritime History of Massachusetts*. In science, we have some readable popularizers in the rousing modern manner, but they are mostly undistinguished writers: Doctor Fishbein, Doctor De Kruif and Doctor Dorsey. Edwin Slosson is rapidly becoming a sort of William Lyon Phelps of scientific culture. The zoölogist William Beebe writes a prose that is shamelessly journalistic; but he is a man of some literary ability, who deserves to be read by writers. One of his assets is an extraordinary vocabulary, which blends scientific with literary language in such a way that his scientific words are imbued with a new life and color. I doubt, however, whether the cable to the *New York Times* is a very good school of writing. I am sorry not to be able to do justice to our recent political writers. I believe that in this department we are somewhat better off than elsewhere; but it is the one in which I have lately read least.

As for poetry, the new movement of twelve years ago seemed at the time to assume impressive proportions. But who can believe in its heroes now? Edgar Lee Masters did one creditable thing: *The Spoon River Anthology;* but, except for a single fine poem called *Silence,* I have seen nothing by him since that I could read. Vachel Lindsay's best poems, such as his *Bryan,* are spoiled by the incurable cheapness and looseness which are rampant in the rest of his work. Carl Sandburg, unlike Masters and Lindsay, has a genuine talent for language; with a hard-boiled vocabulary and reputation, he offers what is perhaps the most attractive surface of any of the men of the group. But, when we come to read him in quantity, we are disappointed to find him less interesting than we had hoped; his ideas seem rather obvious, his emotions rather meager. The work of Amy Lowell is like a great empty cloisonné jar; that of John Gould Fletcher a great wall of hard descriptive prose mistakenly presented as poetry. Conrad Aiken, except in a few of his lyrics, is one of those curious people, like William Vaughn Moody, who can turn out a rich-looking texture of words and who can make at first glance the impression of being true and highly gifted inheritors of the English tradition of the nineteenth century, but who leave us, on closer reading, with a feeling that they have not quite got the "afflatus" that their themes and their style imply. Robert Frost has a thin but authentic vein of poetic sensibility; but I find him excessively dull, and he certainly writes very poor verse. He is, in my opinion, the most generally overrated of all this group of poets. Ezra Pound, who deserves all honor as a champion and pioneer, has worked conscientiously and stubbornly as one who understands very well, and as few of his contemporaries do, in what the highest poetry consists, but who has rarely been able to affect us as the highest poets do. His cantos of a "poem of considerable length," so ambitious and so full of fine passages, passages that, standing by themselves, might lead us to believe them mere ornaments from a masterpiece on the great scale, seem entirely composed of such fragments; a mosaic which fails to reveal a pattern, a monument, in its lack of cohesion, its lack of driving force or a center, to a kind of poetic bankruptcy. The other poets of the literary Left, though, like Pound, they can often write, seem to suffer from a similar sterility. Marianne Moore, for example, is sometimes very fine; but, as she herself has shrewdly noted in choosing a title for her collected verse, the bulk of her work answers better to the description of "Observations," than to that of poetry. From a slag of intellectual processes that has only a viscous flow, there emerge intense and vivid images that seem to have been invested with a sharp emotional meaning but that are rarely precipitated out in such a way as to make the piece a poem. H.D., like Carl Sandburg, writes well; but,

like Sandburg, there is not much in her. Wallace Stevens
has a fascinating gift of words that is not far from a gift
of nonsense, rather like that of Edith Sitwell, and he is a
charming decorative artist. Alfred Kreymborg has his dry
distinction, but he tends fatally toward insipidity. I think
I prefer the oddity of his early work, frankly prosaic and
dry, to his later more pretentious sonnets. E. E. Cummings
possesses, in some respects, a more remarkable lyric gift
than any of the poets reviewed above; his feeling is always
spontaneous, and his words run naturally into music. But,
as in his rather limp line-drawings, the hand does not seem
very firm: all sorts of ideas and images have come stream-
ing into his head, and he doesn't know how to manipulate
them to make them artistically effective. W. C. Williams
and Maxwell Bodenheim I have tried my best to admire,
but I have never been able to believe in them.*

Since these poets made their first reputations, the general
appetite for poetry seems to have somewhat abated. Among
the younger poets, for example, even those of most brilliant
promise are having difficulty in getting their poems printed,
not by the publishers only, who have evidently come to the
conclusion that poetry is bound to be unprofitable, but even
by the magazines. The editors of the magazines, who have
brought out, since the poetic revival, two or three crops
of poets, seem content now to close the canon, and have
no place for the poetry of unknown men—even if so obviously gifted as Phelps Putnam or Allen Tate—who cannot
be found in Mr. Untermeyer's anthologies or among the
original contributors to the *Dial*.

I have left aside the women lyric poets in order to discuss them as a group by themselves. On the average,
though less pretentious, I think I find them more rewarding
than the men: their emotion is likely to be more genuine

---

* It was at about this time that Maxwell Bodenheim described
me in some such phrase as "a fatuous policeman, menacingly
swinging his club." In rereading this essay—in which I have
qualified or softened some of the original judgments—I have
sometimes been reminded of this.

and their literary instinct surer. Miss Lizette Woodworth
Reese, the dean of the guild, astonishes one by continuing
to write, not only with the same fine quality, but almost
with the same freshness, as forty years ago. Sara Teasdale,
the monotony of whose sobbing note caused her to become
rather unfashionable when a more arrogant race of young
women appeared, has made definite progress in her art
since her earlier books of poems and has recently written
some of her most charming lyrics. Miss Edna St. Vincent
Millay has now, in turn, grown so popular that she, too, is
in danger of becoming unfashionable; but she remains the
most important of the group and perhaps one of the most
important of our poets. Like Mencken, the prophet of a
point of view, she has, like him, become a national figure;
nor, as in the case of some other prophets, is her literary
reputation undeserved. With little color, meager ornament
and images often commonplace, she is yet mistress of
deeply moving rhythms, of a music which makes up for the
ear what her page seems to lack for the eye; and, above all,
she has that singular boldness, which she shares with the
greatest poets and which consists in taking just that one
step beyond where one's fellows stop that, by making a
new contact with moral reality, has the effect of causing
other productions to take on an aspect of literary convention. Elinor Wylie, in the best of her verse and in her
novel *Jennifer Lorn*, gives expression to a set of emotions
quite different from those of Miss Millay, but one which
has also its typical interest and its own kind of intensity.
Her literary proficiency is immense: she is never at a loss
for a clever rhyme, a witty reference or a brilliant image;
she can command all the finest fabrics, the choicest works
of art, the most luxurious sensations, the most amusing
historical allusions and the most delicious things to eat.
And, as a consequence, her inferior work is almost as well-
written as her best; and her best work has both a style
and a splendor of a kind very rare in America—where, even
when these qualities do appear together, as they did to
some extent in Amy Lowell, they too often remain hollow

and metallic from the lack of a heart at the core. Edna Millay's inferior work has no such embroidery to deck it; and, save in her vein of classical austerity, she has for her best but the imagery of the sorrel or mullein stalk of the barren and rocky pastures, the purple wild sweetpea dragging driftwood across the sand, the dead leaves in the city gutters, the gray snow in the city street, the kettle, the broom, the uncarpeted stairs and the dead father's old clothes—grown strange and disturbing now, to this reader's sense, at least, as the prison cell of Verlaine or Catullus's common crossroads. Louise Bogan plucked one low resounding theme on tensely strung steel strings, but it is now the vibrations of this rather than a further development that are ringing still in the air. Léonie Adams's *Those Not Elect* is a very remarkable book, of which the language, which seems to branch straight from the richest seventeenth-century tradition, strikes music from the calm summer starbreak, the bright-washed night after rain or the blue translucence of evening, where a gull or a pigeon that flies alone, seeking freedom in that space and clarity, is lost in a confusion of cloud and light. An anthology of these women poets should include, besides those named above, the *Cinquains* of the late Adelaide Crapsey and the best of Miss Genevieve Taggard, Miss Babette Deutsch and several others, of whom the younger Laura Gottschalk may turn out to be one of the most interesting and in whose company Dorothy Parker, long known as a humorous writer, has recently, it seems to me, fully proved her right to belong.

I have left to the last the two poets whom, among the men, I admire most: T. S. Eliot and E. A. Robinson. T. S. Eliot, though heavily infected with the Alexandrianism of the Left, has been able to imbue with a personal emotion, not only his inveterate literary allusions and his echoes of other poets, but even the lines that he has borrowed from them. He deserves, both as critic and as poet, his present position of influence. I deplore the fatigued and despondent mood that seems lately to have been drying up both his criticism and his poetry; but I cannot believe that a passion for poetry so serious and so intense can be permanently stifled or numbed. E. A. Robinson is the last and, artistically (leaving the happiest flashes of Emerson aside), the most important of the New England poets. Though he has recently run much into the sands of long and arid blank-verse narratives, I believe that he is one of the poets of our time most likely to survive as an American classic. He and Eliot both, though there are times when they disappoint us by the tendency of their motors to stall and times when they get on our nerves by a kind of hypochondria of the soul, have possessed the poetic gift and the artist's mastery of it.

The subject of Mr. Robinson may lead us to some more general observations. I have said that E. A. Robinson is the last of the New England poets, and it is true that he really belongs to an earlier period than the present and has little in common with the writers in whose company the anthologists now place him. (He is closer to Hawthorne and Henry James.) When we look back on the literary era which preceded the recent renascence, we are surprised, after all that has been written about its paleness, its tameness and its sterility, to take account of the high standard of excellence to which its best writers attained. When we consider Henry James, Stephen Crane and even such novelists of the second rank as George W. Cable and William Dean Howells, with such critics as Irving Babbitt, W. C. Brownell and Paul Elmer More, who belong essentially to the same era, we are struck with certain superiorities over our race of writers today. It may be said of these men, in general, that, though their ideas were less "emancipated," they possessed a sounder culture than we; and that, though less lively, they were better craftsmen. They were professional men of letters, and they had thoroughly learned their trade. Note the intense concentration, the incapacity for careless writing, of even Stephen Crane, who passed for a clever newspaper man and an outlaw to respectable literature, but whose work astonishes us now by an excellence of quality by no means incomparable—as how much of our present fiction is?—to the best European work in the same kind.

Another writer who, like Mr. Robinson, is bound closely, through her craftsmanship and her culture, to this earlier American tradition, but who, by reason of her critical point of view, makes a connecting link with our own, is Edith Wharton. Often described as an imitator of Henry James, she was really, in her important novels, a writer of a different kind. Henry James, except at very rare moments, was never a preacher or a bitter social satirist; but Mrs. Wharton was perhaps the first American to write with indignant passion *against* American values as they had come to present themselves by the end of the last century. Her recent books, since *The Age of Innocence*, have been of rather inferior interest; but, in her prime, she produced what I strongly believe are the best examples of this kind of fiction that we have had in the United States. She was soon followed by Van Wyck Brooks, who represented a similar reaction against a world either brutal and commercial or moribund and genteel. One of the prophets of the present generation, he belongs to the older and more sober tradition and has never, for better or for worse, learned any of the methods of the new.

Join these writers with the others I have mentioned and it will be seen that they make a remarkable group. They have provided both a picture and a criticism of one period of American life. The writing of our own age will hardly, I fear, present so dignified or so firm a front. We have the illusion of a stronger vitality and of a greater intellectual freedom, but we are polyglot, parvenu, hysterical and often only semi-literate. When time shall have weeded out our less important writers, it is probable that those who remain will give the impression of a literary vaudeville: H. L. Mencken hoarse with preaching in his act making fun of preachers; Edna St. Vincent Millay, the soloist, a contralto with deep notes of pathos; Sherwood Anderson holding his audience with naïve but disquieting bedtime stories;

Theodore Dreiser with his newspaper narrative of commonplace scandals and crimes and obituaries of millionaires, in which the reporter astonishes the readers by being rash enough to try to tell the truth; T. S. Eliot patching from many cultures a dazzling and variegated disguise for the shrinking and scrupulous soul of a hero out of Henry James. Let us remember, however, that vaudeville has always been an American specialty; and that the writers we value most highly in the pre-Civil War period have not in general been such as I have mentioned above as typical of the generation just before our own. Emerson, Whitman, Poe; *Walden* and *Moby Dick:* they are all independent one-man turns, and who can say that we may not find their peers among our present bill of comic monologuists, sentimental songsters and performers of one-act melodramas?

June 30, 1926

Mencken's Democratic Man

H. L. MENCKEN's *Notes on Democracy* adds nothing that is new to his political philosophy: its basic ideas are precisely those which he has been preaching for many years and which already appear in his book on Nietzsche, published in 1908. The human race, according to Mencken, is composed of "gentlemen" and "boobs"; the gentlemen, by virtue of their superiority, have made themselves masters of the good things of the world; and the peasants, who, by virtue of their ineptitude, remain fettered to the plough and the bench, are embittered by envy of "their betters." It is this envy which supplies all the issues of politics in a democracy: it is the desire on the part of the peasants to rob the superior classes of rewards unattainable by themselves or to restrain them from the enjoyment of activities that they are unable to understand. The superior classes possess a monopoly not merely of property and pleasure but of the higher virtues as well: they embody all the learning, all the taste, all the fortitude, all the intelligence, all the sense of personal honor and all the sense of social obligation. A government by the people, therefore—that is to say, a government by persons characterized by the opposites of these qualities—is sure to be a scandal and a farce. The United States is such a farce and scandal.

Mr. Mencken has here expounded this thesis in greater detail and in more connections than he ever has done before; and he has invoked more authorities to support it. He thus makes the gesture of discussing systematically the machinery of democratic government; he attempts to find corroboration in behavioristic psychology; and he at last receives into his bosom the conclusions of the Binet tests, which he had previously denounced but which he sees now can serve his turn by apparently demonstrating that the majority of the population possess the mentality of schoolboys. Yet, for all this, his book is not really an inquiry: it is Mencken's same old melodrama, with the gentleman, the man of honor, pitted against the peasant and the boob. We are not told what makes people gentlemen or what makes people boobs, or of how it is that both these species happen to belong to the same human race, or of how it is that we often find them merging or becoming transformed into one another. With his fierce inflexibility of mind, Mr. Mencken is capable neither of the sympathy of the historian, of the detachment of the scientist nor of the subtlety of the philosopher. And his new book is not to be taken as a contribution to political science: it is simply another of his "prejudices," treated on a larger scale than the rest.

Yet although these *Notes on Democracy* are not precisely politics, they are quite remarkable as literature. Poe said of his treatise *Eureka* that it was to be taken as neither science nor philosophy, but as what he called a "prose poem," which was, nevertheless, in its own way, true. The same thing might be said about Mencken's *Notes*, which is a sort of obverse of *Leaves of Grass*. Let us, therefore, accept its assumptions and find out what validity it has. Now, it is plain that a population composed, as Mr. Mencken says ours is, almost exclusively of beings without courage, ability, honor or aspiration could never have settled, however crudely, either the West or the East of the United States or established, let alone maintained, however unenlightened a federal government—could never, in fact, have made the efforts or carried out the calculations that are needed for a single street of shops, could never have preserved the discipline that is needed to run a first-rate office or a theater or factory or bank, let alone train an army, a navy, a medical profession, a church, a bar or the personnel of any of our good universities. But let us accept the world that Mencken imagines as we do the country of the Houyhnhnms or the country of Erewhon, and we shall find that it has its reality as these other imaginary places have.

This world which, as I say, has its reality, is simply an abstraction from *our* world of all those features of American life that fall short of Mr. Mencken's standards. What these standards of Mencken's are I have indicated, and we can accept them as more or less sound. But the point is that Mencken's emotions in connection with the things he admires are rarely of a positive kind: they are negative emotions at missing them, and they take the form of rage and scorn for the people who do not represent them. This animus has never been more effectively—perhaps never so effectively—expressed by Mencken than it is in this latest book. The *Notes* lack the cumulative power of a pamphlet by Swift or Shaw, because they do not have the drive of close reasoning to carry us along to the end; and, as a result, the last of the three sections becomes rather repetitious and disappointing. But, as a whole, the *Notes on Democracy* is unquestionably one of the best-written and most intensely felt of Mr. Mencken's books: with *The American Language* and *A Book of Prefaces*, it constitutes the core of his work, that part of Mr. Mencken's writing that, whatever else of his we may skip, certainly ought to be read. He has been saying the same thing for years, but

he has never before succeeded in saying it in so pungent
and so terse a language or with a satiric force so nearly
tragic.

These emotions of contempt and anger have projected,
as everyone knows, a ridiculous but terrifying bugaboo:
the great American boob. Some of the items in this latest
indictment of the fabulous Menckenian dunce may sound
perhaps a little fatuous: "What he knows of histology," we
learn, "or protozoölogy, or philology or paleontology is
precisely nothing. Such things lie beyond his capacity for
learning, and he has no curiosity about them. . . . Even
those applied sciences which enter intimately into his everyday existence remain outside his comprehension and interest. Consider, for example, chemistry and biology. The
whole life of the inferior man, including especially his so-
called thinking, is purely a biochemical process, and exactly
comparable to what goes on in a barrel of cider, yet he
knows no more about chemistry than a cow and no more
about biology than its calf. . . . He is more ignorant of
elementary anatomy and physiology than the Egyptian
quacks of 4000 B.C. . . . He has never so much as heard
of ethnology, pathology or embryology. Greek, to him, is
only a jargon spoken by boot-blacks, and Wagner is a
retired baseball player. He has never heard of Euripides,
of Hippocrates, of Aristotle or of Plato. Or of Vesalius,
Newton and Roger Bacon. The fine arts are complete blanks
to him. He doesn't know what a Doric column is, or an
etching, or a fugue. He is as ignorant of sonnets and the
Gothic style as he is of ecclesiastical politics in Abyssinia.
Homer, Virgil, Cervantes, Bach, Raphael, Rubens, Beethoven—all such colossal names are empty sounds to him,"
etc., etc. This all sounds a little like M. Jourdain giving
Mme. Jourdain the benefit of his recent instruction in the
pronunciation of the vowels (to say nothing of Mr.
Mencken's own notions of the conceptions of modern
biology—the barrel of cider, etc.). Nevertheless, the *Notes
on Democracy* contain what is up to date the author's most
effective description of his "Democratic Man." This char-

acter is an ideal monster, exactly like the Yahoo of Swift, and it has almost the same dreadful reality. This "boob" has impressed himself on the imagination of our general public in a way that has not been equalled by any other recent literary creation, with the possible exception of Scott Fitzgerald's flapper. Sinclair Lewis's *Babbitt* and the inhabitants of his *Main Street* must have been at least partly inspired by Mencken, and they present themselves as merely species of the genus *American boob*. In the current *New Masses,* one finds a cartoon with the caption "Immaculate Conception," in which the editor of the *American Mercury* is seen suckling "the American superman," a rudimentary one-hundred-percent American, who has been born with a pair of bone spectacles; and this accurately satirizes the situation. The conception of the national boob has, one realizes, been firmly planted, not only in the minds of our writers, but also in the minds of all those, all the otherwise undistinguished citizens, who are to be seen in every state of the Union with the *Mercury* under their arms. We may not always like the heavy-footed superman, who for Mencken is the positive inference to be drawn from the negative caricature, as we sometimes encounter him in Mencken's pages, and we may like him even less when we run into attempts to live up to him on the part of Mencken's admirers; but we must grant that to have made the Americans feel the menace of this super-boor and repudiate their fellowship with him is an achievement of some importance.

December 15, 1926

The Sportsman's Tragedy

THE REPUTATION of Ernest Hemingway has, in a very short time, assumed such proportions that it has already become fashionable to disparage him. Yet it seems to me that he has received in America very little intelligent criticism. One finds Mr. Lee Wilson Dodd, for example, in the *Saturday Review of Literature*, with his usual gentle trepidation in the presence of contemporary vitality, deciding with a sigh of relief that, after all, Mr. Hemingway (a young man who has published only three books) is not really Tolstoy or Shakespeare, and describing his subjects as follows: "The people he observes with fascinated fixation and then makes live before us are . . . all very much alike: bull-fighters, bruisers, touts, gunmen, professional soldiers, prostitutes, hard drinkers, dope-fiends. . . . For what they may or may not be intellectually, aesthetically, or morally worth, he makes his facts ours." In the *Nation*, Mr. Joseph Wood Krutch, whose review is more sympathetic than Mr. Dodd's, describes Mr. Hemingway as follows: "Spiritually the distinguishing mark of Mr. Hemingway's work is a weariness too great to be aware of anything but sensations. . . . Mr. Hemingway tells us, both by his choice of subject and by the method which he employs, that life is an affair of mean tragedies. . . . In his hands the subject-matter of literature becomes sordid little catastrophes in the lives of very vulgar people." I do not know whether these critics of *Men without Women* have never read Mr. Hemingway's other two books or whether they have simply forgotten them. Do the stories in *In Our Time* and *The Sun Also Rises* actually answer to these descriptions? Does *Men without Women* answer to them? The hero of *In Our Time*, who appears once or twice in this new volume of stories, and the hero of *The Sun Also Rises* are both highly civilized persons of rather complex temperament and extreme sensibility. In what way can they be said to be "very vulgar people"? And can the adventures of even the old bull-fighter in such a piece as *The Undefeated* correctly be called a "sordid little catastrophe"?

One of the stories in *Men without Women* also appeared in the *American Caravan*, and was thus twice exposed to the reviewers; yet in all the reviews I have read I cannot remember one which seemed to me to give an accurate account of it. *An Alpine Idyl* has usually been mentioned as a simple tale of horror or a tale of brutality, or something of the sort. Let us examine this story a moment. Two young men have been skiing in the Alps. It is spring and the sun is terrifically strong; but in the shade, the sweat freezes in their underclothes. They have begun to find this oppressive and are glad to get down to an inn. On their way, they have passed a funeral, and at the inn they hear the story behind it. The woman who is dead was a peasant's wife who had died during the winter, but the house had been snowbound, and the husband had not been able to bring her out till spring. The man had put the body in the woodshed, laying it on a pile of logs; but when he had had to use the wood, he had stood the corpse up in a corner, and had later got into the habit of hanging the lantern in its mouth. Why, we ask ourselves now for a moment, have we been told about the skiing expedition? Then, immediately, we realize that Hemingway, with his masterly relevance in indirection, has, by telling us of the tourists' oppression, supplied us with the explanation of the brutalization of the peasant. But it is not the mere fact of this brutalization that makes the point of the story. We do not see the point till the end. The peasant comes on to the inn, but he refuses to drink with them there and goes on to another inn. " 'He didn't want to drink with me,' said the sexton. 'He didn't want to drink with me, after he knew about his wife,' said the innkeeper." In a similar way, it is true that *A Pursuit Race* is, as Mr. Dodd would say, a story about a dope-fiend; but what is much more important, it is also a story of a man who has just lost a desperate moral struggle. It is given its point by the final paragraph, in which the manager of the burlesque show, understanding that the struggle has been lost and pitying his recreant advance man, goes away without waking him up. So, in *A Simple Inquiry*—a glimpse of one aspect of army life: that strange demoralization that may bring with it a kind of stoicism—the significance of the incident lies in the fact that the major refrains from dismissing the boy who has just refused his advances.

It would appear, then, that Hemingway's world is not quite so rudimentary as Mr. Krutch or Mr. Dodd represents it. Even when he is dealing with primitive types—as he by no means always is—his drama almost always turns on some principle of courage, of pity, of honor—in short, of sportsmanship, in its largest human sense—which he is able to bring to light in them. I do not say that the world that Mr. Hemingway depicts is not, on the whole, a bad world; it *is* a bad world, and a world where much is suffered. Mr. Hemingway's feelings about this world, his criticism of what goes on in it, are, for all his misleadingly simple and matter-of-fact style, rather subtle and complicated; but he has, it seems to me, made it plain enough what sort of ideas and emotions he is trying to communicate. His first book was called *In Our Time*, and it was a sequence of short stories about a sensitive and healthy boy in the American Northwest. We were, I take it, to contrast these two series. When Mr. Hemingway gave them this title, he meant to tell us that life was barbarous even in the twentieth century; and that the man who sees the cabinet ministers shot and who finds himself potting the Germans from behind the "absolutely topping" barricade has had to come a long way from the boy who, with the fresh responses of youth, so much enjoyed the three days' fishing trip at Big Two-Hearted River. Yet *has* he really come so far? Is not the principle of life itself essentially ruthless and cruel? What is the difference between the gusto of the soldier shooting down his fellow humans and the gusto of the young fisherman hooking grasshoppers to catch trout? Ernest Hemingway is primarily preoccupied with these problems of natural cruelty and its inevitable obverse of suffering.

The barbarity of the world since the war is also the theme of his next book, *The Sun Also Rises*. By his title and by the quotations which he prefixes to this novel, he makes it plain what moral judgment we are to pass on the events he describes: "You are all a lost generation."

What gives the book its profound unity and its disquieting effectiveness is the intimate relation established between the Spanish fiesta, with its revelry, its bull-fighting and its processions, and the atrocious behavior of the group of holiday-making British and Americans who have come down from Paris to enjoy it. In the heartlessness of these people, in their treatment of one another, do we not find the same principle at work as in the pagan orgy of the festival? Is not the brutal persecution of the Jew as much a natural casualty as the fate of the man who is gored by the bull on his way to visit the bull-ring? The whole interest of *The Sun Also Rises* lies in the attempts of the hero and the heroine to disengage themselves from this world, or rather to arrive at some method of living in it in such a way as to satisfy some code of their own. The real story is that of their attempts to do this—attempts by which, in such a world, they are always bound to lose out in everything except honor. I do not agree, as has sometimes been said, that the behavior of the people in *The Sun Also Rises* is typical of only a small special class of American and British expatriates. I believe that it is more or less typical of certain phases of the whole Western world today; and the title *In Our Time* could have been applied to it with as much appropriateness as it was to its predecessor.

Ernest Hemingway's attitude, however, toward the cruelties and treacheries he describes is quite different from anything else that one remembers in a similar connection. He has nothing of the liberating impulse involved in the romantic's indignation:* he does not, like Byron, identifying himself with the Prisoner of Chillon, bid the stones of any earthly cell "appeal from tyranny to God"; nor, like Shelley, invite the winds to "wail for the world's wrong." Nor has he even that grim and repressed, but still generous, still passionate feeling which we find in the pessimist-realists—in Thomas Hardy's Tess, in Maupassant's *Boule de Suif*, even in those infrequent scenes of Flaubert by which

* This liberating impulse, however, was later to be brought out in Hemingway by the Spanish Civil War.

one's resentment is kindled at the spectacle of an old farm
servant or of a young working-class girl at the mercy of the
bourgeoisie. In his treatment of the war, for example, Mr.
Hemingway is as far as possible from John Dos Passos or
Henri Barbusse. His point of view, his state of mind, is a
curious one, and one typical, I think, of "our time"; he
seems so broken in to the human agonies, and, though even
against his will, so impassively, so hopelessly, resigned to
them, that the only protest of which he is capable is, as
it were, the grin and the curse of the sportsman who loses
the game. Nor are we always quite sure on which side
Mr. Hemingway is betting. We do sometimes feel a suspicion that the conflict we are witnessing is a set-up, with the
manager backing the barbarian. Yet to speak in these terms
of Mr. Hemingway is really to misrepresent him. He is not,
of course, a moralist staging a melodrama, but an artist
exhibiting situations the values of which are not simple. Mr.
Hemingway enjoys bull-fighting, as he enjoys skiing, racing
and prize-fights; and he is unremittingly conscious of the
fact that, from the point of view of life as a sport, all that
seems most painful in it is somehow very closely bound up
with what he finds to be most enjoyable. The peculiar conflicts of feeling which arise in a temperament of this kind are
the subject of Mr. Hemingway's fiction. The most remarkable effects of this fiction, effects unlike those of anyone
else, are those, as in the fishing-trip in *The Sun Also Rises*,
by which we are made to feel, behind the appetite for the
physical world, the tragedy or the falsity of a moral relation. The inescapable consciousness of this does not arouse
Hemingway to passionate violence; but it poisons him and
makes him sick, and thus invests with a sinister quality—a
quality perhaps new in fiction—the sunlight and the green
summer landscapes of *The Sun Also Rises*. Thus, if Hemingway is oppressive, as Mr. Dodd complains, it is because
he himself is oppressed. And we may find in him—in the
clairvoyant's crystal of a polished incomparable art—the
image of the common oppression.

December 14, 1927

Thornton Wilder

Now THAT MR. THORNTON WILDER has become both a
best-seller and a Pulitzer prize-winner, he is in an unfortunate situation. On the one hand, the literary columnists
have accepted him as a Reputation and gossip about him
with respect but without intelligence; and, on the other,
the literary snobs have been driven by his tremendous popularity, by the obsequious gossips themselves, into talking
as if they took it for granted that there must be something
meretricious about him. Mr. Wilder remains, however, a
remarkably interesting writer, with a good deal to be said
about him which no one, so far as I know, has said.

One of the things about Mr. Wilder that I do not think
has yet been said is that he seems to be the first American
novelist who has been influenced deeply by Proust. In devoting some attention to this subject, I do not at all mean
to imply a lack of originality on Mr. Wilder's part: on the
contrary, it is quite extraordinary that a novelist so young
should display, from the first page of his very first book,
so accomplished a mastery of a form and a point of view
so much his own. The Proust influence seems simply the
influence of a first-rate senior writer on a first-rate junior
one. And what Mr. Wilder has learned from Proust is not
merely Proust's complex impressionism: the side of Proust
that Sacheverell Sitwell imitated in *All Summer in a Day*
does not figure in Mr. Wilder at all. He has listened to
Proust's very heart, and his own has been timed to its beat.
It is not so much a formula of style that Thornton Wilder
has taken, though there are echoes of Proust's style, too,
but a formula of emotion, of the criticism of life. And in
order to estimate his work, we should try to discover which
part of it represents the poet Wilder himself, from whom
quite un-Proustian things may eventually be expected, and

which part is mere repetition of cadences caught from the asthmatic master.

One of Proust's favorite formulas, then—which we find in almost every situation of *A la Recherche du Temps Perdu*—is that of an abject and agonizing love on the part of a superior for an inferior person, or at least on the part of a gentle person for a person who behaves toward him with cruelty. Mr. Wilder seems infatuated with this, and he leans on it a little too heavily. It figures less conspicuously in *The Cabala* than in *The Bridge of San Luis Rey;* but the episode of Alix in the former book, which seems to me also the episode that carries the least conviction, is simply a reversal of the Proustian relationship in which we are shown a charming and sensitive man breaking his heart for an unworthy woman: the part played for Swann by Odette, for Saint-Loup by Rachel and for Proust's hero by Albertine, is played for Alix by Blair. One finds, also, everywhere in *The Cabala* unmistakable Proustian turns of phrase; the author has even taken over a favorite expression of Proust's—a sort of proverbial phrase in French, which I have never seen before in English: he likes to talk about somebody or other "making the fair weather" of somebody else, as Swann made *"la pluie et le beau temps"* of the Duchesse du Guermantes. And one finds in *The Cabala,* also, one passage where the typical Proustian note of hypochondriacal melancholy is brought almost to the point of burlesque: a Helen Darrell, a famous beauty, enters the story suddenly like one of those unannounced characters in Proust's social scenes. We are not told precisely what is wrong with her, but, like so many of the characters in *A la Recherche,* she is ill and very soon to die; none of her dearest friends dares to kiss her: they feel that she is blighted and doomed. "She was like a statue in solitude. She presuffered her death." Yet the unfortunate Alix envies her: "He would have loved me," she breathes in the hero's ear, "if I had looked like that. . . . She is beautiful. She is beautiful," he hears her mutter. "The world is hers. She will never have to suffer as I must."

The dying beauty asks, before she goes, to be taken to say good-by to a saintly old French poet, who is also about to die. "One wonders what they said to one another as she knelt beside his chair: as he said later, they loved one another because they were ill." I have cited this passage at length because it shows Thornton Wilder when he has slipped into writing pure Proust and when, as it seems to me, he is least successful. Proust's characters are always ill, and Proust thinks that a languishing illness is the most pathetic thing on earth—but he has in French the special advantage of words made for him: *malade* and *maladie*, which he is able to introduce with a mournful and ominous accent that prevents us from becoming impatient with his eternal incurable invalids. Now, the words *ill* and *sick* hardly lend themselves to any such mournful magic: when, in English, you hear that someone is ill, you at once ask what treatment he is taking.

In *The Bridge of San Luis Rey*, the Proustian spirit pervades the book. The Marquesa de Montemayor is made to distil marvellous literature from her love for her selfish daughter, just as Vinteuil in Proust is made to distil marvellous music from his insulted love for his. The Marquesa, furthermore, is evidently a transposition from Mme. de Sévigné, who plays herself such an important role in Proust. The bad feature here, however, is that Mr. Wilder has followed Proust in exaggerating the cruelty of the beloved to the lover. This is sometimes hard to swallow in Proust himself, but then there is in Proust a bitterness that seems derived from hard experience; whereas with Mr. Wilder we feel that this violence is merely an effective device. I cannot quite believe, for example, in the harrowing scene in which Esteban is dressing Manuel's wound while Manuel abuses him so harshly, and I cannot believe at all in the scene where La Périchole refuses, after twenty years, to allow Uncle Pio to address her by her first name. Isn't there, also, something rather forced about the pining of Captain Alvarados for his daughter? Isn't it one case of hopeless love too many? At one point, Mr. Wilder allows himself to be carried into rewriting the death of Bergotte (by a natural attraction, certainly: no doubt, like Strachey's death of Victoria, it is destined to be imitated many times): "We come from a world where we have known incredible standards of excellence, and we dimly remember beauties which we have not seized again, and we go back to that world." (*"Toutes ces obligations qui n'ont pas leur sanction dans la vie présente semblent appartenir à un monde différent, fondé sur la bonté, le scruple, le sacrifice, un monde entièrement différent de celui-ci, et dont nous sortons pour naître à cette terre, avant peut-être d'y retourner. . . ."*)

This is not, I must repeat, that Proust has been anything other for Wilder than the inevitable elder master that every young writer must cling to before he can stand on his own feet. Since I have cited so many passages in which Mr. Wilder has filled in with Proust, I must quote at least one in a similar key which Proust would never have written and which, in Mr. Wilder's own work, has a quite distinct ring of artistic authenticity: "He regarded love as a sort of cruel malady through which the elect are required to pass in their late youth and from which they emerge, pale and wrung, but ready for the business of living. There were (he believed) a great repertory of errors mercifully impossible to human beings who had recovered from this illness. Unfortunately there remained to them a host of failings, but at least (from among many illustrations) they never mistook a protracted amiability for the whole conduct of life, they never again regarded any human being, from a prince to a servant, as a mechanical object."

The effect of Thornton Wilder is, in any case, not at all like the effect of Proust, or like the effect of anyone else one remembers. From what one hears about him, one may get the impression that he is one of those contemporary writers who seem still to date from the nineties—that he is simply another "stylist," another devotee of "beauty"—that one will find him merely a pretty or a precious writer; but Mr. Wilder, when one comes to read him, turns out to be something quite different from this. He possesses that quality of "delightfulness" of which George Saintsbury has said that Balzac did not possess it but that Gérard de Nerval did. But he has, also, a hardness, a sharpness, that sets him quite apart from our Cabells, our Dunsanys, our Van Vechtens and our George Moores. He has an edge that is peculiar to himself, an edge that is never incompatible with the attainment of a consummate felicity. This felicity, which has nothing of the pose, of the self-conscious effort to "write beautifully," of the professional beautiful writer, is felt through the whole of his work and as much in the conception of the characters and the development of the situations as in the structure of the sentences themselves. It is the felicity of a true poet—not merely the contrived "style" of a literary man with a yearning for old unhappy fancy far-off things—and it makes possible for Thornton Wilder a good many remarkable feats that we should not have expected to see brought off. Mr. Wilder, for example, I understand, has never been in Peru, and ordinarily there are few things more deadly than the dream-country of the twentieth-century novelist. Yet the author of *The Bridge of San Luis Rey* has been able to give us a Peru that is solid, incandescent, distinct. Here is the Marquesa's pilgrimage to Cluxambuqua: "a tranquil town, slow-moving and slow-smiling; a city of crystal air, cold as the springs that fed its many fountains; a city of bells, soft and musical and tuned to carry on with one another the happiest quarrels. If anything turned out for disappointment in the town of Cluxambuqua the grief was somehow assimilated by the overwhelming immanence of the Andes and by the weather of quiet joy that flowed in and about the side-streets. No sooner did the Marquesa see from a distance the white walls of this town perched on the knees of the highest peaks than her fingers ceased turning the beads and the busy prayers of her fright were cut short on her lips." Then the church, the hawks, the llama. . . . It is the city of a fairy-tale, of course; but it is almost of the same quality as *Kubla Khan*. It is not without its preciosity; but this preciosity of Thornton Wilder's is at least as sound as that of *Vathek*.

Mr. Wilder has also a form of his own, which is highly individual and which seems to me to promise more than he has hitherto been able to accomplish. In *The Cabala*, the several heroes of the several episodes seem at first to have nothing in common save the accident of all being observed by the American who is telling the story; then we learn that they are the ancient gods fallen on evil times, and we realize that there is also a significance in their relations with the young American. In *The Bridge of San Luis Rey*, the different characters appear to have in common merely the fact that they were killed by the fall of the bridge; then gradually we are made to understand that their deaths at that moment had meaning, and that there is a meaning in the relations of the people who fell to the people who were left alive. *The Bridge of San Luis Rey* is more ingenious than *The Cabala*, and more completely worked out; but I do not find it completely satisfying. God works in too obvious a way. It is hard to believe that the author believes in the God of his book. The real higher power at work here is the author's aesthetic ideal, which is struggling to incarnate itself.

One ought to say something more about *The Cabala*, which has received less attention than *The Bridge* but which seems to me, in some ways, more interesting. The circle of clever people in Rome turn out to be the gods grown old; Christianity and modern society have finally proved too much for them. The Puritanism of the young American gives Pan (or Priapus?) such a feeling of guilt that he is driven to suicide; and Aphrodite breaks her heart for an American Adonis who pays no attention to her. A brilliant peasant Cardinal, who has spent most of his life as a missionary to China, robs Artemis—if, as I suppose, Astrée-Luce is Artemis—of her pagan religious faith. These are the gods of Europe contending with the influences of alien races. In the end, the young American goes to call on the Cardinal, whom he finds with *Appearance and Real-*

ity, Spengler, *The Golden Bough*, *Ulysses*, Proust and Freud on the table beside him. In the course of the conversation, the Cardinal pushes them all to the floor: "Yes, I could write a book," he says, "better than this ordure that your age has offered us. But a Montaigne, a Machiavelli . . . a . . . a . . . Swift, I will never be." The moment after, as the visitor is going, the Cardinal remarks that he would like for his birthday a small Chinese rug. The young American departs for the States: "Why was I not more reluctant at leaving Europe? How could I lie there repeating the *Aeneid* and longing for the shelf of Manhattan?" The shade of Virgil appears to him. "Know, importunate barbarian," says the poet, "that I spent my whole lifetime under a great delusion—that Rome and the house of Augustus were eternal. Nothing is eternal save Heaven. Romes existed before Rome and when Rome will be a waste there will be Romes after her. Seek out some city that is young. The secret is to make a city, not to rest in it." . . . "The shimmering ghost faded before the stars, and the engines beneath me pounded eagerly towards the new world and the last and greatest of all cities."

Mr. Wilder himself, however, next turns up in Peru. I have already praised this fairy-tale country. I am told that it owes part of its vividness to its grasp of the Spanish character. Thornton Wilder's feeling for national temperaments—French, Italian and American—had already appeared in *The Cabala* as one of his most striking gifts. But I wish, for our sakes, and perhaps for his own, that he would now follow Virgil's advice and return for a time to New York. I wish that he would study the diverse elements that go to make the United States, and give us *their* national portraits. Mr. Wilder already knows Europe, and he also knows something of the Orient; and now we need him at home. I believe that this player on plaintive stops has more than one tune in his flute.

August 8, 1928

The Death of Elinor Wylie

ELINOR WYLIE died on the night of December 16, 1928. The account of this given me by her husband, William Rose Benét, was somewhat fuller than that which appears in the memoir of her sister, Miss Nancy Hoyt (*Elinor Wylie: The Portrait of an Unknown Lady*). It had been Sunday, and, after a good deal of going out, they had decided to stay at home for the evening. The day before, Elinor had put in order the manuscript of her last book of poems, *Angels and Earthly Creatures,* which was to go to the publisher on Monday. She had picked up her own novel *Jennifer Lorn* and had read in it for a while; then had closed it in her definite way, saying, "Yes: *Jennifer Lorn is* better than *The Venetian Glass Nephew!*" and had gone to the kitchen to get them some supper. In a moment, her husband heard her call, and went in and found her fainting. She asked for a glass of water and when he gave it to her—I learn from Miss Hoyt—said, "Is that all it is?" He carried her to her bedroom, where she died.

The sense of loss expressed in the following article was felt by a good many people. Elinor Wylie had meant to us more than we had always been aware of at the time she was living. With her fine bindings, her formal furniture, her old-fashioned dining-room still-life and her old-fashioned literary culture that made one remember that her godfather had been Horace Howard Furness, the Philadelphia scholar who made the great Variorum Edition of Shakespeare, and her talk that had both style and wit, she occupied a unique position in the region below Fourteenth Street, where, as Frank Crowninshield wrote about her later, she "liked to pretend that she was a Bohemian, but the sham was at all times apparent." Yet it was not this shell that she carried about that gave her her peculiar prestige: it was the fact that, living inside it, she managed to remain a free spirit as few Bohemians are. I was trying to convey this; and the eloquent tone of my article is also explained by the fact that Elinor was the first to die of my close literary friends, the commemoration of whose passing is a recurrent and, I fear, rather depressing feature of this chronicle and its successor.

The death of Elinor Wylie hardly yet seems a real event. When people whom we know die, we have usually been prepared for their deaths by some weakening or decay of personality. But in Elinor Wylie's case, a personality still vigorous and vivid suddenly went out of being. A mind alive with thoughts and images, at what seemed its point of fullest activity, was annihilated at a stroke. In a letter she wrote me from England, just before her return in December, she told me that she had never been so happy, had never loved life so much: she had written forty poems, she said—an unusual rate of production for her. I was out on the West Coast at the time of her death, and I found that, even after the news had reached me, I kept unconsciously looking forward to seeing her in New York again. A part of my mind still kept turning toward her—for she had left New York with no farewell, but, on the contrary, with salutations and with the promise that I should see her soon.

It was true that, of recent years, she had been suffering severely from high blood-pressure, and had been warned by the doctors of the danger of a stroke such as that which actually ended her life. She had been told that, if she wished to escape it, she must diet, abstain from coffee and alcohol, be careful not to overtax herself, etc. But she paid little heed to these admonitions, and, as year followed year, used to laugh at her defiance of medical advice and her obstinate survival in spite of it.

In these latest doomed years of her life, her energy seemed actually to increase. When I first knew her, only five years ago, Elinor Wylie was a brilliant amateur, who had produced a few striking poems and started a novel or two, but who had never worked with much application. Yet by the time *Jennifer Lorn* was published, she had become one of the most steadily industrious and most productive writers of my acquaintance. She had always first composed her poems in her head and then simply written them down (in many cases, she never afterwards changed a word); but she now sat at her typewriter day after day, and turned out novel after novel, as well as a good deal of miscellaneous journalism. With a mind that seemed never to flag, she continued up to the last to go out night after night and to meet and talk to all sorts of people. In the meantime, she read insatiably. All her fiction was more or less historical and required special research. For her novel about Shelley, she collected and mastered a whole library. Her labor, in this case, was double, for she had to get up the American West in the pioneering days as well as the English nineteenth-century background. She had authority even for her landscapes, which she would prettily rework in her own colored silks from the narratives of old books of travel. And she seemed to find time, besides, to get through all the poetry and fiction of any distinction or interest that appeared in either England or America.

It was, no doubt, partly her very abnormal condition that so sped up her energy and imagination. Her vitality, during the years after she had come to live in New York, triumphed and flourished at the cost of desperate nervous strain. Though she had sometimes enjoyed fairly long periods of tranquillity, comfort and leisure, her life had been broken up by a series of displacements and emotional dislocations which might have destroyed a weaker nature. In Elinor Wylie's case, it had left her like one of those victims of the war who recover from critical operations and are sent out into life again, but whose condition is a little precarious. Irritation of the old wounds would at once cloud her mind with distress and terror; and one had to remember where they were. Yet in that still scarred and shaken being, who had had to live so long at the mercy of fate and under the domination of others, exasperated inescapably by the recurrent necessity to struggle, there came to birth, in these later years, what seemed to be a new and more powerful personality.

It was like the possession of a poor human life by some strong and non-human spirit, passionate but detached, all-worldly-wise and yet unworldly, generous without devotion, ruthless without spite, laughing with unbiased intelligence over the disasters of the hurt creature it inhabited, and the mistress of a wonderful language, in which accuracy, vigor and splendor seemed to require no study and no effort and in which it spoke sometimes simply of its own divine estate, sometimes fled to bright and cooling visions for forgetfulness of its human exile, and sometimes tried to entertain by inventing the kind of tales, lending itself to the kind of sentiments, that maudlin human beings enjoy.

Such a spirit, among human beings, can nowhere find itself at home. Received in the conventional world with aversion, suspicion and fear, it creates in that other world where people avowedly live by their wits and their imaginations, an embarrassment almost equally uncomfortable. Yet the inhabitants of both worlds stand in awe of it, for they know that they must look to it for the values which they attach to the things of their worlds, for their very opinions of themselves and for their hopes of life itself. And the presence of such a spirit makes illness and death seem unreal. There are beings—and sometimes among the noblest—who pass their lives in the shadow of death. Putting all faith in the ecstasy of the senses, they cannot but fear the moment when the senses must fade: when the body fails, for them, the world ends. But for a spirit like Elinor Wylie's, death can never quite seem serious. The doctors can never dismay it. And when such a spirit drops its abode, we do not feel in its departure any pathos. Yet in its absence, we find ourselves blank: its vanishing has thrown us out more than we might have expected. It is almost as if the intellect that orders, the imagination that creates—those abstractions which have come to seem to us to have some sort of existence of their own, independent of any individual—had themselves been suddenly cut off. We are here among doubtful human creatures, all quarrelling or herding together, knowing little and thinking less, vague, pig-headed, purblind and violent. We come almost to wonder at last whether that spirit has really been among us—whether it may not have been merely, like the others, a blind, violent and crippled human life. Then we remember that harsh unflurried, that harsh unembittered laughter, and we look up the lovely lines in the book; and we know that in this sea without harbors, our compass must still be set by such magnets as the jest and the verse.

February 6, 1929

Signs of Life: *Lady Chatterley's Lover*

THIS FINE NOVEL of D. H. Lawrence's has been privately printed in Florence, and it is difficult and expensive to buy. This is a pity, because it may very well be one of the author's best books. About the erotic aspect of *Lady Chatterley's Lover*, which has prevented it from being circulated except in this subterranean fashion, I shall have something to say in a moment. But one ought to begin by explaining that the novel is something more than the story of a love affair: it is a parable of post-war England.

Lady Chatterley is the daughter of a Scotch R.A., a robust and intelligent girl, who has married an English landowner from the Midlands coal-mining country. Sir Clifford is crippled in the war, and returns to his family estate, where he lives amid the unemployment of the decaying industrial towns. He occupies himself at first with writing, sees the literary people in London and publishes some short stories, "clever, rather spiteful, and yet, in some mysterious way, meaningless"; then later he applies himself feverishly to an attempt to retrieve his coal-mines by working them with modern methods: "Once you started a sort of research in the field of coal-mining, a study of methods and means, a study of by-products and the chemical possibilities of coal, it was astounding the ingenuity and the almost uncanny cleverness of the modern technical mind, as if really the devil himself had lent a fiend's wits to the technical scientists of industry. It was far more interesting than art, than literature, poor emotional half-witted stuff, was this technical science of industry."

But Sir Clifford, semi-paralytic, is in the same unhappy situation as the hero of *The Sun Also Rises;* and his attractive wife, in the meantime, has been carrying on an affair with the gamekeeper—himself a child of the collieries, but nevertheless an educated man, who has risen to a lieutenancy during the war, and then, through inertia and disillusion, relapsed into his former status. There has been an understanding between Sir Clifford and his wife Connie, that, since he cannot give her a child himself, he will accept an illegitimate child as his heir. But Connie has finally reached a point where she feels that she can no longer stand Sir Clifford, with his invalidism, his arid intelligence and his obstinate class-consciousness. She has fallen in love with the gamekeeper; and when she finally discovers that she is going to have a child, she leaves her husband and demands a divorce. We are left with the prospect of the lady and her lover going away to Canada together.

Now, Lawrence's treatment of this subject is not without its aspects of melodrama. It is not entirely free from his ill-mannered habit of nagging and jeering at those of his characters who arouse his contempt or resentment. Poor Sir Clifford, whom his shrill creator cannot refrain from baiting, was, after all, however disagreeable, a man in a pathetic situation for which he was in no way to blame. And, on the other hand, Mellors, the gamekeeper, has his moments of romantic bathos. Yet the characters do, in general, maintain a certain heroic dignity, a certain symbolical importance, which enable them to carry off all this. D. H.

Lawrence's theme is a high one: the self-affirmation and the triumph of life in the teeth of all the sterilizing and demoralizing forces—industrialism, physical depletion, dissipation, careerism and cynicism—of modern English society; and the drama he has set in motion against the double contrasting background of the collieries and the English forests has both solid reality and poetic grandeur. It is the most inspiriting book from England that I have seen in a long time; and—in spite of Lawrence's occasional repetitiousness and his sometimes rather overdone slapdash tone—one of the best written. D. H. Lawrence is indestructible: censored, exiled, denounced, snubbed, he still possesses more vitality than almost anyone else. And this one of his books which has been published under the most discouraging conditions and which must have been written in full knowledge of its fate—which can, indeed, hardly yet be said to have seen the light at all—is one of his most vigorous and brilliant.

D. H. Lawrence, in *Lady Chatterley's Lover*, has thrown over the Anglo-Saxon conventions and, in dealing with sexual experience, has decided to call things by their common names. The effect of this, on the whole, is happy. I will not say that the unlimited freedom which Lawrence for the first time enjoys does not occasionally go to his head: the poetic sincerity of the gamekeeper does not quite always save his amorous rhapsodies over certain plain old English terms from being funny at the wrong time; and one finds it a little difficult to share the author's exaltation over a scene in which the lovers are made to decorate one another with forget-me-nots in places where flowers are rarely worn. But, on the other hand, he has greatly benefited from being able, in dealing with these matters, to dispense with circumlocutions and symbols. It gets rid of a good deal of verbosity, the apocalyptic grandiloquence, into which this subject has so often led him, and it keeps the love scenes human. It may, in fact, probably be said that these scenes in *Lady Chatterley's Lover* contain the best descriptions of sexual experience that have yet been written in English. It is certainly not true, as is sometimes asserted, that erotic sensations either cannot or ought not to be written about. D. H. Lawrence has demonstrated here how interesting and how varied they are, and how important to the comprehension of emotional situations in which they play a part.

The truth is simply, of course, that in English we have had, since the eighteenth century, no technique, no vocabulary even, for presenting such scenes in a novel. The French have been writing directly about sex, in works of the highest dignity, ever since they discarded the proprieties of the age of Louis XIV. For this purpose they have adopted a vocabulary which is conventional and classically abstract; and they have even, for a long time, in their realistic fiction, been printing the vulgar language of the farmyard, the street and the bar. But James Joyce and D. H. Lawrence are the first modern English-speaking writers to put this language into serious books; and the effect, in the case of *Ulysses*, at least, has been shocking to English readers to an extent that must seem very strange to a French literary generation who read Zola, Octave Mirbeau and Huysmans in their youth. But, aside from this question of coarseness in faithfully reporting colloquial speech, we have in English, as I have said, the problem of dealing with sexual matters at all. We have not evolved any equivalent for the literary vocabulary of the French. We have only, on the one hand, colloquial words that will deeply offend some people and no doubt be unintelligible to others, and, on the other hand, the technical words used in works on biology and medicine. Neither kind goes particularly well in a love scene intended to generate an illusion of charm or romance.

This is the problem that Lawrence has tried to solve in *Lady Chatterley's Lover*, and, on the whole, he has been successful. He deserves a special medal from the Republic of Letters for his courage in facing the obloquy to which his experiment was sure to expose him, to say nothing of the other kinds of losses he must take for it—for he cannot have had printed in Italy many copies of the original edition or have made very much money by selling them, and he can claim no rights in the pirated edition that is being printed and sold over here. But there can be no advance in this prohibited direction without somebody's taking losses; and no writer of first-rate merit has done so since Joyce's *Ulysses,* in which it was a question rather of allowing the characters to use certain words than of genuine pioneering in the description of sexual intercourse. All serious writers in the English-speaking countries are much in Lawrence's debt, for even the limited circulation of *Lady Chatterley's Lover* cannot fail to make it easier in future to disregard the ridiculous taboo that the nineteenth century imposed on sex.

July 3, 1929

Dostoevsky Abroad

A TRANSLATION has just appeared—*The Diary of Dostoevsky's Wife*—of the journal of Dostoevsky's second wife during the spring and summer of 1867, when Dostoevsky had been forced to leave Russia to escape from his own and his brother's creditors. From this account, it would appear that the Dostoevskys spent most of their time in Germany quarrelling with waiters over tips, quarrelling and making up with each other, and pawning their belongings to pay the bills when Dostoevsky had lost his money gambling. Anna Grigorevna is simple and touching; Dostoevsky's own complicated character here appears to its worst advantage: he is selfish, disagreeable and silly. It was the range of Dostoevsky's intelligence and the brilliance of his conversation which made people forgive him these qualities. When, for example, we read Baron Wrangel's account of his talks with Dostoevsky in Siberia, or the description of him by Sonia Kovalevsky, the woman mathematician, with whose sister Dostoevsky was in love, we have a vision of a quite different person. Anna Grigorevna, though she frequently speaks of long conversations with her husband, and notes exactly how much everything costs, almost never puts down his opinions. Yet from Dostoevsky's letters of this time, we know that he was already preoccupied with the ideas with which he was afterwards so profoundly to impress himself on Russian thought.

Perhaps the nearest that Mme. Dostoevsky comes to touching on these ideas is in her record of the already famous quarrel between Dostoevsky and Turgenev. Here is her report of the former's account of the visit he paid the latter in Baden-Baden:

"According to him, he is very embittered, even to the point of being venomous and talks the whole time about his new novel, which Fyodr never even so much as mentioned. Turgenev is furious over the notices in the papers, saying he has been most fearfully cut up in *Golos* and *Vaterländischen Nachrichten*, as well as in other publications. He also said that the Russian aristocracy, at the instigation of Philip (?) Tolstoy, had done their best to exclude him from their society, but that none the less nothing had come of it. He added, moreover: 'If you only knew how delighted I should have been!' Fyodr, as usual, treated him none too gently, telling him to procure himself a telescope, for, since he always lived in Paris, he couldn't otherwise expect to know what was happening in Russia, let alone understand it. Turgenev declared he was a realist, and Fyodr said he only thought he was. When Fyodr declared he found the Germans extremely stupid and very apt to be dishonest, Turgenev promptly took offense, assuring Fyodr he had irreparably insulted him, for he himself had now become, not a Russian any more, but a German. Fyodr said he hadn't known that and greatly deplored the fact. Fyodr said that for the most part he had spoken in a facetious tone of voice, which had obviously annoyed Turgenev considerably, and that he had quite openly told him that his novel had met with no success. But on the whole they parted friends, and Turgenev promised to give him the book. Of all the curious men—how could he possibly be proud of being a German instead of a Russian? I should have thought that no Russian writer on earth would want to repudiate his country and least of all to declare himself a German! What, when all's said and done, has he got to be grateful to Germany for, seeing that he has grown up in Russia, which has supported him and done its very utmost to encourage his talent. And now he breaks right away from it and declares that if Russia were to go under, the world would not be the loser! Of all the appalling things for a Russian to say! Enough of the whole matter—but I know that this conversation with Turgenev has excited Fyodr beyond words, and that he always gets beside himself when people repudiate their fatherland."

It is clear from the first part of this account that Turgenev on this occasion had special reasons for being irritable; and it is equally true that Dostoevsky had special reasons for resenting Turgenev: Dostoevsky had borrowed two years before fifty thalers from the richer man and had never paid them back. Yet there was something more important and interesting than appears from Mme. Dostoevsky's description at the bottom of the quarrel between the two writers, who were contemporaries in age and who had had, as young men in St. Petersburg, their first successes at the same time. Dostoevsky belonged, like Turgenev, to the Russian educated class; but his imprisonment in Siberia had modified his point of view profoundly. The Russian governing classes spoke French, and they looked habitually toward Western Europe for culture and ideas; they regarded Russians as barbarians, and could not sometimes, according to Dostoevsky, even write their own language correctly. Their liberal aspirations, when they had them, were derived from Republican France. Dostoevsky had had himself this sort of education and had at one time shared these ideas. He had belonged to a political and literary club composed of Russian intellectuals of this type, and, as a member of this club, he had been convicted of conspiracy against the Tsar and sent for four years to prison. He had found there that, as an educated man, he was regarded by the ordinary Russians with hatred and suspicion. It had seemed to him then that the gulf between the educated class and the people was so deep as to make it impossible for even the most sympathetic artists, for even the reformers themselves, to contribute anything really valuable to the development of the national life. Russian novelists wrote about Russia, as he himself in his early fiction had done, from a Western European point of view, from a point of view derived from writers who had been dealing with societies quite unlike the Russian; and Russian reformers behaved as if a solid and enlightened bourgeoisie, such as had engineered the French Revolution, could be counted on to take over in Russia. Neither knew Russian life at firsthand; both, by their very education, were unfitted to understand it; and both inhabited worlds of illusion. Contemptuous or despairing of the antiquated social system and the semi-savage population from which they themselves had sprung, they had removed, either actually or spiritually, to the other end of Europe; and, even when intelligent and benevolent, had persistently succeeded in evading the realities of the national life. The correspondence of Dostoevsky, during these years of his own enforced exile, is full of hunger for Russia: he devours the Russian newspapers; he complains again and again that a novelist cannot create in exile. For him, Turgenev was a gifted Russian who had run away from Russia, who had too easily given up as hopeless a world that he feared to face, and who patronized the fellow-countrymen whom he had made his reputation by writing about.

When we read Dostoevsky on this problem, we come to realize that a good deal of what he says applies equally to expatriate Americans in Europe. We feel that the difficult position of the artist or intellectual who turns his back on a provincial country with which he cannot make any wide contact has never—not even by Brooks in *The Pilgrimage of Henry James*—been studied more profoundly than by Dostoevsky. There is, in many respects, a striking analogy between the situation of Russia in respect to Western Europe and the situation of the United States; and it is of special interest to Americans to see how Dostoevsky deals with it.

The course recommended by Dostoevsky was for educated Russians, as far as possible, to clear their minds of preconceived ideas from abroad and, from a firsthand realistic examination of their country and its institutions, to try to understand the Russian character and the Russian point of view. Now, the conditions of Russian life are, and were, very different from our own; but they resemble our own in this: that both are fundamentally different from the conditions of Western Europe. Like the Russians of Dostoevsky's day, we have been used to looking to Europe for ideas; and the ideas with which we have been supplied have, as in Dostoevsky's Russia, been imperfectly suited to our needs. This has always been the problem in America: simultaneously to adapt European culture to the alien conditions of American life and to cultivate from our own peculiar and un-European resources an original culture of our own. But our situation, since the war, has, in some respects, become more serious. Since the war, we have been importing from Europe the emotions and the points of view appropriate to bankruptcy and exhaustion—resignation, futility and despair—into a country full of money and health; while Europe seems herself to be looking to us, as she never has done before: the very books that she sends us denouncing us seem to suggest that she has been disappointed. Yet what America sends Europe, in her famine, are still principally scientific researches uninspired by creative theory and works of art, often illiterate and usually secondhand, imitated from European models. The principal philosophy, so far as one can see, that America has exported abroad during the period since the war, has been Watson's behaviorism—the invention of an experimental psychologist who is certainly not a great thinker and who has since, as a matter of fact, gone into the advertising business.

If, however, we pursue the conclusions to which Dostoevsky's position led him, we come upon a further analogy between the Russian situation and our own. When Dostoevsky had set his face away from Western Europe to direct his attention toward Russian institutions, he found himself confronted by the Tsardom, the feudal system of landowning and the Greek Orthodox Church; and there is something both heroic and embarrassing in the spectacle of one of the most intelligent men of his time making the effort to swallow all these. Thus, in a somewhat similar way, an American who would turn for sustenance to contemporary American institutions will find himself confronted by elements not easy to assimilate. He will find the Chamber of Commerce, the Rotary Club, the American political machine, all apparently the willing instruments of the nationwide commercial solidarity which harasses American communities with company spies and informers and dragoons them on occasion with strong-arm men; which persecutes without justice or mercy Sacco and Vanzetti and how many others!; and the upholders of which it sufficed for an honest municipal servant like Al Smith to speak out with a moderate common sense and a by no means unhampered frankness to strike with panic and fire with resentment.

Yet Dostoevsky's instinct was sound: the fact that the American problem seems a particularly formidable one is no excuse for fleeing or evading it. We must, of course, take European ways of thinking along with our language, our alphabet; but we must try to stick close to the realities of our contemporary American life, so new, and so different perhaps from anything that has ever been known, that, if we cannot find out for ourselves what we want and where we are going, it is improbable, with Europe declining, that anybody else can tell us. Of all this, more presently.

January 30, 1929

Citizen of the Union

THE PUBLICATION of *George W. Cable: His Life and Letters* by his daughter, Lucy Leffingwell Cable Bikle, reminds us how completely this once-popular novelist has now passed into eclipse. Few people read Cable today; and the critics never discuss him. Yet in the eighties and the nineties he was enormously read both at home and abroad; and he deserved the high standing he was given. The decline of Cable's reputation is, I believe, mainly due to the general lack of interest, on the part of the critics of the new generation, in the American literature of the period just behind them. We are rediscovering Irving Babbitt and Paul Elmer More, but we have not yet discovered John Jay Chapman; we leave Stephen Crane in half-shadow, and George Cable in complete eclipse.

The prevalent notion of Cable today seems to be that he was a romantic novelist, of a species now obsolete, who made a good thing of exploiting the sentiment and charm, the quaintness and picturesqueness, of a New Orleans long gone to decay. This idea seems, indeed, to some extent, to have been shared by the public who read Cable, that public for whom taste and intellect were represented by Richard Watson Gilder, the editor of the *Century Magazine*. When George Cable was presented with an honorary degree of Master of Arts by Yale, it was "with the desire of recognizing publicly the eminent success which you have achieved in embalming in literature a unique phase of American social life which is rapidly passing away." Yet Cable himself had no idea that he was engaged in embalming anything: he supposed himself to be dealing with the realities of contemporary life—and, in the work of his best years, this was true.

The New Orleans of George Cable's time—and even the

New Orleans of today—is a laboratory where certain American situations present themselves, if not in a form necessarily more acute than elsewhere, at least in more vivid colors. Louisiana, originally French, was transferred in 1762 to Spain, with the result of arousing extreme hostility between the French and the Spanish inhabitants. At the beginning of the nineteenth century, it was transferred back from Spain to France, and then sold by Napoleon to the United States, with the result of provoking a new kind of hostility, this time between the original Latin Americans, Spanish and French, on the one hand, and the Anglo-Saxon Americans who had come in to take possession, on the other. At the same time, the mingling of the whites with the large Negro element of the population had resulted in a class of mulattoes who constituted a special problem. Thus, one found in New Orleans simultaneously in a concentrated field and in intensified form, the conflict of European nationalities, as between the Spanish and the French; the conflict of the Latins and the Anglo-Saxons; and the conflict of two totally different races, as between the Negroes and the whites. Add to this the sectional conflict at the time of the Civil War, of the American South with the North, a conflict felt so much more painfully and for so much longer a time after the war by the South than by the North. The whole American problem of diversity and unity was here, and no writer ever studied it more thoroughly or thought about it more intelligently than George Washington Cable did.

For Cable was essentially a sociologist. He was not in the least a fancier of lavender and old lace. He was a good deal closer to Upton Sinclair than he was to Myrtle Reed. He had a real sense of beauty, but there was too much of the Puritan in him—his mother had been a New Englander, and it was only comparatively late in life that Cable was able to make up his mind that the theater was not immoral—to allow him much to cultivate his sensibility. Though his books have their own sort of atmosphere, which seems to have enchanted his readers, it is certainly not the atmosphere of Cable's novels which appears most successful today. Compare one of Cable's Louisiana descriptions with a description of the same region by Lafcadio Hearn. The lush background that Hearn is so good at investing with color and glamor has a way of turning flat in Cable. Beneath the floridity of the Southerner and his courteous and affable manner, we catch a glimpse of William Wetmore Story and his statue of Cleopatra. And so, though Cable had a most remarkable, an almost unexcelled ear for human speech, though he reported it with the most scrupulous accuracy, he did little to make it attractive. Just as he listened with attention to the songs of birds and transcribed them into musical notation, so he studied the different varieties of the French, Spanish and Negro Creole dialects and the language of the Acadians, both English and French, with a scholarly exactitude that must be as valuable to the phonetician as it is forbidding to the ordinary reader. This rendering, with pitiless apostrophes, of these special pronunciations was complained of even in the period of Cable's greatest popularity, and it constitutes a formidable obstacle to appreciating him today.

Cable's own conception of his craft comes out plainly in certain of the letters included in this biography. Of *The Grandissimes*, he writes that the editors of *Scribner's*, in which it first appeared, did not know "that the work I should by and by send them was going to have any political character. But that was well-nigh inevitable. It was impossible that a novel written by me then should escape being a study in the fierce struggle going on around me, regarded in the light of that past history—those beginnings —which had so differentiated Louisiana civilization from the American scheme of public society. I meant to make *The Grandissimes* as truly a political work as it has ever been called. . . . My friends and kindred looked on with disapproval and dismay, and said all they could to restrain me. 'Why wantonly offend thousands of your own people?' But I did not intend to offend. I wrote as near to truth and justice as I knew how, upon questions that I saw must be settled by calm debate and cannot be settled by force or silence."

The Grandissimes was the first full-length instalment of Cable's anatomy of Southern society. He prepared at about the same time for the United States Census of 1880 a report on the "social statistics" of New Orleans which was specially commended by the authorities; and it was this blending of what may perhaps be taken as a New England respect for facts with a humanism quite alien to New England which left Louisiana, in Cable's writings, perhaps the most satisfactorily studied of nineteenth-century American communities. For Cable, who had never been in France, had read and spoken French all his life and who, brought up as a Presbyterian, had come to manhood in a Catholic community, could penetrate Louisiana in every layer and all directions.

In *The Grandissimes* Cable incorporated a story that he had never been able to sell to the "family" magazines of the period and that had consequently not been included in the popular *Old Creole Days*. The reason for rejecting this manuscript that had been given by George Parsons Lathrop, writing for William Dean Howells, then editor of the *Atlantic Monthly*, was "the unmitigatedly distressful effect of the story." This was the *Story of Bras-Coupé*, the adventures of an African king sold into slavery in the United States. When Bras-Coupé is brought to Louisiana and taken into the fields, and he first comes to understand that it is intended for him to work with common Negroes, he hits the foreman over the head with his hoe, picks up one of the other slaves and bites him in the leg and throws him away, and raises havoc till the overseer shoots him down. A woman slave, who speaks his language, is brought to interpret to him, and he instantly falls in love with her and allows himself to be ruled through her. He demands to marry her; and, on the night of his wedding, gets drunk and forgets his status; he knocks down his master, who has already resented being treated by him as king to king. He is brutally hunted to death. As a study of what man can make of man, of the deformation of human relations by unnatural social institutions, the story of Bras-Coupé is as powerful in its smaller scope as *Uncle Tom's Cabin* itself. With the story of Mme. Lalauré in *Strange True Stories of Louisiana* and some other detached episodes, it almost puts Cable in the class of the great Russian chroniclers of serfdom.

For it is not the love stories in Cable's fiction that really interest Cable: it is the social and political situations. It is human life throttled in the web of society that arouses all his emotion, at the same time that he can trace with nicety every one of the tangled strands and explain the necessities that have strung it. One of the features of this biography is a hitherto unpublished account by Cable of the development of his political ideas. He had fought in the Confederate Army, but had afterwards come to unorthodox conclusions in regard to the Negro question and the relations of the North and the South. About the time that he began to give public expression to his opinions on these subjects, he moved his family from New Orleans to New England. The real occasion for this change of residence was the ill-health of Cable's wife; but, in spite of the fact that he made it a rule never to publish an opinion in the North which he had not first put forward in person from a public platform in the South, returning there expressly for the purpose, there can be no doubt that Cable's native city was no longer very comfortable for him. He was one of the clearest-minded Americans of his time, and in the South, after the Civil War, so detached and realistic an intelligence was uncommon and unwelcome. It was not common or welcome anywhere. Cable understood both South and North; the American and the European; the white man and the Negro; and he would not become the partisan of any of them. What he believed in were democratic principles of the kind that he understood the American Republic to have been founded to put into practice; and he devoted all his study and art to the attempt to impress their importance on a public that were occupied for the most part—during our period of industrial development after the Civil War—with aims that ran counter to these. The moral of Cable's stories is always that distinctions between human beings on social or national or racial grounds must be regarded as merely provisory; that there can never be a true equilibrium, that there can only be conflict and agony, where such discriminations are used as pretexts for unequal privilege.

February 13, 1929

Dos Passos and the Social Revolution

JOHN DOS PASSOS's *Airways, Inc.*, was produced in March as the last play of the second season of the New Playwrights' Theater, and almost entirely failed to attract attention. This was due, principally, I believe, to the fact that by that time the critics had become rather discouraged with the revolutionary drama of Grove Street and that the New Playwrights themselves were so low in funds that they could not afford proper publicity. None the less, *Airways, Inc.*, was a remarkable play, perhaps the best that the New Playwrights have done; and though this is not the place to speak of the merits of the Grove Street production, which I thought were considerable, the published text of the play demands attention as a work of literature.

Airways is, like the group's other plays, a social-political-economic fable; but Dos Passos is more intelligent than most of his associates—he is able to enter into more points of view—and he is a much better artist. His play is neither a naturalistic study nor a vaudeville in the manner of John Howard Lawson, though it has some of the elements of both; it is rather a sort of dramatic poem of contemporary America. With great ingenuity, Dos Passos had assembled on a single suburban street-corner representatives of most of the classes and groups that go to make up our society.

We concentrate upon the life of a single middle-class household, but this is submerged in a larger world: its fate is inextricably bound up with a current real-estate boom; a strike that eventually gives rise to a Sacco-Vanzetti incident; and the promotion of a commercial aviation company. Nor, as is likely to be the case in this kind of play, are the social types merely abstractions which never persuade the imagination. Dos Passos has succeeded in producing the illusion that behind the little suburban street-corner of the Turners lies all the life of a great American city—all the confusion of America itself; and *Airways* made the meager stage of the bleak little Grove Street Theater seem as big as any stage I have ever seen. Dos Passos has also given the household of the Turners an extension in time as well as in space: he has provided a chorus of two old men, an American inventor and a Hungarian revolutionist, whose role is to relate what we see to what has gone before in history and to what may be expected to come after.

It is in the construction of this sort of sociological fable that Dos Passos particularly excels. The strength of his novel, *Manhattan Transfer*, lay in the thoroughness and the steady hand with which he executed a similar anatomy on the city of New York as a whole. As a dramatist he is less expert; and *Airways* suffers in certain ways from comparison with *Manhattan Transfer*. Dos Passos sometimes interrupts his action with long passages of monologue, which, though they might go down easily in a novel, discourage our attention in the theater; and his last act, though the two separate scenes are excellent in themselves, fails to draw the different strands together as we expect a third act to do. But, on the other hand, *Airways*, at its best, has an eloquence and a spirit that *Manhattan Transfer* largely lacked. It is one of the best-written things that Dos Passos has so far done—perhaps freer than any other of his productions both from rhetoric doing duty for feeling and from descriptions too relentlessly piled up. Dos Passos is probably only now arriving at his mature prose style.

So much for the purely artistic aspect of *Airways*. It is impossible to discuss it further without taking into account Dos Passos's political philosophy. Dos Passos is, one gathers from his work, a social revolutionist: he believes that, in the United States as elsewhere, the present capitalistic regime is destined to be overthrown by a class-conscious proletariat. And his disapproval of capitalist society seems to imply a distaste for all the beings who go to compose it. In *Manhattan Transfer*, it was not merely New York, but humanity that came off badly. Dos Passos, in exposing the diseased organism, had the effect, though not, I believe, the intention, of condemning the sufferers along with the disease; and even when he seemed to desire to make certain of his characters sympathetic, he had a way of putting them down.

Now, in *Airways*, there are several characters whom Dos Passos has succeeded in making either admirable or attractive, but these are, in every case, either radicals or their sympathizers. His bias against the economic system is so strong that it extends beyond its official representatives to all those human beings whose only fault is to have been born where such a system prevails and to be so lacking in courage or perspicacity as not to have allied themselves with the forces that are trying to fight it. In Dos Passos, not only must the policeman not fail to steal the money with which the street-kids have been playing craps; but even the young people of *Airways* who, however irresponsible and immoral, might be expected to exhibit something of the charm of youth—become uglier and uglier as the play proceeds, till they finally go completely to pieces in a drunken restaurant scene which is one of Dos Passos's masterpieces of corrosive vulgarity. It is especially curious to note the treatment which the American aviators receive at the hands of both Dos Passos and Lawson. The aviator is one of the authentic heroes that our American civilization now produces. But for Lawson or Dos Passos, an aviator cannot be an authentic hero, or even, apparently, a genius, because he is not on the side of the revolution. The truth is, of course, that the aviator of the type of Lindbergh or Byrd never troubles himself with these questions at all and, even when, as in the case of Lindbergh, he is exploited for a time by the government, he exists and performs his achievements in a world independent of politics. But to a Lawson or a Dos Passos, he is suspect: they cannot let him get away with anything, and eventually, in what they write, they succeed in destroying or degrading him. In Lawson's play, *The International*, another New Playwrights production, the Lindbergh character appears as a drunken taxi-driver—or perhaps as a drunken bum in a taxi—amid the débâcle of the capitalist state; and in *Airways*, the young aviator is sent up by the agents of his capitalist employers to scatter leaflets on a strikers' meeting. He is drunk, and falls and breaks his back.

Now, the life of middle-class America, even under capitalism and even in a city like New York, is not so un-attractive as Dos Passos makes it—no human life under any conditions can ever have been so unattractive. Under however an unequal distribution of wealth, human beings are still capable of enjoyment, affection and enthusiasm—even of integrity and courage. Nor are these qualities and emo-tions entirely confined to class-conscious workers and their leaders. There are moments in reading a novel or seeing a play by Dos Passos when one finds oneself ready to rush to the defense of even the American bathroom, even the Ford car—which, after all, one begins to reflect, have perhaps done as much to rescue us from helplessness, ignorance and squalor as the prophets of revolution. We may begin to reflect upon the relation, in Dos Passos, of political opinions to artistic effects. Might it not, we ask ourselves, be possible—have we not, in fact, seen it occur —for a writer to hold Dos Passos's political opinions and yet not depict our middle-class republic as a place where no birds sing, no flowers bloom and where the very air is almost unbreathable? For, in the novels and plays of Dos Passos, everybody loses out: if he is on the right side of the social question, he has to suffer, if he is not snuffed out;

if he is on the oppressors' side, his pleasures are made
repulsive. When a man as intelligent as Dos Passos—that is,
a man a good deal more intelligent than, say, Michael
Gold or Upton Sinclair, who hold similar political views—
when so intelligent a man and so good an artist allows his
bias so to falsify his picture of life that, in spite of all the
accurate observation and all the imaginative insight, its
values are partly those of melodrama—we begin to guess
some stubborn sentimentalism at the bottom of the whole
thing, some deeply buried streak of hysteria of which his
misapplied resentments represent the aggressive side. And
from the moment we suspect the processes by which he has
arrived at his political ideas, the ideas themselves become
suspect.

In the meantime, whatever diagnosis we may make of
Dos Passos's infatuation with the social revolution, he remains one of the few first-rate figures among our writers
of his generation, and the only one of these who has made
a systematic effort to study all the aspects of America and
to take account of all its elements, to compose them into
a picture which makes some general sense. Most of the
first-rate men of Dos Passos's age—Hemingway, Wilder,
Fitzgerald—cultivate their own little corners and do not
confront the situation as a whole. Only Dos Passos has
tried to take hold of it. In the fine last speech of *Airways*,
he allows the moral of his play to rise very close to the
surface. The spinster sister of the Turner household has
just received the news that the strike leader, with whom she
has been in love and who has been made the victim of a
frame-up, has finally been electrocuted: "Now I'm beginning to feel it," she says, "the house without Walter, the
street without him, the city without him, the future that
we lived in instead of a honeymoon without him, everything stark without him. Street where I've lived all these
years shut up in a matchwood house full of bitterness. City
where I've lived walled up in old dead fear. America, where
I've scurried from store to subway to church to home,
America that I've never known. World where I've lived

without knowing. What can I do now that he is gone and that he has left me full of scalding wants, what can I do with the lack of him inside me like a cold stone? The house I lived in wrecked, the people I loved wrecked, around me there's nothing but words stinging like wasps. Where can I go down the dark street, where can I find a lover in the sleeping city? At what speed of the wind can I fly away, to escape these words that burn and sting, to escape the lack that is in me like a stone?"

It is true that the lack of real leadership is felt by us today as a stone. It is Dos Passos's recognition of this—his relentless reiteration of his conviction that there is something lacking, something wrong, in America—as well as his insistence on the importance of America—that gives his work its validity and power. It is equally true, of course, of H. L. Mencken that he finds something lacking and something wrong; but the effect of Mencken on his admirers is to make them wash their hands of social questions. Mencken has made it the fashion to speak of politics as an obscene farce. And Dos Passos is now almost alone among the writers of his generation in continuing to take the social organism seriously.

April 17, 1929

T. S. Eliot and the Church of England

For Lancelot Andrewes by T. S. Eliot contains essays on Lancelot Andrewes and John Bramhall, two seventeenth-century English divines, and on Machiavelli, F. H. Bradley, Baudelaire, Thomas Middleton, Crashaw and Irving Babbitt. They all display the author's unique combination of subtle and original thinking with simple and precise statement, and will be read by everybody interested in literature. T. S. Eliot has now become perhaps the most important literary critic in the English-speaking world. His

writings have been brief and few, and it is almost incredible
that they should have been enough to establish him as an
intellectual leader; but when one tries to trace the causes
of the change from the point of view of the English criticism of the period before the war to the point of view of
our own day, one can find no figure of comparable authority. And we must recognize that Eliot's opinions, so
cool and even casual in appearance, yet sped with the force
of so intense a seriousness and weighted with so wide a
learning, have stuck oftener and sunk deeper in the minds
of the post-war generation of both England and the United
States than those of any other critic.

For Lancelot Andrewes, however, is not, like The Sacred
Wood, a book merely of literary criticism. The essays
which it contains have been selected by Eliot for the purpose of indicating a general position in literature, politics
and religion. This position, he tells us in his preface, "may
be described as classicist in literature, royalist in politics,
and Anglo-Catholic in religion"; and it is further to be
expounded in "three small books," called respectively The
School of Donne, The Outline of Royalism and The Principles of Modern Heresy.

Mr. Eliot's ideas, in For Lancelot Andrewes, appear
chiefly by implication; and we run the risk of misrepre-
senting them in attempting to discuss them on the basis
of this book. Still, Eliot has invited us to read this slender
collection of essays as a prelude to the trilogy mentioned
above, and it is difficult to know how else to deal with it.
The clearest and most explicit statement on the subject of
religion I can find is the following from the essay in which
Eliot points out the deficiencies of Irving Babbitt's humanism: "Unless by civilization you mean material
progress, cleanliness, etc. . . . if you mean a spiritual and
intellectual coördination on a high level, then it is doubtful
whether civilization can endure without religion, and religion without a church." One recognizes a point of view
which is by way of becoming fashionable among certain
sorts of literary people, yet this usually presents itself

merely as a sentiment that it would be a good thing to believe rather than as a real and living belief. And, though Eliot lets us know that he does believe, his faith, in so far as we find it expressed in these essays and in his recent poems, seems entirely uninspired by hope, entirely unequipped with force—a faith which, to quote his own epigraph, is merely "ready to die."

Now, no one will dispute that, at the present time, our society is in need of the kind of ideals which the churches were once able to supply; but the objection to Eliot's position is simply that the churches are now out of the question as a solution to our present difficulties, because it is so difficult to get educated people to accept their fundamental doctrines—and that, even if a few first-rate ones can convince themselves that they do, one does not see how they can possibly hope for a revival general enough to make religion intellectually important again. I agree that, without a church, you cannot have a real religion; and I sympathize with Mr. Eliot's criticism of certain substitute religions, like that of H. G. Wells, which try to retain the benefits of faith while doing away with the necessity of believing. You cannot have real Christianity without a cult of Jesus as the son of God. But since it has plainly become anachronistic to accept the prophet Jesus in this role, it seems that we must reconcile ourselves to doing without both the churches and religion. The answer to Mr. Eliot's assertion, that "it is doubtful whether civilization can endure without religion" is that we have got to make it endure. Nobody will pretend that this is going to be easy; but it can hardly be any more difficult than persuading oneself that the leadership of the future will be supplied by the Church of England or by the Roman Catholic Church or by any church whatsoever.

Nothing seems to me more sadly symptomatic of the feeble intellectual condition of a good many literary people, of their unwillingness or incapacity to come to terms with the world they live in, than the movement back to Thomas Aquinas—or, in Eliot's case, back to Bishop Andrewes. It is not, of course, a question of the wisdom or the spiritual authority of Aquinas or Andrewes in his own day, when it was still possible for a first-rate mind to accept the supernatural basis of religion. But to argue, as in the literary world one sometimes finds people doing, that, because our society at the present time is badly off without religion, we should make an heroic effort to swallow medieval theology, seems to me utterly futile as well as fundamentally dishonest. If the salvation of our civilization depends on such religious fervor as our writers are capable of kindling—if it depends on the edifying example of the conversion of Jean Cocteau and the low blue flame of the later Eliot—then I fear that we must give up hope.

I was writing last week of John Dos Passos and his mirage of a social revolution. It seems to me that T. S. Eliot is a case of much the same kind: Eliot, like Dos Passos, is a highly cultivated American who does not care for contemporary America; but, instead of escaping from the American situation by way of Greenwich Village radicalism and the myth of a serious-minded and clear-eyed proletariat, as Dos Passos attempts to do, Eliot has gone to England and evolved for himself an aristocratic myth out of English literature and history. Eliot's classicism, royalism and Anglo-Catholicism, from the notion I get of them in his recent writings, seem to me as much academic attitudes, as much lacking in plausibility, as Dos Passos's cult of the class-conscious proletariat: it is as hard to imagine royalty and the Church becoming more instead of less important, even in England, as it is to imagine the American employees becoming less instead of more middle-class. Most Americans of the type of Dos Passos and Eliot —that is, sensitive and widely read literary people—have some such agreeable fantasy in which they can allow their minds to take refuge from the perplexities and oppressions about them. In the case of H. L. Mencken, it is a sort of German university town, where people drink a great deal of beer and devour a great many books, and where they respect the local nobility—if only the Germany of the Empire had not been destroyed by the war! In the case of certain American writers from the top layer of the old South, it is the old-fashioned Southern plantation, where men are high-spirited and punctilious and women gracious and lovely, where affectionate and loyal Negroes are happy to keep in their place—if only the feudal South had not perished in 1865! With Ezra Pound, it is a medieval Provence, where poor but accomplished troubadours enjoy the favors of noble ladies—if only the troubadours were not deader than Provençal! With Dos Passos, it is an army of workers, disinterested, industrious and sturdy, but full of the good-fellowship and gaiety in which the Webster Hall balls nowadays are usually so dismally lacking—if only the American workers were not preoccupied with buying Ford cars and radios, instead of organizing themselves to overthrow the civilization of the bourgeoisie! And in T. S. Eliot's case, it is a world of seventeenth-century churchmen, who combine the most scrupulous conscience with the ability to write good prose—if it were only not so difficult nowadays for men who are capable of becoming good writers to accept the Apostolic Succession!

Among these, the writers like Dos Passos and Mencken stay at home and denounce America, while the writers like Eliot and Pound go abroad and try to forget it. It is peculiarly hard for such men to get an intellectual foothold in our world: New York, in particular, just now, is like the great glass mountain of the *Arabian Nights,* against which the barques of young writers are continually coming to grief. And this is true not merely of the United States, but more or less of the whole Western world. Industrially, politically and socially, Europe itself is becoming more and more like America every day; and the catastrophe of the war has demoralized America, too. It is up to American writers to try to make some sense of their American world —for their world is now everybody's world, and, if they fail to find a way to make possible in it what T. S. Eliot desiderates: "a spiritual and intellectual coördination on

a high level," it is improbable that any one else will be
able to do it for them. That world is a world with a number
of religions, but not amenable to the leadership of a single
church—and it is a world in which, whatever reorganization
one may prophesy for the democratic state, the restoration
of the monarchic principle seems improbable to the last
degree. It is a world in which Eliot's program would not
appear very helpful. We shall certainly not be able to lean
upon the authority of either Church or King, and we shall
have to depend for our new ideals on a study of contemporary reality and the power of our own imaginations.

April 24, 1929

Dahlberg, Dos Passos and Wilder

In *The Woman of Andros*, Thornton Wilder has turned
Terence's *Andria* into a fable of the world without Christianity. At some indeterminate date before the birth of
Christ, the son of a well-to-do merchant on the Greek
island of Brynos falls in love with the sister of an hetaira
and gets her with child. But it has been arranged for him
by his family to marry a girl of his own class, and he is in
doubt as to what to do about his mistress. The intelligent
and sympathetic father leaves it up to the young man, who
seeks enlightenment in a religious fast and vigil. In the
meantime, however, the hetaira's household—the hetaira
herself having died—has been sold to a visiting pimp, and
by the time the father has succeeded in buying Glycerium
back and the son has returned from the temple with his
mind firmly made up to marry her, the poor girl has been
overcome by the strain of her situation, and both she and
her baby die.

Thornton Wilder has achieved his effect with accomplished technical skill: he has induced us to follow his story
with sympathy and suspense, but he has kept us from

understanding the full significance of the incidents we have been witnessing until we read the final sentence of the book, which is repeated from the first paragraph, where it has seemed to have only a casual interest, but which now retrospectively illuminates all that has come between: "But behind the thick beds of clouds the moon soared radiantly bright, shining upon Italy and its smoking mountains. And in the East the stars shone tranquilly down upon the land that was soon to be called Holy and that even then was preparing its precious burden." Looking back, we now understand that we have been watching a world in half-darkness: these people have been groping and perplexed—they have as yet known no revelation, they can depend upon no authority, to justify their impulses toward charity, toward putting the instinct of brotherhood before those of convention and interest. We see now that the cultivated hetaira—who, in conformity with the tradition of Wilder's novels, is secretly and hopelessly in love with the boy—in her acceptance of disappointment and death, and her final philosophical reflections: "I want to say to someone . . . that I have known the worst that the world can do to me, and that nevertheless I praise the world and all living. All that is, is well. Remember some day, remember me as one who loved all things and accepted from the gods all things, the bright and the dark" —we see that Chrysis is supposed to represent the highest culture and moral wisdom which, before the coming of Christ, the pagan world could attain, and that she has already, in making her house an asylum for simpleton, pauper and cripple, anticipated a new and deeper morality. We see that the asceticism of the priest of Apollo anticipates that of the Christian priesthood, that the merchant and his son are groping for principles that only the gospel of Christ can supply, and that the dead mother and child are a symbol for the death of the pagan world, which another mother and child, in "the land soon to be called Holy," are to waken to another life.

This moment before the advent of Christianity has

already been exploited as a theme for fiction; it has even been a favorite theme. Its popularity has been due, I suppose, partly to the influence of Renan, who, in his *Origines du Christianisme,* subtly creates the impression that the Graeco-Roman culture was itself tending independently toward all that was best in Christianity, and that it had, also, virtues of its own that were more attractive than most of the Christian ones. Pater's *Marius the Epicurean* seems to have taken its subject and mood from the final volume of the series, which describes the reign of Marcus Aurelius; but Pater slightly shifted the emphasis: he gave Christianity a certain advantage. The Gospel is with Pater, as with Wilder, the word for which humanity has been waiting, the only thing needful that the ancient world has lacked. Anatole France followed Renan, also, but, with a livelier malice than Renan's, he tipped the scales against Christianity, and delighted, in *Sur la Pierre Blanche,* in showing how Paul before Gallio at Corinth had not really, as Renan had said, represented in his unprepossessing person the imminent future of Europe, of which the cultivated Roman had no suspicion, but had been merely the fanatical product of a semi-barbarous interlude —since, when Europe should have recovered from the Middle Ages, she was to aim, in her civilization, at Gallio's ideals, not Paul's.

Now, Wilder has picked up this pagan-Christian theme and, tipping the balance, as Pater did, in favor of Christ again, has written a book which belongs to the period of Pater and Anatole France. *The Woman of Andros,* though it is very well done, strikes me as being a kind of thing that there is no longer much point in doing. I am sure that, in revisiting the ancient world, the author has intended to tell us, as every writer must do, something interesting about our own. We gather from Wilder's play *The Angel That Troubled the Waters* that he himself is a believer in the Christian creed, and I assume that in *The Woman of Andros* he is trying to show us the sorrows and doubts that we ourselves must experience if we live without the Christian religion. There is behind many a page of this book a broken-hearted Proustian sob which has welled up, all too unmistakably, from the peculiar sentimentality of our own time and not from any state of mind that one can associate with the Greeks; and there are also some admirable passages that speak to us directly of ourselves: "From time to time she peered into her mind," Wilder writes of the dying hetaira, "to ascertain what her beliefs were in regard to life after death, its judgments or its felicities; but the most exhausting of all our adventures is that journey down the long corridors of the mind to the last halls where belief is enshrined." But the further Thornton Wilder withdraws into the past, the more imitative he becomes. This ought not necessarily to be true; but the fact is that, ever since the romantic revival set the fashion of re-creating the past, the writers have been ringing the changes on the Christian-pagan theme, loading the dice for one or the other, and that dealing with the past, for Wilder, means not merely going back to Greece, not merely going back to Terence, but going back to the Paris of yesterday. His new book, for all the charm of its style, the grace of narrative and the spare firm outline which Wilder never fails of, as it is paler than his other books, comes closer to seeming mawkish. Wilder announced, or made his hero announce, at the conclusion of *The Cabala* that he was returning with high hopes to New York. But he was next heard from in Cluxambuqua, and he now hails us with rather a far faint voice from a Greek island of some vague date B.C. One always reads with pleasure and edification anything that Thornton Wilder writes—but just because he is evidently a first-rate man, one would like to see him more at home.

Edward Dahlberg, the author of *Bottom Dogs*, is, on the other hand, very close to us—he is closer to us, indeed, than we quite care to have literature be. *Bottom Dogs* is the back-streets of all our American cities and towns. Mr. Dahlberg, as a writer, has nothing in common with the consummate sophistication of Thornton Wilder, and his narrative is sometimes dull; but what he has brought in from the obscurer sections of Los Angeles, Cleveland, Kansas City is something more than an interesting document—it is a work of literature that has the stamp of a real and original gift. The prose of *Bottom Dogs* is partly derived from the language of the streets itself, but to say this may give a misleading impression: Dahlberg's prose is primarily a literary medium, hard, vivid, exact and racy, and with an odd kind of street-lighted glamor. I do not agree with D. H. Lawrence, who has written for this sordid story a curious and suggestive introduction, that the dominating feeling of the book is repulsion. It would be easy for a writer of another kind to make Dahlberg's kind of experience repulsive, but I do not feel that Dahlberg has done so: the temperament through which he has strained his orphan homes, his barber shops and bakeries, his dance-halls and Y.M.C.A.'s, though he is always realistically observant, seems a gentle and unassertive, and, consequently, an unembittered one. We read the book, at any rate, with wonder to see how the rawest, the cheapest, the most commonplace American material may be transmuted by a man of talent, so submerged in it that he can only speak its language, yet acting upon it so strongly, so imbuing it with his own tone and color and texture, that he can make it yield a work of distinction.

Now, John Dos Passos, in *The 42nd Parallel*, has consciously and deliberately worked out a medium similar to Dahlberg's. *The 42nd Parallel*—which it seems to me Dos Passos's publishers have made a serious mistake in not announcing for what it is: the first section of a large-scale novel—is to deal with the role of the United States in relation to the rest of the world during the early years of the present century; but though it is written from the point of view of an unusually internationally minded American of unusually wide culture, the author has been able to immerse himself in the minds and the lives of his middle-class characters, to identify himself with them, to a degree that must astonish any reader of Dos Passos's other novels. In this respect, *The 42nd Parallel* is quite different from *Manhattan Transfer* and marks a striking advance beyond it. *Manhattan Transfer*, after all, might almost have been written by a very intelligent and very well-documented foreigner: the characters are seen from the outside and do not always seem organically human. But in this new work of fiction, Dos Passos has abandoned the literary baggage that encumbered his exploration of New York. Here one finds no elaborate backdrops and no Joycean prose-poems. For the method of *The 42nd Parallel*, Dos Passos has perhaps gone to school to Ring Lardner and Anita Loos; he is, at any rate, the first of our writers —with the possible exception of Mark Twain—who has successfully used colloquial American for a novel of the highest artistic seriousness. This has enabled him to keep us close to the characters as we never were in *Manhattan Transfer*. He still has moments of allowing his people to contract into two-dimensional caricatures of qualities or forces he hates; but, in general, we live their lives, we look at the world through their eyes.

These characters of *The 42nd Parallel* belong mostly to the white-collar class. Almost all of them begin as obscure and more or less mediocre-appearing people, who, from the ordinary American point of view, are anxious to improve their condition. Neither the gentle spinster stenographer from Washington, the amiable publicity director from Wilmington nor the sharp woman interior decorator from Chicago, has an intimation of any other values than those of the American business office, of the American advertising game, of the American luxury trade, out of which they make their salaries and in terms of which they conceive their ambitions. Only the nephew of the radical Irish printer reacts against the habits of the white-collar class and tends to identify his interests with those of a proletariat. The author introduces separately each one of his five principal characters—we have of each a continuous history from childhood. For this, he has invented a narrative method which enables him to cover a great deal of ground with astonishing rapidity and ease, yet to give us the illusion of finding out all about his people's lives: their friends and the members of their families, their amusements and their periods of stagnation, the places where they work and how much they get, the meals they eat, the beds they sleep in. And without any explicit commentary, each of these sequences of data and incident is made to create a character. Eleanor Stoddard's cold-blooded shrewdness and passionate appetite for refinement or J. Ward Moorehouse's unconscious charlatanry is presented entirely in terms of *things*. And when these commonplace individuals, who have first been presented to the reader independently of one another, are finally brought together, they take on a further significance—we realize that what we have been witnessing is the making of our contemporary society. And as Dos Passos can indicate in masterly fashion the shift from one city to another, so that we understand, without having been overtly told, the difference between the way people behave and feel in Chicago and the way they behave and feel in New York, in Washington, Minneapolis, Pittsburgh or Mexico City; so—also, apparently, without being told—we at last seem to understand the national character of America. The author has sandwiched in, between the sections of the life-histories of his characters, what he labels as "newsreels"—that is, medleys of newspaper-clippings—that give us a picture of the public consciousness running parallel with the private events of the lives that are narrated in detail; as well as a series of brief biographies (very well done) of eminent contemporary Americans, all shown as hampered, stunted or perverted by that same commercial society in which the characters of the novel are submerged. And at the end of this first instalment, with the entrance of the United States into the war and the appearance of the last of the characters, a young garage man from North Dakota, who in his wanderings has fallen in with a rich and drunken cracker from Okeechobee City and been persuaded by him that he ought to go over and get a load of the fun in Europe "before the whole thing goes belly-up"—Dos Passos, in the perfectly aimed final paragraphs, reveals this character suddenly as a symbol for the American people, adventurous and well-intentioned but provincial and immature, voyaging out from its enormous country into a world of which it knows nothing.

This novel, when it has been completed, may well turn out to be the most important that has yet been produced by any American of Dos Passos's generation. Dos Passos seems the only one of the novelists of this generation who is concerned with the large questions of politics and society; and he has succeeded in this book in bridging the gap, which is wider in America than anywhere else and which constitutes a perpetual problem in American literature and thought, between the special concerns of the intellectual and the general pursuits and ideas of the people. The task of the intellectual is not merely to study the common life but to make his thoughts and symbols *seem* relevant to it—that is, to express them in terms of the actual American world without either cheapening them or rendering them vapid. Dos Passos, who has read as much and traveled as widely as Wilder, does not always avoid spinning literature—especially in the first section, which has a flavor of *Huckleberry Finn;* and, in consequence, he is sometimes flimsy, where Dahlberg, in dealing with a similar subject, would be authentic and dense. But, though in neither intensity nor skill is Dos Passos superior to Hemingway, *The 42nd Parallel* seems to me, from the point of view of its literary originality and its intellectual interest, by far the most remarkable, the most encouraging American novel that I have read since the end of the war.

March 26, 1930

Notes on Babbitt and More

THE FOLLOWING NOTES deal with the essays by Irving Babbitt and Paul Elmer More which appeared in the humanist symposium called *Humanism and America.*

Humanism: An Essay at Definition

By Irving Babbitt

(1) *The law of measure on which it [humanism] depends becomes meaningless unless it can be shown to be one of the "laws unwritten in the heavens" of which Antigone had the immediate perception, laws that are "not of to-day or yesterday," that transcend in short the temporal process.*

This seems to me a grotesque misapplication of the famous speech from Sophocles. Let me point out, in the first place, that what Antigone says is "ἄγραπτα κἀσφαλῆ θεῶν νόμιμα"—"unwritten and unfailing laws of the gods"—and that Professor Babbitt, in changing "gods" to "heavens" (which is particularly inappropriate in this case, since Antigone has just specified the gods of the underworld), is following the Victorian tradition of Jebb and Jowett, who, by substituting such Christian words as "God" and "heaven" for the pre-Christian conceptions of the Greeks, almost succeeded in giving Sophocles and Plato the aspect of pious English dons. But Babbitt has turned Sophocles into something worse and even more alien to his true nature: he has turned him into a Harvard humanist. In the scene in question, Antigone is not talking about the law of measure or anything remotely resembling it—she has disobeyed Creon's edict by performing funeral rites for her brother and she is justifying herself for her in-

subordinate conduct. There is no self-control about Antigone's behavior: she has committed an act of passionate
personal loyalty, regarded as excessively rash and wrong-
headed by everybody else in the play, including her own
sister, whose "inner check" is more highly developed than
Antigone's. When Creon demands how Antigone has dared
to break the law, she answers fiercely that such a law as
his edict is contrary to the laws of the gods.

The romantic might, in fact, turn this scene against
the humanist with more appropriateness than the humanist
can use it against the romantic. Antigone has the same
hasty insolent intemperate nature as her father Oedipus—
we are told so explicitly in the play—and she is asserting
her individual will in defiance of law and expediency—she
is making an impulsive and desperate gesture. Aristotle—
"a true humanist," according to Babbitt—says of this passage, in showing the distinction between conventional and
natural law, that Antigone vindicates the latter in asserting
"ὅτι δίκαιον, ἀπειρημένον, θάψαι τὸν Πολυνείκη, ὡς φύσει ὂν
τοῦτο δίκαιον,"—that her act, though it violated the prohibition, had the sanction of natural right, was "right
according to nature." Now Antigone, of course, is not a
nineteenth-century romantic, and Aristotle does not mean
by "nature" quite the same thing that Rousseau does. But
what Rousseau means does have something in common
with what Aristotle means that Antigone means, whereas
what Antigone means can't by any possible stretch be
associated with Babbitt's "law of measure." Babbitt grossly
misrepresents Sophocles when he applies Antigone's speech
in this way: "The laws unwritten in the heavens" is one of
Babbitt's favorite quotations: he has used it again and
again in order to give us the impression that Sophocles
has endorsed the humanist "will to refrain." Yet, as I say,
if it is a question of slinging classical texts, the old-fashioned
romantic who is Babbitt's bugbear—if there be any such
still alive—might turn Antigone's outburst against Babbitt
—and, relapsing into the truculence of the age of Bentley,

which the manners of the humanists invite, might add, as Antigone does:

σοὶ δ' εἰ δοκῶ νῦν μῶρα δρῶσα τυγχάνειν,
σχεδόν τι μώρῳ μωρίαν ὀφλισκάνω.

Babbitt elsewhere in this essay says that Sophocles "ranks high among occidental humanists," though he admits—making reservations in regard to the opinion of Matthew Arnold—that "perfect poise is no doubt impossible; not even Sophocles succeeded in seeing life steadily and seeing it whole." I don't know in precisely what respect Professor Babbitt considers Sophocles to have fallen short of perfect poise; but it is certainly true that Sophocles' characters are usually remarkable for anything but poise—they are as violent and as harsh as the people in the plays of Eugene O'Neill. Where the "law of measure" comes in is certainly not in connection with the conduct of Sophocles' people—the hot-headed overconfident Oedipus; the "fierce child of a fierce father," Antigone; the relentless and morbid Electra, etc.—but in Sophocles' handling of his material— the firmness of his intellectual grasp, the sureness of his sense of form, the range of psychological insight which enables him to put before us the rages, the ambitions, the loyalties, of so many passionate persons, that spend themselves against one another and expire in the clear air, leaving only with the echo of their tirades the vibration of the taut verse. In a world dominated by the law of measure, there would, however, be no humanist masterpieces such as the tragedies of Sophocles—since Babbitt claims them, with reservations, as humanist masterpieces—because there would be no violent passions to write about. This might be a good thing—perhaps we ought to be glad to do without the Sophocleses if we could get rid of the unruly passions. But, on the other hand, we ought perhaps to think twice before letting ourselves in for a world where the sole masterpieces were humanist symposia.

(2) *It would not be easy to argue with any plausibility that the typical modernist is greatly concerned with the*

law of measure; his interest, as a glance at our newspapers should suffice to show, is rather in the doing of stunts and the breaking of records, in "prodigies, feats of strength and crime," the very topics that, according to the traditional report, Confucius banished from his conversation.

In this respect, our age is no worse than any other. What is done today for the people by the newspapers was done formerly by the composers of ballads, and ballad literature has always been occupied with prodigies, feats of strength and crime. The *Iliad* itself was presumably made out of ballads—and, in any case, there can be no question that it deals with prodigies, feats of strength and crime. The Greek dramatists, including Sophocles, got their themes from Homer or similar sources. It is true that the genuine poet is able to do with such stories something that the simple reporter is not usually able to do, but the material that he deals with is the same. And the general run of the ballads of any age has been as crude as newspaper stories. The sages of our own time—Professor Babbitt, for example—are, I should say, as little preoccupied with the prodigies and crimes of the newspapers as Confucius was with the common gossip.

(3) *In the case of such encroachments [of naturalism upon the domains of humanism or religion] there is not only a quarrel between the naturalist and the humanist, but a quarrel of first principles. When first principles are involved the law of measure is no longer applicable. One should not be moderate in dealing with error.*

It has apparently never occurred to Professor Babbitt that one's moderation ought to extend to not being too sure that one is absolutely right and that others are absolutely wrong—though Mr. More, in his companion essay, quotes from Whitehead, against the dogmatists of Darwinism, Cromwell's, "My brethren, by the bowels of Christ I beseech you, bethink you that you may be mistaken!" We might have thought that if the law of measure were valuable anywhere, it would be valuable in the domain of ideas, where the failure sufficiently to respect it has notoriously bred war and oppression since the beginning of the world. Babbitt surely did not learn from Plato, whom he invokes in the next paragraph, that we should feel so sure of our own opinions that we need not be moderate with other people who happen to have different ones. The hero of Plato's novel of ideas is, of course, Socrates, but Plato's dialogues are a novel, none the less, and the impression, I think, that most people get from them, though they may be persuaded by Socrates' opinions, is that the world has a good many aspects and that there is a good deal to be said on all sides. The people in Plato who follow Babbitt's precept that we "should not be moderate in dealing with error" are the judges of Socrates. I doubt whether even Aristotle was so sure that he was right as Babbitt. If Mr. Babbitt wants to find a tradition for his policy in dealing with error, he must look not to the Academy and the Lyceum, but to the councils of the Inquisition, the revolutionary tribunal of the Terror and—to come closer to Professor Babbitt's home—Dedham Courthouse and Boston State House.*

(4) *Positively one may define it [the higher will] as the higher immediacy that is known in its relation to the lower immediacy—the merely temperamental man with his impressions and emotions and expansive desires—as a power of vital control* (frein vital).

So Paul Elmer More asserts (in *Aristocracy and Justice*) that if a man "retires into himself and examines his own motives and the courses of his self-approval and discontent . . . he will discover that there is a happiness of the soul which is not the same as the pleasure of fulfilled desires, whether these be for good or for ill, a happiness which is not dependent upon the results of this or that choice among our desires, but upon the very act itself of choice and self-control."

Now, why on earth is virtue, with the humanists, always

* This refers to the Sacco-Vanzetti case.

made to reside exclusively in what Babbitt calls the "will to refrain"? "Humanism," says Professor Babbitt, in making a distinction between humanism and religion, "is not primarily enthusiastic." So far as I can see, it is not enthusiastic at all. Professor Babbitt goes on to say that the humanist, though he "cannot afford to be an enthusiast in Rousseau's sense, on the other hand should not neglect the truth of Rousseau's saying that 'cold reason has never done anything illustrious.'" But the writings of the humanists strike us with a chill even more mortal than that of reason. And how can one be seriously impressed by a philosophy which enjoins nothing but negative behavior?—as if humanity were not, now as always, as much in need of being exhorted against coldness and indifference and routine as against irresponsible exuberance—especially Anglo-Saxon humanity. As if it were not obvious that Boston and New York, Manchester and London, were not suffering rather from a lack of normal human fellowship and normal human hope and joy than from any demoralizing effects of unbridled "humanitarian" sympathies, indiscriminate emotional "expansiveness" or universal orgiastic dissipation—as if our clerks, our factory workers and our respectable professional and business classes were all in danger of falling victims to the rhapsodical enthusiasm and the lawless individualism of romanticism! If it is merely a question of refraining, these people are all good humanists: they have either been compelled by society to refrain from most of the enjoyments, from the exercise of most of the faculties, that make the amenity of human life, or they refrain because their education has been too limited to enable them to conceive their own aesthetic and emotional possibilities, or because their natures are too poor to have any.

As a matter of fact, however, Professor Babbitt, as I have noted above, has managed to exempt his own professional activities from the law of measure, the duty to refrain. He makes it plain that, in "dealing with error," we are no longer obliged to be moderate; and as Professor Babbitt, in his writings, hardly ever deals with anything but error, he is rarely obliged to be moderate. Professor Babbitt—and the other humanists—are permitted to drop their ideal of decorum the moment they put pen to paper. It is not decorous to look for nothing but mistakes in the writings of your contemporaries; it is not decorous always to call attention to these mistakes with a sneer; it is not decorous to take a word like humanism, which has formerly been applied to the great scholars, philosophers, satirists and poets of the Renaissance, and to insist that it ought to be regarded as the property of a small sect of schoolmasters so fatuous that they do not hesitate to assign schoolmasters' A's, B's and C's in humanism to "Homer, Phidias, Plato, Aristotle, Confucius, Buddha, Jesus, Paul, Virgil, Horace, Dante, Shakespeare, Milton, Goethe, Matthew Arnold, Emerson and Lowell" (I quote a list of their preferred great figures); it is not decorous to assume that you yourselves are the only persons who have taken seriously the vices and woes of your own time and that everybody except yourselves is engaged either perversely or stupidly in trying to make them worse. The exercise of decorum by the humanists is evidently confined to their private lives, where the public cannot benefit by it.

(5) *This movement has, from the eighteenth century and in some respects from the Renaissance, been marked by a growing discredit of the will to refrain. The very word renunciation has been rarely pronounced by those who have entered into the movement. The chief exception that occurs to one is Goethe (echoed at times by Carlyle). Any one who thinks of the series of Goethe's love affairs, prolonged into the seventies, is scarcely likely to maintain that his Entsagung was of a very austere character even for a man of the world, not to speak of a saint.*

It seems to me that assumptions are here being made in regard to sexual morality which require a good deal of proving on Professor Babbitt's part. He goes on to say, a little further, that "the real humanist consents, like Aristotle, to limit his desires only in so far as this limitation can be shown to make for his own happiness." If one disapproves of Goethe's love affairs, but if the end to be achieved is happiness, one would have to show first that these love affairs failed to make Goethe happy. It seems to me that Mr. Babbitt should shoulder this burden of proof and argue that it did not do Goethe good at the same time that it did the ladies no harm for him to fall in love after he was seventy. But these are questions which Babbitt and More will never consent to argue, as to which they simply make assumptions—just as they assume that virtue is identical with the will to refrain—for the reason that these opinions are not really conclusions from evidence, but the mere unexamined prejudices of a bigoted Puritan heritage which these gentlemen—for all their voyaging through the varied realms of the mind—have never succeeded in sloughing off, and which they persist in mistaking for eternal and universal laws, because—they have put this forward as an overwhelming justification—when they look into their own natures, they find them there.

The Humility of Common Sense
By Paul Elmer More

(1) *It is a nice question to ask whether belief in the absolute irresponsibility of the artistic temperament has engendered the modern ideal of absolute art, or the contrary. . . . The point I would make is the falseness and futility of the logical deduction that art can . . . dispense with the stuff of humanity or nature, or can weigh anchor and sail off into a shoreless sea of unreality.*

In the first part of Mr. More's essay, marked by his usual intellectual arrogance, which he incongruously entitles *The Humility of Common Sense,* he is occupied with the old "art for art's sake" doctrine as it has recently been formulated by some of its champions. Now, one may agree with Mr. More that the artist should not be irresponsible and that he cannot dispense with humanity and nature—one may even agree that "art for art's sake" has given rise to a good deal of nonsense, as indeed what doctrine has not? But it is obvious that Mr. More fails to see how this point of view is the natural and inevitable product of a particular situation. Art is, of course, a profession like medicine, law or banking, a trade like market-gardening or carpentry, that supplies certain human needs; it is one of our human devices for adjusting ourselves to the world and for mastering it in a way that the other animals cannot do. It is preposterous, certainly, for artists to talk as if they were able to work *in vacuo* or as if it were possible for them to remain indifferent to the effects of their work on human life. But in the course of the nineteenth century, they were goaded into talking in this way, into making a cult of art for its own sake, by the progress of the industrial revolution and the rise of the middle class. It was one of the fatal defects of industrial-commercial society that it neglected or discouraged the appetites for which the artists had formerly provided; and as the market value of art depreciated to the point where its practitioners found themselves pushed almost into the role of outlaws, they became embittered and desperate. They swore, if they had any spirit, that they were going to work at their craft even though nobody wanted their wares, and they thus arrived at the slogan that has irritated so many people. The fact that they should have felt the necessity for asserting the value of what they were doing was a sign of their maladjustment, of the abnormality of their situation; but, given this situation, the very faith in aesthetic values, the dogged devotion to art, not infrequently called forth qualities of heroic endurance and self-denial. It was to some extent true, of course—especially toward the end of the century—that the isolation of the artist, his consciousness of swimming against the current, had sometimes the effect of deforming his work. But what student of literature who is not content naïvely to praise or blame while referring works from different periods to the same ideal standards, what critic aware of art in its relation to the other forces of the society

in which it is practised, will assert that even the poet of
the fin de siècle could or should have done otherwise?
In the generation of the middle century, even so great a
man as Flaubert had found it possible to save his soul only
through the cult of art. Yet the notion that the cynical
Flaubert and the diabolistic Baudelaire could have exercised, in their novels and poems, the most exacting kind
of self-discipline, exerted, in dealing with the materials
supplied them by their imaginations, a rigorous will to
refrain; that their work might thus fortify their readers
as well as entertain them—this is something Mr. Paul Elmer
More seems incapable of conceiving. He apparently believes that the only way in which it is possible for a reader
or a writer to school himself in these bad days is to read
or write literary criticism of the type of his own and
Babbitt's, which, though based on thorough reading and
distinguished by sound writing, has obviously not required
a discipline a tenth as difficult as that which has gone to
produce some of the works it so loftily castigates.

Even aside, however, from its meaning in this special
situation, the slogan of "art for art's sake" has a meaning
which would still remain valid even in an age which did
not, as our own does, freeze out the artists and make them
defiant. From this point of view, Mr. More's attitude is
open to the same sort of criticism as that of the not insensitive but rather unintelligent socialist of the type of Upton
Sinclair. Upton Sinclair disapproves of works of art which
do not point explicitly a socialist moral, as Paul Elmer
More disapproves of works of art which do not point explicitly the moral of self-control. Each insists on denouncing
as irresponsible and evil or futile all the writers in which
it is impossible for him to find his own particular moral
stated in his own particular terms. Now, aside from the fact
that reality presents a variety of aspects and may be expected to suggest more than one kind of moral, and aside
from the fact that fine workmanship itself always contains
an implicit moral, it should further be borne in mind that
in the arts as in the sciences a certain freedom for experi-

mentation is necessary: one must allow a good deal of apparently gratuitous, and even empty or ridiculous work, if one wants to get masterpieces. Gregor Mendel was dead eighteen years before anyone had even suspected that his hobby of interbreeding green peas was anything other than a harmless monastic diversion; Gauss's non-Euclidean geometry, which he had been too timid to publish, as well as Ricci and Levi-Civita's calculus, had seemed the idlest of mathematical exercises till Einstein found them just the tools he needed, ready to his hand. But, in general, the gratuitous experimentation of the scientific world is known only inside its own laboratories, whereas the corresponding work of the literary world is likely to be circulated more widely. When it happens to fall under the eye of an Upton Sinclair or a Paul Elmer More, he is infuriated by what seems to him its fatuity: he demands at once to know what these writers imagine they are good for. Well, they may not be good for anything, but, on the other hand, they may be valuable—one has to wait and see what comes of them, what other writers may get out of them. Virgil, a poet in high repute with Mr. More and the other humanists, had laid under contribution not merely Homer but also the romantic rebel Apollonius Rhodius, whose innovations, in Alexandria, had had no important results, but from whom, two and a half centuries later, Virgil was partly to derive his misty and subtle feeling for nature and human life. The Alexandrians—as, for different reasons, the poets of the end of the century—were denied participation in the life of a great society, and they cultivated art for art's sake. In view of their having kept alive the poetic tradition of Greece as well as having made contributions to the later poetry of Rome, will Paul Elmer More contend today that the work of these writers was futile?

(2) They ["a few restless souls" among the "radical writers of to-day"] hold deliberation to be the foe of liberation. Hence the later theory, exemplified in English by James Joyce, that art shall not reproduce a picture of life

*as the humanist sees it, or even from the point of view of
the realist, but for its subject matter shall descend to what
they call the pure "stream of consciousness." The hero of
fiction shall have no will, no purpose, no inhibition, no
power of choice whether for good or evil, but shall be
merely a medium through which passes an endless, un-
checked, meaningless flux of sensations and memories and
emotions and impulses.*

But Joyce does not exemplify anything of the sort: his
characters are all going about their business like the characters of any other novelist. Bloom, Dedalus, Mrs. Bloom
and the others do have their wills, their purposes, their
inhibitions, and they make their moral decisions—indeed,
these moral decisions are the crucial events of *Ulysses*.
What has probably misled Mr. More is Joyce's method of
dealing with the human mind, not by telling us what it
does, but by trying to present it directly in the terms in
which it is aware of itself from hour to hour, from moment
to moment. The minds of the people in Joyce are sometimes relaxed or confused, at other times intent and lucid:
it depends on the character and the situation. The principal
way in which *Ulysses* differs from the kind of novel to
which Mr. More is accustomed is not in Joyce's depriving
his characters of moral sense or will, but simply in his
showing us their consciousnesses as if they were beehives
under glass, and of making us watch them through the
whole of a day—it is a difference of technique, and of pace
and scale. But I cannot suppose, as a matter of fact—from
the extreme inappropriateness of Mr. More's remarks about
Joyce—that he has ever done anything more than look into
him, and I will venture to say that this high-handed habit
on the part of the humanist critics of attempting to dispose
of contemporary writers whom they obviously haven't read
by supercilious classroom jeers is an even more serious
scandal to their cause than their misrepresentation of the
ancients, whom they have at least carefully studied. So
Mr. More, in *The Demon of the Absolute*, has described
Dos Passos's *Manhattan Transfer* as "an explosion in a cess-

pool" without apparently the faintest suspicion that Dos Passos intends his novel as an indictment of the same social conditions of which Mr. More himself has always taken so gloomy a view. But not only is Mr. More unable to recognize in *Manhattan Transfer* the work of a man who, like himself, has been "deafened," as he once wrote of his own state of mind, "by the 'indistinguishable roar' of the streets" and can "make no sense of the noisy jargon of the market place," and who finally causes his hero to escape from the modern American city with as much relief as ever Mr. More did when he went into his celebrated retreat at Shelburne; he has not even succeeded in informing himself from any other sources than this novel as to Dos Passos's general point of view. If Dos Passos had been a second-rate eighteenth-century essayist, Mr. More would know everything about him, including his political opinions—if he had been the most obscure New England poet (of the seventeenth century, that is), Mr. More would have read him through.

(3) *"The only way of mitigating mechanism," he [A. N. Whitehead] says, "is by discovery that it is not mechanism." And so, instead of admitting humbly that mechanism is mechanism while beside it there exists something of a totally different nature, and that the ultimate nexus between these two fields of experience surpasses our comprehension, he must demonstrate mechanism out of the world altogether.*

But why *should* Whitehead admit humbly that mechanism is mechanism and that humanity exists beside it as something of a totally different nature? Why *should* he assume that the ultimate nexus between these two fields of experience surpasses our comprehension? I do not feel with Mr. More that the effect of Whitehead's metaphysics is to "make a travesty of the inorganic world," that it threatens "to deprive humanity of what is distinctly human." Why should Mr. More take for granted that to change our idea of humanity necessarily means to degrade it? There can be no advances in philosophy without the altering of old conceptions. And I cannot, for the life of me, see that Mr. More has any other real objection to Whitehead's ideas than that they would, as he believes— and I am not sure that he is right even here—tend to discredit the distinction between "man" and "thing" upon which his own humanistic philosophy is based. He makes no attempt to show that Whitehead's speculations are not justified, that his arguments are not sound; he makes no effort whatever to discuss the scientific findings—the conception of the "event," for example, as the ultimate unit of both the organic and the inorganic worlds—upon which Whitehead has based his metaphysics and which he did not himself invent. He merely asserts that Whitehead should never have undertaken at all to account for the relations between the organic and the inorganic worlds. He says that he "admits" this "humbly," but one gathers from his tone that he would, if he could, get out an injunction against all wanton metaphysics directed to this end, just as he would, if he could, get out an injunction against all experimentation in the arts. Yet it is plain that if the philosophers of the past had been content to accept so incuriously the apparent paradoxes of experience, we should not have any philosophy at all, and Mr. More would have no Plato and no Platonists to beguile his academic retirement. One cannot avoid the conclusion that the primary difficulty for Mr. More is to admit that it is possible for anyone, either in art or in science, to find out anything new, and I cannot explain this state of mind except on the hypothesis that Mr. More is really an old-fashioned Puritan who has lost the Puritan theology without having lost the Puritan dogmatism. Mr. More is more certainly than Professor Babbitt a man of some imagination; he is able, up to a point, to follow the thought of the modern world, as appears from his not unintelligent and often sensitive expositions of the ideas of other writers (if they are not absolutely contemporaries); but some iron inhibition seems inevitably to come into play to restrain Mr. More from agreeing with anything in modern philosophy or from accepting anything in art. Everything he encounters here seems to have the effect of alarming him, even when, as in the case of White-head, one would think he ought to find it reassuring. One law for man and another law for thing is the whole of philosophy for More, as the will to refrain is the whole of morals. Outside these—anywhere, that is, except among the brave little band of humanists—he sees only perdition, chaos. It is as if Mr. More, on one of his sides, were capable of meeting on his own ground the great modern philosopher or poet, but as if some other element in his nature—which he tries to foist upon us, too, as the universal law of the "inner-check"—had operated to make him shy away from philosophy and poetry themselves, so that, in spite of his vigorous intellect and his genuine sensibility, he is unable to allow himself to profit by any book not written sufficiently long ago to have acquired an academic sanction almost equivalent to a religious one.

A certain passage from Whitehead's *Science and the Modern World* is quoted by Mr. More as follows: "When Darwin or Einstein proclaim[s] theories which modify our ideas, it is a triumph for science." Mr. More is going on to criticize this passage, but in the meantime he has observed that Whitehead has been so indiscreet as to write "pro-claim" as a plural verb after two subjects connected by "or," and where any ordinary critic would either have left Whitehead's sentence as he wrote it or have made him a present of the singular ending without calling the reader's attention to it, Mr. More has put it in brackets, as who should comment scornfully "[sic!]." Mr. More may not be able, or may not dare, to imagine, as Whitehead has done, a metaphysical explanation of the relations between the organic and the inorganic worlds, but he can, and, by Heaven, he will, correct this philosopher's grammar!

March 19, 1930

The Nietzschean Line

NORMAN DOUGLAS has been aroused by *Mother India* to
write an attack on Western civilization called *Good-bye to
Western Culture: Some Footnotes on East and West* (the
English title is *How about Europe?*). His notes on the
tyrannies and manias of European as contrasted with Hindu
life make an entertaining book; but they represent a line
of criticism which is no longer so impressive as it once was.

The oppression of our laws, in the West, says Douglas,
is much worse than that of an oriental despot. The latter
"is uncertain," (he is here quoting another writer) "and
leaves to the oppressed chances and hopes of escaping it;
it varies with the individual; and those who suffer, if not
benefited, are, at least, consoled by the vengeance that,
sooner or later, overtakes the guilty. The tyranny of law
is a dead and immovable weight, that compresses at once
the activity of the limb and the energy of the mind; leaves
no hope of redress, no chance of escape; is liable to no
responsibility for its acts or vengeance for its crimes." And
in Europe, "an air of pointless preoccupation hangs about
like influenza, infecting the sanest and most self-possessed
of us. You encounter it in every walk of life and every
grade of society: complications and glumness, with feverish streaks in between; in a word, fluster. There is as much
grace and dignity in a European existence just now as there
is in a fat bourgeoise running after an omnibus. The Ameri-
canization of life on this continent may have contributed
its share; it has infused a note of impermanence. Gregarious
and homeless, fearing solitude as never before, our European is losing his idiosyncrasy. Hustle is his opiate, his
refuge from self. . . . Hindus are not afflicted with the
fidgets. . . . They do not imagine, like Europeans, that
they are driving a machine because they happen to be

tangled up in its works." "Why," he finally demands, "does one belong to such a race, so sad and yet so ferocious?"

So far we may heartily agree; but Norman Douglas's farewell to Europe is like Clive Bell's book on "Civilization" and the tirades of H. L. Mencken (both of whom Mr. Douglas invokes). We ask, What then?—and we get no answer. What does Mr. Douglas want to do with Western society? How does he propose to bring it back to those virtues which it has abandoned and which he is still able to admire in the East. Mr. Douglas would reply, I suppose, that he does not propose to do anything: he is content to live in Capri and keep away from it all. He is content to occupy himself with the animals and the birds of the Greek anthology, about which he has written a learned book. So Clive Bell merely wants to be let alone to enjoy beautiful pictures and fine wines; and so Mencken asks for nothing but his Brahms, his beer and his books, and the hilarious spectacle of his neighbors. When we look for a central point of view in Douglas, we find much the same thing that we do in Mencken: a diluted and inconsistent Nietzscheanism (he has a good deal to say about Nietzsche, and his book is dedicated to Oscar Levy, Nietzsche's English translator). Like Mencken, Norman Douglas believes that the illiterate should be left illiterate; that the poor should be left poor; that the socially inferior should be kept in their places. The caste system is one of the things that he most approves of in India; and, like Mencken, he has a good deal to say about the scarcity in Europe of "gentlemen." (Mencken, of course, as an American, thinks that Europe is full of gentlemen, but Norman Douglas, being a European, thinks the gentlemen are all in the East.) For Mr. Douglas, one of the great merits of the caste system seems to be that it unfailingly provides for European gentlemen travelling in the East devoted, efficient and handsome servants.

Here are Douglas's final conclusions as to what is wrong with the Western world: "I become more and more convinced, with increasing years, that the roots of the mischief lie far back, in the Roman point of view. The shoddiness of our ideals—the shoddiness of all our ideals, social and political—is a heritage from those unimaginative Roundheads, with their ingrained vulgarity, their imperialism, their pernicious doctrine of the *raison d'état,* and the welcome they gave, as vulgarians naturally would give, to imported pinchbeck like Christianity." The religious wars and the Spanish Inquisition have "consumed our mental fiber to this day, and blunted our apperception of finer issues"; and Christianity has led to "our cult of those fetid 'masses' whom, in accordance with New Testamentary injunctions, we are now breeding as carefully as if they were Pekingese spaniels, and who, in return, have imposed on us by law their own fatuous and degrading aspirations." The pernicious political results of Rome are, first, that "that tiresome standardizing mania of theirs [has] destroyed the more delicate tissues in the national character of people subject—however superior intellectually—to themselves"; and second, that "the state idolatry of the Romans, their toga tomfoolery, has converted European races into a pack of mongrels snarling at each other."

It will be seen that the vein is a familiar one. Norman Douglas, who writes so clearly, does not think any more clearly than any other dilettante of epicurean tastes who desires to figure as a champion of all the moral and aesthetic values without being willing to deal with the problem of how these values are created or lost. The passages I have quoted are full of such words and phrases as "shoddiness," "ingrained vulgarity," "vulgarians," "pinchbeck," "coarsened our mental fiber," "our apperception of finer issues," "those fetid 'masses,' " "destroyed the more delicate tissues,"—phrases which are calculated to convince us of Norman Douglas's "ingrained" refinement and to establish between him and us—Mencken and Clive Bell do the same thing—a genial understanding that he and we belong to a rare superior order of beings; that we are, in fact, "aristocratic," and that the other people don't matter. The way in which writers of this kind persuade us to accept their opinions is precisely similar to the methods by which "quality" advertising is conducted—by which a picture, for example, of a smart-looking woman eating paté de foie gras and a smart-looking man with a monocle, with some smartly printed text about "these charming people" who are "always so casually yet successfully pioneering in the realm of enjoyment," is used as a bait to make people spend their money on "menthol-cooled cigarettes." If the reader can be induced to imagine himself one of these charming people, he may not even know whether or not he enjoys cigarettes that are flavored with menthol, just as the reader of Norman Douglas may fail to notice that vulgarity and delicacy, fetidness and refinement, are treated as if they were God-given qualities, independent of other factors— as if they had no relation to questions of money and education. But what makes people "vulgar" or "fine"? And in a civilization like our present one—the creation of a single class, the middle class, of that eighteenth-century society whose passing Mr. Douglas laments, in the course of the exploitation of a single human aptitude, mechanical invention, for the purpose of getting rich—in a civilization like our own, how can you tell whether they are fine or not? From the island of Capri, it may not be possible to see them very clearly; and from the point of view of one engrossed in the birds and the beasts of the Greek anthology, it may not be easy to appreciate the peculiar sort of refinement—refinement in the various mechanical and scientific techniques—that our industrial society has certainly achieved.

The Nietzschean of Norman Douglas's type is moreover always trying to have it both ways: he always attempts to combine a ruthless and contemptuous attitude toward those aspects of ordinary humanity that happen to be distasteful to him with a sympathetic and even sentimental one toward those aspects that happen to appeal to him. Mr. Douglas, for example, is all against our cult of "those fetid 'masses' whom," in accordance with New Testamentary injunctions, he alleges we are now "breeding as carefully as if they were Pekingese spaniels." Very well: should he not, as a Nietzschean, be willing to let them die? Yet in an earlier part of the book, he made a point of wringing our hearts with an account of the wretched children in English and French reformatories. These children do not, as a rule, belong to Mr. Douglas's class: they belong to "those fetid 'masses.'" So why should Mr. Douglas worry about them? If it is true that the "filthy and damp walls exude misery and vice," this is a condition appropriate to the fetid. If it is true that young girls are put in strait jackets and made to lap up their food from the floor, a punishment from which they sometimes suffocate—this certainly does not err in the direction of breeding them like Pekingese. Why on earth should Mr. Douglas care whether the reformatories are cleaned up or not? If it is true, as he says, that there are six thousand French convicts "rotting in French Guiana" and that "the whole [penal] system is riddled with cruelties and abuses and absurdities," what should that matter to a resolute Nietzschean, who elsewhere refers to the unemployed as "scum" and objects to paying taxes for poor relief?

The few constructive suggestions that are offered by Mr. Douglas, with a great air of realism and common sense, appear to me more or less frivolous. "In England we build 165,000 new houses every year, and yet, in London alone, there are said to be 130,000 persons living in insanitary dens. An ex-Mayor of Manchester has lately written a book on *How to Abolish the Slums*. I have not read it, but can suggest a solution of the problem that would not cost a half-penny: stop this breeding. And the point to notice is this, that the breeding would stop automatically were it not officially encouraged." What makes Mr. Douglas so sure of this? "They manage these things better, out East," he declares. You think that he is going on to tell us that in India they exterminate the poor; but it turns out that he is thinking of the fact that the East is full of beggars and that begging is there a recognized profession. But how can you make English working people beg even when they are out of work? And do they deserve, for their reluctance to do so, to be described by Mr. Douglas as "dregs," inferior to the beggars of the East?

In spite of Mr. Douglas's denunciations of the meddlesomeness and absurdity of law-making, it is curious to note that, the moment it is a question of anything that he himself has an interest in seeing done or not done, he is as prompt to appeal to legislation as any other modern European. He protests against some English by-law which makes it necessary to get a license for a dog-kennel, but later on he becomes equally indignant over the lax enforcement of another by-law which makes "the fouling of footways by dogs" an offense liable to a fine. Only eight people, it seems, have so far been convicted. "When eighty thousand have been fined," says Douglas, "that downcast look of the cockney will begin to disappear." This is a matter about which he feels strongly, so call in the police by all means.

I have considerable respect for Norman Douglas. His career has been an honorably independent one. He has lived in a variety of countries and is not easily intimidated by the conventions of his own place and time. But the kind of social criticism represented by *Good-bye to Western Culture*—and, as I say, we have had a good deal of it—seems to me essentially trivial.

October 22, 1930

Lytton Strachey

IT IS SOMETIMES the case with first-rate people that their lives seem to come to an end—sometimes very suddenly—just when they have finished performing their function. This was the case with Lytton Strachey. Lytton Strachey's chief mission, of course, was to take down once for all the pretensions of the Victorian Age to moral superiority. His declaration in the preface to *Eminent Victorians*, "Je

n'impose rien; je ne propose rien: j'expose," was certainly
not justified by the book that followed. His irony here
was so acid that it partly dehumanized his subjects. The
essays on Manning and Dr. Arnold, though the technique
gives an effect of detachment, have a force of suppressed
invective; and the essays on Florence Nightingale and
Gordon, written with the same metallic accent, make the
subjects less sympathetic than they probably deserve to be.
In attempting to destroy, for example, the sentimental
reputation that had been created for Florence Nightingale,
he emphasized her hardness to such a degree as to slight
her moral seriousness and the deep feeling for suffering
that drove her. Only at moments does he let these appear:
"O Father," he quotes her as writing, "Thou knowest that
through all these horrible twenty years, I have been supported by the belief that I was working with Thee who wast
bringing everyone, even our poor nurses, to perfection";
and "How inefficient I was in the Crimea, yet He raised
up from it trained nursing." Such a woman must have been
more than the mere demon of energy that Lytton Strachey
tried to make her appear.

But from *Eminent Victorians* on, the ferocity of Strachey
abates. Queen Victoria is already a different matter. In this
book, both Victoria and Albert become human and not
unattractive figures. He is said to have approached them
originally in the mood of *Eminent Victorians* and then
found himself relenting. Victoria is not caricatured as
Florence Nightingale is: she is presented simply as a
woman, living, for all her exalted position and her public
responsibility, a woman's limited life. To Strachey's Victoria, the role of queen is a woman's personal experience,
a matter of likes and dislikes, of living up to social obligations. This is the force of the famous deathbed scene,
which has been imitated so often by people who have
tried to reproduce the cadences without understanding
the point: that Victoria has lived through the Victorian
Age, has stood at the center of its forces, without knowing
what it was all about.

But in Strachey's next biography, *Elizabeth and Essex*, he produces a somewhat similar effect without the same ironic intention. *Elizabeth and Essex* seems to me the least satisfactory of Strachey's books. His art, so tight and so calculated, so much influenced by the French, was ill-suited to the Elizabethan Age. His Elizabeth, though a fine piece of workmanship like everything he did, is worse than metallic, it is wooden. It concentrates so narrowly on the personal relation between the Queen and her favorite that we wonder, glancing back to the earlier book, whether it really was Victoria who lacked interest in the politics and thought of her time, whether it was not perhaps Strachey himself. Certainly Elizabeth lived in a larger intellectual world than Victoria, yet we get almost none of it in Strachey. In general, we do not feel that the individual fates of the characters are involved with the larger affairs of history. The personal story is told with insight, but then, after all, Michelet tells a thousand such stories, taking them in his stride. And we here, for the first time with Strachey, become disagreeably aware of the high-voiced old Bloomsbury gossip gloating over the scandals of the past as he ferrets them out in his library. Lytton Strachey's curious catty malice, his enjoyment of the discomfiture of his characters, is most unpleasantly in evidence in *Elizabeth and Essex*. His attitude toward women—Florence Nightingale, Mme. du Deffand, Queen Victoria or Queen Elizabeth—was peculiar in this, that he was fascinated by their psychology without feeling any of their attraction, and rather took pleasure in seeing them humiliated. The feminine subjects he chose were certainly lacking in feminine charm, and he seemed to do everything possible to make them unappetizing. His study of Queen Elizabeth in the light of modern psychology brings her character into sharper focus, but the effect of it is slightly disgusting; it marks so definitely the final surrender of Elizabethan to Bloomsbury England.

The revolt against Victorian pretenses thus ends in faintly scabrous psychology; and in his next book Lytton

Strachey recapitulates his view of history—a view with which Flaubert and Anatole France, Henry Adams and T. S. Eliot have already made us familiar and which assumes that modern society, in relation to the societies of the past, represents some sort of absolute deterioration. In *Portraits in Miniature*, which seems to me one of Strachey's real triumphs, he gives glimpses, through a series of thumbnail sketches of for the most part minor historical and literary personages, of the evolution of modern society from the Elizabethan to the Victorian Age. These personages, by very reason of their special interest or small capacity, supply cultures particularly clear of the social and intellectual bacteria at work during the periods in which they lived. The first specimen is Sir John Harrington, the Elizabethan inventor of the water-closet; then we are shown some seventeenth-century types: an amateur scientist, a truculent classical scholar, an ambitious university don, the leader of an uncouth Protestant sect, and a few eighteenth-century types: a French abbé who consorted with the philosophers, a French magistrate and country gentleman who insisted on his rights, a lady of sensibility; and we end with Mme. de Lieven, whose liaison with the bourgeois Guizot marks for Strachey the final surrender of the splendid aristocratic qualities he had admired in Queen Elizabeth. A second series of miniatures reviews the British historians from the eighteenth-century Hume to the Victorian Bishop Creighton, and suggests a similar moral. The industrial, democratic, Protestant, middle-class world is a come-down, says Strachey by implication, from Queen Elizabeth, from Racine, from even Voltaire (these last two are favorites of Strachey's, on whom he has written more than once). When one considers the great souls of the past, the present seems dreary and vulgar—the Victorian Age in particular, for all its extraordinary energy, was a disgrace to the human spirit. This is the whole of the message of Strachey; and when he had said it as pointedly as possible in the fewest possible words, he died.

But not only did Strachey in his writings point an historical moral: he illustrated one himself. In his gallery of English historians, he himself should fill out the series. Certainly one of the best English writers of his period, he makes us feel sharply the contrast between Shakespeare's England and his. Shakespeare is expansive and untidy and close to the spoken language. Lytton Strachey, whose first-published book was a history of French literature, is so far from being any of these things that one of his chief feats consists in having managed to achieve in English some of the effects of French. His biographical method, though novel in England, was already an old story in France. Sainte-Beuve was the great master of it, and Strachey's ironic tone has something in common with his. The weaknesses as well as the virtues of Strachey's style are the result of his imitation of French models. He is lucid and cool and precise, but he is terribly given to clichés. The penalty of trying to reproduce in English the chaste and abstract vocabulary of French is finding one's language become pale and banal. No wonder the age of Shakespeare turned rigid and dry in Strachey's hand. And by the time he had reached *Portraits in Miniature,* he was importing belatedly to England a point of view that since the middle nineteenth century had become a commonplace in France.

The real force and audacity of Lytton Strachey are therefore seen best, as I have indicated, at the beginning of his career. In *Eminent Victorians,* which was published just at the end of the war, he stripped forever of their solemn upholstery the religion, the education, the statesmanship and the philanthropy of the society which had brought it about. The effect in the English-speaking countries was immediate and swiftly pervasive. The biographers turned at once to the easy game of exposing accepted celebrities, and this soon became a bore and a nuisance. The harshness of *Eminent Victorians* without Strachey's wide learning and bitter feeling, the intimate method of *Queen Victoria* without his insight into character, had the effect of cheapening

history, something Strachey never did—for, though he was
venomous about the Victorians, he did not make them any
the less formidable. He had none of the modern vice of
cockiness; he maintained a rare attitude of humility, of astonishment and admiration, before the unpredictable spectacle of life, which he was always finding "amazing" and
"incredible." But neither the Americans nor the English
have ever, since *Eminent Victorians* appeared, been able to
feel quite the same about the legends that had dominated
their pasts. Something had been punctured for good.

September 21, 1932

André Malraux

NOBODY ON OUR SIDE of the Atlantic has yet written anything, so far as I know, about André Malraux, the French
novelist; and, though I have read only two of his half-
dozen books and am unable to deal with his work in any
thoroughgoing fashion, I want to bring this fascinating and
profitable writer to the attention of American readers. If
the recent apotheosis of André Gide has been tending to
discourage you with French literature, you will be glad to
see the French genius cropping up again in a field where
you would least expect it. A fault of much French writing
lately has been that it has all seemed to be steeped in the
atmosphere of the literary world of Paris, with its smug
and self-conscious dependence on the French literary tradition. But M. André Malraux turns up a long way from
Paris, and he nowhere—at any rate, in either of the books
I have read—pays his pious respects to Racine.

M. Malraux first visited the orient at the age of twenty-
three as head of an archeological expedition to Indo-China;
but he presently dropped the cultural problems of ancient
Cambodia for the political problems of the present. The
orient that Malraux writes about is not the orient of

Madame Butterfly. He published in 1928 a novel called *Les Conquérants,* which dealt with the events of the Chinese revolution in 1925. The reader who picked up this book was dazzled by an unhoped-for searchlight into a region which had previously seemed distant and dim. Here was a picture, based evidently on intimate knowledge, of the conflict of forces in modern China, with every figure, oriental or European, thrown into brilliant relief, every Chinese water-front or street—junks and steamers, pagodas, bars and banks—made distinctly and solidly visible. And here was something even more remarkable— something one had not yet found in contemporary fiction to the same degree: the psychological atmosphere of stress, with its own peculiar passions and moralities, its tense and sustained attitudes, which is coming to be felt throughout the world.

A translation of *Les Conquérants (The Conquerors)*— made, I am told, at Aldous Huxley's suggestion—has been brought out in England, but seems to have had no success at all. I do not know whether the odious role that is played in the book by the British has had anything to do with this. The novel has done no better here. Harcourt, Brace brought over sheets and sold only eight hundred copies. Yet I urge American and English publishers—especially now that reviewers are beginning to take Jules Romains as solemnly as he takes himself—to consider bringing out a translation of Malraux's new and even more important novel, *La Condition Humaine.*

I have spoken of Malraux's achievement in conveying the sense of strain produced by the antagonism of modern society. The publication of *Les Conquérants* was followed, in *La Nouvelle Revue Française,* by a controversy between Malraux and Trotsky. (Trotsky's two papers are included in his *Problems of the Chinese Revolution.*) It was Trotsky's complaint that Malraux, though he had chosen a revolutionist for hero, had "introduced into his observations a small note of blasé superiority, seeming to excuse himself for his transient contact with the insurrection of the Chinese people, as much perhaps to himself as to the academic mandarins in France and the traffickers in spiritual opium." This is putting it a little too strongly; but it is true that Malraux's hero, Garin, has a certain alloy of old-fashioned romanticism. There are moments when he gives the impression of being simply another René or Manfred, somber, tortured, terrifying, a solitary savage rebel, seeking in the revolution what René had sought in the American forests, grasping at his bureau of propaganda with the same sort of desperation that Byron had brought to Greece. Part Swiss and part Russian, formerly an anarchist, Garin hates the bourgeoisie without real fellow-feeling for the masses: " 'I don't love humanity. I don't love even the poor, the people—those, in fact, for whom I am fighting.' 'But you like them better than the others.' . . . 'I like them better, but only because they're beaten. Yes: on the whole, they have more feeling, more humanity, than the others—they have the virtues of the beaten. What's absolutely certain, however, is that I have nothing but hatred and disgust for the bourgeoisie from which I come. But as for the others, I know very well that they'd become quite abject as soon as we'd conquered together. We have our struggle in common—that's clear, at any rate.' " His dominant passion, he admits, is for power, and in the final scenes of the story, worn out with his work and dying of malaria and dysentery, he declares in his delirium that he now regrets having chosen to serve the Communists instead of England, since it is England that commands the real power. Yet in spite of his doubt and his egoism, he sticks by the revolution and is receiving, on the final page, the dispatches that bring the news of victory. Trotsky has expressed the opinion that what Garin needed was "a good inoculation of Marxism." Malraux retorted to this that there was something of Garin in Trotsky—pointing out that when you read in Trotsky's autobiography "the moving account of his fall, you forget that he is a Marxist, and perhaps he forgets it himself." He also protested that *La*

Condition Humaine was not—what Trotsky had called it—
a "novelized chronicle" of the Chinese revolution. "The
principal emphasis," he says, "is on the relation between
individuals and a collective action, not in the collective
action alone." "The book," he explains, "is first of all a
presentation of the human situation (*une accusation de la
condition humaine*)."

André Malraux's new novel has this phrase for its title,
La Condition Humaine, and it develops in a more explicit way the ideas implicit in *Les Conquérants. La Condition Humaine* is a much more ambitious and a more
remarkable book than *Les Conquérants.* In the latter,
Garin pretty well holds the spotlight, and there is an "I"
who plays the role of Dr. Watson, deeply agitated by his
hero's every utterance and standing by, indefatigably wide-
eyed, while Garin receives portentous telegrams. He also
plays the role of Conrad's Marlow. He is, in fact, our
old friend the fictional observer who, from a more or less
conventional point of view, looks on at a mystery or a
moral problem. In this new book, however, the novelist
gets rid of his European observer and, meeting Trotsky's
challenge, attacks the revolution directly. Dealing with
cultures the most diverse, moral systems the most irrecon-
cilable, he establishes a position outside them which enables him to dispense with the formulas alike of the
"academic mandarins" and of the orthodox Communists.
I do not know of any modern book which dramatizes so
successfully such varied national and social types. Beside
it, even E. M. Forster's admirable *A Passage to India*
appears a little provincial; you even—what rarely happens
nowadays to the reader of a French novel—forget that the
author is French. You see juxtaposed the old Buddhist
China and its half-Europeanized children; the vaporing
imagination of ruined aristocratic Europe and the single-
minded will to money of the European business king; the
American Calvinist missionary unwittingly building the
character of the young Chinese terrorist; and—growing
up under all the rest like the elm that splits the pavement—

the new world of the revolutionary Marxist which is re-orienting all the moralities. Nor is this handled in the manner of the journalist, as Paul Morand might have done it. The personalities of Malraux's characters are organically created and thoroughly explored. We not only witness their acts and see them in relation to the forces of the social-political scene: we share their most intimate sensations.

The handling of this huge and complicated subject must have given the author a good deal of trouble. He evidently sat down like an engineer to the problem of designing a structure that would meet a new set of conditions; and an occasional clumsiness of mechanics appears. The device of presenting in dramatic scenes the exposition of political events, to which we owe Garin and his eternal dispatches, here appears as a series of conversations so exhaustive and so perfectly to the point in their function of political analysis as—in spite of the author's efforts to particularize the characters—occasionally to lack plausibility. And we are sometimes thrown off the track when a thesis that deals with psychology comes butting into a paragraph devoted to explaining the "objective conditions" or when a description that had seemed as external as a colored picture post-card of Shanghai takes a sudden subjective turn.

Yet, on the whole, the author has met these problems with amazing originality and skill. He has a genius for effects of contrast. The opening of *La Condition Humaine*, which follows the activities of a Communist group—a Chinese, a half-breed Jap, a Belgian and a Russian—the night before the insurrection, is a masterly dramatization. The initial inability of Tchen to bring himself to murder the man from whom he must steal the orders for the guns and his immediate realization afterwards of his terrorist's vocation; Baron Clappique's romances in the night club and his subsequent revelation of his ignoble trade; the confession of Kyo's wife that, on the eve of the insurrection, she has been unfaithful to him, and its repercussions on revolutionary solidarity; Tchen's report of what he has done and felt to his Buddhist-sociologist master, Gisors, and

Gisors' prompt liquidation of his own anxiety and horror in an opium dream, in which the ripples from a boat on a lake full of water-lilies spread out to sweep all horror and anxiety into the purity and peace of the Divine—followed immediately by the spectacle of the real boat putting out in the Shanghai harbor to steal the guns for the insurrection: each one of these shocks is a flash that illuminates the conflicts and anomalies of the tense international city.

I have spoken of Malraux's success in avoiding conventional formulas. Where, however, is his own center? What is his frame of reference? What he wants to show us, he says, is the human situation. What is his view of the human situation? What every human being wants, he makes his philosopher Gisors explain, is not the object of his ambition itself, but to escape from the conditions of life, to give oneself the illusion of being God. Gisors attains this through opium; Tchen through assassination—an act in which he immolates himself, is the destroyed as well as the destroyer; Ferral, the French business man, tries to reach it through his sexual relations, in which he imagines himself in the roles of both possessed and possessor; even the rickety Baron Clappique finds it at the gambling table, where he identifies himself with the roulette ball, the master of both gain and loss; Kyo, the Japanese, rises above life when, for the sake of the revolution, he commits hara-kiri with cyanide; and Katov, the Russian Communist, gives his cyanide to brother Communists whose morale is weaker than his, when they have all been condemned to be burnt in the furnace of a locomotive. Tchen, Malraux lets us know, has saved his soul; Kyo has saved his, and more nobly; and Katov most nobly of all, because he can only fulfil himself by sacrificing himself to others.

There is, then, something else in the book besides the mere theme of escape from the human situation. The events described in *La Condition Humaine*, which occurred in 1927, must still have been going on while *Les Conquérants* was being written. At the end of the earlier novel, the Chinese revolution—there presented as the work of Garin as well as of Chiang Kai-shek—is assumed to be already victorious; in the later, the Communists fail, sold out by Chiang Kai-shek to the interests of Western capital and paralyzed by the faulty policy of the Comintern itself. Malraux seems, in line with Trotsky's advice, to have made some progress in Marxism. His interpretation of recent events seems now essentially Marxist—though he never, as I have said, slips into the facile formulas; and though the criticism his characters make of the line of the Comintern is more or less that of Trotsky, he maintains in relation to Trotsky, too, an attitude of independence. Marxism, Gisors observes, is not a doctrine but a will; and it is simply that, in Malraux's world, the only men he respects are animated by the Marxist will. *La Condition Humaine* ends with Gisors, who has lost his son Kyo, sinking back into the culture of the East and lighting up the opium pipe, while May, Kyo's widow, sets out for Moscow.

August 9, 1933

M. Malraux, on reading this article, wrote me the following letter:

n.r.f.   Le 2 oct.

Monsieur—Je trouve à mon retour à Paris l'article que vous voulez bien me consacrer.

Comme je vous réponds en suivant cet article permettez-moi d'abord quelques précisions. Je n'ai publié, en plus des livres que vous avez lus, qu'un livre et une plaquette (que je vous envoie)—le reste est très court et sans importance. D'autre part, mon père n'était pas fonctionnaire en Indochine.* Je suis allé en Asie à 23 ans, comme chargé de mission archéologique. J'ai alors abandonné l'archéologie, organisé le mouvement Jeune-Annam, puis suis devenu commissaire du Kuomintang en Indochine et enfin à Canton.

Il y a du vrai dans ce que dit Trotsky de Garine, et

* This corrects an erroneous statement that I had made in the original version of my article.

dans ce que vous en dites vous-même. Peut-être faudrait-
il pourtant tenir compte d'une certaine objectivité. Que ce
personnage soit marxiste, certes non. Peut-être a-t-il tort,
mais c'était ainsi. Il y avait à Canton en 1927 (ce fut très
différent en 1927) singulièrement plus d'aventuriers révo-
lutionnaires que de marxistes. Et lorsque Borodine discutait
avec Sun-Yat-Sen, il n'était jamais question de lutte de
classes.—Je ne voudrais pas faire de cela un argument,
mais une nuance. Car il est fort vrai que le rôle joué dans
mes livres par l'objectivité n'est pas de premier plan, et que
Les Conquérants sont un roman "Expressioniste" comme,
toutes proportions gardées, *Wuthering Heights* ou les
Karamazoff.

Vous dites très justement que *La Condition humaine*
développe certaines idées implicites dans *Les Conquérants*.
Et aussi que le livre est meilleur (à la verité, du moins,
c'est le seul que j'aime). Ma construction, en effet, ne
pourrait rejoindre celle d'un écrivain comme Morand: ses
types reposent sur l'observation ironique, le mien sur le
besoin de traduire à travers des personnages un certain
ordre de valeurs éthiques.

Ne voyez en ce semblant de discussion qu'un moyen de
remercier plus longuement le premier critique, en Amé-
rique, qui s'intéresse à ce que j'écris et croyez, je vous prie,
Monsieur, à ma sympathie artistique, car je suis depuis
longtemps l'effort de la *New Republic*.

André Malraux

The Literary Worker's Polonius

A BRIEF GUIDE FOR AUTHORS AND EDITORS

Nature of Magazines and Editors

THE PRIMARY FACT to be grasped about editors is that they
are not independent agents, but function as parts of the

larger organisms known as magazines. Magazines, like other living organisms, develop according to certain laws and pass through regular life-cycles. These cycles may vary in length from a few to many years; but they all complete the same cycle (unless they meet untimely ends); they have a youth, a maturity and an old age. In its earliest years, a magazine may seem spontaneous, novel and daring; but by the time it has reached its maturity it has, as the French say, "taken its fold," and it succumbs to a force of inertia against which the youngest and freshest editor is as powerless as the oldest and stalest. Thereafter, it grows old, declines and dies.

Magazines derive their principle of being from a relation between some part of the mind of the editor and some part of the mind of the public. They rarely represent the whole of the editor or the editor at his best; and they do not usually give the public all it wants. But the relationship, once established, apparently cannot be altered. Both editor and reader may be bored by the contents of the magazine; but at this point it will be impossible to introduce any real novelty or to make any serious new departure. To his readers as well as to his contributors, the editor may seem timid, pedantic, unimaginative, obsessed by formulas. But anyone who has had anything to do with magazine offices knows that there is always a Higher Power which decides all important issues: the magazine as an entity in itself. And this entity takes on eventually a purely metaphysical character: it has nothing to do with commercial considerations. It can often be demonstrated that a drastic change in policy would increase the circulation of the magazine; but such a change is no more possible to effect than the transformation, by grafting on wings or claws, of one kind of animal into another.

Magazines cannot be born again. The most that can be done with a magazine is to subject it to a sort of face-lifting process, which, though it may improve its look at long distance, only exposes it, on closer examination, in a more hideous state of senility. Or, as in the case of the old

Dial, a magazine can be deliberately killed off, and the name taken over for a new one. But, otherwise, the most that can be hoped is that a magazine may pass its old age in something like comfort and peace without lapsing from its original standards. All too often it must linger on in a dotage or a cheapened form which disgusts its former readers.

Duties of the Editor to the Contributor

The scope within which it is possible for the editor to exercise independent volition is thus seen to be narrowly circumscribed. It is limited, in fact, to the purely business aspects of his dealings with his contributors. The selection of material is determined by the higher will of the magazine; but the editor can be more or less prompt in registering and conveying to the contributor the decisions thus arrived at. And the prompt communication of decisions is one of the editor's prime duties to his writers. The editor has a regular job; the writer very often has not, and he may even depend for the necessities of life on selling what he has written. He usually wants an immediate decision even though it may be adverse; such a decision would at least make it possible for him to send his manuscript elsewhere.

Some editors are efficient about this: Mencken and Nathan, for example, were remarkable for the definiteness and promptness of their decisions. But many editors are either the victims of badly organized offices or lack consideration for writers, and cause by their negligence or irresolute stalling an immense amount of depression, exasperation and sometimes even actual privation.

A piece of writing, once accepted, should be paid for on the nail (if the finances of the paper permit it); and, once accepted, it should be printed. In the first connection, the ideal method is that of one of the New York weeklies, which sends the check with the letter of acceptance. In the matter of printing, it ought to be said that there are sometimes extenuating circumstances, which the writer should understand and allow for. One of the editors may have pressed a decision in favor of accepting a manuscript which one or more of the other editors may afterwards consciously or unconsciously sabotage; or an editor may sabotage a manuscript which he has been responsible for accepting himself. Allowing, however, a certain small margin for sincere doubts and differences on the part of editors, it must be asserted, as a general thing, that the writer has just cause for complaint when an editor accepts his manuscript and then suppresses it by leaving it in the "barrel."

Connected with this is another matter which has probably caused between the editor and the writer more misunderstanding and bitterness than any other aspect of their relations, and which has often for the writer, and sometimes for the editor, resulted in serious loss. This is the question of ordering things in advance. The problem of making these decisions clear and afterwards keeping them straight is entirely in the hands of the editor, and it is sometimes not the least difficult of his problems, since the writer, through his eagerness for the order, will sometimes unconsciously do his best to mistake an expression of possible interest for a commitment to buy what he writes; but any editor with a primary grasp of the duties of his position will school himself never to leave any doubt as to whether or not an article is ordered and to stick by his engagement, once it has been made. If the manuscript turns out too badly, he is not absolutely bound to print it; but he is certainly bound to pay for it and to give it back to the writer, so that the latter may have a chance of publishing it elsewhere.

Duties of the Writer to the Editor

On the other hand, the writer should allow the editor a reasonable length of time in which to decide and should not pester him with letters and telephone calls till a maximum of, say, two weeks has elapsed.

The writer should always have his manuscript typed, and he should never send it in to the magazine accompanied by a long letter, or, unless he knows one of the editors, by any letter at all. In the first place, these letters are rarely read; and, in the second place, they usually have the effect of prejudicing the editor against the piece instead of stimulating his interest in it. This prejudice may sometimes result in unfairness on the part of the editor, if the writer is inexperienced and has thought it the natural thing to address himself directly to the editor— since he is used to being addressed by the editor, in the editorial department of the magazine, in a friendly and even confidential manner. But such writers should be warned that manuscript-reading is one of the most trying of an editor's tasks and that the notion of reading long letters in addition is one that he rejects with impatience. Manuscripts must speak for themselves; letters can never help them. If the writer should happen to know one of the editors, who he imagines may be sympathetically disposed toward him, he may address his manuscript to this editor (though some magazines have tried to bar this): he may possibly get prompter consideration. But he should never write more than a line.

Nature of Authors

The relations between authors and reviewers are a constant source of anxiety to authors. To understand why this should be so, we must first examine the nature of authors.

Authors in the main are persons who are preoccupied with constructing and peopling individual intellectual worlds. They may be roughly divided into three classes:

1. *Fiction-Writers.* Novelists and short-story writers are writers who make up fantasies about imaginary people.

Such writers may in certain instances be on fairly good terms with one another, but the imaginary worlds they inhabit tend to be mutually exclusive. As a result, they seem ungenerous to one another, and it is sometimes superficially concluded that they are exceptionally vain and envious people. This is, however, not always the case. The pure type of fiction-writer who merely reacts to the stimuli of life with no broad philosophical or historical interest will feel naturally that the work of another such writer, especially if he is dealing with the same material, is a monstrous misrepresentation or even a deliberate imposture.

2. *Poets.* Poets are today imaginative writers who use the technique of verse. This technique, though employed by the ancients for almost every form of utterance and record, from songs to dramas and epics, from legal codes to medical treatises, has come to be confined in our epoch to functions of a specialized kind. Where the novelist deals in character, adventure and situation, the poet is usually limited to the expression of emotion and mood or to the simple description of people and objects. As a consequence, being a poet is rarely a full-time job, and the poet has large spaces in his life which are not filled by his literary activity proper and in which he is likely to occupy himself with a kind of professional politics. Poets form into groups, which in their combinations, disruptions and recombinations, their debates, practical jokes and fierce battles, tend to keep them in a state of excitement. In this group instinct they somewhat resemble painters—though painters, by reason of the fact that they practise a genuine handicraft instead of a purely intellectual métier, have a certain amount of physical work to tire them and are not so erinaceous as poets. The reactions of groups of poets toward one another may be said to correspond more or less to the reactions of individual novelists.

3. *Scientific, philosophical and critical writers.* This class includes all those writers who are occupied with the attempt to present or to interpret known events, or to investigate the nature of reality. They are sometimes capable

of a kind of collaboration hardly known among novelists and poets, for the reason that, where the materials are facts themselves, it usually requires more than one person to ascertain what the facts are and to organize them, and where the field is that of mathematical or metaphysical theory, a staff of several persons may be enlisted to develop the ramifications of a subject. But though it is possible for a number of experts to work together on some special subject, it not infrequently happens that monopolies are attempted by the groups themselves or by powerful authorities in some department, and these may lead to stupendous combats like the brawlings of Leviathan and Behemoth. It should be added that literary critics may develop the worst characteristics of any of these other classes of writers.

(It may be suggested that the writers of fictionized biography and history constitute a fourth class, which should be listed between classes 1 and 2; but the truth is that producers of books of this type are not genuine writers at all, but merely a kind of chimera believed in during the Boom by publishers.)

It will be seen, then, that all classes of authors tend to assume that their personally created worlds have some kind of general validity, and that they are likely to be disturbed when an attempt is made by anyone else to question or upset this assumption.

The author is most often upset in this way by the people who review his books. For an author, the reading of his reviews, whether favorable or unfavorable, is one of the most disappointing experiences in life. He has been laboring for months or for years to focus some comprehensive vision or to make out some compelling case, and then finds his book discussed by persons who not only have not understood it, but do not even in some instances appear to have read it. In twenty-two reviews out of two dozen, either the reviewer has attempted nothing more than to give a description of the contents of the book, not even doing this correctly (and these reviews are often copied word for word from one another), or his comments, either praise or blame, seem to the author to have little or no relevance to the book he believes he has written. The reading of his reviews, indeed, is so likely to let the author down after the excitement and satisfaction of finishing his book that there is a good deal to be said for the practice of those writers who go off on trips to remote parts of the world as soon as their last proofs have been corrected.

In order to understand why the reviewer thus disappoints the author, we must inquire as to who reviewers are and under what circumstances they do their work.

Nature of Reviewers

Reviewers may be classified under five heads:

1. *People who want work.* Every magazine office is a clearing-house for people who need money or jobs: the waiting-rooms are always full of college graduates, indigent radicals, escaped débutantes and wives, young boys who have just bummed their way from the Coast, and many other types of persons who want to write or to associate themselves with writing, as well as personal friends of the editors in difficulties. These people should be given considerate attention, if only because it sometimes turns out that there is a really good writer among them; and it is customary on magazines with literary sections to try them out on writing book reviews. These book reviews are often very bad and not far, if at all, removed from school exercises. But the editor will want to pay for them if he knows that the writer needs money, and when he has paid for them, he will feel that he ought to print them if by any means they can be made presentable. The best solution to this problem is probably that adopted by one of the New York weeklies. This magazine sells the extra books which come into the office for review and provides

a permanent fund for the relief of needy writers, thus rendering it unnecessary to purchase from them reviews which may turn out to be either unprintable or printable only at the expense of a great deal of drudgery on the part of the editor.

To the groups mentioned above should be added the impoverished novelist or poet who, though gifted and expert in his own field, may have no aptitude for or practice in reviewing.

2. *Literary columnists.* The writer of a newspaper literary column has to read and talk about one or more books a day for five or six days of the week. To go through all these books conscientiously and comment upon them thoughtfully is a task beyond human capacity; and, in consequence, it is not to be expected of these writers that they should give us much serious criticism. Not all of them are interested in books: some are literary columnists merely by accident; others may be well-equipped persons who have to write so much and so fast that they are not able to do themselves justice. But in any case one should judge these writers, not as essayists or critical authorities, but as chroniclers of the literary news, who are managing more or less sensibly and more or less entertainingly to give, by a selection of excerpts or a swift résumé of a book's contents, a more or less adequate idea of the events of the publishing season.

Where the newspaper reviewer is most likely to go wrong is in explaining the purport or the significance of a book. A short and concentrated piece of writing such as one of Ernest Hemingway's short stories is very quickly read (these reviewers are naturally delighted when they strike something easy to get through), and the chances are that the reviewer will miss many things that the author has worked hard to make implicit in it, that he will, in fact, miss the point. And in the case of a long book, he is likely to be forced to skip through it, and so not only mistake the author's intention, but make blunders as to what has been said. When André Malraux's *Man's Fate* came out in English, for example, the newspaper accounts of the characters and the story seemed to me so different from what I remembered from reading it in French that I was driven to look up the translation. But the translator had in general been accurate: it was the reviewers who had sometimes been confused from having had to deal hurriedly and briefly with so crowded and complex a work. Yet it is also true that even in the case of Thornton Wilder's *Heaven's My Destination*, one of the newspaper reviewers managed to mix up the characters. It may perhaps be demanded of the newspaper reviewer that he avoid this sort of literal inaccuracy, but even that is demanding a good deal and the most, probably, that one should expect.

3. *People who want to write about something else*. Book-reviewing is frequently exploited, especially by the young, as a pretext for writing an essay of one's own on the subject dealt with by the book or for neglecting the book altogether and writing an essay on some other subject. Such reviews are often bitterly resented both by authors and by conscientious critics; but anyone who has ever been an editor must regard them, if they are interesting in themselves, with a certain amount of leniency: it is so relatively rare for an editor to get really interesting articles of any kind that he cannot afford to discourage them even on those occasions when they displace proper reviews. The author may console himself with the thought that the review he might otherwise have had would probably have been as poor as most reviews.

We may also treat under this head the problem of young people in general. Should a brilliant but inexperienced young writer be allowed to treat a mature writer unfairly in a brilliant but uncomprehending review? The young must be given a chance, and their point of view is sometimes important, even when what they say is entirely aside from the mark. Older writers have sometimes to resign themselves to being mistreated by youth. And there are also, of course, the embittered old who are irked at being driven to write reviews and who take it out in putting the young in their places and in undermining their more prosperous contemporaries.

4. *Reviewer experts.* The so often unsatisfactory results of having books of poetry reviewed by persons who have never written verse, works of philosophy by persons with no philosophical training, and so forth, have led editors to try to get poets to write about poets, philosophers to write about philosophers. The trouble with this, however, is that the philosopher or the poet is likely to belong either to the same school or to some opposing school, so that in either case the review may be biased and produce for the outside reader a misleading impression of the book.

5. *Reviewer critics.* These are extremely rare. Most people who are capable of first-rate criticism do not want to interrupt their other work for jobs as unremunerative as book reviews. Exceptional cases were Van Wyck Brooks and H. L. Mencken; but the former was rather narrowly specialized, and the latter has always tended to use book-reviewing as a way of putting over his own personality and his opinions on all sorts of subjects. The only American writer who has tried recently to do this kind of thing the way, ideally, it ought to be done was a second-rate man, Stuart P. Sherman. Such a reviewer should be more or less familiar, or be ready to familiarize himself, with the past work of every important writer he deals with and be able to write about an author's new book in the light of his general development and intention. He should also be able to see the author in relation to the national literature as a whole and the national literature in relation to other literatures. But this means a great deal of work, and it presupposes a certain amount of training. Sainte-Beuve had to work all week—hardly taking time out for lunch—for each of his *Causeries du Lundi.* But Sainte-Beuve was perhaps a unique case. Has there ever been another example of a man of Sainte-Beuve's abilities devoting so large a part of his life to weekly articles on miscellaneous subjects?

I want to suggest, however, that it might be a profitable

idea for some editor to get a really able writer on literature and make it worth his while to do a weekly article. For a man who should combine a sound education with intelligence and literary ability he would probably best go to the universities, where the *Herald Tribune* got Stuart Sherman and the *New Masses* Granville Hicks. Let him take, say, a Newton Arvin or a Haakon Chevalier, impose upon him no duties that would impede his weekly articles—Burton Rascoe's articles evidently suffered, when he ran the *Herald Tribune* book section, from his having too much to do—and pay him enough to live on. He should not be expected to cover what is published, but to write each week of a man or a book. I believe that such a feature would prove valuable to the magazine that installed it and an excellent thing for the literary world in general.

Attitude of the Author toward the Reviewer

It will thus be seen that the author has no justification for expecting serious criticism from reviewers, and that, in becoming elated or indignant over anything that is written about his books, he is wasting his nervous energy.

His reviews, if he knows how to read them, may have for the author a certain interest; but he will not be able to find out from them very much about the value of his work. For this he will have to depend on other sources, such as remarks made in casual conversation and evidences of his effect on other writers—always bearing in mind, however, that the true excellence or badness of what he has written may never really be grasped during his lifetime —a hazard for which we must all be prepared. And in the meantime he should read his reviews, not as the verdict of a Supreme Court of critics, but as a collection of opinions by persons of various degrees of intelligence who have happened to have some contact with his book. Considered from this point of view, there is occasionally something to be learned from them.

Special Psychology of Reviewers

The reviewer, like other kinds of writers, has his ego; and, since he is continually occupied with other people's books, it is somewhat peculiarly difficult for this ego to assert itself. One of the best ways in which a reviewer can give himself a vicarious sense of creation is by encouraging and presenting new writers who have previously been unknown; but when a writer is already known, the reviewer may procure the sensation of power by making the gesture of putting him down. This psychology must always be reckoned with. In the literary world in the last few years, one has seen a number of writers cried up at the time when they were still obscure, by the more discerning critics, and then afterwards disparaged by them. This has happened in turn to Eugene O'Neill, Edna St. Vincent Millay, Ernest Hemingway and Thornton Wilder. It is the rarest thing in the world at the present time to find a word of intelligent critical comment on any of these important writers. And the unfortunate Mr. Saroyan has been put through the cycle in record time. He was first discovered by the editors of *Story* and acquired a reputation among its readers. Then, when his book was published, he got some prompt enthusiastic reviews. But he had now been triumphantly brought out, and after this there was nothing left for the later reviewers of his books but to try to make him ashamed of himself.

Duties of the Reviewer to the Author

On the other side, however, the reviewer has certain obligations in relation to the author.

I have recommended lenience toward reviewers who use the books they are supposed to be reviewing as pretexts for expressing themselves; but only in cases where their articles—what happens comparatively rarely—are interesting in themselves. There is no excuse at all for an uninteresting review that tells nothing about the book. The reviewer, at the very least, should be expected to supply information. The retelling of the story of a novel, the summary of an historical or philosophical book, the selection of representative passages and the attempt to communicate the quality of a poet, is the most boring part of the reviewer's business, but it is an absolutely essential part. The reader should be given a chance to judge whether or not he would be interested in the book, irrespective of what the reviewer may think of it; and it is an indispensable discipline for the reviewer, or any critic, to give the gist of the book in his own words. The reviewer, when he sets about this task, is quite likely to find that there is more in the book, or less in it, or something different in it, than he imagined when he first went through it. If the author is incoherent or woolly, the critic will be able to detect it. If the reviewer is incompetent, his incompetence will be evident to his more acute readers when they find out he cannot tell them what is in the book.

The failure to follow this procedure is one of the factors responsible for those opaque pretentious essays, aesthetic, metaphysical or social, that, especially in the highbrow reviews, are sometimes hung on the titles of books. The reader has no means of knowing, if he has not himself read the books, whether they prove the critic's points or not: the titles play the role of counters to which, from the reader's point of view, no value has been assigned. It is as vitally important for the critic to establish definite identities for the books that he discusses in an essay as it is for the novelist to establish them for the characters who figure in his story.

Attitude of the Author toward His Public

Another class of persons toward whom the poised author should adopt an unemotional attitude are the people who write him letters. Most of these fall into the following categories:

1. *Insane people and cranks.* The author should be able to spot these and should remember that people in abnormal states of mind are likely to be set off by anything.

2. *Lonely women and persons in provincial isolation.* Of these, even when they are sane, very much the same thing may be said: the fact that they write authors letters shows merely that they need to communicate with somebody and does not necessarily imply any interest or merit in the author's books.

3. *Young people who want the author to read their manuscripts.*

4. *People who want the author's autograph.* These, for the most part, either want it for a collection, and have no interest in the author's books, or want it in order to sell it.

Along with a good many of these, the author will receive a few letters from people who are interested in what he has written and have something to say to him about it. But, in general, it may be assumed that the letters written to authors mean nothing. No writer who has been an editor can ever take letters so seriously as is often done by writers who have had no such experience. Every editor has seen almost incredible evidence that one cannot publish anything in a magazine so bad that some reader will not write in to say that it has changed his life, or so good that it will not cause someone to cancel his subscription.

Duty of the Public toward the Author

One should never send manuscripts to authors. They have enough to do writing their books. If authors read the manuscripts sent them, they would never be able to do anything else. The author of a manuscript who desires advice should send it to a publisher or editor: they pay people for this kind of work.

Duty of Authors to Other People

The author should not make a practice of sending out to his friends, or to persons whom he admires but does not know, large quantities of his books, inscribed. In the first place, he will be out of pocket if he exceeds the publisher's quota of free copies. In the second place, inscribed books from authors are likely to prove a nuisance: the person to whom the book has been sent is likely to feel that he ought to read it and yet at the moment may not be able to; he will go around having it on his conscience that he ought to have written to the author. And when he does get around to reading it, he may feel that the flattering or affectionate inscription obliges him, whether he likes it or not, to say something nice about it. Such a present is really a bribe that is likely to prevent the reader from coming out with the candid opinion which the author imagines he values.

Duty of the Novelist to the Public and the Profession

The novelist should never put at the end of his novel a date of the following kind:

Boulogne-sur-Mer-Hoboken
December 1934–*January* 1935

This kind of thing has been in fashion ever since Joyce dated *Ulysses*:

Trieste-Zurich-Paris 1914–1921

but it is rarely justified. In Joyce's case, the book took seven years, and the date has a special point, for Stephen Dedalus in 1904 is made to tell the Dubliners of the novel that he will produce something important in ten years' time. But it is usually a mistake for other writers to imitate this, for the reasons that, in the first place, it is dangerous to suggest a comparison with Joyce; and, in the second place, that such dates are irrelevant. In the case of a poem, date and place may in certain instances be in order if they add something that helps in understanding it and that cannot be conveniently put into the poem. But if a novelist is really successful, he will have interested us in characters and happenings that are supposed to have nothing to do with himself; he will have induced us to accept their reality, and it is therefore an impertinence to his own creation to remind us of himself and where he has worked. If the novelist has been unsuccessful, the reader, when he has got through the book, will not care to be reminded of the author and his sojourn at Boulogne-sur-Mer.

June, 1935

Letter to the Russians about Hemingway

WHEN I VISITED the Soviet Union, I was assigned as a guide and advisor by the cultural liaison organization VOKS Sergei Tretyakov, then a well-known literary figure. I knew him already as the author of an effective melodrama, which had been done in New York under the title *Roar, China!* He was tall, very sober and a little rigid; he wore spectacles and had shaved his gray hair; and he rather resembled, as was sometimes said of him, a professor or a Protestant pastor. But in literature he was earnestly Leftist. He was a great participator in groups. He had passed through futurism and the group called LEF, in both of which—he was very proud of this—he had been associated with Mayakovsky. He was at that time one of the great champions of "fact literature" as distinguished from "plot literature"; he declared that the Soviet newspaper was the *War and Peace* of the present, and he was engaged in writing a novel about the collective farms, which was a matter of pure documentation that took him into the country on fact-gathering excursions. Though Tretyakov was theoretically one of the most intransigent of Soviet writers, who had declared his scorn of fellow-travellers, I found him both mild and polite. He did his best to be helpful to me, and I ate some good dinners in his apartment, where he would show me the old files of the LEF magazines. On one occasion, he prepared me for meeting his father by saying, "He's a real peasant!," but when I was presented to the elder Tretyakov, he seemed to me a well-bred old gentleman, whose mustaches and small Van Dyke beard must always have been carefully tended.

I wanted to buy books. There was some difficulty about this, due to restrictions and my lack of money; and Tretyakov suggested that I contribute an article to the Russian edition of *International Literature* and have the Writers' Union pay me in books. There was a considerable excitement about Hemingway in the Soviet Union then, and it was agreed that I should write about his latest book, which had not yet been translated. Just before I left Moscow, Tretyakov took me to a bookseller in the ancient Tverskaya, now rechristened Ulitsa Gorkovo, who dealt in pre-Soviet books. To enter it was something of a shock, for one seemed to step out of the new Russia and land in a pocket of the past. The proprietor, with his skull-cap, his ivory pallor, his tarnished green velvet jacket, his archaic fringe of red beard that ran under his chin from ear to ear, might have been a contemporary of Gogol's. These old books, especially in good editions, were rather rare in the Soviet Union, and it was forbidden to take them out of the country, unless one bought them for valuta at Intourist emporiums and could show a certificate for them; but the amiable Tretyakov, with his slightly complacent official air, promised to arrange all this. I chose a set of Turgenev that was rather expensive and several other things, and I left with the bookseller some books that I had already acquired elsewhere and that I wanted to have sent with the others, including a large-paper two-volume edition of Taine's *Théorie de l'Intelligence,* which had been given me by a friend in Leningrad. Few of these I ever saw again, either my old books or the new purchases. When a package finally reached me in America, I found, instead of the set of Turgenev, one very badly battered volume of a Soviet edition on cheap paper: Volume XII, the last, which contained a miscellaneous collection of Turgenev's reviews and speeches. The only thing I had ordered that they sent me was a volume of Mayakovsky's drawings. The Taine had disappeared. So not only have I never been paid for the article that follows by the Soviet periodical that ordered and ran it, but I was robbed of my Taine on account of it. Poor Tretyakov vanished in the purge, along with almost everyone else who represented the Leninist tradition of socialist idealism. His obstinate loyalty to it may well have seemed to his inquisitors stupid. He had staked his whole career on the iconoclasm—which was bound to be for Tretyakov not an uproarious but a solemn matter—of his brilliant ally Mayakovsky; he had sworn on Marx and Lenin a life-long devotion to the doctrine that an up-to-date report on industrial work in progress was the highest form of literature. I felt very badly about him. It outrages one's sense of justice that a man should be encouraged by the government to maintain an official attitude and then punished for doing so when this attitude is repudiated by the government. Such people as Tretyakov, industrious, pious and a little absurd, have been among the most pathetic victims of Stalin's soul-destroying reign.

Letter to the Russians about Hemingway

I have been very much disappointed by the new book by Ernest Hemingway. *Green Hills of Africa* is certainly far and away his weakest book—in fact (leaving out of consideration the burlesque *Torrents of Spring*), the only really weak book he has written.

Green Hills of Africa is a narrative of an actual hunting expedition, in which "the writer has attempted," as
Hemingway says, "to write an absolutely true book to see
whether the shape of a country and the pattern of a month's
action can, if truly presented, compete with a work of the
imagination." In my opinion, he has not succeeded. The
sophisticated technique of the fiction-writer comes to look
artificial when it is applied to a series of real happenings;
and the necessity for sticking to what really happened prevents the writer from supplying the ideal characters and
incidents which give meaning to a work of fiction. The
book is thus an instructive experiment: it brings out very
clearly the difference between actual experience and the
imaginary experience of fiction, but it is a warning of reefs
to steer clear of.

Aside from this—or perhaps for the very reason that he
has chosen to treat his material in the wrong way—the
literary personality of Hemingway here appears in a
slightly absurd light. He delivers a self-confident lecture
on the high possibilities of prose-writing, with the implication that he himself, Hemingway, has realized or hopes to
realize these possibilities; and then produces what are
certainly, from the point of view of prose, the very worst
pages of his life. There is one passage which is hardly
even intelligible—the most serious fault for a writer who
is always insisting on the supreme importance of lucidity.
He inveighs with much scorn against the literary life and
the professional literary men of the cities; and then manages to give the impression that he himself is a professional
literary man of the most touchy and self-conscious kind. As
a newspaper reviewer has said of Hemingway, he went all
the way to Africa to hunt, and then when he thought he
had found a rhinoceros, it turned out to be Gertrude Stein
—an old friend and admiration of Hemingway's, who wrote
of him disparagingly in her recent autobiography and upon
whom, in *Green Hills of Africa*, he has taken the opportunity to revenge himself. He affirms in accents of defiance
his perfect satisfaction with the hunter's life and his pas-

sionate enthusiasm for Africa; and then turns out the only book I have seen that makes Africa and its animals seem dull.

When the Soviet critic, I. Kashkin, who has contributed to the English edition of *International Literature* a very able essay on Hemingway—what is, in fact, perhaps so far the only serious full-length study of him that has yet been made—when Kashkin comes to read *Green Hills of Africa*, he will no doubt find much confirmation for his theory that the author of *In Our Time* has been becoming more sterile in proportion as he has become more detached from the great social issues of the day. And it is true that one of the things which strikes us most and which depresses us as we read *Green Hills of Africa* is the apparent drying-up in Hemingway of his interest in his fellow-beings. Wild animals can, of course, be made extremely interesting; but the animals in this book are not interesting. We do not learn very much more about them than that Hemingway wants to kill them. Nor do we learn much about the natives: there is, to be sure, one fine description of a tribe of marvellous runners, but the principal impression we carry away is that the Africans were simple people who enormously admired Hemingway. Nor do we learn much more about his hunting companion than that the latter had better luck than Hemingway and inspired Hemingway with envy; nor much more about Mrs. Hemingway than that she is fond of Hemingway. Nor does the author seem, in any really serious way, even to take very much interest in himself; the self-dramatized Hemingway we get has the look of having been inspired by some idea of what his public must expect after reading his rubbishy articles in the men's-wear magazine, *Esquire*.

Yet I am not by any means sure that—as Kashkin perhaps would conclude—it is Hemingway's material which is here at fault. It is not the fact that, in *Green Hills of Africa*, he is dealing with an African hunting expedition instead of with the American class struggle that is really at the bottom of its failure; but rather the technical approach of the writer to his subject, and the psychological attitude that follows from it. One can imagine the material of *Green Hills of Africa* being handled quite successfully in short stories or as a background to one of Hemingway's novels. But for reasons which I cannot attempt to explain, something dreadful seems to happen to Hemingway as soon as he begins to write in the first person. In his fiction, the conflicting elements of his nature, the emotional situations which obsess him, are externalized and objectified; and the result is an impersonal art that is severe and intense, deeply serious. But as soon as he speaks in his own person, he seems to lose all his capacity for self-criticism and is likely to become fatuous or maudlin. The artist's ideas about life, or rather his sense of what happens and the way in which it happens, is in his stories kept deep below the surface and conveyed not by argument or preaching but by directly transmitted emotion: it is turned into something as hard as a crystal and as disturbing as a great lyric. When he expounds this sense of life, however, in his own character of Ernest Hemingway, the Old Master of Key West, he has a way of making himself ridiculous. It may be that he himself is imposed on by the American publicity legend which has been created about him and which, as Kashkin has pointed out, has very little to do with what one actually finds in his stories. But, in any case, among his creations, he is certainly his own worst-drawn character, and he is his own worst commentator. His very prose style goes to pot— or rather, he writes a different prose style from the one he has perfected in his fiction, which seems to me to be without question one of the finest we have had in America and one of the finest in the world today.

This vein of Hemingway maudlin, this vein of unconscious burlesque, had already broken out in the personal interludes of *Death in the Afternoon,* his book on the Spanish bull-fight, but in that book there was so much objective writing, so much solid information, that these monologues could not spoil it. *Green Hills of Africa* is almost all such an interlude—and I doubt whether it is anything more than an interlude in Hemingway's work as a whole. His latest collection of stories, *Winner Take Nothing*, showed certainly a further development rather than any degeneration of his art. One of them, a simple anecdote of a man who goes out to plunder a wreck and finds that he cannot even crack open the porthole—this short story, with its implications of the irreducible hazards and pains of life and of the private code of honor that one has to evolve to live among them, is worth the whole of the *Green Hills of Africa*.

These moral implications of Hemingway, as one finds them in this story, for example, it seems to me that Kashkin underestimates. The Marxist must no doubt maintain that no hazards and pains are irreducible. But these will not be eliminated next year, nor even five years from now, nor even after five years more. And in the meantime, if Hemingway were to address himself to writing about the social conflict, there is no reason to believe that his stories would not continue to illustrate the same personal tragic sense of the way in which things happen. We can get some idea of what we might expect from the introductory note he has written to the exhibition of drawings by the Spanish revolutionary painter, Luis Quintanilla. He has an acute sense of the cost and the danger involved in doing anything worth doing, including revolution; and he knows that people do not always live to get the benefit of what they pay for. "The world breaks everyone and afterward many are strong in the broken places. But those that will not break it kills. It kills the very good and the very gentle and the very brave impartially. If you are none of those you can be sure that it will kill you too but there will be no special hurry"—says the hero of *A Farewell to Arms*. This is not in the least the same thing as saying that there is no use in being good or brave. The truth is that, though, as Kashkin says, Hemingway is very much given to writing about the end of things, the effect of what he writes is bracing rather than dispiriting. His short story, *The Un-defeated*, which describes the humiliating death of a super-annuated bull-fighter, is, as its title indicates, not really a tale of defeat. The old man's courage in itself constitutes a victory. It is true that Hemingway writes about de-cadence, but there is always something else that is pitted against the decadence. It is true that he writes about death, but in order to write tellingly about death, you have to have the principle of life in you.

Can it not be said that on the highest plane of imagina-tive literature, the plane on which Hemingway must be considered, what is written about an old bull-fighter is written, also, about other kinds of men? Is not real genius of moral insight a motor that will start any engine? The non-Marxist who reads a banal Marxist fable, written with-out real insight or feeling, does not feel or imagine any-thing. The Marxist who reads a story presenting a dramatic conflict, though the conflict may be as far from the class struggle as the battle between a man and a bull, will surely, if the story is written with sympathy, passion and skill, identify himself with the hero. Do we not translate what moves us in literature into terms of whatever we do in our lives?

But that, Kashkin might reply, is an extremely dangerous doctrine. Suppose the hero of the story in question is frankly a counter-revolutionary. How can we be sure that the reader will translate counter-revolutionary courage into terms of revolutionary activity? How do we know that he will not be persuaded to admire the counter-revolution? We cannot know this, of course. But we may be assured that wherever the main current of human hope and prog-ress runs, the readers will get out of all kinds of literature the kind of inspiration they need for their own particular activities, the kind of consolation they require for their own particular defeats. That the Soviets assume this to be true is indicated by the fact that they are at present translating wholesale the classics both of antiquity and of the modern world and republishing their own classics with pious care. I observed, when I was recently in Russia, that even the novels of the counter-revolutionary Dostoevsky were still of interest to Soviet readers and that the government was bringing out his note-books. And surely there is something more to the increasing popularity of Shakespeare in Russia than a desire on the part of the Soviet audiences to study the failures of feudal princes. Individuals in Russia still fail; they still suffer their griefs and frustrations; and people still go to the theater to have their souls purged through pity and terror.

I feel that Soviet critics, as well as many Marxist critics elsewhere, sometimes underestimate the positive qualities of the modern non-Marxist masters. A writer like Kashkin might answer that today the only positive forces are those which are working for the destruction of the rotten old capitalist world and for the liberation through socialism of stunted and cramped human powers. I can only adduce, as an example of the law of moral interchangeability which I would invoke on behalf of Hemingway, that on my recent visit to Russia the passage from contemporary literature that I found came most often to mind, that seemed to me to express most eloquently the effect of the Revolution on all kinds and conditions of people in the Soviet Union, was from the writings of that arch-bourgeois, arch-snob, arch-aesthete and arch-decadent, Marcel Proust. It is that passage at the end of the section describing the death of the novelist Bergotte in which Proust speaks of the moral obligations that make themselves felt in spite of everything, and that seem to have reached humanity from some source outside its own wretched self—obligations "invisible only to fools—and are they really even to them?" Proust was speaking here of the artist's obligations—for him, in his world of dissolving values, art was the only element which seemed to keep its validity and last. But when I was travelling in the Soviet Union, these words would come back into my mind, and I would find that the obligations involved in the ideal of the Leninist tradition, permeating even those parts of society, motivating even those individuals, by whom at first sight it seemed least to be felt, had substituted themselves for the obligations involved in Marcel Proust's ideal of art. "Invisible only to fools—and are they really even to them?"

December 11, 1935

This article, which came out in the *New Republic* of the date given above, appeared later in Russian in issue No. 2 for 1936 of *Internatsionalnaya Literatura* (the two texts are slightly different). It was accompanied by an editorial rejoinder, which I here translate (the italics are the writer's):

We are glad to print the interesting article by Edmund Wilson written by him especially for Soviet readers. Wilson is one of the most considerable critics who have appeared in the post-war generation of American literature. He has of recent years taken an active part in the Left movement of the intelligentsia, and though he has not arrived in the camp of revolutionary literature, stopping halfway, he has nevertheless accomplished a significant evolution toward the Left. The article written by E. Wilson, after a visit (last summer) to the Soviet Union, constitutes a new link in the development of Soviet-American literary relations.

It would be out of place here to attempt a general discussion with Wilson on the fundamental problems of Marxist criticism, especially since, in formally replying to the article on Hemingway by I. Kashkin, Wilson is actually arguing against very primitive theses that he has picked up somewhere or other and that sound rather like a *parody* of Marxist criticism. Over these theses E. Wilson is able to score an easy enough victory.

What interests us more is the positive part of E. Wilson's article. In connection with this we shall allow ourselves to make two observations.

Hemingway's book before the last, *Winner Take Nothing*, was met with fixed bayonets by the American bourgeois critics. Hemingway, they said, was "repeating himself," and this fact annoyed them extremely. When *Green Hills of Africa* came out, a book that was really bad, a regular Witches' Sabbath took place in the literary departments of the newspapers and magazines. The critics, frothing at the mouth, demonstrated that Hemingway was "finished." They could not have been more anxious about this if they had been the hired agents of publishing houses who were competing with Hemingway's publisher.

The article by E. Wilson does not belong to this *vulgarly commercial* type of criticism. On the contrary, it is obvious that Wilson likes and esteems Hemingway and that he is saddened by his creative collapse. All the more striking, then, is *the shirking of the task of analysis of the contradictions in Hemingway's work* which constitutes, as it were, the invisible axis of Wilson's article.

That Hemingway has lost the ability to embody the contradictions by which he is torn in harmonious artistic form, has unmistakably been shown by Wilson. Wilson cannot be suggesting seriously that the central problem by which Hemingway is confronted is the recovery of his lost artistic quality on the basis of his former contradictions. Now, come: is this really possible? Has E. Wilson read Hemingway's article on the veterans,* in which the writer speaks in the first person, as he does in *Green Hills of Africa*, and is no less "intense and severe" than in the best of his artistic productions.

Not to speak out about these questions amounts to a betrayal of the fact that one takes even less interest in Hemingway's fate than the malice-breathing newspaper critics. To limit oneself to a consideration of the "aesthetic factors" means to alienate oneself from the living processes of literature, to dissociate oneself from political and moral responsibility for the artist's fate in the disintegrating bourgeois world. An article by Granville Hicks which we read in the *New Masses* not long ago on the same subject

* An article by Hemingway called *Who Killed the War-Veterans in Florida?* which appeared in *Internatsionalnaya Literatura*, No. 12, 1935.

as Wilson's article expressed a deep concern for the artist and did its best to discover ways by which Hemingway might escape from his creative blind alley. Here you may see at once the advantage of Marxist criticism over the passively contemplative kind.

And now, one more observation.

The attempt to judge artistic questions *sub specie aeternitatis* has the defect that, even when accompanied by good intentions about dealing with the facts, it must lead to excessive generalizing. Thus Wilson is correct in pointing out that *courage* is one of the elements in Hemingway's "moral code." But his further discussion of the role of Hemingway's creative activity under conditions of socialist culture is definitely not correct. The courage of Hemingway's heroes is the *courage of despair*. It may inspire the respect, even the admiration, of the Soviet reader, but it is powerless to awaken in him any valid social and psychological conceptions, because it is entirely lacking in the *dynamic optimism* that constitutes the *fundamental characteristic of the courage of the socialist world-view in life and in art.*

The "over-all" theory of the psychology of the mechanism of response to art which is involved in Wilson's idea that the reader identifies himself passively with *any* fully realized character in an artistic production, independently of this character's intellectual content, is *absolutely false.*

In the response to works of art, as in the creation of works of art, there is always an intellectual and moral element; the Marxist reader, in his approach to bourgeois literature, pits himself against it, actively selecting the feelings and ideas that he recognizes as close to his own, and rejecting the alien and hostile ones.

This does not mean that the Soviet publishers bring out the works of Hemingway or Proust for the sole purpose of demonstrating "bourgeois decay." Every genuine work of art—and such are the productions of Hemingway and Proust—enriches the reader's knowledge of life and heightens his artistic sensibility and his emotional culture

—in a word, it figures in the broad sense, as a factor of educational value. Liberated socialist humanity inherits all that is beautiful, elevating and sustaining in the culture of previous ages. Such are the laws of historical development.

I do not know which now seems more touching: my conviction that the Leninist idealism was sure to command universal respect in the Soviet Union of the thirties or my critic's belief that their "liberated humanity" would be allowed to help itself freely to the cultural treasures of the past.

It's Terrible! It's Ghastly! It Stinks!

I HAVE LAUGHED a good deal in reading a new book—*The Great Goldwyn* by Alva Johnston—about Sam Goldwyn, the Hollywood producer. It is fun to hear how Mr. Goldwyn, when told that a script was "too caustic," said: "To hell with the cost! We'll make it anyway!"; and how he brought Maeterlinck to Hollywood in a private car and then, after seeing his first script, rushed out of the room screaming: "My God, the hero is a bee!" Alva Johnston, who is an adept at this kind of personal sketch, has handled his subject with deftness. He has turned out a good piece of light reading, through which the Goldwyn gags are sprinkled in such a way as to give the whole story a certain comic sparkle.

And yet this book makes one slightly sick. It has the slave-brand of Hollywood upon it. Instead of being able to present Sam Goldwyn as the rich humorous character he undoubtedly is, with whatever credit for energy and enterprise he deserves, Mr. Johnston seems to feel forced to flatter him. Mr. Johnston does not, to be sure, offer up his homage to Goldwyn with quite the piety of a denizen of the studios. He is used to writing "profiles" for the *New Yorker,* and he makes a point of turning his paeans off with quick winks and light changes of tone. But the flattery is there just the same. One gets very definitely the impression that Mr. Johnston has written his sketch in such a way that Mr. Goldwyn will be able to read it or to have certain selected passages read to him and imagine that he has been apotheosized by Mr. Johnston, while at the same time Mr. Johnston will be let out with his friends in New York by the delicate irony which he has aimed in their direction but which may not be perceptible to Mr. Goldwyn. Or it may be all a special kind of publicity designed to give more serious weight to Mr. Goldwyn by scaling down his colossal vanity and ignorance, and what sounds from Mr. Johnston's account like a lack of ordinary sportsmanship and decency, to the proportions of amusing foibles which only endear him the more to his friends.

I will quote only two examples—the whole book is written in the same way. "It has been said," says Mr. Johnston, "that if Shakespeare were alive today, Goldwyn would have him. It is an interesting notion; some of the bad plays, like *Cymbeline, Troilus and Cressida* and *Pericles,* might have been tightened up into great dramas if the playwright had had a producer over him to tell him, 'It stinks, Wagspeare. It's lousy. It's terrible. It's ghastly. You're ruining me, Wagstaff.'" Very funny about Goldwyn talking to Shakespeare; but what is Mr. Johnston's object in asserting that the defective plays of Shakespeare could have been converted by Mr. Goldwyn into "great dramas"? Mr. Johnston must know as well as anybody that Mr. Goldwyn would not be able to do anything for the least of Shakespeare's plays except turn it into something different and worse. And here is the conclusion of *The Great Goldwyn:* "Last year was Sam's twenty-third in the movie business; his press department at that time spotted him two years and celebrated the completion of his quarter-century in the business. Next year is Sam's real silver jubilee. It is something for everybody to feel patriotic about. The U.S.A. leads the world by a wider margin in pictures than anything else, and one of the chief reasons is the Great Goldwyn."

Well, I for one will be damned if I will feel patriotic about Sam Goldwyn's silver jubilee, which his agents have been unable to restrain themselves from celebrating two years too early. In what sense does the United States lead the world in moving pictures? We make more of them than any other country and are, I suppose, more proficient technically, but have we ever turned out anything that was comparable artistically to the best German or Russian films? I can think of nothing except Charlie Chaplin, who is his own producer and produces simply himself. There was a time—up to, say, 1930—when our pictures seemed to be improving. There were new actors brought in from Europe and from the speaking stage in New York; there was mechanical experimentation and an aesthetic attention to photography; intelligent directors were given their chance.

But then the depression fell; the producers were frightened and forced to retrench; and the whole movie business seemed to harden into something immovably banal. It nailed down its favorite formulas in all their vulgarity and falsity, and almost entirely abandoned any attempt to make the old situations seem lifelike or to point them up with novel direction. The actors who were brought to Hollywood were handled with extreme stupidity, and, if they stayed there, almost invariably ruined. A lot of talent has been fed into the studios, and what have our pictures to show for it? How shall we ever know now, for example, whether Katharine Hepburn—or, for that matter, Greta Garbo—ever really had anything in her? They set the talented Emil Jannings to performing over and over again wretched parodies of his German masterpieces, with everything that had given them reality and made them human and moving bleached out by the insipid Hollywood sun, until he could stand it no longer and departed. Charles Laughton has also escaped and has returned to England and the Old Vic. Marlene Dietrich, who must have had some ability at least as a night club singer, because she has made marvellous phonograph records in German, has been turned into something in the nature of one of those loose-jointed dolls designed to be propped up against the pillows in boudoirs with sateen bedspreads, and has been made to appear in pictures so foolish, so unsightly and of such horrible taste that the most beautiful woman in the world could not play in them without looking ridiculous. But the only mirrors, apparently, in which film actors can look at themselves are the magazines that exploit the glamor of the trade and are edited for adolescent school-girls. That able Soviet actress Anna Sten the Great Goldwyn was unable to use at all; and I see that she is now making for another producer pictures with such titles as *Love Me Again*, *Gorgeous* and *Orchid Girl*. Mae West, whose peculiar attraction was that she worked up her own material and created a legendary world of her own, now has to have savorless imitations written for her by Hollywood hacks, who have quickly converted her fantasies into run-of-the-mill goods. The vultures of the Coast get them all. A director like King Vidor who has serious aspirations ends by turning out the worst kind of monstrosity: the bad serious picture. The shimmering polish of Lubitsch ends as a veneer on the awful old formulas. We have actually got to a point where features like Tarzan and Charlie Chan are the most satisfactory things one can go to. They are absurd, they are fairy tales; but they do have a certain independent existence.

The other day, after long abstinence from the movies, the result of having seen nothing but bad films for a year, I went to one for the first time in months. I had assumed that the Marx brothers were indestructible. True, I had been reading the publicity stories about their new picture, *A Day at the Races*: how it had first been taken all over the country in the form of a stage entertainment, with a view to weeding out every gag that could not be immediately appreciated by the audience of the average town of over two or three thousand inhabitants. (This was partly, apparently, the work of Mr. George S. Kaufman, who, years ago, after his first experience of Hollywood, wrote *Once in a Lifetime* as a satire on it but later went back to learn the trade.) But I hadn't foreseen that the result of this would be to deprive the Marx brothers of all their natural vitality and spontaneity. As if even popular comic art, if this is really to capture the public, were not more a matter of putting over on an audience (as Charlie Chaplin and Walt Disney have) something from one's own imagination than of finding an infallible formula to provoke its automatic reactions! The idea of establishing and exploiting the lowest common denominator of audiences has finally killed the movies. They are absolutely sterile and static. And even the Marx brothers are no longer the Marx brothers. Their corporate élan has been deadened by unnatural selection of their dullest gags; and they now fall asunder helpless. It would be amusing if *A Day at the Races*, after all the special trouble taken with it, should turn out to be a total flop.

And the writers. Before the vultures have picked the bones of theatrical talent, the big white worms of the studios have grown fat on the decaying flesh. But the vultures get the worms, too. Have we not all had needy friends who have gone West with a smile on their lips and who have never returned again?—from whom we have ceased to hear and whose names we no longer mention, whom we remember as young people of promise, wondering what they have found to do and never thinking to connect them with the processed stuff we hear croaked out, between kisses and pistol-shots, by the smooth-faced gigantic phantoms, when we are foolish enough to go to the movies? It is true, as Mr. Johnston tells us, that Sam Goldwyn always wants the best writers; and there they are out on the Golden Coast, cooped up in their little cells, like school children in study-hour. Teacher is the supervisor, and one hopes to be teacher's favorite. There they are, blowing in their money on goofy Los Angeles houses and on ostentatious cocktail parties, at which they talk about their salaries and their options and always speak of their superiors with admiration, while they submit to being spied upon and having their correspondence opened. Those who do not care to admit surrender pretend to be uncompromising Leftist, getting together in little groups to give three discreet cheers for Stalin and to shed a tear for Republican Spain. But when the Writers' Guild was organized, it took only one woof from Schulberg to send them running like prairie-dogs—leaving the job to the technicians and the actors. And now the blacklisted leaders are creeping back, having become so profoundly habituated to high salaries for low work that, no matter how radical they claim to be, they don't know how to get along without them.

I remember only one American critic who has seemed to me to do full justice to this subject of the Hollywood producers: Mr. George Jean Nathan in the *Smart Set*. Mr. Nathan had the rich and reckless language for it; I am sorry that my own powers are relatively feeble. That was ten years or more ago; but it is plain that today's producers, including the Great Goldwyn and the late lamented Irving Thalberg, are the same megalomaniac cloak-and-suit dealers that their predecessors were. You have only to look at their products. You have only to look at their staffs. From the servant you may know the master. Mr. Johnston can have had only a brief submergence, and look at the book he has written.

July 21, 1937

Twilight of the Expatriates

The Tropic of Cancer, by Henry Miller, was published in Paris four years ago, but nobody, so far as I know, has ever reviewed it in the United States, and it seems to me to deserve some notice.

Every phase of literary opinion is responsible for its critical injustices. During the twenties, this book would have been discussed in the *Little Review,* the *Dial* and *Broom.* Today the conventional critics are evidently too much shocked by it to be able to bring themselves to deal with it—though their neglect of it cannot wholly have been determined by the reflex reactions of squeamishness. A book bound in paper and published in Paris has no chance against a book bound in cloth and brought out by a New York publisher, who will buy space to announce its appearance. The conservative literary reviews have not been so easily outraged that they would not give respectful attention to John O'Hara's *Butterfield 8* or squander space on the inferior Hemingway of *To Have and Have Not.* As for the Left-Wingers, they have ignored *The Tropic of Cancer* on the ground that it is merely a product of the decadent expatriate culture and can be of no interest to the socially minded and forward-looking present.

Expatriate Mr. Miller certainly is: he is the spokesman, par excellence, for the Left Bank; but he has produced the most remarkable book which, as far as my reading goes, has come from it in many years. *The Tropic of Cancer* is a good piece of writing; and it has also a sort of historical importance. It is the epitaph for the whole generation of American writers and artists that migrated to Paris after the war. The theme of *The Tropic of Cancer* is the lives of a group of Americans who have all more or less come to Paris with the intention of occupying themselves with literature but who have actually subsided easily into an existence almost exclusively preoccupied with drinking and fornication, varied occasionally by the reading of a book or a visit to a picture exhibition—an existence for which they muster the resources by such expedients as pimping for travellers, playing gigolo to rich old ladies and sponging on one another. The tone of the book is undoubtedly low; *The Tropic of Cancer,* in fact, from the point of view both of its happenings and of the language in which they are conveyed, is the lowest book of any real literary merit that I ever remember to have read; it makes Defoe's Newgate Calendar look like Plutarch. But if you can stand it, it is sometimes quite funny; for Mr. Miller has discovered and exploits a new field of the picaresque.

The disreputable adventures of Mr. Miller's rogues are varied from time to time with phosphorescent flights of reverie devoted to the ecstasies of art or the doom of European civilization. These passages, though old-fashioned and rhetorical in a vein of late romantic fantasy reminiscent of *Les Chants de Maldoror,* have a youthful and even ingenuous sound in queer contrast to the cynicism of the story. And there is a strange amenity of temper and style which bathes the whole composition even when it is disgusting or tiresome. It has frequently been characteristic of the American writers in Paris that they have treated pretentious subjects with incompetent style and sordid feeling. Mr. Miller has done the opposite: he has treated an ignoble subject with a sure hand at color and rhythm. He is not self-conscious and not amateurish. And he has somehow managed to be low without being really sordid.

The last episode of *The Tropic of Cancer* has a deadly ironic value. A friend of the narrator called Fillmore, who is unique among these cadgers and spongers in enjoying a small regular income, becomes entangled in an affair with a French girl, who is pregnant and declares him responsible. Poor Fillmore first drinks himself into an insane asylum; then, emerging, falls straight into the clutches of the girl and her peasant family. They reduce him to utter abjection: he is to marry her, set her father up in business. The girl quarrels with him every night over dinner. The narrator suggests to Fillmore that he run away and go back home. For the latter, the glamor is all off Paris: he has been up against the French as they really are (in general these émigrés see nobody but one another); he realizes at last that the French regard Americans as romantic idiots; and he is weepily homesick for America.

He allows himself to be sent off on a train, leaving the narrator a sum of money to provide for the girl's accouchement.

But as soon as Fillmore is gone, the helpful hero, left to himself, with the money for the girl in his pocket, decides that good old Paris, after all, is a wonderful place to be. "Certainly never before," he thinks, "had I had so much in my fist at one time. It was a treat to break a thousand-franc note. I held it up to the light to look at the beautiful watermark. Beautiful money! One of the few things the French make on a grand scale. Artistically done, too, as if they cherished a deep affection even for the symbol." Ginette need never know about it; and, after all, suppose her pregnancy was all a bluff. He goes for a drive in the Bois. Does he want to take the money, he asks himself, and return to America too? It is the first opportunity he has had. No: a great peace comes over him now. He knows that for half an hour he has money to throw away. He buys himself an excellent dinner and muses on the Seine in the setting sun. He feels it flowing quietly through him: "its past, its ancient soil, the changing climate." It is only when they are looked at close-to that human beings repel one by their ugliness; they become negligible when one can put them at a distance. A deep feeling of well-being fills him.

In retelling this incident from *The Tropic of Cancer*, have I made it more comic than it is meant to be? Perhaps: because Mr. Miller evidently attaches some importance to the vaporings of his hero on the banks of the Seine. But he presents him as he really lives, and not merely in his vaporings or his poses. He gives us the genuine American bum come to lead the beautiful life in Paris; and he lays him away forever in his dope of Pernod and dreams.

March 9, 1938

Mr. Miller, in reply to this review, wrote the *New Republic* the following letter, which appeared in the issue of May 18. I regret that I am unable to restore a passage cut by the editors.

Sir: There are several inaccuracies in Mr. Wilson's review of *Tropic of Cancer* . . .

First of all, I should like it to be known that the book has been reviewed before, by Professor Herbert West. It has been mentioned numerous times in a sensational manner by so-called reputable magazines in America. . . . The theme of the book, moreover, is not at all what Mr. Wilson describes: the theme is myself, and the narrator, or the hero, as your critic puts it, is also myself. I am not clear whether, in the last paragraph of his review, Mr. Wilson meant to imply that Fillmore is the genuine American bum, or myself. If he means the narrator, then it is me, because I have painstakingly indicated throughout the book that the hero is myself. I don't use "heroes," incidentally, nor do I write novels. I am the hero, and the book is myself. . . .

Perhaps the worst mistake which the eminent critic makes in his review is to say that because a book is bound in paper and published in Paris, it has no chance against a book bound in cloth and sold in New York. This is the very contrary of the truth. Without any hocus-pocus of the American publicity agents, almost entirely by word-of-mouth recommendations, *Tropic of Cancer* has already gone into several editions at a price which for Europe is prohibitive. It is now being translated into three languages. It may be procured at leading bookstores in practically every important city of the world excepting those of America, England, Germany and Russia. It has been reviewed enthusiastically by some of the foremost critics of Europe. If it has not yet brought me riches, it has at any rate brought me fame and recognition. And, whether it is given notice by American reviewers or not, Americans coming to Europe buy it, as they once bought *Ulysses* and *Lady Chatterley's Lover*.

A conspiracy of silence, like censorship, can defeat its own ends. Sometimes it pays *not* to advertise. Sometimes the most effective, realistic thing to do is to be impractical, to fly in the face of the wind. The Obelisk Press took my book on faith, against all commercial wisdom. The results have been gratifying in every way. I should like to add that the Obelisk Press will publish any book of quality which the ordinary commercial publisher refuses, for one reason or another, to handle. Any writer with guts who is unable to get a hearing in America might do well to look to Paris. And damn all the critics anyway! The best publicity for a man who has anything to say is silence.

Henry Miller

Paris, France

The Boys in the Back Room

"Set 'em up for the boys in the back room."

1. James M. Cain

RISING from a long submergence in the politics and literature of the nineteenth century, during which I read almost nothing that people were reading, I have just regaled myself with practically the complete works of James M. Cain, Horace McCoy, Richard Hallas, John O'Hara, William Saroyan, John Steinbeck and Hans Otto Storm. These writers are all of fairly recent arrival; they have most of them been influenced by Hemingway; they all live or have lived in California, and they have all, to a greater or lesser extent, written about that State. They thus constitute a sort of group, and they suggest certain generalizations.

Let us begin with Mr. Cain and his school. *The Postman Always Rings Twice* came out in 1934; and Mr. Cain's second novel, *Serenade*, in 1937. They were followed by other similar novels which apparently derived from Mr. Cain. The whole group stemmed originally from Hemingway, but it was Hemingway turned picaresque; and it had its connections also with the new school of mystery writers of the type of Dashiell Hammett.

Mr. Cain remained the best of these novelists. Horace McCoy, the author of *They Shoot Horses, Don't They?* and *I Should Have Stayed Home*, had a subject with possibilities: the miserable situation of movie-struck young men and women who starve and degrade themselves in Hollywood; and the first of his books is worth reading for its description of one of those dance marathons that were among the more grisly symptoms of the early years of the depression. But the faults of Mr. McCoy's first novel—lack of characterization, lack of motivation—show up much more nakedly in the second. *You Play the Black and the Red Comes Up*, by a writer who calls himself Richard Hallas, is a clever pastiche of Cain which is mainly as two-dimensional as a movie. It is indicative of the degree to which this kind of writing has finally become formularized that it should have been possible for a visiting Englishman— the real author is Eric Knight—to tell a story in the Hemingway-Cain vernacular almost without a slip.

The hero of the typical Cain novel is a good-looking down-and-outer, who leads the life of a vagrant and a rogue. He invariably falls under the domination—usually to his ruin—of a vulgar and determined woman from whom he finds it impossible to escape. In the novels of McCoy and Hallas, he holds our sympathy through his essential innocence; but in the novels of Cain himself, the situation is not so simple. Cain's heroes are capable of extraordinary exploits, but they are always treading the edge of a precipice; and they are doomed, like the heroes of Hemingway, for they will eventually fall off the precipice. But whereas in Hemingway's stories, it is simply that these brave and decent men have had a dirty deal from life, the hero of a novel by Cain is an individual of mixed unstable character, who carries his precipice with him like Pascal.

His fate is thus forecast from the beginning; but in the meantime he has fabulous adventures—samples, as it were, from a *Thousand and One Nights* of the screwy Pacific Coast: you have jungle lust in roadside lunch-rooms, family motor-trips that end in murder, careers catastrophically broken by the vagaries of bisexual personality, the fracas created by a Mexican Indian introduced among the phonies of Hollywood.

All these writers are also preëminently the poets of the tabloid murder. Cain himself is particularly ingenious in tracing from their first beginnings the tangles that gradually tighten around the necks of the people involved in those bizarre and brutal crimes that figure in the American papers; and is capable even of tackling—in *Serenade*, at any rate—the larger tangles of social interest from which these deadly little knots derive. Such a subject might provide a great novel: in *An American Tragedy*, such a subject did. But as we follow, in a novel by Mr. Cain, the development of one of his plots, we find ourselves more and more disconcerted at knocking up—to the destruction of illusion —against the blank and hard planes and angles of something we know all too well: the wooden old conventions of Hollywood. Here is the Hollywood gag: the echo of the murdered man's voice reverberating from the mountains when the man himself is dead, and the party in *Serenade*, in which the heroine stabs the villain under cover of acting out a bull-fight; the punctual Hollywood coincidence: the popping-up of the music-loving sea-captain, who is the *deus ex machina* of *Serenade;* the Hollywood reversal of fortune: the singer who loses his voice and then gets it back again, becoming famous and rich in a sequence that lasts about three minutes.

Mr. Cain is actually a writer for the studios (as are also, or have also been, Mr. Hallas and Mr. McCoy). These novels are produced in his off-time; and they are a kind of Devil's parody of the movies. Mr. Cain is the *âme damnée* of Hollywood. All the things that have been excluded by the Catholic censorship: sex, debauchery, unpunished crime, sacrilege against the Church—Mr. Cain has let them loose in these stories with a gusto as of pent-up ferocity that the reader cannot but share. What a pity that it is impossible for such a writer to create and produce his own pictures!

In the meantime, *Serenade* is a definite improvement on *The Postman*. It, too, has its trashy aspect, its movie fore-shortenings and its too-well oiled action; but it establishes a surer illusion. *The Postman* was always in danger of be-coming unintentionally funny. Yet even there brilliant moments of insight redeemed the unconscious burlesque; and there is enough of the real poet in Cain—both in writ-ing and in imagination—to make one hope for something better than either.

2. John O'Hara

John O'Hara also derives from Hemingway, and his short stories sound superficially like Hemingway's. His longer stories, like Cain's, have it in common with Hemingway that the heroes and heroines are doomed. But O'Hara's main interest in life is of an entirely different kind from Hemingway's, and his writing really belongs to a different category of fiction.

O'Hara is not a poet like Hemingway, but primarily a social commentator; and in this field of social habits and manners, ways of talking and writing letters and dressing, he has done work that is original and interesting. It is essen-tially the same kind of thing that Henry James and his fol-lowers developed, but the center of attention has shifted. The older novelists dealt almost exclusively with a well-to-do upper stratum, and the chief contrast he had to depict was between the American upper classes and the European upper classes, or between the established and cultivated people and the vulgar *nouveaux riches*. John O'Hara sub-jects to a Proustian scrutiny the tight-knotted social web of a large Pennsylvania town, the potpourri of New York night-life in the twenties, the nondescript fringes of Holly-wood. In all this he has explored for the first time from his peculiar semi-snobbish point of view a good deal of interesting territory: the relations between Catholics and Protestants, the relations between college men and non-college men, the relations between the underworld and "legitimate" business, the ratings of café society; and to read him on a fashionable bar or the Gibbsville country club is to be shown on the screen of a fluoroscope gradations of social prestige of which one had not before been aware. There is no longer any hierarchy here, of either cultivation or wealth: the people are all being shuffled about, hardly knowing what they are or where they are headed, but each is clutching some family tradition, some membership in a select organization, some personal association with the famous, from which he tries to derive distinction. But in the meantime, they mostly go under. They are snubbed, they are humiliated, they fail. The cruel side of social snobbery is really Mr. O'Hara's main theme. Only rarely, as in the excellent story called *Price's Always Open*, do the forces of democracy strike back.

This social surface, then, Mr. O'Hara analyzes with delicacy, and usually with remarkable accuracy. His grasp of what lies underneath it is not, however, so sure. His point of view toward his principal characters tends to be rather clinical; but even where his diagnosis is clear, we do not share the experience of the sufferer. The girl in *Butterfield 8* is a straight case of a Freudian complex, somewhat aggravated by social maladjustment; but we don't really know her well. Julian English of *Appointment in Samarra* is apparently the victim of a bad heredity worked upon by demoralizing influences; yet the emotions that drive him to suicide are never really shown. The whole book is in the nature of an explanation of why Julian threw the highball in the face of the Irish climber; yet the explanation doesn't convince us that the inevitable end for Julian would be the suicide to which his creator brings him. As for Mr. O'Hara's latest novel, *Hope of Heaven*, a story of Hollywood, I have not been able to fathom it at all—though here, too, there seems to be discernible a Freudian behavior-pattern. One wonders whether the personality of the script-writer who is telling the story is intended to play some role of which he himself is unaware, in connection with the conduct of the other characters, or whether the author himself does not quite know what he is doing.

One gets the impression—confirmed by a statement which Mr. O'Hara is reported to have made—that he improvises more or less and never reworks or revises. His longer stories always sound like first drafts which ought to be trimmed and tightened up—which might be turned into very fine little novels, but which, as it is, remain rather diffuse and rather blurred as to their general intention. What is the relevance to the story, for example, of the newspaperwoman in *Appointment in Samarra*, whose career is described on such a scale? The account of her beginnings is amusing, but the part she plays in the drama doesn't seem to warrant this full-length introduction. What is the point of the newspaper reporter who suddenly gets into the picture, and more or less between us and it, at the end of *Butterfield 8*? What on earth is the justification—aside from establishing the atmosphere for a drama of general crookedness—of the long story about the man who stole the traveller's checks at the beginning of *Hope of Heaven*? If Mr. O'Hara has definite ideas about the meaning of these characters in his scheme, I can't see that he has brought it out. He seems merely to be indulging his whims. He happens, however, to be gifted with a clean, quick and sure style, which by itself gives an impression of restraint; and the unfaltering neatness of his writing carries him over a good deal of thin ice. But he appears, in perfecting this style, to have been following, from the point of view of architecture, a line of least resistance. Each of his novels has been less successful, less ambitious and less well-disciplined than the one that went before; but while the long stories have been deteriorating, the short stories have been improving: in the most successful of them he has achieved his characteristic effects as he has hardly been able to do in his novels. The best of his work, in my opinion, consists of *Appointment in Samarra*, the admirable long short story called *The Doctor's Son* in the collection of that name, and the short pieces of *Files on*

Parade (though there are also a few memorable ones in the early volume—such as *Ella and the Chinee*).

As for *Pal Joey*, his last-published book, it is funny, well-phrased, well-observed; but, heel for heel, Pal Joey is a comedown after Julian English. *Appointment in Samarra* is a memorable picture both of a provincial snob, a disorganized drinking-man of the twenties, and of the complexities of the social organism in which he flourished and perished. But Pal Joey is merely an amoeba of the night-life of the jitter-bug era; and he is a little amoeba-monster. It is not that one objects to O'Hara's creating a monster—*Pal Joey* is successful as satire precisely because the author is not afraid to go the whole hog; but that he seems to represent a contraction of John O'Hara's interests.

The truth is perhaps that O'Hara has never really had his bearings since he dropped Gibbsville, Pa. He was all awash in *Butterfield 8* in the night-life of New York—though he still kept some capacity for judgment; and in *Hope of Heaven* he showed serious signs of suffering from Hollywood lightheadedness. He partly retrieved himself by becoming the outstanding master of the *New Yorker* short-story-sketch; but we expected, and still expect, more of him.

3. William Saroyan

The refrain becomes monotonous; but you have to begin by saying that Saroyan, too, derives from Hemingway. The novelists of the older generation—Hemingway himself, Dos Passos, Faulkner, Wilder—have richer and more complex origins, they belong to a bigger cultural world. But if the most you can say of John O'Hara is that he has evidently read Ring Lardner and F. Scott Fitzgerald as well as Hemingway, the most you can say of Saroyan is that he has also read Sherwood Anderson (though he speaks of having looked into a book which he bought for a nickel at a bookstore and which was in Swedish and had pictures of churches). When you remember that Lardner and Anderson were among the original ingredients in Hemingway, you see how limited the whole school is.

But what distinguishes Saroyan from his fellow disciples is the fact that he is not what is called hard-boiled. What was surprising and refreshing about him when he first attracted notice, was that, although he was telling the familiar story about the wise-guy who went into the bar, and I said and the bartender said and I said, this story with Saroyan was never cruel, but represented an agreeable mixture of San Francisco bonhomie and Armenian Christianity. The fiction of the school of Hemingway had been full of bad drunks; Saroyan was a novelty: a good drunk. The spell exerted in the theater by his play, *The Time of Your Life,* consisted in its creating the illusion of friendliness and muzzy elation and gentle sentimentality which a certain amount of beer or rye will bring on in a favorite bar. Saroyan takes you to the bar, and he produces for you there a world which is the way the world would be if it conformed to the feelings instilled by drinks. In a word, he achieves the feat of making and keeping us boozy without the use of alcohol and purely by the stimulus of art. It seems natural that the cop and the labor leader should be having a drink together; that the prostitute should prove to be a wistful child, who eventually gets married by someone that loves her; that the tall tales of the bar raconteur should turn out to be perfectly true, that the bar millionaire should be able to make good his munificent philanthropical offers—that they should be really Jack the Giant-Killer and Santa Claus; and that the odious vice-crusader, who is trying to make everybody unhappy, should be bumped off as harmlessly as the comic villain in an old-fashioned children's "extravaganza."

These magical feats are accomplished by the enchantment of Saroyan's temperament, which induces us to take from him a good many things that we should not accept from other people. With Saroyan the whole trick is the temperament; he rarely contrives a machine. The good fairy who was present at his christening thus endowed him with one of the most precious gifts that a literary artist can have, and Saroyan never ceases to explain to us how especially fortunate he is: "As I say, I do not know a great deal about what the words come to, but the presence says, Now don't get funny; just sit down and say something; it'll be all right. Say it wrong; it'll be all right anyway. Half the time I *do* say it wrong, but somehow or other, just as the presence says, it's right anyhow. I am always pleased about this. My God, it's wrong, but it's all right. It's really all right. How did it happen? Well that's how it is. It's the presence, doing everything for me. It's the presence, doing all the hard work while I, always inclined to take things easy, loaf around, not paying much attention to anything, much, just putting down on paper whatever comes my way."

Well, we don't mind Saroyan's saying this, because he is such an engaging fellow; and we don't mind his putting down on paper whatever happens to come his way. It is true that he has been endowed with a natural felicity of touch which prevents him from being offensive or tiresome in any of the more obvious ways; and at their best his soliloquies and stories recall the spontaneous songs of one of those instinctive composers who, with no technical knowledge of music, manage to finger out lovely melodies. Yet Saroyan is entirely in error in supposing that when he "says it wrong," everything is really all right. What is right in such a case is merely this instinctive sense of form which usually saves him—and even when he is clowning— from making a fool of himself. What *is* wrong, and what his charm cannot conceal, is the use to which he is putting his gifts. It is a shock for one who very much enjoyed *The Daring Young Man on the Flying Trapeze* to go back to reading Saroyan in his latest collection, *The Trouble with Tigers.* There is nothing in the book so good as the best things in *The Flying Trapeze*, and there is a good deal that is not above the level of the facility of a daily columnist. A columnist, in fact, is what William Saroyan seems sometimes in danger of becoming—the kind of columnist who depends entirely on a popular personality, the kind who never reads, who does not know anything in particular about anything, who merely turns on the tap every day and lets it run a column.

It is illuminating to compare this inferior stuff with the contents of a less well-known collection published in California. This volume, *Three Times Three*, consists mainly of miscellaneous pieces which the author seems to regard as not having quite come off. The result is something a great deal more interesting than the slick and rather thin stuff of *Tigers*. One of these pieces, *The Living and the Dead*, of which the author rightly says that it is not so good as it ought to be, seems to me, in spite of the fact that it miscarries to some degree, one of the best things Saroyan has written. The scene with the Armenian grandmother after the departure of the money-collecting Communist is of a startling and compelling beauty. This theme of the foreign-born asserting in modern America the virtues of an older society is one of the principal themes in Saroyan; whenever it appears—as in the short story called *70,000 Assyrians*—it takes his work out of the flat dimensions of the guy watching life in the bar; and here he has brought it into play for one of his most poignant effects. This is followed by an admirable scene, in which the young man walks out on the street and sees a child crying at a window, and reflects that for "the children of the world eternally at the window, weeping at the strangeness of this place," where the Communist must always look forward to a perfected society of the future, where his grandmother must always look backward to a world that has gone with her youth and that could never really have been as she remembers it, it is natural enough to escape into the "even more disorderly universe" of drunkenness, a state sad enough in itself. But the conception, with its three motifs, required a little doing; and Saroyan, as he confesses, did not quite bring it off. He would have had to take the whole thing more seriously and to work it out with more care;

and he knows that he can get away with an almost infinite number of less pretentious pieces without having their second-rateness complained of.

Rudyard Kipling said one very good thing about writing: "When you know what you can do, do something else." Saroyan *has* tackled in his plays something larger and more complicated than his stories; but these plays seem now to be yielding to a temptation to turn into columns, too. The three that have been acted and printed have many attractive and promising features in a vein a little like J. M. Barrie's; but George Jean Nathan in the *American Mercury* has given a disquieting account of no less than five new plays by Saroyan that have already been unsuccessfully tried out. There was a rumor that Mr. Nathan had been trying to induce Saroyan to take the trouble to acquaint himself with a few of the classics of the theater, but it sounds as if the attempt had come to naught.

In the meantime, Saroyan goes on with his act, which is that of the unappreciated genius who is not afraid to stand up for his merits. This only obscures the issue. Most good artists begin by getting bad reviews; and Saroyan, in this regard, has been rather remarkably fortunate. So let him set his mind at rest. Everybody who is capable of responding to such things appreciates what is fine in his work. The fact that a number of people who do not know good theatrical writing from bad or whose tastes lie in other directions have failed to recognize Saroyan is no excuse for the artist to neglect his craft. He will be judged not by his personality act or by his ability to get produced and published—which he has proved to the point of absurdity; but by work that functions and lasts.

With his triumph there has crept into Saroyan's work an unwelcome suggestion of smugness. One has always had the feeling with his writing that, for all its amiability and charm, it has had behind it the pressure of a hard and hostile environment, which it has required courage to meet, and that this courage has taken the form of a debonair kidding humor and a continual affirmation of the funda-

mental kindliness of people—a courage which, in moments
when it is driven to its last resources and deepest sincerity,
is in the habit of invoking a faith in the loyalties of straight
and simple people—Armenians, Czechs, Greeks—surviving
untouched by the hatreds of an abstract and complex
world. In Saroyan the successful playwright, for whom
that pressure has been partially relieved, there seems to
be appearing an instinct to exploit this theme of loving-
kindness and of the goodness and rightness of things; and
there is perhaps a just perceptible philistinism. If Saroyan,
in *Love's Old Sweet Song,* has hit upon precisely the right
way to make fun of *Time* magazine, he has, on the other
hand, here, in what sounds like a skit on *The Grapes of
Wrath,* at least grazed the familiar complacency which
declares the unemployed are all bums. This is the path
that leads to Eddie Guest, Professor William Lyon Phelps
and Dr. Frank Crane; and let not Mr. Saroyan deceive
himself: no writer has a charmed life.

4. Hans Otto Storm

With Hans Otto Storm and John Steinbeck, we get into
more ambitious writing.

The work of Mr. Storm has been presented to the public
in a curious and probably misleading way. His first two
books, *Pity the Tyrant* and *Made in U.S.A.* (the latter published only in a limited edition), attracted relatively little
attention. They were both novelettes. *Pity the Tyrant,* one
of those stories about an "I" who travels and loves and
runs risks and reflects with a sardonic detachment on the
things that go on around him, seemed to attach itself to
the general school of Hemingway. *Made in U.S.A.* had no
"I" and was an exercise in objectivity: a story about people
on a ship that ran aground, worked out as a social fable.
Both stories had a concentration of form and a kind of con-
scientiousness in their approach to their material that
were rare enough to excite interest in the author.

These books were followed in the fall of 1940 by a very long novel, *Count Ten*, which was enormously advertised by the publishers. To the surprise of Mr. Storm's readers, this book turned out, however, to be very much inferior on the whole to the ones that had gone before and to show what seemed internal evidence of having been written earlier than they. *Count Ten* gives distinctly the impression of being one of those autobiographical novels that young men begin in college and carry around for years in old trunks, keeping them at the back of their minds as refractors for their subsequent experience, but returning to work on them after intervals so long that the texture of the book is always changing, and that the story, when it finally appears, fluctuates between callowness and maturity, literal fact and developing invention. The characters encountered by the hero of *Count Ten* have a sort of goofy unreality which lets us down in an embarrassing way after the pretty well-observed social types of Mr. Storm's other novels; and the book is full of violent incidents which occur, as it were, offstage, in the blank lines between one chapter and the next, and which have no real emotional effect on what follows. The hero preserves a certain consistency; but the story of his adventures rambles on with little proportion, composition or climax. The writing, too, is far below the level of the author's earlier published novels. His style has always been hampered by an uncertainty about idiomatic English and a proclivity for German locutions, and, though his instinct for expressing himself has its own kind of sensitive precision, his language is always here a little cockeyed.

Yet *Count Ten* is not uninteresting to read. Implausible though a good deal of it is, it evidently makes use of actual experience; and the experience of Hans Otto Storm has been of a kind rather unusual among our fiction-writers. In the first place, Mr. Storm, though a radical, is not, like so many other novelists, a radical of the depression vintage. He is—one gathers from *Count Ten*—the descendant of German refugees of the Revolution of 1848 settled in

Southern California. The hero of his novel, at any rate, begins by going to jail for resisting the draft in the last war and ends by going to jail again as the result of his activities as campaign manager for a movement evidently drawn from Upton Sinclair's EPIC. He has, in the meantime, had a successful career as an agent of the mining interests. Mr. Storm's perspectives from the Left are obviously a good deal longer than those of the ordinary California Communist: he is both practically more sophisticated and historically better informed.

Mr. Storm is unusual in another way. These youthful autobiographical fictions usually tell the stories of young men who want to be writers, and they do not as a rule get far from the literary life itself. But Mr. Storm is neither a journalist nor a script writer, not a man who has made his living by writing at all: he is a trained engineer; and his hero builds and flies planes, works on a construction gang, sails a ship, runs a furniture business in which he manufactures the furniture himself, and becomes a mining prospector in South America. An engineer who thus goes in for literature is such a novelty that Hans Otto Storm is able to carry us with him because we have never listened to precisely his story before. His writing about the sea—in *Made in U.S.A.* and in the episode of the yacht in *Count Ten*—without the parade of technical knowledge which is the betrayal of the layman in Kipling, gives us a much more intimate sense of living the life of the ship than we get from *The Ship That Found Herself* or *The Devil and the Deep Sea*.

Add to this equipment—to this first-hand knowledge of aspects of American life which few American writers know at all—a mentality which is culturally closer to Europe than that of most American writers (there is a suggestion of Conrad about him); and you get something quite unique in our fiction. Mr. Storm has so far, it seems to me, done his best work in *Pity the Tyrant*. Both the earlier published books show an application of engineering aptitude to the technique of constructing novels which is strangely absent in *Count Ten;* but *Pity the Tyrant* has a freshness and vividness which do not appear to the same degree in *Made in U.S.A.,* a more systematic affair. The South American episodes in *Count Ten* sound like mere juvenile sketches for it. Here in this story of an American technician involved in a Peruvian revolution and sorely perplexed between his job, his proletarian political sympathies and a love affair with a South American lady, Mr. Storm does succeed in dramatizing one of those cases of social conscience which do not come off so well in *Count Ten.* Here he really attains intensity; and *Pity the Tyrant*—though not quite in the class with Hemingway and Stephen Crane—belongs among the more distinguished products of this tradition of American story-telling.

5. John Steinbeck

John Steinbeck is also a native Californian, and he has occupied himself more with the life of the State than any of these other writers. His exploration in his novels of the region of the Salinas Valley has been more tenacious and searching than anything else of the kind in our recent fiction, with the exception of Faulkner's exhaustive study of the State of Mississippi.

And what has Mr. Steinbeck found in this country he knows so well? I believe that his virtuosity in a purely technical way has tended to obscure his themes. He has published eight volumes of fiction, which represent a variety of forms and which have thereby produced an illusion of having been written from a variety of points of view. *Tortilla Flat* was a comic idyl, with the simplification almost of a folk tale; *In Dubious Battle* was a strike novel, centering around Communist organizers and following a fairly conventional pattern; *Of Mice and Men* was a compact little drama, contrived with almost too much cleverness, and a parable which criticized humanity from a non-political point of view; *The Long Valley* was a series of short stories, dealing mostly with animals, in which poetic symbols were presented in realistic settings and built up with concrete detail; *The Grapes of Wrath* was a propaganda novel, full of preachments and sociological interludes, and developed on the scale of an epic. Thus attention has been diverted from the content of Mr. Steinbeck's work by the fact that when his curtain goes up, he always puts on a different kind of show.

Yet there is in Mr. Steinbeck's fiction a substratum which remains constant and which gives it a certain weight. What is constant in Mr. Steinbeck is his preoccupation with biology. He is a biologist in the literal sense that he interests himself in biological research. The biological laboratory in the short story called *The Snake* is obviously something which he knows at first hand and for which he has a strong special feeling; and it is one of the peculiarities of his vocabulary that it runs to biological terms. But the laboratory described in *The Snake*, the tight little building above the water, where the scientist feeds white rats to rattlesnakes and fertilizes starfish ova, is also one of the key images of his fiction. It is the symbol of Mr. Steinbeck's tendency to present human life in animal terms.

Mr. Steinbeck almost always in his fiction is dealing either with the lower animals or with humans so rudimentary that they are almost on the animal level; and the relations between animals and people are as intimate as those in the zoöphile fiction of David Garnett and D. H. Lawrence. The idiot in *The Pastures of Heaven*, who is called Little Frog and Coyote, shows his kinship with the animal world by continually making pictures of birds and beasts. In *Tortilla Flat*, there is the Pirate, who lives in a kennel with his dogs and has practically forgotten human companionship. In *In Dubious Battle*, there is another character whose personality is confused with that of his dogs. In *The Grapes of Wrath*, the journey of the Joads is figured at the beginning by the progress of a turtle, and is accompanied and parodied all the way by animals, insects and birds. When the expropriated sharecroppers in

Oklahoma are compelled to abandon their farm, we get an extended picture of the invasion of the house by the bats, the weasels, the owls, the mice and the pet cats that have gone back to the wild. Lennie in *Of Mice and Men* likes to carry around pet animals, toward which as well as toward human beings he has murderous animal instincts. The stories in *The Long Valley* are almost entirely about plants and animals; and Mr. Steinbeck does not give the effect, as Lawrence or Kipling does, of romantically raising the animals to the stature of human beings, but rather of assimilating the human beings to animals. *The Chrysanthemums, The White Quail* and *The Snake* deal with women who identify themselves with, respectively, chrysanthemums, a white quail and a snake. In *Flight*, a young Mexican boy, who has killed a man and run away into the mountains, is finally reduced to a state so close to that of the beasts that he is apparently mistaken by a mountain lion for another four-footed animal; and in the fantasy *Saint Katy the Virgin*, in which a vicious pig is made to repent and become a saint, the result is not to dignify the animal as the *Little Flowers of Saint Francis* does, for example, with the wolf of Agubbio, but to make human religion ridiculous.

Nor does Steinbeck love his animals as D. H. Lawrence does. The peculiar point of view is well analyzed in connection with Thomas Wayne in *To a God Unknown:* "He was not kind to animals; at least no kinder than they were to each other, but he must have acted with a consistency beasts could understand, for all creatures trusted him. . . . Thomas liked animals and understood them, and he killed them with no more feeling than they had about killing each other. He was too much an animal himself to be sentimental." And Steinbeck does not even dwell much, as Lawrence likes to do, on the perfections of his various beasts each after its own kind. It is the habits and behavior of the animals, not the impression they make, that interests him.

The chief subject of Mr. Steinbeck's fiction has been

thus not those aspects of humanity in which it is most thoughtful, imaginative, constructive, nor even those aspects of animals that seem most attractive to humans, but rather the processes of life itself. In the ordinary course of nature, living organisms are continually being destroyed, and among the principal things that destroy them are the predatory appetite and the competitive instinct that are necessary for the very survival of eating and breeding creatures. This impulse of the killer has been preserved in a simpleton like Lennie of *Of Mice and Men* in a form in which it is almost innocent; and yet Lennie has learned from his more highly developed friend that to yield to it is to do something "bad." In his struggle against the instinct, he loses. Is Lennie bad or good? He is betrayed as, the author implies, all our human intentions are, by the uncertainties of our animal nature. And it is only, as a rule, on this primitive level that Mr. Steinbeck deals with moral questions: the virtues like the crimes, for him, are still a part of these planless and almost aimless, of these almost unconscious, processes. The preacher in *The Grapes of Wrath* is disillusioned with the human moralities, and his sermon at the grave of Grampa Joad, so lecherous and mean during his lifetime, evidently gives expression to Mr. Steinbeck's own point of view: "This here ol' man jus' lived a life an' jus' died out of it. I don't know whether he was good or bad, but that don't matter much. He was alive, an' that's what matters. An' now he's dead, an' that don't matter. Heard a fella tell a poem one time, an' he says, 'All that lives is holy.'"

The subject of *The Grapes of Wrath*, which is supposed to deal with human society, is the same as the subject of *The Red Pony*, which is supposed to deal with horses: loyalty to life itself. The men who feel themselves responsible for having let the red pony die must make up for it by sacrificing the mare in order that a new pony may be brought into the world alive. And so Rose of Sharon Joad, with her undernourished baby born dead, must offer her milk, in the desolate barn which is all she has left for a shelter, to another wretched victim of famine and flood, on the point of death from starvation. To what end should ponies and Oakies continue to live on the earth? "And I wouldn' pray for a ol' fella that's dead," the preacher goes on to say. "He's awright. He got a job to do, but it's all laid out for 'im an' there's on'y one way to do it. But us, we got a job to do, an' they's a thousan' ways, an' we don' know which one to take. An' if I was to pray, it'd be for the folks that don't know which way to turn."

This preacher who has lost his religion does find a way to turn: he becomes a labor agitator; and this theme has already been dealt with more fully in the earlier novel, *In Dubious Battle*. But what differentiates Mr. Steinbeck's picture of a labor movement with radical leadership from most treatments of such subjects of its period is again the biological point of view. The strike leaders, here, are Communists, as they are in many labor novels, but *In Dubious Battle* is not really based on the formulas of Communist ideology. The kind of character produced by the Communist movement and the Communist strategy in strikes (of the Communism of the day before yesterday) is *described* by Mr. Steinbeck, and it is described with a certain amount of admiration; yet the party member of *In Dubious Battle* does not talk like a Marxist of even the Stalinist revision. The cruelty of these revolutionists, though they are working for a noble ideal and must immolate themselves in the struggle, is not palliated by the author any more than the cruelty of the half-witted Lennie; and we are made to feel all through the book that, impressive though the characters may be, they are presented primarily as examples of how life in our age behaves. There is developed in the course of the story—especially by a fellow-traveller doctor who seems to come closer than the Communist to expressing Mr. Steinbeck's own ideas—a whole philosophy of "group-man" as an "animal."

"It might be like this, Mac: When group-man wants to move, he makes a standard. 'God wills that we recapture the Holy Land'; or he says 'We fight to make the world safe for democracy'; or he says, 'We will wipe out social injustice with communism.' But the group doesn't care about the Holy Land, or Democracy, or Communism. Maybe the group simply wants to move, to fight, and uses these words simply to reassure the brains of individual men. . . ."

"How," asks Mac, "do you account for people like me, directing things, moving things? That puts your group-man out."

"You might be an effect as well as a cause, Mac. You might be an expression of group-man, a cell endowed with a special function, like an eye cell, drawing your force from group-man, and at the same time directing him, like an eye. Your eye both takes orders from and gives orders to your brain."

"This isn't practical," objects Mac. "What's all this kind of talk got to do with hungry men, with lay-offs and un-employment?"

"It might have a great deal to do with them. It isn't a very long time since tetanus and lockjaw were not con-nected. There are still primitives in the world who don't know children are the result of intercourse. Yes, it might be worth while to know more about group-man, to know his nature, his ends, his desires. They're not the same as ours. The pleasure we get in scratching an itch causes death to a great number of cells. Maybe group-man gets pleasure when individual men are wiped out in a way."

Later, when the mob of striking fruit-pickers begins to get out of hand, the Communists themselves begin to think of them in these infra-human terms:

"They're down there now. God, Mac, you ought to of seen them. It was like all of them disappeared, and it was just one big animal, going down the road. Just all one animal." . . .

"The *animal* don't want the barricade. I don't know what it wants. Trouble is, guys that study people always think it's men, and it isn't men. It's a different kind of animal. It's as different from men as dogs are. Jim, it's swell when we can use it, but we don't know enough. When it gets started it might do anything."

So the old pioneer of *The Leader of the People* describes a westward migration which he himself once led as "a whole bunch of people made into one big crawling beast. . . . Every man wanted something for himself, but the big beast that was all of them wanted only westering."

This tendency on Steinbeck's part to animalize humanity is evidently one of the causes of his relative unsuccess at creating individual humans. The *paisanos* of *Tortilla Flat* are not really quite human beings: they are cunning little living dolls that amuse us as we might be amused by pet guinea-pigs, squirrels or rabbits. They are presented through a special convention which is calculated to keep them cut off from any kinship with the author or the reader. In *The Grapes of Wrath*, on the other hand, Mr. Steinbeck has summoned all his resources to make the reader feel his human relationship with the family of dispossessed farmers; yet the result of this, too, is not quite real. The characters of *The Grapes of Wrath* are animated and put through their paces rather than brought to life; they are like excellent character actors giving very conscientious performances in a fairly well-written play. Their dialect is well managed, but they always sound a little stagy; and, in spite of Mr. Steinbeck's efforts to make them figure as heroic human symbols, one cannot help feeling that these Okies, too, do not exist for him quite seriously as people. It is as if human sentiments and speeches had been assigned to a flock of lemmings on their way to throw themselves into the sea. One remembers the short story called *Johnny Bear*. Johnny Bear is another of Steinbeck's idiots: he has exactly the physique of a bear and seems in almost every way subhuman; but he is endowed with an uncanny gift for reproducing with perfect mimicry the conversations he overhears, though he understands nothing of their human meaning.

It is illuminating to look back from *The Grapes of Wrath* to one of the earliest of Steinbeck's novels, *To a God Unknown*. In this book he is dealing frankly with the destructive and reproductive forces as the cardinal principles of nature. In one passage, the hero is described by one of the other characters as never having "known a person": "You aren't aware of persons, Joseph; only people. You can't see units, Joseph, only the whole." He finds himself, almost unconsciously and in contravention of Christianity, practising a primitive nature cult, to which, in time of terrible drought, he sacrifices first his wife, then himself, as blood offerings to bring the rain. This story, though absurd, has a certain interest, and it evidently represents, on the part of Steinbeck just turned thirty, an honorably sincere attempt to find expression for his view of the world and his conception of the powers that move it. When you husk away the mawkish verbiage from the people of his later novels, you get down to a similar conception of a humanity not of "units" but lumped in a "whole," to a vision equally grim in its cycles of extinction and renewal.

Not, however, that John Steinbeck's picture of human beings as lemmings, as grass that is left to die, does not have its striking validity for the period in which we are living. In our time, Shakespeare's angry ape, dressed in his little brief authority, seems to make of all the rest of mankind angry apes or cowering rodents. The one thing that was imagined with intensity in Aldous Huxley's novel, *After Many a Summer Dies the Swan*, was the eighteenth-century exploiter of the slave-trade degenerating into a fetal anthropoid. Many parts of the world are today being flooded with migrants like the Joads, deprived of the dignity of a human society, forbidden the dignity of human work, and made to flee from their houses like prairie-dogs driven before a prairie fire. Aldous Huxley has a good deal to say, as our American "Humanists" did, about a fundamental moral difference which he believes he is able to discern between a human and an animal level, and the importance of distinguishing between them; and, like the Humanists, he has been frightened back into one of those synthetic cults which do duty for our evaporated religions. The doctor of *In Dubious Battle* is made, on the contrary, to deprecate even such elements of religion as have entered into the labor cause at the same time that he takes no stock in the utopianism of the Marxists. When he is depressed by the barbarity of the conflict and is reminded by the neophyte Jim that he "ought to think only of the end: out of all this struggle a good thing is going to grow," he answers that in his "little experience the end is never very different in its nature from the means . . . It seems to me that man has engaged in a blind and fearful struggle out of a past he can't remember, into a future he can't foresee nor understand. And man has met and defeated every obstacle, every enemy except one. He cannot win over himself. How mankind hates itself." "We don't hate ourselves," says Jim. "We hate the invested capital that keeps us down." "The other side is made of men, Jim, men like you. Man hates himself. Psychologists say a man's self-love is balanced neatly with self-hate. Mankind must be the same. We fight ourselves and we can only win by killing man."

The philosophy of Mr. Steinbeck is obviously not satisfactory in either its earlier or its later form. He has nothing to oppose to this vision of man's hating and destroying himself except an irreducible faith in life; and the very tracts he writes for the underdog let us see through to the biological realism which is his natural habit of mind. Yet I prefer his approach to the animal-man to the mysticism of Mr. Huxley; and I believe that we shall be more likely to find out something of value for the control and ennoblement of life by studying human behavior in this spirit than through the code of self-contemplation that seems to grow so rootlessly and palely in the decay of scientific tradition which this latest of the Huxleys represents.

For the rest, Mr. Steinbeck is equipped with resources of observation and invention which are exceptional and sometimes astonishing, and with color which is all his own but which does not, for some reason, possess what is called magic. It is hard to feel that any of his books, so far, is really first-rate. He has provided a panorama of California farm-life and California landscape which is unique in our literature; and there are passages in some ways so brilliant that we are troubled at being forced to recognize that there is something artistically bad about them. Who has ever caught so well such a West Coast scene as that in *To a God Unknown* in which we visit the exalted old man, with the burros, who has built his hut high on the cliff so that he can look down on the straight pillars of the redwoods and off at the sea far below, and know that he is the last man in the western world to see the sun go down? What is wrong here is the animal sacrifice which the old man performs at this moment and which reminds us of the ever-present paradox of the mixture of seriousness and trashiness in the writing of Mr. Steinbeck. I am not sure that *Tortilla Flat*, by reason of the very limitations imposed by its folk-tale convention, is not artistically his most successful work.

Yet there remains behind the journalism, the theatricalism and the tricks of his other books a mind which does seem first-rate in its unpanicky scrutiny of life.

6. Facing the Pacific

Contemporary California has thus been described by our novelists on a very extensive scale. It has probably had as much attention as any other part of the country. Yet the California writers—and this is true even of Steinbeck, the most gifted of them—do not somehow seem to carry a weight proportionate to the bulk of their work.

Why is this? All visitors from the East know the strange spell of unreality which seems to make human experience on the Coast as hollow as the life of a troll-nest where everything is out in the open instead of being underground.

I have heard a highly intelligent Los Angeles lawyer who had come to California from Colorado remark that he had periodically to pinch himself to remind himself of the fact that he was living in an abnormal, a sensational, world which he ought to get down on paper, but that he could never pull out of the trance sufficiently to react and to judge in what he still at the back of his mind considered the normal way. There is in one of these Hollywood novels, *You Play the Black and the Red Comes Up*, a veracious account of the feelings of a man leaving Southern California. The hero has just crossed the mountains after a great career of love and crime. And yet "it was like all I had done in California was just a dream. And at first it felt good, and then it felt worse, because Sheila was only a dream with everything else. And that was bad. I could remember everything about California, but I couldn't feel it. I tried to get my mind to remember something that it could feel, too, but it was no use. It was all gone. All of it. The pink stucco houses and the palm trees and the stores built like cats and dogs and frogs and ice-cream freezers and the neon lights round everything."

This is partly no doubt a matter of climate: the empty sun and the incessant rains; and of landscape: the dry mountains and the void of the vast Pacific; of the hypnotic rhythms of day and night that revolve with unblurred uniformity, and of the surf that rolls up the beach with a beat that seems expressionless and purposeless after the moody assaults of the Atlantic. Add to this the remoteness from the East and the farther remoteness from Europe. New York has its own insubstantiality that is due to the impermanence of its people, of its buildings, of its business, of its thoughts; but all the wires of our western civilization are buzzing and crossing here. California looks away from Europe, and out upon a wider ocean toward an Orient with which as yet any cultural communication is difficult.

This problem of the native Californian to find a language for the reality of his experience is touched upon in Hans Otto Storm's *Count Ten*. "If things now and then did not look real to you; if you were bothered by that particular question, Eric thought, then you ought certainly to keep off the Gulf of California. It hadn't looked real the time they did or did not bathe their feet in it and eat the clams, and it certainly did not look real now, this deadish place where no ships ever came and where the waves move with such an unutterable weariness." The hero is puzzled but his interest is pricked by an Easterner he meets at Berkeley, who misses the New England seasons and tries to explain to him the dramatic character which they impart to the cycle of the year; and when, gazing over San Francisco bay, he quotes Heine to one of his girls, she objects: " 'That isn't Heine any more. It's a hakku. It makes me think of tea-cakes without salt.' She shivered a little. 'It's getting cold. No, that doesn't click in California. In California you can't sit and meditate on through the sunset.' " The young man applies himself to learning Chinese.

Add to this that the real cultural center, San Francisco, with its cosmopolitanism and its Bohemian clubs, the city of Bret Harte and Ambrose Bierce, was arrested in its natural development by the earthquake of 1906, and that thereafter the great anti-cultural amusement-producing center, Los Angeles, grew up, gigantic and vulgar, like one of those synthetic California flowers, and tended to drain the soil of the imaginative life of the State. (It is a question how much the movies themselves have been affected by the California atmosphere: might they not have been a little more interesting under the stress of affairs in the East?) In this city that swarms with writers, none yet has really mustered the gumption to lay bare the heart and bowels of the moving-picture business. The novels I have mentioned above only trifle with the fringes of Hollywood, as the stage comedies like *Boy Meets Girl* only kid it in a superficial way. A novel on a higher level of writing than any of those I have mentioned—*The Day of the Locust* by Nathanael West—is also mostly occupied with extras and gives mere glimpses into the upper reaches. Aldous Huxley's California novel, *After Many a Summer Dies the*

Swan, does not get even so far into the subject as his compatriot Mr. Eric Knight, the author, under a pseudonym, of *You Play the Black,* etc. Mr. Huxley here seems well on his way to becoming a second-rate American novelist. Satirizing in more or less conventional fashion the Hearstian millionaire, the vapid Hollywood beauty and the burlesque pomps of a Los Angeles cemetery, he has succumbed to one of the impostures with which the Golden State deludes her victims: the Burbankized West Coast religion; and Mr. Huxley and his ally, Mr. Gerald Heard, will be lucky if they do not wake up some morning to find themselves transformed into Yogis and installed in one of those Wizard-of-Oz temples that puff out their bubble-like domes among the snack bars and the lion ranches.

The novel about Hollywood with most teeth in it is still that intrepid satire by Miss Anita Loos called *The Better Things of Life,* which came out serially in the *Cosmopolitan* and was repeatedly announced by her publishers, but which never appeared between covers. It seems to be true, in general, of Hollywood as a subject for fiction that those who write about it are not authentic insiders and that those who know about it don't write.*

But, as I say, it is not merely in Los Angeles that the

* The relation between the movies and prose fiction works in two ways. There are the actual writers for the pictures like Mr. West and Mr. Cain who produce sour novels about Hollywood. And there are the serious novelists who do not write for the films but are influenced by them in their novels. Since the people who control the movies will not go a step of the way to give the script-writer a chance to do a serious script, the novelist seems, consciously or unconsciously, to be going part of the way to meet the producers. John Steinbeck, in *The Grapes of Wrath,* has certainly learned from the films—and not only from such documentary pictures as those of Pare Lorentz, but from the sentimental symbolism of Hollywood. The result is that *The Grapes of Wrath* has poured itself onto the screen as easily as if it had been written in the studios, and that it is probably the sole serious story on record that seems almost equally effective as a book and as a film. Ernest Hemingway's *For Whom the Bell Tolls,* which also has elements of movie romance, was instantly snapped up by Hollywood.

purposes and passions of humanity have the appearance of playing their roles in a great open-air amphitheater which lacks not only acoustics to heighten and clarify the speeches but even an attentive audience at whom they may be directed. The paisanos of *Tortilla Flat* also eat, love and die in a golden and boundless sunlight that never becomes charged with their energies; and the rhapsodies of William Saroyan, diffused in this non-vibrant air, pass without repercussions. Even the monstrous, the would-be elemental, the would-be barbaric tragedies which Robinson Jeffers heaps up are a little like amorphous cloud-dramas that eventually fade out to sea, leaving only on our faces a slight moisture and in our ears an echo of hissing. It is probably a good deal too easy to be a nihilist on the coast at Carmel: your very negation is a negation of nothing.

One theme does, however, it must be said, remain serious for the California novelists: the theme of the class war. The men and women of the Cain-O'Hara novels are doomed: they are undone by their own characters or by circumstances. But in time—as in Cain's *Serenade* and O'Hara's *Hope of Heaven**—the socialist diagnosis and the socialist hope begin to appear in the picture. This has been true, of course, during the thirties, of our American fiction in general; but the labor cause has been dramatized with more impact by these writers of the Western coast than it has been, on the whole, in the East, where the formulas of Marxist theory have been likely to take the place of experience. I do not mean the Hollywood Stalinism which is satirized by Mr. McCoy in the swimming-pool scene of *I Should Have Stayed Home:* I mean the tradition of radical writing which Californians like Storm and Steinbeck are carrying on from Frank Norris,† Jack London and Upton Sinclair.

---

* O'Hara is not yet a Californian either by birth or by adoption. Except in *Hope of Heaven*, he had always had the Eastern edge and tension.

† Steinbeck's close relationship with Norris is indicated by what is evidently a borrowing from *McTeague* in *Of Mice and Men*.

This tradition dates from Henry George, who witnessed, in the sixties and seventies, the swallowing-up of the State —in what must have been record time—by capital; and California has since been the scene of some of the most naked and savage of American labor wars. The Mc-Namaras, Mooney and Billings, the Wobblies and Vigilantes, the battles of the longshoremen and the fruit-pickers, the San Francisco general strike—these are names and events that have wrung blood and tears in the easy California climate; and it is this conflict that has kept Mr. Storm afloat in the Pacific vacuum, fixed securely in his orientation toward the east of the social world, and that has communicated to Mr. Steinbeck the impetus that has carried the Joad jalopy into the general consciousness of the nation.

Here the novelists of California know what they are talking about, and they have something arresting to say. In describing their special mentality, I do not, of course, in the least, mean to belittle their interest or value. The writing of the Coast, as I say, may seem difficult to bring into focus with the writing that we know in the East. But California, since we took it from the Mexicans, has always presented itself to Americans as one of the strangest and most exotic of their exploits; and it is the function of the literary artist to struggle with new phases of experience, and to try to give them beauty and sense.

The conversation that is so often repeated between Norris's Polish junk dealer and the cracked Spanish-American girl, in which he is always begging her to describe for him the gold table service she remembers from her childhood, must have suggested the similar dialogue that recurs between Lennie and George, in which the former is always begging the latter to tell him more about the rabbit farm they are going to have together. Steinbeck's attitude toward his rudimentary characters may, also, owe something to Norris—who, like him, alloys his seriousness with trashiness.

Postscript

These notes were first written during the autumn and early winter of 1940. Since then, several events have occurred which require a few words of postscript.

On December 21, 1940, F. Scott Fitzgerald suddenly died in Hollywood; and, the day after, Nathanael West was killed in a motor accident on the Ventura boulevard. Both men had been living on the West Coast; both had spent several years in the studios; both, at the time of their deaths, had been occupied with novels about Hollywood.

The work of Nathanael West derived from a different tradition than that of these other writers. He had been influenced by those post-war Frenchmen who had specialized, with a certain preciosity, in the delirious and diabolic fantasy that descended from Rimbaud and Lautréamont. Beginning with *The Dream Life of Balso Snell*, a not very successful exercise in this vein of phantasmagoria, he published, after many revisions, a remarkable short novel called *Miss Lonelyhearts*. This story of a newspaper hack who conducts an "advice to the lovelorn" department and eventually destroys himself by allowing himself to take too seriously the sorrows and misfortunes of his clients, had a poetic-philosophical point of view and a sense of phrase as well as of chapter that made it seem rather European than American. It was followed by *A Cool Million*, a less ambitious book, which both parodied Horatio Alger and more or less reproduced *Candide* by reversing the American success story. In his fourth book, *The Day of the Locust*, he applied his fantasy and irony to the embarrassment of rich materials offered by the movie community. I wrote a review of this novel in 1939, and I shall venture to append it here—with apologies for some repetition of ideas expressed above—to make the California story complete:

Nathanael West, the author of *Miss Lonelyhearts*, went to Hollywood a few years ago, and his silence had been causing his readers alarm lest he might have faded out on the Coast as so many of his fellows have done. But Mr. West, as this new book happily proves, is still alive beyond the mountains, and quite able to set down what he feels and sees—has still, in short, remained an artist. His new novel, *The Day of the Locust*, deals with the nondescript characters on the edges of the Hollywood studios: an old comic who sells shoe polish and his film-struck daughter; a quarrelsome dwarf; a cock-fighting Mexican; a Hollywood cowboy and a Hollywood Indian; and an undeveloped hotel clerk from Iowa, who has come to the Coast to enjoy his savings—together with a sophisticated screen-writer, who lives in a big house that is "an exact reproduction of the old Dupuy mansion near Biloxi, Mississippi." And these people have been painted as distinctly and polished up as brightly as the figures in Persian miniatures. Their speech has been distilled with a sense of the flavorsome and the characteristic which makes John O'Hara seem pedestrian. Mr. West has footed a precarious way and has not slipped at any point into relying on the Hollywood values in describing the Hollywood people. The landscapes, the architecture and the interior decoration of Beverly Hills and vicinity have been handled with equal distinction. Everyone who has ever been in Los Angeles knows how the merest aspect of things is likely to paralyze the aesthetic faculty by providing no *point d'appui* from which to exercise its discrimination, if it does not actually stun the sensory apparatus itself, so that accurate reporting becomes impossible. But Nathanael West has stalked and caught some fine specimens of these Hollywood lepidoptera and impaled them on fastidious pins. Here are Hollywood restaurants, apartment houses, funeral churches, brothels, evangelical temples and movie sets—in this latter connection, an extremely amusing episode of a man getting nightmarishly lost in the Battle of Waterloo. Mr. West's surrealist beginnings have stood him in good stead on the Coast.

The doings of these people are bizarre, but they are also sordid and senseless. Mr. West has caught the emptiness of Hollywood; and he is, as far as I know, the first writer to make this emptiness horrible. The most impressive thing in the book is his picture of the people from the Middle West who, retiring to sunlit leisure, are trying to leave behind them the meagerness of their working lives; who desire something different from what they have had but do not know what they desire, and have no other resources for amusement than gaping at movie stars and listening to Aimee McPherson's sermons. In the last episode, a crowd of these people, who have come out to see the celebrities at an opening, is set off by an insane act of violence on the part of the cretinous hotel clerk, and gives way to an outburst of mob mania. The America of the murders and rapes which fill the Los Angeles papers is only the obverse side of the America of the inanities of the movies. Such people—Mr. West seems to say—dissatisfied, yet with no ideas, no objectives and no interest in anything vital, may in the mass be capable of anything. The day-dreams purveyed by Hollywood, the romances that in movie stories can be counted on to have whisked around all obstacles and adroitly knocked out all "menaces" by the time they have run off their reels, romances which their fascinated audiences have never been able to live themselves—only cheat them and embitter their frustration. Of such mobs are the followers of fascism made.

I think that the book itself suffers a little from the lack of a center in the community with which it deals. It has less concentration than *Miss Lonelyhearts*. Mr. West has introduced a young Yale man who, as an educated and healthy human being, is supposed to provide a normal point of view from which the deformities of Hollywood may be criticized; but it is also essential to the story that this young man should find himself swirling around in the same aimless eddies as the others. I am not sure that it is really possible to do anything substantial with Hollywood except by making it, as John Dos Passos did in *The Big Money*, a part of a larger picture which has its center in a larger world. But in the meantime Nathanael West has survived to write another distinguished book—in its peculiar combination of amenity of surface and felicity of form and style with ugly subject matter and somber feeling, quite unlike—as *Miss Lonelyhearts* was—the books of anyone else.

Scott Fitzgerald, who at the time of his death had published only short stories about the movies, had been working for some time on a novel* in which he had tackled the key figure of the industry: the successful Hollywood producer. This subject has also been attempted, with sharp observation and much humor, by Mr. Budd Schulberg, Jr., whose novel *What Makes Sammy Run* has been published since my articles were written. But Mr. Schulberg is still a beginner, and his work in *What Makes Sammy Run* does not rise above the level of a more sincere and sensitive George Kaufman; whereas Scott Fitzgerald, an accomplished artist, had written a considerable part of what promised to be by all the odds the best novel ever devoted to Hollywood. Here you are shown the society and the business of the movies, no longer through the eyes of the visitor to whom everything is glamorous or ridiculous, but from the point of view of people who have grown up or lived with the industry and to whom its values and laws are their natural habit of life. These are criticized by higher standards and in the knowledge of wider horizons, but the criticism is implicit in the story; and in the meantime, Scott Fitzgerald, by putting us inside their group and making us take things for granted, is able to excite an interest in the mixed destiny of his Jewish producer of a kind that lifts the novel quite out of the class of this specialized Hollywood fiction and relates it to the story of man in all times and all places.

* Later published as *The Last Tycoon*.

Both West and Fitzgerald were writers of a conscience and with natural gifts rare enough in America or anywhere; and their failure to get the best out of their best years may certainly be laid partly to Hollywood, with its already appalling record of talent depraved and wasted.

1940–41

Alexander Woollcott of the Phalanx

ALEXANDER WOOLLCOTT is dead; and a hostile obituary in the New York *Herald Tribune,* which dwelt on his disagreeable traits, has prompted me to try to pay some tribute to his more attractive ones.

I knew Woollcott only slightly, but my relations with him were based on an aspect of him which may not have been very well known. He was born at the North American Phalanx near Red Bank, New Jersey, and I was born at Red Bank. The North American Phalanx was one of the longest-lived of the socialist communities that flourished in the middle of the last century, and Woollcott's grandfather was for many years the head of it. My family knew all his family, and my grandfather, who was a doctor at Eatontown, brought Woollcott into the world.

When I first came to New York and met Woollcott, I did not connect him with the Woollcotts of Red Bank or the curious old Fourierist building, half barracks and half hotel, to which I had been taken, as a child, to call. At that time, when I had just started working in the office of *Vanity Fair,* to which he was a distinguished contributor, I saw his more erinaceous side. I provoked him to ferocity one day by asking him who the Father Duffy was to whom he was in the habit of referring as if he were the Apostle Paul. I had spent a year and a half in France during the war but had not been aware of Father Duffy; and I had not grasped the fact that Woollcott had created for himself a calendar of saints whose glory must not be questioned. But one day at the Algonquin he asked me whether I was the son of Lawyer Wilson of Red Bank, and we talked about the Phalanx. He told me about a Fourierist uncle who had devoted himself to painting with so much single-mindedness and so little material success that he had finally had to go into bankruptcy. My father had extricated him from his troubles; and I presently discovered that a picture that hung in my mother's house—the old phalanstery building itself dimly looming behind the fresh green of the straight-stemmed New Jersey forest—was one of this uncle's productions, which at that time he had given my father. I had been struck, when Woollcott told me of this incident, by the evident admiration he felt for the completeness of his uncle's unworldliness: not only for the immense number of pictures he had painted but for the enormous sum of money he had failed for.

From then on our relations were cordial. When a play of mine was done at the Provincetown Playhouse in the early nineteen twenties, Alec, then the dramatic critic of the *Times*, wrote a rather sympathetic review of it, but ended by explaining that his judgment might possibly have been somewhat softened by the fact that thirty-odd years before a certain kindly old country doctor had been called on a snowy night to attend Mrs. Woollcott of the Phalanx, etc. When he found out later on that the kindly old doctor had gone to Hamilton College, of which Alec was one of the most loyal alumni, my grandfather came to figure, from his connection with Alec's birth, as a species of Angel of the Annunciation; and I was surprised to find myself involved in one of those sentimental myths on which he fed the unsatisfied affections that had for objects only his heroes, his friends and the memories of his family.

This myth would occasionally crop up in his writings, and even after I ceased to see him, I would hear from him from time to time. One day I ran into him in New York in the street somewhere in the West Forties. He was going very fast, but stopped a second and said brusquely, "I'm having a play produced!" I asked him what it was called. "*The Crime in the Whistler Room*," he snapped and passed on. *The Crime in the Whistler Room* had been the title of my play at the Provincetown. Later on, when I published a study of Kipling, he wrote me several long letters on the subject, about which he had some sober and shrewd ideas. I had also, however, been writing about Dickens and praising his gloomy later novels; and this elicited from Alec a sulky "I do not care to discuss Dickens with you." He did, nevertheless, indicate his preferences; and I could see him as a child in the phalanstery lying in the hammock on a summer day with *Pickwick* or *David Copperfield*. His point of view was perfectly infantile. It turned out that he did not like *Bleak House* simply because it was the only one of the novels which he had not read as a child.

In the meantime, however, in the years of the depression, I had had with him a curious interview. I had been travelling around the country doing articles on labor and economic conditions, and he wrote me that he had been reading these articles and said he would like to talk to me. I invited him to dinner, but he answered that he was a much older man than I and that I ought to come to him. So I called on him at Sutton Place, where he occupied a splendid apartment looking out on the East River. As soon as I entered the room, he cried out, without any other greeting: "You've gotten very fat!" It was his way of disarming, I thought, any horror I might have felt at his own pudding-like rotundity, which had trebled since I had seen him last. He did not rise and was wearing a dressing-gown, so I asked whether he had been ill. He shortly replied that he hadn't; and wanted to know whether I thought he was ill because he was wearing a dressing-gown. There were other guests, and they kept coming and going. Drinks were brought by a butler: Woollcott never stirred from his chair; and there was a backgammon board, at which people were playing. A secretary in a room beyond was typing an article for him; and he would rap out from time to time peremptory orders to the butler, who was feeding a phonograph in a neighboring room with Gilbert and Sullivan records.

He made no attempt to talk to me, and I wondered why he had wanted to see me. At last there came a moment, however, when all the guests had gone and there was nobody but him and me. His demeanor changed entirely. He began to speak naturally and frankly: a note of uncertainty came into his voice, and a look of distressful anxiety tightened his brows above his spectacles. He asked me about the Communist movement in America. I told him a little, and he went on to talk about the North American Phalanx —on which he had been collecting material and about which he meant some day to write. He said that he had always known that labor was going to be the great force in the modern world; and he told me about the Labor Day rites at the Phalanx, over which his grandfather had presided. He said that the kind of reporting that I had been doing for the *New Republic* was the kind of thing he should like to do himself: he should like to go around the country and see what was going on—he had friends in the West and the South whom it would be easy for him to visit; and the only consideration that had prevented him from carrying out this project was the fact that, reduced as his income was, he had difficulty in finding a chauffeur who could also do dictation and typing.

Then another batch of guests came in, and Woollcott resumed his role in that theatrical-journalistic world in which he was both a "personality" of print and a "star" in an eccentric part. I wasn't sure that anybody but me could recognize in his anagrams and croquet, his Dickens and Gilbert and Sullivan, his idealization of the stars of the early nineteen hundreds such as the Barrymores and Mrs. Fiske, and his general wide-eyed excitement of the semi-suburban Jerseyman over all that was going on in New York—could recognize in this the persistence of the atmosphere and the habits of an old-fashioned childhood, but seemed quite exotic, a pose, in the modern New York of the thirties.

When *The Man Who Came to Dinner* was done on the stage, I was rather depressed to hear that Alec was acting in the West the character drawn from himself. But when I saw the play in New York, I ceased to be troubled by this. Kaufman's comedy was stupid enough; and it was slightly offensive, like most of his things, because it was an exploitation by an expert contriver of curtains and exploder of firecracker laughs of an idea that had better possibilities. But its very comic-supplement mechanics made Woollcott's participation in it a relatively innocent matter. Kaufman had put on the stage some of Woollcott's superficial idiosyncrasies without ever even attempting to do anything with his real personality. The bad side of the Kaufman character was simply a combination of fiendishness and childishness, while the better side was simply a stage Santa Claus, straight out of the last act of a George Arliss play. A portrayer of the actual Woollcott would have had to show how his arrogance and venom arose from the vulnerability of an excessively sensitive man rather badly favored by nature and afflicted by glandular disorders. When Woollcott addressed his friends as "Repulsive," it was like his receiving me with a hoot at my increasing weight: he was afraid you were going to find him so. And a serious portrait of Woollcott would have had to show the lifelong inspiration for him of the Fourierist background of the Phalanx.

His interest in communism, so far as I know, did not have any practical upshot; but a certain queer moral authority which he exerted throughout his career was derived from the idealism that had bankrupted the Phalanx; and what made him seem impossible to editors, to producers whose plays he reviewed and to the arrangers of radio programs, were not entirely his fits of bad temper but also a boldness and an independence, learned in the same school, that made him intolerant of other people's policies when they conflicted with his own judgment, and prevented him from hesitating a moment about throwing up any job, no matter how fraught with prestige, when principle demanded a choice between submission and resignation. The idea that "social betterment" and the "elevating" effects of the arts were the most important things in the world and causes to be served gratuitously was always alive in his mind; and one might be very far from sharing a good many of his enthusiasms and very much dislike his way of expressing them, and yet feel that his lights were not vulgar ones and that Alec had not betrayed them.

He had it, moreover, in common with the older American radicalism that, in the days of totalitarian states and commercial standardization, he did not hesitate to assert himself as a single unique human being: he was not afraid to be Alexander Woollcott; and even when Alexander Woollcott was horrid, this somehow commanded respect. In *The Man Who Came to Dinner,* it made him a kind of folk-hero.

February 6, 1943

Mr. Joseph E. Davies as a Stylist

I HAVE JUST been reading *Mission to Moscow,* Mr. Joseph E. Davies' book, after seeing the film of the same title. The picture, I find, coincides with the book in almost no respect. The real Mr. Joseph Davies, for example, is a shrewd corporation lawyer who contributed to the Roosevelt campaign fund and was appropriately rewarded with an ambassadorship. The Davies of the Warner Brothers picture is a plain rugged American business man, played by Mr. Walter Huston rather like a more elderly version of Sinclair Lewis's Dodsworth, who demurs with a touching humility when the President asks him to go to Russia, and protests that he is really not qualified because he has had no diplomatic training. The real Mr. Davies was sent for the perfectly specific purpose of discussing a trade agreement and arranging for the settlement of debts contracted by the Kerensky government. But these objectives do not figure in the film. The Hollywood Mr. Davies is simply entrusted with a mission of reporting on the Soviet

Union. The real Mr. Davies was troubled by the tyrannies of the Stalinist police state. "No physical betterment of living standards," he wrote in *Mission to Moscow*, "could possibly compensate for the utter destruction of liberty of thought or speech and the sanctity of the individual . . . The government is a dictatorship not 'of the proletariat,' as professed, but 'over the proletariat.' It is completely dominated by one man." One could quote him in this sense at length.

There is one point, however, in which the film is quite faithful to the real Mr. Davies. When the Davies of Walter Huston is made to attend the Moscow trials, he enunciates the following statement: "Based on twenty years of trial practice, I'd be inclined to believe these men's testimony." The trials themselves, it is true, are represented falsely, and this is not precisely the kind of thing that Mr. Davies was saying about them at the time; but the undependable syntax of the Warner Brothers' Davies is absolutely true to life. I should say, indeed, from reading the book, that the author of *Mission to Moscow* is, so far as my knowledge extends, the greatest master of bad official English since the late President Harding.

The prose style of President Harding has been analyzed by H. L. Mencken in his admirable little paper, *A Short View of Gamalielese;* and this piece, which I have lately been rereading, has stimulated me to try to do some justice to the beauties of Mr. Davies' writing.

Let me begin with one of the cultural notes with which Davies the connoisseur and man of taste diversifies his record of affairs of state, a passage which illustrates brilliantly his skill in producing the effect of surprise:

"For weeks there have been celebrations of the centenary of Pushkin's death all over the country. He is a combination of Byron and Shakespeare for the Russian people. He was a liberal in thought and married to a noblewoman who, it is alleged, was a mistress of the tsar. He was killed in a duel, which, as the story goes, was a frame-up. Both the opera and the ballet were based on Pushkin's works and the music was by the great Tchaikovsky. The opera was *Eugen Onegin,* a romantic story of two young men of position whose friendship was broken up over a misunderstanding and lovers' quarrel which resulted in a duel in which the poet was killed. It was significant of Pushkin's own end and oddly enough was written by him."

The sequence of relative pronouns here in the sentence before the last, each one depending on the one before, is a very fine bit of writing, but it only prepares for the climax. It drags us, by a series of hitches, up an incline like the hump on a roller-coaster, from the top of which we suddenly dip into a dizzying and breath-depriving excitement. What is it that makes the next sentence so startling? Not syntax, for the syntax is normal. Not logic: no mere fallacy is involved. We cannot assign this slight to any of the familiar categories of rhetorical or logical error. The device is original and daring; it takes us a moment to grasp it; but then we become aware that the trick consists of first explaining that the opera which Mr. Davies calls *Eugen Onegin* (though this is neither the Russian nor the English form of the title) is based on Pushkin's poem; then of indicating a striking parallel between the circumstances of Pushkin's death and the poem; and then of suddenly making the point that, by some scarcely believable coincidence, the poem was written by Pushkin. But to paraphrase the passage thus is to rob it of all its thrill. The whole effect depends on the quickness of the shift in the sense and on the simple phrase *oddly enough,* at once arresting and casual. Only a bad writer of special gifts could have hit upon and placed this phrase. It is as if a long red carpet upon which we had been walking, on our way to some ceremony of state, had suddenly been pulled out from under us.

There is, however, one example even bolder of Mr. Davies' ability to baffle and to dazzle:

"The peace of Europe, if maintained, is in imminent danger of being a peace imposed by the dictators, under conditions where all of the smaller countries will speedily rush in to get under the shield of the German aegis, and under conditions where, even though there be a concert of power, as I have predicted to you two years ago, with 'Hitler leading the band.'"

Here the opening is weighty and portentous: a veteran man of affairs with a large experience of Europe is about to deliver a considered opinion. The first indication of anything queer comes with *the shield of the German aegis;* but although this gives us pause for a moment, we immediately reassure ourselves by concluding that Mr. Davies surely knows that a shield is an aegis, and has allowed himself the little tautology, in the exuberance of his enjoyment of his official position, as a mere rhetorical flourish. But then we come to the *as I have predicted to you two years ago.* The tense here is incorrect: it should be *as I predicted to you two years ago.* We conclude that Mr. Davies does not know this, but that, even though he does not know it, the instinct of his genius has guided him to hit upon the perfect deviation which, by adding to the solemnity of the tone at the same time as to the absurdity of the writing, will lead the way to the final effect. And what an effect it is! The sentence never comes to a conclusion. It is a new sort of aposiopesis—an aposiopesis with a full-stop at the end. Yet the grammatical impossibility has with wonderful art been half-concealed. The writer has first given us an adverbial clause beginning with *under conditions where,* which completes itself in the logical way, but then he has gone on to another clause, which begins in the same way: *and under conditions where.* Since we have just seen the first one brought off, we are prepared for the fulfilment of the second. But this second clause is never completed. Mr. Davies, by a rare stroke of art, starts another subordinate clause, *even though there be,* etc., and at the end of this clause he stops. On first reading, we fail to grasp it; we go back and read the sentence again. The use of the subjunctive here, *even though there be,* is another of his fine manipulations to give us confidence in the structure of his thought. We find it very hard to believe that a man who can use the subjunctive in this noble traditional way would be capable of leaving his sentence with one end sticking out in the air, like the rope in the Indian rope trick. And yet Mr. Davies *has* left it so, and we can only accept and wonder, just as we can only accept and wonder at his giving the public his word for the authenticity of all the testimony that is supposed to be quoted, in his film, from the records of the Moscow trials and that includes a confession by Tukhachevsky imagined and written by Hollywood; at his flying back from Moscow on his second mission with the advertisement *Mission to Moscow* painted, in English and Russian, in large yellow letters on his plane; and at his watching with gratification, in the company of Stalin and his retinue, while this film was shown in the Kremlin.

Let me finally quote a passage less distinguished by brilliance of language than by the felicity with which it mirrors the qualities of the man himself. Mr. Davies is reporting an interview with a representative of the Soviet Foreign Office, at which the trade agreement and the debts were discussed:

"He stated that they were having difficulty, in connection with guaranteeing $4,000,000 of purchases in the United States. . . . I stated quite frankly, however, that while, personally, I made these admissions to him 'and against interest,' that [*sic*] quite frankly I had absolutely no tolerance for a position that would haggle over an increase of $10,000,000 in purchases (from $30,000,000 to $40,000,000) in view of both the equities and the practicalities of this situation; that in my opinion it was not an evidence of approaching the matter in a broad-minded and appreciative attitude of the position which Secretary

Hull had taken so fairly and in such a large-minded way on this particular problem."

The style here, of course, is remarkable, as Mr. Davies' style always is. The superfluous *that* is good. The *broad-minded* and *large-minded* are like the flourish of persuasive hands brushing doubts and inhibitions aside; and in the next sentence but one we already see the spell that is cast by the verbal incantation, taking effect on the Soviet department head:

"Mr. Neymann manifested a very fair-minded attitude in reply and stated in conclusion that he would not be disposed to quarrel with that point of view . . ."

But there glints through in this passage, when the figures are named, the relentless *fortiter in re*—to resort to a kind of ornament much relished by Mr. Davies—which always lurks behind his *suaviter in modo*. Mr. Davies is of Welsh blood, he tells us, and, like a Welshman, he knows how to combine an elevated and shimmering eloquence with a certain subtlety of practical shrewdness. The glint is half lost in the mist; the purpose is half obscured by the shower of flattering words that, meaningless though most of them are, rather soothe us and please us as we read. These words may perhaps have made it easier for Mr. Davies, at the time of his embassy, to further the interests of the United States; but there are moments when the metallic gleam that pierces from time to time the shifting lights of Mr. Davies' language, has the look of an eye fixed intently on opportunities for conspicuous self-dramatization.

Winter, 1944

The Life and Times of John Barrymore

IF you merely take a glance at *Good Night, Sweet Prince*, Gene Fowler's biography of John Barrymore, you may suppose that it is a cheap journalistic job.

Certainly the style couldn't be more journalistic in a flowery old-fashioned way, which has sometimes a tinge of O. Henry, sometimes a tinge of Woollcott ("A block to the east of the Arch Street Theatre lay the wise bones of Benjamin Franklin"). For Mr. Fowler, Broadway is inevitably "this street of fickle lustre," a distiller a "maker of spirituous delicacies," and Shakespeare "Stratford's first gentleman"; cigarette-smoking is "bronchial debauchery," hair on the chest "torsorial upholstery" and the men's washroom "ammoniac grottos" equipped with "cracked and homely porcelains." When he wants to convey the idea that some white mice were multiplying rapidly, he says that the "snowy rodents were fruitful"; and when Barrymore sets out to play Hamlet, or take on "the Danish assignment," Mr. Fowler says that he "announced . . . his decision to draw on the black tights of the classic Scandinavian." His notion of syntax and the meaning of words is also of the vaguest. When it is a question of anybody's conduct, the word "behaviorism" is always summoned: "After the passing of his grandmother he entered upon a bouncing behaviorism"; and when, in reporting an interview with Alexander Woollcott, he seems to feel that he should make an effort to have this celebrator of Hamilton College talk like an educated man, he produces the following tribute to grammar: " 'And when you write of him, as I fear you shall, for heaven's sake remember one thing.' "

The language of Mr. Fowler has no structure and no harmonics. It is something that is exhaled like breath or exuded like perspiration. And yet the fuzzy raffish style of this book has its special appropriateness to the subject: it is a literary equivalent for the atmosphere in which the events take place. What we get here is the folklore of the Barrymores; and, as you read, you can smell the aroma of the manhattans and highballs and cigars of the old Hoffman House and the Knickerbocker bar, you seem to drift on the long late conversations at the Players club and the Lambs on which the Barrymore mythology was nourished. John Barrymore did in a sense live his legend; but you cannot really feel its validity unless you see it presented in terms of the smoking room, the city room, the green room, of the mirrors behind the bar and the shaded lamps at the club, all elements of urban life themselves rather remotely associated with the realities of common day. In this world of nocturnal fancy, Jack Barrymore was a fabulous character: a great drinker, a great man with women, a great comedian of public and private life, and finally a great maker of money. Gene Fowler, with his word-slinging jargon and his husky-throated sports-writer humor, is the right person to tell this story which might otherwise never have been told; and his book contains a most entertaining collection of funny theatrical anecdotes, phantasmagoric binges and what would in the days of the Knickerbocker bar have been described as "gorgeous yarns."

Yet this *Life and Times of John Barrymore* is absorbing for another reason, too; and the author has put into it something more than the favorite tales of a raconteur. The truth is that you get from this chronicle a much more convincing picture of its subject than you usually expect to find in either a fan or an official biography. Gene Fowler shows both insight into Barrymore and delicacy in handling his difficult case; and the piecing together of the record becomes fascinating because it is directed by a definite conception, always sympathetic but also quite realistic, of the man inside the reputation.

To begin with: the evidence of this book establishes indubitably a fact which the more fanatical admirers of the Barrymores are sometimes rather loath to admit. The generation of the Barrymore family that included John, Lionel and Ethel never really wanted to be on the stage. Their father, an Englishman named Blythe, who had assumed the stage name of Barrymore, was the son of an officer in India and had been educated at Harrow and Oxford. It was expected that he would read for the law, and his taking to the stage was a kind of a lapse, which, in spite of the long theater tradition on the mother's side of the family, the children seemed anxious to retrieve. "We became actors," says Ethel Barrymore, as reported by Mr. Fowler, "not because we wanted to go on the stage but because it was the thing we could do best." And Lionel corroborates this: "Neither Jack nor myself preferred the stage. We both wanted to become painters. Yet it seemed that we had to be actors. It was as if our father had been a street-cleaner and had dropped dead near a fire hydrant, and we went to pick up his shovel and broom to continue his work. Perhaps we didn't clean the corners well, but we did a better job at it than someone who never had been in the environment. What other thing could we have done better?"

This covers the case precisely. The Barrymores have occupied a position which has been at least as much social as theatrical. Seeing them on the stage was not always so very much different from meeting them in private life; and there was a tendency on the part of the public to imagine that the events of the play were happening to John or Ethel. They were none of them, even John, great actors, because they never had the actor's vocation. You see it very clearly if you compare them with their uncle John Drew, who, glass of fashion and mold of form though he was, took the theater with professional seriousness, and even in his later years, at his blindest and most arthritic, kept his cast and himself up to scratch with the rigor of an old general at maneuvers; whereas, as Gene Fowler tells us, the father of the three, Maurice Barrymore, used to neglect to memorize his lines and "contrive amazing excursions from the text," and John carried this cavalier treatment of the conventions and discipline of the stage to what must have been unprecedented lengths—breaking up his fellow-actors with elaborate and cruel jokes, stepping out of his character to denounce the audience and, in general, doing everything possible to sabotage an occupation he scorned.

The artistic deficiencies of the Barrymores were thrown into striking relief at the time—the season of 1922–23—when the Moscow Art Theater first visited America. That was also the season when the Barrymores were attempting their most ambitious roles: that fall John had opened in *Hamlet* and Ethel in Hauptmann's *Rose Bernd;* but when one compared these productions with the Russian ones, they had almost the aspect of private theatricals. Kachalov, of the Moscow Art Theater, was by way of being the Russian John Barrymore—that is, he was a good-looking and popular actor with a romantic reputation, who was supposed to do a good deal of drinking. But, if you went to see Kachalov in a play, you would find the dilapidated baron of Gorky's *The Lower Depths* or the elderly and bourgeois Stockmann of Ibsen's *An Enemy of the People.* If you had failed to look at the program, you might sit through a couple of acts before you recognized Kachalov at all: you had absolutely had the illusion that you were watching the creation of the dramatist. When you went to see John Barrymore in *Hamlet,* however, what you found was John Barrymore in *Hamlet.* His voice was better-trained than it had been and he had cultivated a new kind of vehemence; but he was obviously the same engaging fellow who had been playing around with the stage for years; and as the run of the show continued—one story Mr. Fowler does not tell—he would kid with the audiences at Shakespeare's expense by substituting, in the play scene, "Hollywood, Hollywood!" for "Wormwood, wormwood!" So Ethel, as Rose Bernd, a part in which a Russian actress would completely have incorporated herself, made a conscientious effort for a scene or two to impersonate a country girl who had been gotten with child by her master, then would drop the whole thing and smile graciously and become her delightful self.

Yet John Barrymore was a gifted person, and he counted for something in the life of his time. The extracts from his letters and diaries which Mr. Fowler has included in this book show his wit and his sensibility, and a refractory integrity of character which has nothing in common with the temperament of the ordinary popular actor. He belonged to an American tradition of the high-strung man of talent who makes hay of the American standards—runs amuck, takes to dissipation and is broken down young. But poor Barrymore never realized himself in either his painting or his acting as, say, Poe or Stephen Crane did in his writing, and he never found the right thing to do or be. It was only when some aspect of a character he was playing coincided with some aspect of his own personality that he was really creative on the stage: the scenes in which Hamlet takes his bitterness out in baiting the various figures of the Court, the opening of *Richard III*—one of the moments he came closest to greatness—in which the young Richard, full of envy as he sees how his deformities must cripple his life, vows himself, with a young man's spirit that moves us for the moment with its passion, to revenge upon normal humanity. Though I saw John Barrymore, through the years, in most of his important parts, from *The Fortune Hunter* to *Hamlet*, I can remember, leaving aside the light comedies, only one in which he seemed indistinguishable from the character he was impersonating: the bank clerk in Galsworthy's *Justice*, who commits a forgery out of love for a woman and is sentenced to solitary confinement. This came at the beginning of the period when Barrymore's friends were trying to persuade him to take his dramatic abilities more seriously, and it gave him a chance, I suppose, to identify with the character he was playing all that shrinking and uncertainty of his nature which, according to Mr. Fowler, made a lady who knew him well call him "a confused child."

He tried hard to find some role in life itself that he could count on and that would express him; and this biography is the story of his successive attempts. A disturbing and saddening story; for whenever, through exercise of will, he had achieved a high point of intensity by imposing on life his personal dream, the role always failed and let him down with a crash. First there was the effort of hard training that raised him to his Shakespearean roles, which he tired of and discarded so soon; then there was the quite different effort, inspired, when he was forty-three, by his idealization of Dolores Costello, to find at last some high and enduring ground as lover, husband, father. John Barrymore's solitary voyage on his yacht, as recorded by himself in his diary, when he is exalted by his vision of his love, yet living with his own thoughts and obviously happier alone with them than he is ever likely to be in his relations with other people, makes an attractive episode in his story but contains its tragic implications. The dream went to pieces when he tried to embrace it, as he had evidently the premonition it would do, and he had lost forever now the fine dignity of his independence, which had been partly sustained by the dream. It is quite plain from Mr. Fowler's account that the débâcle of John Barrymore's final years was almost as much the result of an actual loss of his faculties as the complete mental breakdown which his father had had at about the same age; yet in this hideous self-parody and self-ruination there was also perhaps a kind of arrogance, a paroxysm of contempt for the stage, and a last desperate effort in an inverted form to achieve that extreme intensity that enables one to realize oneself.

January 22, 1944

"Never Apologize, Never Explain": The Art of Evelyn Waugh

I DID NOT READ Evelyn Waugh at the time when he was first attracting attention. I never got started on him till a year ago, when I picked up a reprint of *Decline and Fall* and was so much exhilarated by it that I went on to *Vile Bodies,* and then read his four other novels in the order in which they were written. I may thus lay claim to a fresh impression of Evelyn Waugh's work—an impression, I believe, not much influenced by any journalistic interest that work may have had, appearing at the end of the twenties, as a picture of the delirium of that period. Nothing can taste staler today than some of the stuff that seemed to mean something then, that gave us twinges of bitter romance and thrills of vertiginous drinking. But *The Great Gatsby* and *The Sun Also Rises* hold up; and my feeling is that these novels of Waugh's are the only things written in England that are comparable to Fitzgerald and Hemingway. They are not so poetic; they are perhaps less intense; they belong to a more classical tradition. But I think that they are likely to last and that Waugh, in fact, is likely to figure as the only first-rate comic genius that has appeared in English since Bernard Shaw.

The great thing about *Decline and Fall*, written when the author was twenty-five, was its breath-taking spontaneity. The latter part of the book leans a little too heavily on Voltaire's *Candide*, but the early part, that hair-raising harlequinade in a brazenly bad boys' school, has an audacity that is altogether Waugh's and that was to prove the great principle of his art. This audacity is personified here by an hilarious character called Grimes. Though a schoolmaster and a "public-school man," Grimes is frankly and even exultantly everything that is most contrary to the British code of good behavior: he is a bounder, a rotter, a scoundrel, but he never has a moment of compunction. He is supplemented by Philbrick, the butler, a graduate of the underworld, who likes to tell about revolting crimes. This audacity in Waugh's next book, *Vile Bodies*, is the property of the infantile young people who, at a time "in the near future, when existing social tendencies have become more marked," are shown drinking themselves into beggary, entangling themselves in absurd sexual relationships, and getting their heads cracked in motor accidents. The story has the same wild effect of reckless improvisation, which perfectly suits the spirit of the characters; but it is better sustained than *Decline and Fall*, and in one passage it sounds a motif which for the first time suggests a standard by which the behavior of these characters is judged: the picture of Anchorage House with its "grace and dignity and other-worldliness," and its memories of "people who had represented their country in foreign places and sent their sons to die for her in battle, people of decent and temperate life, uncultured, unaffected, unembarrassed, unassuming, unambitious people, of independent judgment and marked eccentricities."

In *Black Mischief* there is a more coherent story and a good deal of careful planning to bring off the surprises and shocks. There are descriptions of the imaginary black kingdom of Azania, which is the principal scene of action, that are based on the author's own travels and would not be out of place in a straight novel. We note that with each successive book Evelyn Waugh is approaching closer to the conventions of ordinary fiction: with each one—and the process will continue—we are made to take the characters more seriously as recognizable human beings living in the world we know. Yet the author never reaches this norm: he keeps his grasp on the comic convention of which he is becoming a master—the convention which makes it possible for him to combine the outrageous with the plausible without offending our sense of truth. It is a triumph for him to carry from book to book the monsters of *Decline and Fall* and to make us continue to accept them as elements in later novels that touch us or stir us with values quite different from those of the earlier ones. There are two important points to be noted in connection with *Black Mischief*. The theme of the decline of society is here not presented merely in terms of night-club London: it is symbolized by the submergence of the white man in the black savagery he is trying to exploit. The theme of audacity is incarnated here, not in a Philbrick or a Grimes, but in a bad-egg aristocrat, who steals his mother's emeralds to run away from England, manipulates the politics of Azania by talking modern ideas to the native king and, forced at last to flee the jungle, eats his sweetheart unawares at a cannibal feast.

A Handful of Dust, which followed, is, it seems to me, the author's masterpiece. Here he has perfected his method to a point which must command the admiration of another writer even more perhaps than that of the ordinary non-literary reader—for the latter may be carried from scene to scene of the swift and smooth-running story without being aware of the skill with which the author creates by implication an atmosphere and a set of relations upon which almost any other novelist would spend pages of description and analysis. The title comes from T. S. Eliot's line, "I will show you fear in a handful of dust," but, except on the title page, the author nowhere mentions this fear. Yet he manages to convey from beginning to end, from the comfortable country house to the clearing in the Brazilian jungle, the impression of a terror, of a feeling that the bottom is just about to drop out of things, which is the whole motivation of the book but of which the characters are not shown to be conscious and upon which one cannot put one's finger in any specific passage. A charming woman of the aristocracy deserts a solid county husband and a high-spirited little boy to have a love affair with the underbred and uninteresting son of a lady interior decorator; the child is killed at a hunt; the husband runs away to Brazil and ends as the captive of an illiterate halfbreed, who keeps him for years in the jungle reading the novels of Dickens aloud. The audacity here is the wife's: her behavior has no justification from any accepted point of view, whether conventional or romantic. Nor does the author help out with a word of explicit illumination. He has himself made of audacity a literary technique. He exemplifies, like so many of his characters, the great precept of Benjamin Jowett to young Englishmen just starting their careers: "Never apologize, never explain."

The next novel *Scoop* is not quite so good as the ones just before and just after it, but it has in it some wonderful things. A quiet country gentleman, who writes nature notes for a big London paper called the *Daily Beast,* gets railroaded, through a confusion of identities, to another of Waugh's Negro countries, where he is supposed to act as war correspondent. The story is simpler than usual, and it brings very clearly to light a lineup of opposing forces which has always lurked in Evelyn Waugh's fiction and which is now even beginning to give it a certain melodramatic force. He has come to see English life as a conflict between, on the one hand, the qualities of the English upper classes, whether arrogant, bold and outrageous or stubborn, unassuming and eccentric, and, on the other, the qualities of the climbers, the careerists and the commercial millionaires who dominate contemporary society. The story of William Boot comes to its climax when the grown-up public-school boy faces down the Communist boss of Ishmaelia, who is trying to get him off the scene while a revolution takes place: "'Look here, Dr. Benito,' said William. 'You're being a bore. I'm not going.'" And the book has a more cheerful moral than any of its predecessors: William succeeds in holding his own against the barbarisms both of Africa and of London, and in the end he returns to the country, where they cannot get him again and where he continues to write his notes about the habits of the local fauna—though "outside the owls hunted maternal rodents and their furry broods." If this book is less exciting than the others, it is perhaps because the theme of audacity appears mainly in connection with the *Daily Beast*, with which the author cannot feel any sympathy.

Waugh's most recent novel, *Put Out More Flags*, written during and about the war, has an even more positive moral. Basil Seal, the aristocratic scoundrel who has already figured in *Black Mischief*, exploits the war to his own advantage by informing against his friends and shaking down his sister's county neighbors with threats of making them take in objectionable refugees, but finally he enlists in the Commandos, who give him for the first time a legitimate field for the exercise of his resourcefulness and nerve. Evelyn Waugh's other well-born wastrels are already in the "corps d'élite," somewhat sobered after years of "having fun." "There's a new spirit abroad. I see it on every side," says stupid old Sir Joseph Mainwaring. "And, poor booby," says the author, "he was bang right." We see now that not only has the spirit of audacity migrated from the lower to the upper classes, but that the whole local emphasis has shifted. The hero of *Decline and Fall* was a poor student reading for the church, whose career at Oxford was wrecked by the brutality of a party of aristocratic drunks: "A shriller note could now be heard rising from Sir Alastair's rooms; any who have heard that sound will shrink at the recollection of it; it is the sound of the English county families baying for broken glass." And at the end he is addressed as follows by another and more considerate young nobleman: "You know, Paul, I think it was a mistake you ever got mixed up with us; don't you? We're different somehow. Don't quite know how. Don't think that's rude, do you, Paul?" But it is now this young man, Percy Pastmaster, and Sir Alastair Digby-Vaine-Trumpington and the English county families generally who are the heroes of *Put Out More Flags*. Evelyn Waugh has completely come over to them, and the curious thing is that his snobbery carries us with it. In writing about Harold Nicolson, I remarked on his fatal inability to escape from the psychology of the governing class, which was imposed on him by birth and office. The case of Waugh is the opposite of this: he has evidently approached this class, like his first hero, from somewhere outside, and he has had to invent it for himself. The result is that everything is created in his work, nothing is taken for granted. The art of this last novel is marvellous. See the episode in which Basil Seal blackmails the young married woman: the attractiveness of the girl, which is to prompt him to try a conquest, and her softness, which will permit his success (Evelyn Waugh is perhaps the only male writer of his generation in England who is able to make his women attractive), are sketched in with a few physical details and a few brief passages of dialogue that produce an impression as clear and fresh as an eighteenth-century painting.

Evelyn Waugh is today a declared Tory and a Roman Catholic convert; he believes in the permanence of the social classes and, presumably, in the permanence of evil. It has been pointed out by Mr. Nigel Dennis in an article

in the *Partisan Review* that this would make him rather a
dubious guide for England after the war. But, after all, he
does not set up as a guide; and his opinions do not damage
his fiction. About this fiction there is nothing schematic
and nothing doctrinaire; and, though the characters are
often stock types—the silly ass, the vulgar parvenu, the old
clubman, etc.—everything in it has grown out of experience
and everything has emotional value. *Put Out More Flags*
leaves you glowing over the products of public schools and
country houses as examples of the English character; but
it is not a piece of propaganda: it is the satisfying expression of an artist, whose personal pattern of feeling no
formula will ever fit, whether political, social or moral. For
the savagery he is afraid of is somehow the same thing as
the audacity that so delights him.

March 4, 1944

What Became of Louis Bromfield

IN THE DAYS of *The Green Bay Tree* and *The Strange
Case of Miss Annie Spragg*, Mr. Louis Bromfield used to be
spoken of as one of the younger writers of promise. By the
time he had brought out *Twenty-four Hours*, it was more
or less generally said of him that he was definitely second-
rate. Since then, by unremitting industry and a kind of
stubborn integrity that seems to make it impossible for him
to turn out his rubbish without thoroughly believing in it,
he has gradually made his way into the fourth rank, where
his place is now secure.

His new novel, *What Became of Anna Bolton*, is one
of his most remarkable achievements. The story begins in
the London season of 1937, and in a succession of brilliant
scenes which, for the density of the social picture, recall
the opening of *War and Peace*, Mr. Bromfield makes us
acquainted with a vivid and varied company from that
international haut monde about which he writes with au-

thority. As we pass among these glittering worldlings, Mr. Bromfield characterizes each one with a magically evocative phrase. There are fading Lady Kernogan, "quite simply a tart, with certain superior qualities"; Major von Kleist from the German Embassy, "with the peculiar erect stiff carriage of Prussian military men"; Lady Haddonfield, "whom the years had turned into a rather handsome bony mare" and who at fifty "loved politics and intrigue and was considered the greatest hostess of the Tory Party." But cynosure of all smart London is the American Anna Bolton, of unknown origins but immense wealth, who stands at the top of the staircase of the great Georgian house she has rented, "triumphant and handsome and hard," welcoming "a gaudy, dying world." "There, side by side," thinks a young American guest, as he sees Lady Haddonfield and Mrs. Bolton, "receiving half of Europe, stand the two hardest, most ambitious bitches in the world!" And yet, he notes, Anna Bolton looks "like a fine race horse in training."

This young American, a foreign correspondent—it is he who tells Anna's story—is the only person present who knows who Anna Bolton is, for he comes from her home town of Lewisburg, Ohio, and went to school with her years ago. Mr. Bromfield, at this point, by a deft device, takes us back to Anna Bolton's childhood; and, brilliant social observer that he is, as much at home among the stratifications of a small American town as among the nuances of rank in a London drawing-room, he shows us the unbridgeable difference between the well-to-do classes of Lewisburg and those who, in a racy colloquial phrase which becomes one of the leit-motifs of the story, live "on the wrong side of the tracks." Anna Bolton, we are startled to hear, was once simply Annie Scanlon, the daughter of an Irish cleaning woman and a drunken Irish brakeman, who lived just beyond the railroad crossing. When little Annie first went to high school, the other children couldn't help noticing her "because of her bold looks and coloring— her red hair and blue eyes and a figure developed beyond her years. It was a figure like that of a young Venus

Genetrix, made for love, made for bearing children." "Even the high-school boys who didn't understand such things felt them by instinct," Mr. Bromfield tells us shrewdly, with one of his revealing insights into the psychology of adolescence.

Annie fell in love with Tom Harrigan, "the very core" of whose attraction "was a kind of healthy animal magnetism," "as good-looking a boy as I have ever seen—the Irish kind with black curly hair and blue eyes and high color, with big heavy shoulders and long straight legs. . . . I suppose he fell in love the same way he did everything else. He knew what it was all about without being told. He knew with the sure instinct of a young male animal what it was he wanted and went for it." He seduced Annie and made her pregnant, but when she told him, "he was not puzzled at all. He said quite simply, with a curious mature wisdom, 'We'll get married. After all that's why we love each other. That's the way things are. That's why people fall in love—to have babies. That's the way it was meant to be.'" But Annie is "shanty Irish" and Tom "lace-curtain Irish," a further shade of social distinction of which Mr. Bromfield makes us aware. Tom's rich parents object, but he marries her, and Tom gets himself a job as an automobile salesman in Pittsburgh, and there their baby is born. They are ideally happy together till one day Tom is killed in a motor accident, and that same year the baby catches measles, develops pneumonia and dies. In the hands of a less skillful artist, the death of Annie's husband and her baby might seem rather impromptu and meaningless, a gratuitous visitation of tragedy, but Mr. Bromfield has taken care to make Tom Harrigan so completely unconvincing a character that we do not complain of or notice any lack of plausibility in his death. Since we have never for a moment believed in him, we are not touched by what happens to him. The important thing is the effect on Anna. "I met her on the street," the narrator says, "the day she came back from the funeral of the baby. Something had happened to her eyes. They were like stone, as if there were no more tears in them." There seems to be an assumption in all this and through the whole of Anna's story that she is the victim of the "intricate, senseless pettiness and wornout traditions" of the town where she was born; yet she had obviously done pretty well for herself, and, though Tom had had his fatal accident while hurrying in answer to a telegram, apparently a pretext to lure him home, announcing that his father was dangerously ill, the disastrous end of her marriage can hardly be charged to small-town snobbery. That Mr. Bromfield should have arranged this accident and have made Anna feel this grievance is of the essence of his tragic conviction, somewhat akin to Thomas Hardy's, of the unpredictability of human events.

And then Anna turns up in Europe with a fortune that a rich second husband has left her, riding the high tide of social success and as if "sitting perpetually in a theater box watching a corrupt but breathless play." For Mr. Bromfield, with his epic sense of social forces, paints around her the larger background of the disintegration of Europe. "It was a world dominated by too many intriguers, by too many small people, a world lost for lack of decency and leadership, with scarcely a statesman in it . . . Vienna was like an old whore who had once been very pretty. . . . In France the people were on the brink of revolt against the corruption and intrigue of their own government. But Rome was worst of all. . . . Rome was the mad carnival of Europe at its worst. . . . And strangest of all there was a mad, sinister vagrant who took the name of Hitler."

But Anna is too vital a creature to fall a victim to this decadence of the Old World, and how she fares when war comes to France makes the chief drama of Mr. Bromfield's story. Leaving the Ritz, which has become her home, she flees Paris before the Nazi invasion, but her escape is held up by an air raid, in which she sees a woman killed. The husband of this woman, though Anna protests, makes her drive him to the nearest town. "He said, in a very quiet voice, 'You're going where I tell you. I know your kind. You're the cause of everything.' And suddenly he slapped her hard on the side of the face." This is the beginning of awakening for Anna. She has recognized already in this arrogant young fellow a resemblance to the man she once loved: "She felt suddenly faint and leaned against the car, letting the torch fall to the ground at her side. For what she had seen was Tom Harrigan—a big man with blue eyes and dark, curly hair." Here again we might be tempted to feel, in the case of a less adroit novelist, that the appearance in Anna's life of a second man who is virtually a replica of the first, with a child who closely resembles her own child, strains a little the legitimate license which we are accustomed to accord to fiction; but since the character of the first Tom Harrigan has the two-dimensional quality of a paper doll, it is not difficult to accept an exact duplicate cut out of the same piece of paper.

This second Tom Harrigan is a Russian, perhaps a better man than the first Tom, for he possesses the simple courage, perfect honesty and vast humanity characteristic of his race. In the love between him and Anna, Mr. Bromfield seems to give us a symbol of the union between Russia and the United States which was cemented at Teheran. Not that the author necessarily accepts the Soviet experiment in toto; for, in spite of Tom II's rude behavior on the occasion of his first meeting with Anna, he turns out to be very well-born, the son of a White Russian émigré, and thus keeps up the high social tone which Mr. Bromfield has taught us to expect in his fiction.

Anna takes in his motherless child and she sets up a canteen for refugees in a town just over the line in then still unoccupied France. She works her high connections in Paris and her acquaintance with the Prussian von Kleist, to get supplies for the despoiled population, but she refuses to marry von Kleist, who wants her, as he tells her, "because I am tired and sick and corrupt and you are strong and healthy and young"—a decision from which, also, it is possible for the politically minded reader to draw a significant moral. She finds that she loves this young

Russian, who is active in the underground movement, and for the first time, after many arid years of pleasure-seeking and worldly notoriety, Anna Bolton at last finds herself. Her companion, Harriet Godwin, puts it eloquently in the memorable scene in which Harriet is dying: "I've seen something happen to you, my dear, something miraculous. . . . I think I've seen you grow a soul." "That is really what this story is about," Mr. Bromfield has already told us, "how Anna changed and came to be born at last as a whole person, without deformity, how Anna learned understanding and humanity, and the value of things of life."

When the United States declares war, Anna's position in France becomes impossible, and she escapes to Algiers with the second Tom. There the narrator meets her again: "She turned toward me and I knew at once the woman was Anna Bolton, yet as I saw her in full face there was something about her that was not Annie Scanlon, at least not the Annie I had known. The hard look was no longer in the eyes. There was no hardness about the mouth. The experience was an extraordinary one." She is married and thoroughly happy. When this old friend sees her Russian husband, "it seemed to me that Tom Harrigan was looking at me. . . . I heard Anna saying, 'You see?' And then softly in English in that warm new voice of hers, she said, 'I am very grateful. God gave me another chance.'"

Mr. Bromfield, in *What Became of Anna Bolton*, has accomplished something in the nature of a miracle. In hardly more than sixty thousand words—a story that recalls, by its length, *A Lost Lady* and *Ethan Frome*—he has produced, by severe compression, a small masterpiece of pointlessness and banality. Most novelists of Mr. Bromfield's rank have some hobby about which they become interesting, some corner of life which they know and about which they have something to tell, some humor or infectious sentimentality or capacity for creating suspense; and it must have cost Louis Bromfield a rigorous labor of exclusion to achieve this smooth and limpid little novel in which there is not a single stroke of wit, not a scene of effective drama, not a phrase of clean-minted expression, and hardly a moment of credible human behavior.

I have been trying to describe this production in the manner appropriate to it—that is, as far as possible, in the language of the ladies who admire Louis Bromfield and who write enthusiastic reviews in the *Times* and the *Herald Tribune*. But the truth is that the book reviewer is baffled when he attempts to give an account of a work which has already turned its back on literature and embarrasses him on every page by stretching out its arms to Hollywood. He comes to feel that what he ought to have done was simply to pass it along to the movie department. For the characters of Louis Bromfield are hardly even precisely stock fiction characters: they are blank spaces like the figures on billboards before the faces have been painted in. When their features are finally supplied, they will be the features of popular actors. Mr. Bromfield seems to have made it easy, by giving Anna a similar name, for his heroine to wear the face of Ann Sheridan, who, not so very far back, in *Kings Row*, was playing just such an Irish girl from the other side of the tracks, in love with a rich young man; and in the same way Eric von Kleist can merge readily into Erich von Stroheim. No doubt the public will see them soon and will not mind if what they are and do has no logic and no motivation, no likeness of any kind to life. But the book reviewer is rather up against it, since he has to have something to take hold of, even to say that a book ought to be better, and *Anna Bolton* completely eludes him because it is really sub-literary and proto-film.

April 8, 1944

A review by Mary Ross, published in the New York *Herald Tribune* after the above article was written, closed with the following paragraph:

"This is a simply told and unassuming story, centered in the figure of a proud Irish girl from an American town, rather than the decadent glitter of pre-war Europe or the contrast of gluttony and misery which followed the fall of France. Mr. Bromfield brings the war close, as the story is told in the first person by David Sorrell, but it will be Anna herself that you will remember. This is an appealing novel which it is hard to lay down, and I think it will be hard to forget."

J. Dover Wilson on Falstaff

I DARE SAY that no other national poet presents quite the same problem as Shakespeare to the academic critics who study him. Goethe and Dante were great writers by vocation: they were responsible and always serious; they were conscious of everything they did, and everything they did was done with intention; they were great students and scholars themselves, and so always had something in common with the professional scholars who were to work over them. And this was hardly less true of Pushkin. But Shakespeare was not a scholar or self-consciously a spokesman for his age as Dante and Goethe were; he was not even an "intellectual." He was what the sports-writers call a "natural," and his career was the career of a playwright who had to appeal to the popular taste. He began by feeding the market with potboilers and patching up other people's plays, and he returned to these trades at the end. In the meantime, he had followed his personal bent by producing some extraordinary tragedies which seem to have got rather beyond the range of the Elizabethan theater and by allowing even his potboiling comedies to turn sour to such a degree as apparently to become unpalatable to his public. But he displayed all along toward his craft a rather superior and cavalier attitude which at moments even verged on the cynical—a kind of attitude which a Dante, or a Dostoevsky, could hardly have understood. He retires as a serious artist—in *Cymbeline* and *The Winter's Tale*—before he has stopped writing and says farewell to his audience, in *The Tempest*, through a delightful and rather thoughtful masque.

It would perhaps be an exaggeration to say, as John Jay Chapman did, that Shakespeare regarded the writing of plays as a harmless kind of nonsense. He had certainly, by the end of his life, come to see himself in the role of Prospero: a powerful and splendid enchanter. But it is difficult for the professional scholar to understand the professional playwright; and there is always the danger that a pedant who does come to direct his attention upon the theatrical tradition behind Shakespeare may end by attempting to resolve him into terms of mere stage conventions. It is equally difficult for the scholarly critic who has been nourished on the moralistic literature of the English or American nineteenth century to understand a pure enchanter for whom life is not real and earnest but a dream that must finally fade like the dramas in which he reflects it. Mr. J. Dover Wilson, the English scholar, whose books on *Hamlet* are well known and who has just published a study of *Henry IV* called *The Fortunes of Falstaff*, is an exception to both these limitations, and he has criticized them with much common sense. A good deal of his recent book is occupied, in fact, with exposing various errors that derive from these sources; and, though always pleasant to read, it is thus not always of especial interest to the ordinary reader or playgoer who is accustomed to getting Shakespeare at first hand and has never been bemused by the atmosphere, so curiously un-Shakespearean, engendered by the dramatist's commentators. It does not occur to us today to try, as was at one time a critical fashion, to examine the creations of Shakespeare as if they were actual persons about whom it would be possible to assemble complete and consistent biographies. Mr. Wilson shows how very different the development of Falstaff is from even the kind of presentation of character that one gets in a modern novelist who has worked out a dossier in advance. He makes us see how the personality of Falstaff is created as the long play progresses, and how it exists only in terms of this play. Nor is the ordinary admirer of Shakespeare very likely to have been misled by the theory of certain critics who cannot bear to admit that Falstaff is a rascal and who have attempted to prove, for example, that he never behaved like a coward: a school of opinion not hard to confute.

Mr. Wilson does occasionally himself fall into another kind of error. He belongs to the rarer group of critics—of whom A. W. Verrall, the Greek scholar, is one of the most conspicuous examples—who have themselves a touch of the creative artist, whose virtue is that they seem to wake the text to a new dynamic life by force of their own imaginations and whose fault is that they sometimes read into it new dramas of their own invention. This last is what has happened, I think, in the case of Mr. Wilson's version of the scene after the Gad's Hill robbery, in which Falstaff boasts of having put to rout a group of assailants whose number increases in the course of the conversation as the boastful mood carries him away. Mr. Wilson has convinced himself that this passage is not merely a comic "gag" of Shakespeare's not quite top vintage—in spite of the fact that these plays, especially *Henry V*, are full of crude and implausible jokes—but a particularly subtle bit of comedy only to be grasped by the most intelligent spectators: Falstaff has been aware all the time, according to Mr. Wilson, that the two men who chased him were the Prince and Poins, and, in boasting to them now of his boldness, he is merely playing up to their joke for reasons which Mr. Wilson leaves rather unclear. If Falstaff really knew all the time that his antagonists were the Prince and Poins, then he must also have been merely pretending when at Gad's Hill he ran away from them roaring—a supposition which is surely absurd and which it seems to me that Mr. Wilson rather slips out of facing. And, as it proceeds, Mr. Wilson's story of the affair of Prince Henry and Falstaff gets slightly at a tangent to Shakespeare's. He is excellent in tracing the phases through which Prince Hal and his companion pass in the two parts of *Henry IV* (the growing sense of responsibility of Hal under pressure of his father's impending death and the simultaneously increasing impudence of Falstaff, what Mr. Wilson calls his "comic hubris," which has been stimulated by the undeserved glory that he has acquired at the Battle of Shrewsbury); and in pointing out that the dramatist has been plotting these curves all along for the moment when they shall intersect, with the inevitable disastrous result. He is contending against the disposition to become sentimental over Falstaff and to denounce the crowned Hal as mean-spirited and harsh when he turns him off at the end so firmly. But I think that Mr. Wilson overdoes his case in trying to reduce the pathos when he talks about the "wicked smile" of Falstaff just after the repudiation, as he says, "Master Shallow, I owe you a thousand pound." The old man has been completely discredited; he must accept his humiliation, and he is sportsmanlike and hence pathetic. It is perhaps Falstaff's greatest line, the first stroke that makes us sympathize with him completely. It prepares the way in turn for the report of Falstaff's death in *Henry V*. And I think that Mr. Wilson goes entirely off the track—since he has already shown the close continuity between the two parts of *Henry IV*—in trying to rule out this deathbed as irrelevant. It is true that in the epilogue to *Henry IV* Shakespeare had announced to his audience an intention of making Falstaff play in *Henry V* a more considerable and more comic role than he does in the play which he actually wrote. But we do not know what Shakespeare may have then thought of writing; we only know what he did write; and he certainly shows Falstaff crushed. This is not a made-to-order sequel like *The Merry Wives of Windsor*: it is the true end of Falstaff's story.

I want to suggest another kind of view of the relation between Falstaff and Hal which has not occurred to Mr. Wilson and which—though my reading in this field is not great—I have never seen expressed. Certainly it is true, as Mr. Wilson insists, that *Henry IV* is not open to criticism on the ground that Prince Hal is the hero and that he is made to behave like a prig. As is usual with Shakespeare, the two main personalities are played off against one another with the full dramatic effectiveness that results from his making us feel that each is fulfilling the laws of his nature and that there is no easy escape from a conflict in which one of them has to break. Mr. Wilson has shown us, furthermore, that the adventures of Prince Hal with Falstaff run true to a traditional formula derived from the "morality" of Everyman or Youth and his temptation by Vanity and Riot, at the end of which the Elizabethan audience would expect to see virtue triumphant. But there is surely something more to this problem. Mr. Wilson, who much invokes Dr. Johnson as a witness to the worthiness of Henry, fails to take account of his remark to the effect that the reader's interest suffers a fatal slump from the moment when Falstaff and his friends fall victims to the new Henry's reforms. Most people probably do feel this. Most people probably feel that *Henry V* is, for Shakespeare, relatively thin and relatively journalistic. But if the dramatist really meant Henry V to be taken as a model of a prince, why should this be the case?

I believe that in Shakespeare's more conventional plays, we must always, in order to understand them, look for a personal pattern behind the ostensible plot. In saying, as I did above, that Shakespeare was a fabricator of potboilers both at the beginning and at the end of his life, I did not of course mean to imply that these pieces, even aside from their magnificent poetry, had nothing in them of serious interest. On the contrary, he could hardly write anything without projecting real emotional conflicts in the form of imagined personalities. Now, these Henry plays just precede *Julius Caesar*, and *Julius Caesar* just precedes *Hamlet*. The great salient patterns of Shakespeare that give us symbols for what is most personal and most profound are beginning to take shape in these chronicles. The reader finds his sympathy weighted (as no doubt the Elizabethans did, since Falstaff became so tremendously popular) for Falstaff as against Hal, because Shakespeare, though he can give us both sides and holds the dramatic balance, is identifying himself with Falstaff in a way he cannot do with the Prince. He has already made us sympathize queerly with those of his characters who have been bent out of line by deformities or social pressures, whose morality is twisted, whose motives are mixed. Faulconbridge runs away with *King John,* and Shylock, the villain of *The Merchant of Venice,* becomes by a single speech a great deal more interesting than Antonio. Has not even Richard III in his horrid way a fascination—as of a Quilp or a Punch whose motives we have been made to understand—which the author could not possibly give Richmond? Falstaff is not deformed in quite the same obvious way as these others, but he is both physically and morally monstrous, and his nature is also mixed. And from Falstaff through Brutus to Hamlet is not such a great step. Hamlet is also complex and also out of tune, though what is wrong with him is less obvious still; like Falstaff, he is at once quick-witted and extremely inept at action, a brilliant and constant talker and a man always at odds with his social group. The opposition between Falstaff and Henry unmistakably reappears in the contrast between Hamlet and Fortinbras; and "Master Shallow, I owe you a thousand pound," with the deathbed scene that follows, is to flower into the tragic eloquence of that series of final scenes in which Shakespeare is to make us feel that Hamlet and Othello and Lear and Antony and Coriolanus, for all their confusion and failure, have been rarer and nobler souls than the opponents, unworthy or worthy, who have brought their destruction about. In *Hamlet,* the Falstaff figure, with changed mask but a similar voice, holds the undisputed center of the stage; Prince Henry has dwindled to Fortinbras, who is felt mainly as an offstage force, but still represents the straight man of action who is destined to take over in the end. But later we shall have Antony and Octavius, Coriolanus and Aufidius. Here, too, the balance

will be evenly held, and we shall never get melodrama.
We are not allowed to sentimentalize over Antony any more
than we are over Falstaff. Octavius is perfectly right: he
does his duty as Henry does; but we shall always like
Antony better, just as we did poor old Falstaff. Falstaff
and Richard II are the two most conspicuous prototypes
of Shakespeare's tragic heroes.

April 29, 1944

A Toast and a Tear for Dorothy Parker

REREADING DOROTHY PARKER—in the Viking Portable
Library—has affected me, rather unexpectedly, with a distinct attack of nostalgia. Her poems do seem a little dated.
At their best, they are witty light verse, but when they
try to be something more serious, they tend to become a
kind of dilution of A. E. Housman and Edna Millay. Her
prose, however, is still alive. It seems to me as sharp and
as funny as in the years when it was first coming out. If
Ring Lardner outlasts our day, as I do not doubt that he
will, it is possible that Dorothy Parker will, too.

But the thing that I have particularly felt is the difference
between the general tone, the psychological and literary
atmosphere, of the period—the twenties and the earlier
thirties—when most of these pieces of Mrs. Parker's were
written, and the atmosphere of the present time. It was
suddenly brought home to me how much freer people
were—in their emotions, in their ideas and in expressing
themselves. In the twenties they could love, they could
travel, they could stay up late at night as extravagantly as
they pleased; they could think or say or write whatever
seemed to them amusing or interesting. There was a good
deal of irresponsibility, and a lot of money and energy
wasted, and the artistic activities of the time suffered somewhat from its general vices, but it was a much more favor-

able climate for writing than the period we are in now.

The depression put a crimp in incomes, and people began to have to watch their pockets. Then they began to watch their politics. The whole artistic and intellectual world became anxiously preoccupied with making sure that their positions were correct in relation to the capitalist system and the imminence or the non-imminence of a social revolution; they spent a good deal of time and print arguing with one another about it. Some writers who had been basing their work on the uproar and glamor of the boom grew discouraged and more or less stopped. The young writers who came out of college were likely to be short of cash and have no prospect of easy jobs; they were obliged to be circumspect. The tougher ones tried to work with the Communists or other radical groups; the more conventional became professors. Some tried to do both at the same time, with uncomfortable and unsatisfactory results, for they found themselves in the situation of being obliged to worry about both their standing with the academic authorities and the purity of their political line.

With the writings of Dorothy Parker you are still as far away from all this as you are with those of Scott Fitzgerald. It is a relief and a reassurance, in reading her soliloquies and dialogues—her straight short stories, which are sometimes sentimental, do not always wear quite so well—to realize how recklessly clever it used to be possible for people to be, and how personal and how direct. All her books had funereal titles, but the eye was always wide open and the tongue always quick to retort. Even those titles were sardonic exclamations on the part of an individual at the idea of her own demise. The idea of the death of a society had not yet begun working on people to paralyze their response to experience.

But the literary movement of the twenties showed a tendency to break down and peter out which we never should have expected at that time, when it seemed to us that American writing had just had a brilliant rebirth. It was a shock to know that Scott Fitzgerald, who had seemed

to be still on his way to fulfilling the promise of imperfect
books, was suddenly and prematurely dead; and we soon
found that this imperfect work had almost the look of a
classic: its value had been heightened by its rarity, since
there was not going to be any more of it either by him or
by anyone else. And we find when we take up this new
volume, which contains Dorothy Parker's complete published works, that a similar shift of feeling occurs. Mrs.
Parker is not yet dead nor has she altogether ceased writing: there are several new stories in this volume, and they
hold up with the earlier ones. But she nowadays produces
little, and she has suffered, to our disappointment, one of
the dooms of her generation. A decade or more ago she
went out to Hollywood and more or less steadily stayed
there, and, once away from her natural habitat, New York,
she succumbed to the expiatory mania that has become
epidemic with film-writers and was presently making
earnest appeals on behalf of those organizations which
talked about being "progressive" and succeeded in convincing their followers that they were working for the
social revolution, though they had really no other purpose
than to promote the foreign policy of the Soviet Union.
She ought, of course, to have been satirizing Hollywood
and sticking pins into fellow-travellers; but she has not,
so far as I know, ever written a word about either. There
are among the new pieces here a couple that deal with the
war—*The Lovely Leave* and *Song of the Shirt, 1941*—but
this collection mostly makes you feel that you are reliving
a vanished era. Except for one sketch of the Spanish War,
the record seems to break off abruptly sometime in the
early thirties.

Yet it, too, this collected volume, has a value derived
from rarity—a rarity like that of steel penknives, good
erasers and real canned sardines, articles of which the
supply has almost given out and of which one is only now
beginning to be aware of how excellent the quality was.
It seems to me, though I shall name no names, that it has
been one of the features of this later time that it produces

imitation books. There are things of which one cannot really say that they are either good books or bad books; they are really not books at all. When one has bought them, one has only got paper and print. When one has bought Dorothy Parker, however, one has really got a book. She is not Emily Brontë or Jane Austen, but she has been at some pains to write well, and she has put into what she has written a voice, a state of mind, an era, a few moments of human experience that nobody else has conveyed. And the format of this volume, as is not always the case, is appropriate to and worthy of the contents. It is compact, well printed, and small, easy to carry and handle: the kind of thing that ought to be encouraged, as distinguished from the more ponderous type of omnibus. The title is simply *Dorothy Parker*.

May 20, 1944

A Treatise on Tales of Horror

THERE HAS lately been a sudden revival of the appetite for tales of horror. First, Pocket Books published *The Pocket Mystery Reader* and *The Pocket Book of Mystery Stories*. Then came *Tales of Terror*, with an introduction by Boris Karloff; *Creeps by Night*, with an introduction by Dashiell Hammett; and *Best Ghost Stories of M. R. James* (all three brought out by World). Finally, Random House has produced a prodigious anthology called *Great Tales of Terror and the Supernatural*, edited by Herbert A. Wise and Phyllis Fraser.

One had supposed that the ghost story itself was already an obsolete form; that it had been killed by the electric light. It was only during the ages of candlelight that the race of ghosts really flourished, though they survived through the era of gas. A candle can always burn low and be blown out by a gust of air, and it is a certain amount of trouble to relight it, as is also the case with a gas-jet. But if you can reach out and press a button and flood every corner of the room, leaving the specter quite naked in his vapor, or if you can transfix him out of doors with a flashlight, his opportunities for haunting are limited. It is true that one of the most famous of ghost stories, Defoe's *Apparition of Mrs. Veal,* takes place in the afternoon; that it is a part of the effectiveness of *The Turn of the Screw* that its phantoms appear outdoors in broad daylight as well as indoors at night; and that the eeriest of all ghost stories supposed to be true, the anonymous book called *An Adventure,* purports to give the experiences of two English ladies visiting Versailles in the afternoon; but these are all in the nature of tours de force on the part of the apparitions or the authors. The common run of ghost needed darkness. It will be noticed in all these anthologies that most of the writers belong by training to the last decades of the nineteenth century, even though a few of their stories have been written in the first years of this.

What is the reason, then—in these days when a lonely country house is likely to be equipped with electric light, radio and telephone—for our returning to these antiquated tales? There are, I believe, two reasons: first, the longing for mystic experience which seems always to manifest itself in periods of social confusion, when political progress is blocked: as soon as we feel that our own world has failed us, we try to find evidence for another world; second, the instinct to inoculate ourselves against panic at the real horrors loose on the earth—Gestapo and G.P.U., tank attacks and airplane bombings, houses rigged with booby-traps—by injections of imaginary horror, which soothe us with the momentary illusion that the forces of madness and murder may be tamed and compelled to provide us with a mere dramatic entertainment. We even try to make them cozy and droll, as in *Arsenic and Old Lace,* which could hardly have become popular or even been produced on the stage at any other period of our history. This craving for homeopathic horror first began to appear some years ago in the movies—with the Frankenstein monsters, the werewolves, the vampires and the insane sadistic scientists, of whom such a varied assortment are now to be seen along West Forty-second Street; and recently, in such films as *The Uninvited*, the pictures, too, have been reaching back to pull toward us the phantom fringe which has been exploited by these anthologies.

The best of these volumes is the new Random House one, because it is the most comprehensive (though the book itself has the fault of so many American omnibuses and anthologies of being too cumbersome to handle comfortably in bed, the only place where one is likely to read ghost stories), and not unintelligently edited. The two collections in the Pocket Book series, both edited by Miss Lee Wright, are, however, quite well selected, and have the merit of costing only a quarter each. And yet one cannot read a large number of pieces in any of these compilations without feeling rather let down. The editors are always building up their authors: "Certain of these stories, like *Lost Hearts* and *The Ash-Tree*," says the foreword to the *Best Ghost Stories of M. R. James*, ". . . should, we think, be skipped altogether by the squeamish and faint of heart"; a story by Robert Hichens is "unsurpassed for its subtle unfolding of a particularly loathsome horror"; and *Caterpillars*, by E. F. Benson, is "brilliantly told, and without doubt . . . one of the most horrifying stories in this collection." Now, I find it very hard to imagine that any of these particular tales could scare anybody over ten. Two of them simply play on the gooseflesh that is stimulated in certain people by the idea of caterpillars or spiders, and demon caterpillars and demon spiders very easily seem absurd. Other stories much esteemed by these anthologists, such as the one mentioned above, by Robert Hichens—*How Love Came to Professor Guildea*—or Helen R. Hull's *Clay-Shuttered Doors*, have promising macabre ideas—a great scientist who has cut himself off from all human relationships but is driven to desperation by an invisible imbecile who loves him; the wife of an ambitious New Yorker, who regalvanizes her decaying body and goes on playing her social role several months after she has been killed in a motor accident—but they are trashily or weakly done and do not realize their full possibilities. In either case, the authors content themselves with suggesting unpleasant sensations. They fail to lay hold on the terrors that lie deep in the human psyche and that cause man to fear himself.

These collections, of course, aim primarily at popular entertainment; they do not pretend to a literary standard. But I should like to suggest that an anthology of considerable interest and power could be compiled by assembling horror stories by really first-rate modern writers, in which they have achieved their effects not merely by attempting to transpose into terms of contemporary life the old fairy-tales of goblins and phantoms but by probing psychological caverns where the constraints of that life itself have engendered disquieting obsessions.

I should start off with Hawthorne and Poe, who are represented in these collections, but I should include, also, Melville and Gogol, who are not. The first really great short stories of horror came in the early or middle nineteenth century, when the school of Gothic romance had achieved some sophistication and was adopting the methods of realism. All four of these authors wrote stories that were at the same time tales of horror and psychological or moral fables. They were not interested in spooks for their own sake; they knew that their demons were symbols, and they knew what they were doing with these symbols. We read the tales of Poe in our childhood, when all that we are likely to get out of them is shudders, yet these stories are also poems that express the most intense emotions. *The Fall of the House of Usher* is not merely an ordinary ghost story: the house—see the opening paragraph —is an image for a human personality, and its fate—see the fissure that runs through the wall—is the fate of a disrupted mind. And as for Gogol, he probably remains the very greatest master in this genre. I should put in at least *Viy* and *The Nose*—the former, a vampire story, one of the most terrific things of its kind ever written, and the latter, though it purports to be comic, almost equally a tale of horror, for it is charged with the disguised lurking meaning of a fear that has taken shape as a nightmare. I should include, also, *Bartleby the Scrivener* of Melville, which oddly resembles Gogol in this vein of the somber-grotesque, as well as *Benito Cereno*, a more plausible yet still nightmarish affair, which ought to be matched farther on by Conrad's *Heart of Darkness*.

In the latter part of the century, however, the period to which Conrad belongs, these fables tend to become impure. There was by that time much more pressure on the artist to report the material and social facts of the nineteenth-century world, and it seems difficult to combine symbolism with the inventories of naturalistic fiction or the discussion of public affairs. You have Stevenson, Kipling, Henry James. In Stevenson's case alone, this pressure did not inhibit his fancy, for he rarely wrote anything but fairy-tales, but he has much less intensity and substance than Conrad or Kipling or James. Nevertheless, though I might do without Jekyll and Hyde, I think I should have to have *Olalla* and *Thrawn Janet* (it is queer that a writer so popular in his time should be represented in none of these collections). But with Kipling you run into the cramping effects of a technical and practical period. I should include a couple of stories of Kipling's—say, *At the End of the Passage* and *Mrs. Bathurst*—as examples of borderline cases of the genuinely imaginative story which is nevertheless not first-rate. In such an early tale of Kipling's as *At the End of the Passage* or *The Phantom Rickshaw*, he is trying to write a mere vulgar ghost story, but something else that is authentic gets in. If we have carefully studied Kipling, we can recognize in the horrors of these tales—the blinded phantom, the wronged woman—obsessions that recur in his work and to which we can find the key in his life. But a story of this kind should convey its effect without our having to track down its symbols. We need nothing but the story itself to tell us that the author of *Viy* has put all the combined fascination and fear with which he was inspired by women into the vigil of the young student in the little wooden church beside the coffin of the farmer's daughter. When Kipling sets out later on to work up a more complex technique and attempts several layers of meaning, he gives us a piece like *Mrs. Bathurst*—the pursuit by a wronged woman, again—in which, however, the main character's sense of guilt is tied up through the symbol of the woman with his duty to the British Empire in connection with the Boer War, and he introduces a political element which seems clumsy and out of place in a ghost story and somehow gives Mrs. Bathurst a slight tinge of the newspaper cartoon. Henry James, a more serious writer, produced a strange special case in *The Turn of the Screw*. He asserted that he, too, had aimed merely at a conventional ghost story intended for a more knowing audience than that susceptible to the ordinary kind; but readers familiar with his work and conscious of his preoccupations have tended to see in the tale something more: the governess is not really, as she tells us, defending the children in her charge against the influence of malevolent spirits, she is frightening them herself with the projections of her own repressed emotions. There are, however, points in the story which are difficult to explain on this theory, and it is probable that James, like Kipling, was unconscious of having raised something more frightening than the ghosts he had contemplated. At any rate, I should put in *The Turn of the Screw,* and also *The Jolly Corner,* which seems to me James's other best ghost story. In this latter case, the author is of course quite conscious of what he is doing, but there is here, as in *Mrs. Bathurst,* an element rather difficult to assimilate (though Henry James does make us accept it) in the issue between England and the United States, a social and historical problem, which provides the moral of the fable.

During this period there were some very good ghost stories done by popular writers of distinction like Conan

Doyle and W. W. Jacobs, but, capital fairy-tales though *The Monkey's Paw* and *Playing With Fire* are, I should not admit them to my ideal collection. Nor should I—on the basis of the specimens I have read—include anything from a different school, which grew up in the late years of the century and which was stimulated perhaps by the encroachments of the spread of the new methods of lighting on the old-fashioned kind of ghost. This school, which is represented abundantly in the Random House collection, derives, I take it, from Arthur Machen, and features, instead of resurrected bodies and insubstantial phantoms, a demonology of ancient cults driven underground by Christianity but persisting into our own day, and exploits the identification of the Devil with the pagan god Pan. Machen's story on this theme called *The Great God Pan* (in the Random House collection) seems to me to sum up in a fatal way everything that was most "ham" in the aesthetic satanism of the *fin de siècle*. M. R. James, a great favorite of these anthologists, played countless variations on this theme and had some really fiendish flashes of fancy, but he never took any trouble to make his stories seem even halfway plausible, so his hobgoblins are always verging on parody.

A better writer is Algernon Blackwood, who belongs to this same general group and has an even greater reputation than M. R. James. He, too, tends to lean on anti-human creatures that embody the forces of nature, but he is interesting for another reason: you can see in him very clearly the shift from a belief in evil spirits as things that come to plague us from outside to a consciousness of terrors inside us that merely take possession of our minds. But where Kipling or Henry James knew how to dramatize these terrors in solid images that command our credence, Blackwood, beginning as a rule with a locale which he has actually observed and which he more or less convincingly describes, invariably transposes the story, from the moment when the supernatural element appears, onto a plane of melting, gliding nightmare where nothing seems really to be taking place. Now, a story of this kind, to

impress us, must *never* seem to be a dream. The tales of
Poe, for all the wildness of their fantasy, are as circumstantial as Swift or Defoe; when Gogol retells a Ukrainian
legend, he so stiffens its texture with authentic detail that
we seem to hear the voices of the peasants and smell the
countryside.

I should, therefore, decline to pass Algernon Blackwood,
but I should certainly admit Walter de la Mare, who sometimes errs in the direction of the too dreamlike but makes
up for it through poetic imagination. His story called
Seaton's Aunt comes close to being a masterpiece in this
genre, and I should include also *Out of the Deep*, which is
equally good in conception though not quite so good in
execution. (The first of these has been included in *The
Pocket Book of Mystery Stories* and the second in the
Random House anthology.) De la Mare, a great admirer
of Poe, has done work that is quite his own in this field of
supernatural fiction; it is in my opinion superior to his verse.
His stories at their best are poetic, psychologically subtle
and creepy to a high degree.

And, finally, I should include Franz Kafka, also absent
from any of these collections. Stories like *The Metamorphosis* and *Blumfeld, an Elderly Bachelor* are among the
best things of their kind. The first of these unpleasant pieces
deals with a young travelling salesman who suddenly wakes
up one morning to find that he has turned into an enormous roach, to the horror of his parents, with whom he
lives and who have been counting on him to pay off their
debts; the second tells of an office worker, a selfish and
bureaucratic upper clerk, who is haunted by two little
bouncing balls that represent his niggardly consciousness
of two children that help him in his office. The stories that
Kafka has written on these two unconventional subjects are
at the same time satires on the bourgeoisie and visions of
moral horror; narratives that are logical and compel our
attention, and fantasies that generate more shudders than
the whole of Algernon Blackwood and M. R. James combined. A master can make it seem more horrible to be

pursued by two little balls than by the spirit of a malignant Knight Templar, and more natural to turn into a cockroach than to be bitten by a diabolic spider. Kafka, who was writing these stories at the time of the last World War, had brought back the tale of terror to the true vein of Gogol and Poe. In his realm of imagination no social or political problems intrude in such a way as to spoil the show. The modern bourgeoisie and the Central European bureaucracy have turned into the enchanted denizens of a world in which, prosaic though it is, we can find no firm foothold in reality and in which we can never even be certain whether souls are being saved or damned. As an artist in this field of horror, Kafka is among the greatest. Living in the era of Freud, he went straight for the morbidities of the psyche with none of the puppetry of specters and devils that earlier writers still carried with them. Whether his making out of these subjects at that time of day the Hoffmannesque fantasies that he did make, and whether the rapt admiration for them in *our* time represents a retrogression or a progress in the development of modern literature in general, I shall not attempt to decide.

May 27, 1944

A Guide to *Finnegans Wake*

A Skeleton Key to Finnegans Wake, by Joseph Campbell and Henry Morton Robinson, is an indispensable book for anyone interested in Joyce and should make many new readers for *Finnegans Wake*.

This last book of James Joyce is a very great poem, one of the top works of literature of our time. It is in some ways, in fact, a more extraordinary production than *Ulysses*—digging deeper into human psychology, breaking new intellectual ground and exhibiting Joyce's musical genius as perhaps none of his other books does. Yet *Finnegans Wake* has acquired the reputation of being inordinately difficult to read, and Joyce has even been accused in some quarters of having perpetrated an insolent hoax or excreted an insane mess of gibberish. Even readers who have admired *Ulysses* have been reluctant to tackle its successor. But the book has now been out five years, and it is time that these doubts and inhibitions were dispelled. The appearance of the Campbell-Robinson key should open a new era in the acceptance and currency of *Finnegans Wake*. In recommending this guide, however, I want to make a few suggestions of my own which are, it seems to me, needed to supplement this introduction.

In the first place, it is an excellent thing, though perhaps not absolutely required, for the reader to be fairly familiar with the other writings of Joyce. Then, it will help this reader immensely if he comes to *Finnegans Wake* with some acquaintance with Virgil, Dante and Milton. It is a better equipment for Joyce to know something of the most accomplished masters of the writing of fiction in verse than to have formed one's ideas of literary art from the reading of modern novels. The art of narrative literature was brought by the great epic poets of the past to a point from which it later declined with the rise of the prose novel. A man like Dante has a command of language, a power to make it render the nuances of atmosphere, color, sound, phases of feeling and traits of personality, in comparison with which the writing of even a respectable novelist of the infancy of the novel, like Fielding, seems quite wooden, hardly writing at all. It was only with the Romantics that the language of prose fiction began to be flexible and sensitive enough to represent directly—by the sound and the look and the connotations of words—the things that it was describing. Flaubert was the first writer of prose fiction to challenge the ancients on this ground, and Flaubert had his limitations: his effects, like his mood, are monotonous. But he was studied and emulated by Joyce, whose range was enormously wider and who turned out to be, in fact, as T. S. Eliot said, the greatest master of language in

English since Milton. *Ulysses* and *Finnegans Wake* are epics which not only perform feats of style hitherto unknown in the novel but also, like the *Æneid* and *The Divine Comedy*, deal with national myths and the destiny of man in a way that is unexpected for the ordinary novel reader. *Ulysses* had still enough of the framework of conventional fiction so that this ordinary reader could navigate it at the cost of a little effort. *Finnegans Wake*, however, though it was more "realistic" than it looked at first sight, seemed completely to have cast off the conventions.

The epic of *Ulysses* consisted of a day in the lives of certain characters; that of *Finnegans Wake* covers the sleeping life of a man during a single night. The next difficulty is to grasp this design. We may understand the purpose of Dante to construct an all-comprehensive poem out of a vision of Hell, Purgatory and Heaven; and we may not be baffled in the least by such literary renderings of dream or trance as De Quincey's opium rhapsodies, Flaubert's *Tentation de Saint Antoine*, Lewis Carroll's Alice books or the dreams in Dostoevsky's novels. Yet we may not be prepared for a book of more than six hundred pages which plunges us into a man's sleeping mind and keeps us still there till he is about to wake up. Nor is it easy at first to realize that Joyce is using the resources of a poet not only to present the billowing emotions and the kaleidoscopic imagery of a dream but also to render with accuracy all the physical states of sleep. I may give a simple example, since the authors of the *Skeleton Key* have not emphasized this aspect of *Finnegans Wake*. The heavy breathing and the snoring of the hero run all through the book and are exploited for poetic effects which it might well be thought that no great poet would be so bold or so absurd as to attempt and which yet are made to contribute triumphantly to some of Joyce's most lyrical writing. The heaving of the four deep breaths which always marks the hero's subsidence into a deeper stratum of sleep provides much grotesque humor, such as the "What a hauhauhauhaudibble thing, to be cause! How, Mutt?" of the inarticulate conversation between the loutish prehistoric men; but it also gives the fall of darkness and the widening of the river at the close of the "Anna Livia Plurabelle" chapter, one of the incomparably beautiful things in the book: "Dark hawks hear us. Night! Night! My ho head halls. I feel as heavy as yonder stone," etc.

The sleeper in *Finnegans Wake* is a man named H. C. Earwicker, who keeps a pub on the Liffey and has a family consisting of a wife, one daughter and twin sons. The nexus of his family relations and Earwicker's career in Dublin are the immediate materials of his dream, but Joyce, with his epic intentions and a kind of modern Jungian conception of a myth-creating mind of the race, has contrived to make his dream universal. How he has done this I need not explain in detail because Campbell and Robinson have explained it better than anybody else has yet done. The dream itself is a myth, with characters and a plot of its own, and though its main elements multiply their aspects with all the shifting metamorphosis of a dream, they are constant and perfectly plain. Do not be put off by the opening pages, which have mysteries for even the adept at Joyce. Earwicker has fallen asleep: he has lost consciousness, but he is not yet dreaming. The moment seems dark and blank, but it is a blur of all his being holds. Joyce has resorted to the device, in *Finnegans Wake*, of conveying the ambiguities and vagueness of the visions and sensations of sleep by the invention of punning portmanteau words like the language of *Jabberwocky*, and these words have here been crammed with meanings to a point where all the many symbols appear hopelessly jumbled and mashed. Messrs. Campbell and Robinson, however, have unpacked a good many of these meanings, so that we can see what was in the portmanteaux of the first paragraphs of *Finnegans Wake*, and thus have eliminated one of the obstacles which have been baffling the willing reader. When you get through this choked defile and the action of the dream begins, you will find yourself among recognizable presences that flicker but speak and move, and the powerful current of language will continue to carry you along even through queer interruptions and eclipses. If you will read the Campbell-Robinson synopsis at the beginning of their *Skeleton Key*, you will see that the large architecture of *Finnegans Wake*, in spite of the complication of detail, is solid, precise and simple, as the principal themes of the book are matters of obvious universal experience, so utterly commonplace that the difficulty in grasping them comes sometimes from the sophisticated reader's unreadiness to accept anything so little esoteric as the basic facts of family life, the mixed moral nature of man and the phenomena of birth, growth and death rather than from the dense psychological web which Joyce has spun among them or the variegated legendry and language with which they have been embroidered.

The great thing is to get the hang and to follow the line of the myth, and this Campbell and Robinson will help you to do. They have provided a paraphrase of Joyce which disentangles and tightens this line. One may not approve every step of their trail, every abridgment, selection or reading, and they have sometimes made actual errors, but they have opened up the book to the public at the cost of much patience and care, and they deserve a citation from the Republic of Letters for having succeeded in bringing it out at this time. Mr. Campbell is a folklore scholar, with considerable knowledge of Ireland, who is particularly qualified to interpret Joyce on his mythological and historical sides; Mr. Robinson, who is an editor of *Reader's Digest*, here applies a special skill acquired in whittling down magazine articles to condensing a masterpiece.

This condensation, of course, is compelled to leave a great deal out. The authors' paraphrase of Joyce necessarily strips away most of the master's magnificent poetry, and thus transmits no idea at all of the *emotional* power of the original, since, where everything is not merely described but represented directly, the style is involved with the content to a degree which is not common with contemporary writers. In the Campbell-Robinson key, you will

find almost no indication of the infinite variation in the
texture and tone of the writing which reflects the various
phases of the night.

Another matter which the authors neglect, in holding on
to the sequence of the myth, is the family situation, which
has its grip on the whole fantasia. The real story behind
the dream story is something that we have to guess at and
which it becomes one of the fascinations of reading *Finnegans Wake* to work out. There are moments when it
breaks through the myth with its insistent and naked facts,
and it is at all times the hidden director which determines
the shape of the dream by its alternate impulsions and
checks, its quick blendings and its sudden reversals. The
sleeper, who passes from fatigue to refreshment, from
death to resurrection, is enacting a universal drama which
is enacted every night by every man in the world; but every
man is a particular man, and this man is a particular Dub-
liner, asleep on a certain night in a room above a certain
pub in the bosom of a certain family. The authors of the
Skeleton Key have pretty nearly combed the real family
away in presenting their simplification of the myth; they
tend to disregard the indications which Joyce is very careful to plant about Earwicker's real situation; and they do
not always seem quite clear about the author's technique
in dealing with the connection between the dream and
these realities. They, for example, simply follow the language of the dream in the question-and-answer chapter,
which is intended, though the real questions and answers
are always just around the corner from the dreamed ones,
to give the reader a very definite statement of the location
and personnel of the household; and they seem to think
that Earwicker, through part of the book, has been lying
drunk on the floor of the pub and that he goes upstairs
to bed at some point, and, later, in the scene before dawn,
when one of the twins wakes the mother and she goes into
his room to calm him, that the husband gets up and goes
in with her and afterwards has intercourse with her;
whereas it is plain that, in the first case, the falling on

the floor and the going upstairs themselves take place in the dream, and that, in the second, he has hardly awakened but, half aware of what his wife is doing, has sunk back into fitful slumber. It is an essential feature of the plan of the book, it makes its artistic unity, that Earwicker shall be always in bed and that he shall never wake up till morning—just the moment after the book ends. The later chapters of the *Skeleton Key* are thus definitely unsatisfactory. The authors prove themselves heroically strong in the cracking of such formidable nuts as the colloquy between St. Patrick and the Archdruid, but they are weak and even misleading on the more obvious human elements which make the end of *Finnegans Wake* one of the greatest things Joyce ever wrote.

In any case, if you have not tried *Finnegans Wake*, you cannot do better than get it and get the Campbell-Robinson key and prepare to have them around for years. A few more last words of guidance. The conditions for reading this book are different, so far as I know, from those for reading any other ever written. You have to take it rather slowly, a section at a time, and you have to keep on rereading it. Joyce worked on it through seventeen years, and it is equivalent to about seventeen books by the ordinary gifted writer. You may think it too much that Joyce should ask you to strain your wits over solving his elaborate puzzles, but the fact is that a good deal of the book, once you see the general pattern, is readable and comprehensible even when the language is queer. Joyce counts on a certain dimness to give the effect of a dream; and for people who do like to solve puzzles, the puzzles are fun to solve. Today, when we are getting so many books in which the style is perfectly clear but the meaning nonexistent or equivocal, it affords a certain satisfaction to read something that looks like nonsense on the surface but underneath makes perfect sense. Admirers of Balzac and Trollope think nothing of devoting years to reading their favorites through, and why should we grudge time to Joyce? The demands that he makes are considerable, but the rewards he provides are astounding. I do not deny that he is tedious at times: I am bored by the relentless *longueurs* of some of the middle chapters of *Finnegans Wake* just as I am bored by those of the latter part of *Ulysses*, and I have found it puts me straight to sleep to try to follow the charting of these wastes which has intrepidly been carried out by the authors of the *Skeleton Key*, just as it did to read Joyce's original. But it is an exciting, a unique experience to find pages that have seemed to us meaningless start into vivid life, full of energy, brilliance, passion. The chance to be among the first to explore the wonders of *Finnegans Wake* is one of the few great intellectual and aesthetic treats that these last bad years have yielded.

August 5, 1944

A Long Talk about Jane Austen

THERE HAVE BEEN several revolutions of taste during the last century and a quarter of English literature, and through them all perhaps only two reputations have never been affected by the shifts of fashion: Shakespeare's and Jane Austen's. We still agree with Scott about Jane Austen, just as we agree with Ben Jonson about Shakespeare. From Scott, Southey, Coleridge and Macaulay (to say nothing of the Prince Regent, who kept a set of her works "in every one of his residences") to Kipling and George Moore, Virginia Woolf and E. M. Forster, she has compelled the amazed admiration of writers of the most diverse kinds, and I should say that Jane Austen and Dickens rather queerly present themselves today as the only two English novelists (though not quite the only novelists in English) who belong in the very top rank with the great fiction writers of Russia and France. Jane Austen, as Mr. Stark Young once said, is perhaps the only English example of that spirit of classical comedy that is more natural to the Latin people than to ours and that Molière represents for the French. That this spirit should have embodied itself in England in the mind of a well-bred spinster, the daughter of a country clergyman, who never saw any more of the world than was made possible by short visits to London and a residence of a few years in Bath and who found her subjects mainly in the problems of young provincial girls looking for husbands, seems one of the most freakish of the many anomalies of English literary history.

In *Speaking of Jane Austen,* by G. B. Stern and Sheila Kaye-Smith, two of Jane Austen's sister novelists have collaborated to pay her homage. Both Miss Stern and Miss Kaye-Smith have read the six novels again and again, and they have at their fingers' ends every trait, every speech, every gesture of every one of Jane Austen's people. Here they discuss, in alternate chapters, which give the effect of a conversation, a variety of aspects of their subject. Miss Kaye-Smith is especially concerned with the historical background of the novels: she turns up a good deal that is interesting about the costume and food of the period and the social position of clergymen, and she traces the reflection, so meager and dim, of the cataclysmic political events that took place during Miss Austen's lifetime. Miss Stern is more preoccupied with the characters, whom she sometimes treats as actual people, classifying them on principles of her own and speculating about their lives beyond the story; sometimes criticizes from the point of view of a novelist who would see the situation in some cases a little differently, modifying or filling out a character or assigning a heroine to a different mate. The two ladies debate together the relative merits of the novels, agreeing that *Pride and Prejudice* belongs not at the top but toward the bottom of the list, and partly agreeing and partly not as to which of the characters are least successful. They have notes on Miss Austen's language and they underline some of her fine inconspicuous strokes. They make an effort to evoke the personalities of characters who are mentioned but never appear, and they have concocted a terrific quiz, which few readers, I imagine, could pass.

The book thus contains a good deal that will be interesting to those interested in Jane Austen, though neither Miss Stern nor Miss Kaye-Smith, it seems to me, really goes into the subject so deeply as might be done. My impression is that the long study of Jane Austen which has lately been published by Queenie Leavis in the English magazine called *Scrutiny* gets to grips with her artistic development in a way that the present authors, who do not mention Mrs. Leavis' essay, have scarcely even attempted to do. Yet *Speaking of Jane Austen*, as an informal symposium, revives the enthusiasm of the reader and stimulates him to think about the questions suggested by Miss Kaye-Smith and Miss Stern. Let me contribute a few comments of my own which will bring certain of these matters to attention:

1. The half-dozen novels of Jane Austen were written in two sets of three each, with an interval of about ten years between the two: *Pride and Prejudice, Sense and Sensibility* and *Northanger Abbey; Mansfield Park, Emma* and *Persuasion.* The first of these lots, both in its satiric comedy and in the pathos of *Sense and Sensibility*, is quite close to the eighteenth century, whereas the second, with its psychological subtlety and such realism as the episode in *Mansfield Park* in which Fanny goes back to her vulgar home, is much closer to what we call "modern." In the second lot, the set comic character of the type of Lady Catherine de Bourgh, who at moments, as Miss Stern points out, falls into the tone of an old-fashioned play, tends to give way to another kind of portraiture—as in the small country community of *Emma*—which is farther from caricature and more recognizable as a picture of everyday life, and in *Persuasion,* a sensitivity to landscape and a tenderness of feeling appear that have definitely a tinge of the romantic. It is not true, as has been sometimes complained, that Miss Austen took no interest in nature, though this last novel is the only one of her books of which one

clearly remembers the setting. Miss Kaye-Smith does note of *Persuasion* that "the weather and scenery have taken on some of the emotional force that permeates the whole book." But both authors seem to treat the novels as if they have always coëxisted in time, instead of forming a sequence. What I miss in *Speaking of Jane Austen* is any account of the successive gradations, literary and psychological, which lead from *Pride and Prejudice* to *Persuasion*.

2. The authors of this book both believe that there is something wrong with *Mansfield Park*, and they have a great deal to say about it. They feel that the chief figure, Fanny Price, a poor relation who immolates herself to the family of a great country house, is too meaching—too "creep-mouse," Miss Kaye-Smith says—to be an altogether sympathetic heroine, and that in this case the author herself, in a way that is not characteristic, adopts a rather pharisaical attitude toward the more fun-loving and sophisticated characters. Miss Kaye-Smith tries to explain this attitude by suggesting that Jane Austen at this period may have come under the influence of the Evangelical Movement, to which two references are to be found in the book.

To the reviewer, this line of criticism in regard to *Mansfield Park* is already very familiar—it seems to represent a reaction which is invariable with feminine readers; yet I have never felt particularly the importance of the objections that are made on these grounds nor been shaken in my conviction that *Mansfield Park* is artistically the most nearly perfect of the novels. It is true that I have not read it for thirty years, so that I have had time to forget the moralizings that bother Miss Kaye-Smith and Miss Stern, but the sensations I remember to have had were purely aesthetic ones: a delight in the focussing of the complex group through the ingenuous eyes of Fanny, the balance and harmony of the handling of the contrasting timbres of the characters, which are now heard in combination, now set off against one another. I believe that, in respect to Jane Austen's heroines, the point of view of men readers is somewhat different from that of women ones. The woman reader wants to identify herself with the heroine, and she rebels at the idea of being Fanny. The male reader neither puts himself in Fanny's place nor imagines himself marrying Fanny any more than he does the nice little girl in Henry James's *What Maisie Knew,* a novel which *Mansfield Park* in some ways quite closely resembles. What interests him in Miss Austen's heroines is the marvellous portraiture of a gallery of different types of women, and Fanny, with her humility, her priggishness and her innocent and touching good faith, is a perfect picture of one kind of woman.

Whatever tone Jane Austen may sometimes take, what emerge and give the book its value are characters objectively seen, form and movement conceived aesthetically. It is this that sets Jane Austen apart from so many other women novelists—whether, like the author of *Wuthering Heights* or the author of *Gone With the Wind,* of the kind that make their power felt by a projection of their feminine day-dreams, or of the kind, from *Evelina* to *Gentlemen Prefer Blondes,* that amuse us by mimicking people. Miss Austen is almost unique among the novelists of her sex in being deeply and steadily concerned, not with the vicarious satisfaction of emotion (though the Cinderella theme, of course, does figure in several of her novels) nor with the skilful exploitation of gossip, but, as the great masculine novelists are, with the novel as a work of art.

3. *Emma,* which both these critics adore, is with Jane Austen what *Hamlet* is with Shakespeare. It is the book of hers about which her readers are likely to disagree most; they tend either to praise it extravagantly or to find it dull, formless and puzzling. The reason for this, I believe, is that, just as in the case of *Hamlet,* there is something outside the picture which is never made explicit in the story but which has to be recognized by the reader before it is possible for him to appreciate the book. Many women readers feel instinctively the psychological rightness of the behavior

attributed to Emma, and they are the ones who admire the novel. Some male readers, like Justice Holmes, who was certainly a connoisseur of fiction yet who wrote to Sir Frederick Pollock that, "bar Miss Bates," he was "bored by *Emma*," never succeed in getting into the story because they cannot see what it is all about. Why does Emma take up her two protégées? Why does she become so much obsessed by her plans for them? Why does she mistake the realities so and go so ludicrously wrong about them? Why does it take her so unconscionably long to reach the obvious rapproachment with Knightley?

The answer is that Emma is not interested in men except in the paternal relation. Her actual father is a silly old woman: in their household it is Emma herself who, motherless as she is, assumes the functions of head of the family; it is she who takes the place of the parent and Mr. Woodhouse who becomes the child. It is Knightley who has checked and rebuked her, who has presided over her social development, and she accepts him as a substitute father; she finally marries him and brings him into her own household, where his role is to reinforce Mr. Woodhouse. Miss Stern sees the difficulties of this odd situation. "Oh, Miss Austen," she cries, "it was *not* a good solution; it was a bad solution, an unhappy ending, could we see beyond the last pages of the book." But among the contretemps she foresees she does not mention what would surely have been the worst. Emma, who was relatively indifferent to men, was inclined to infatuations with women; and what reason is there to believe that her marriage with Knightley would prevent her from going on as she had done before: from discovering a new young lady as appealing as Harriet Smith, dominating her personality and situating her in a dream-world of Emma's own in which Emma would be able to confer on her all kinds of imaginary benefits but which would have no connection whatever with her condition or her real possibilities? This would worry and exasperate Knightley and be hard for him to do anything about. He would be lucky if he did not presently find himself saddled, along with the other awkward features of the arrangement, with one of Emma's young protégées as an actual member of the household.

I do not mean to suggest for *Emma* any specific Freudian formula, but I feel sure that it is the one of her novels in which the author's own peculiar "conditioning" is most curiously and clearly seen. Jane Austen spent all her life with persons related to her by blood—her parents, her five brothers, her single unmarried sister—and the experience behind the relationships imagined by her in her novels is always an experience of relationships of blood, of which that between sisters is certainly the most deeply felt. Miss Stern and Miss Kaye-Smith are agreed with George Moore that Marianne's love for Willoughby in *Sense and Sensibility* is the most passionate thing in Jane Austen; but isn't it rather the emotion of Elinor as she witnesses her sister's disaster than Marianne's emotion over Willoughby of which the poignancy is communicated to the reader? The involvement with one another of the sisters is the real central theme of the book, just as the relation of Elizabeth to her sisters is so vital a part of *Pride and Prejudice*. For, though Miss Austen's intelligence was free to follow and understand other women when they were flirting or comfortably married, hunting husbands or breaking their hearts, she seems always to have been held suspended by the web of her original family ties. To some special equilibrium of the kind, which she never felt the necessity of upsetting, she must partly have owed the coolness, the patience, the poise, the leisure of mind to work at writing for its own sake, that made it possible for her to become a great artist. The solicitude of the sober Elinor Dashwood watching her giddy sister Marianne becomes in time the detached interest of the author looking on at the adventures of her heroines. In the last of her novels, *Persuasion*, one does find a different element and feel a personal emotion of the author's—a tinge of sadness at a woman's self-fulfilment missed—but the pattern is still much the same. Anne Elliot is herself a young sister: she, too, has a big sister, Lady Russell, who, like Emma, has misled her protégée—in this case, by discouraging her from marrying and nearly spoiling her life. Miss Stern and Miss Kaye-Smith do not care much for Lady Russell as a character; but she is worth thinking seriously about as a very important motif in Jane Austen. The comedy of the false sister-relationship of *Emma* has turned into something almost tragic.

June 24, 1944

"You Can't Do This to Me!" Shrilled Celia

The Robe, by Lloyd C. Douglas, has become, from the point of view of sales, one of the greatest successes of publishing history. Published in October, 1942, it stood at one time at the head of the best-seller list for fiction for eleven consecutive months, and is still well up toward the top. It has sold, in less than two years, one million, four hundred and fifty thousand copies, and the publishers estimate that it has been read by five times that number of people. Houghton Mifflin, with their restricted supply of paper, have twice had the book reset in order to reduce the number of pages, and have had to resort to other special economies to meet the demand at all. They have announced, in the *Publishers' Weekly*, a vast new advertising campaign for August, and one sometimes gets the impression that they have ceased to bring out any other books. One of their publicity releases reports that a copy of *The Robe*, auctioned off at the opening of the Fifth War Loan Drive, brought $525,000 in War Bonds.

Never having looked into this book, I lately decided that it was time for me to take cognizance of it. I have procured a copy of *The Robe*, and what I have found in it has been rather surprising. Instead of the usual trash aimed at Hollywood and streamlined for the popular magazines, one is confronted with something that resembles an old-fashioned historical novel for young people. Here is the tone of the opening page: "Because she was only fifteen and busy with her growing up, Lucia's periods of reflection were brief and infrequent, but this morning she felt weighted with responsibility. Last night her mother, who rarely talked to her about anything more perplexing than the advantages of clean hands and a pure heart, had privately discussed the possible outcome of Father's reckless remarks yesterday in the Senate, and Lucia, flattered by this confidence, had declared maturely that Prince Gaius wasn't in a position to do anything about it. But after she had gone to bed, Lucia began to fret. . . . They would all have to be careful now or they might get into serious trouble. The birds had awakened her early. She was not yet used to their flutterings and twitterings; for they had returned much sooner than usual, Spring having arrived and unpacked before February's lease was up. Lucia roused to a consciousness of the fret that she had taken to bed with her. It was still there, like a toothache. . . . For the past year or more, Lucia had been acutely conscious of her increasing height and rapid development into womanhood, but here on this expanse of tessellated tiling she always felt very insignificant. . . . No matter how old she became, she would be ever a child here."

There are five hundred and fifty-six pages of this. It is a story of the Roman Empire in the days of early Christianity, and its appeal is exactly the same as that of *The Last Days of Pompeii*, *Quo Vadis?* and *Ben-Hur*. The surface has been brought up to date by diluting the old grandiose language of the novel of ancient Rome with a jargon which sounds as if Dr. Douglas had picked it up during the years when, as the publishers' leaflet tells us, he was a counsellor of college students at the Universities of Michigan and Illinois. The aristocratic Romans are always saying things like "You're definitely drunk," "But what's the matter with idols? They're usually quite artistic!," "Indeed! Well—she'd better be good!," "I wouldn't know," "What do you mean—'a Christian'?" At one point a lady

of Tiberius' court addresses her noble lover as follows:
"You liked me well enough until you came here and noticed
this Gallus girl's curves! And it's plain to see she despises
you! . . . You can't do this to me! Where will *you* stand
with Sejanus when I tell him you have treated me like an
ordinary trollop?" But, for the rest, it is as leisurely, as
formless and as careful of all the maidenly proprieties as
any novel of the nineteenth century. It differs from Bulwer-
Lytton only in being written worse. Dr. Douglas has woven,
in *The Robe*, an almost unrivalled fabric of old clichés,
in which one of the only attempts at a literary heightening
of effect is the substitution for the simple "said" of other
more pretentious verbs—so that the characters are always
shrilling, barking, speculating, parrying, wailing, wheedling
or grunting whatever they have to say.

It is so difficult, when one first glances into *The Robe*,
to imagine that any literate person with even the faintest
trace of literary taste could ever get through more than
two pages of it for pleasure that one is astounded and ter-
rified at the thought that seven million Americans have
found something in it to hold their attention. What is the
explanation of this? Dr. Douglas himself, in an article distinguished by both modesty and good sense (*Why I Wrote
"The Robe,"* in the June *Cosmopolitan*), has indicated a
part of the answer. In the first place, he says, you can
always score a success by writing a novel about Jesus, if
you take care to avoid the controversies which have split
the later Christians into sects. He cites *Ben-Hur*, which
"sold more than a million copies during one of the most
placid decades in American history," and a novel called
In His Steps, by a clergyman in Kansas. But there is also,
perhaps, he adds, a special reason why a novel about Jesus
should be widely read at this time. It is quite natural that
people should find it a relief to hear about somebody who
was interested in healing the blind and the crippled rather
than in blinding and crippling people, and in comforting
the persecuted rather than in outlawing large groups of
human beings. This must certainly be true, and there are

also special reasons why Dr. Douglas' picture of Jesus should particularly command attention. Dr. Douglas, who is a Congregational minister and the son of a country parson, has an asset which can only be described as old-time Christian feeling. He is a genuine man of God of the type that used to do his best in the American small-town pulpit and that the community felt it could rely on. He is an anachronism, but he represents something that a good many Americans must feel to be reassuring. And, besides this, he has given to *The Robe* one virtue which can make a good bad novel, just as it constitutes a *sine qua non* for every really excellent one: he has imagined the whole thing for himself. *The Robe* has not been made out of other books: Dr. Douglas has lived the story—he has attempted to see for himself how the Christians would look to the Romans and how the Romans would look to the Jews. The fact that this has been done many times before does not deter Dr. Douglas or prevent him from creating in his story a certain atmosphere of suspense and adventure. He has set out to track down a conceivable Jesus in an alien but conceivable world; and his book, on its lower level, has the same kind of dramatic effectiveness as Bernard Shaw's *Saint Joan*. Finally, we must count it to him for righteousness that Dr. Douglas has had the courage to let his hero and heroine, at the end of the story, be executed as martyrs to the new religion instead of leaving them on the threshold of a comfortable marriage with a starry-eyed kiss and a fadeout.

When, therefore, one compares *The Robe* with the frankly faked publishers' goods with which the public are usually fed, one sees that Dr. Douglas' novel is a work of a certain purity and that the author deserves a certain respect. It is rather to the credit of the millions who have been buying or borrowing *The Robe* that they should prefer a long and tedious novel about the influence of the power of Jesus on the Roman who carried out the crucifixion to the livelier and easier productions which have been specially flavored to please them. It demonstrates that the

ordinary reader, even in our ghastly time, does long for
moral light, that he cannot live by bilge alone. But that
seven and a half million Americans should not find it in the
least distasteful to devour five hundred and fifty pages of
Dr. Douglas' five-and-ten-cent-store writing is something
to give pause to anyone who may have supposed that the
generation of Mencken had lifted American taste a little
above the level of Gene Stratton-Porter and Harold Bell
Wright.

August 26, 1944

Katherine Anne Porter

MISS KATHERINE ANNE PORTER has published a new book of
stories, her third: *The Leaning Tower and Other Stories.*
To the reviewer, Miss Porter is baffling because one cannot take hold of her work in any of the obvious ways.
She makes none of the melodramatic or ironic points that
are the stock in trade of ordinary short-story writers; she
falls into none of the usual patterns and she does not show
anyone's influence. She does not exploit her personality
either inside or outside her work, and her writing itself
makes a surface so smooth that the critic has little opportunity to point out peculiarities of color or weave. If he
is tempted to say that the effect is pale, he is prevented
by the realization that Miss Porter writes English of a purity
and precision almost unique in contemporary American
fiction. If he tries to demur that some given piece fails
to mount with the accelerating pace or arrive at the final
intensity that he is in the habit of expecting in short stories,
he is deterred by a nibbling suspicion that he may not
have grasped its meaning and have it hit him with a sudden
impact some minutes after he has closed the book.

Not that this meaning is simple to formulate even after
one has felt its emotional force. The limpidity of the sen-

tence, the exactitude of the phrase, are deceptive in that the thing they convey continues to seem elusive even after it has been communicated. These stories are not illustrations of anything that is reducible to a moral law or a political or social analysis or even a principle of human behavior. What they show us are human relations in their constantly shifting phases and in the moments of which their existence is made. There is no place for general reflections; you are to live through the experience as the characters do. And yet the writer has managed to say something about the values involved in the experience. But what is it? I shall try to suggest, though I am afraid I shall land in ineptitude.

Miss Porter's short stories lend themselves to being sorted into three fairly distinct groups. There are the studies of family life in working-class or middle-class households (there are two of these in *The Leaning Tower*), which, in spite of the fact that the author is technically sympathetic with her people, tend to be rather bitter and bleak, and, remarkable though they are, seem to me less satisfactory than the best of her other stories. The impression we get from these pieces is that the qualities that are most amiable in human life are being gradually done to death in the milieux she is presenting, but Miss Porter does not really much like these people or feel comfortable in their dismal homes, and so we, in turn, don't really much care. Another section of her work, however, contains what may be called pictures of foreign parts, and here Miss Porter is much more successful. The story which gives its name to her new collection and which takes up two-fifths of the volume belongs to this category. It is a study of Germany between the two wars in terms of a travelling American and his landlady and fellow-lodgers in a Berlin rooming house. By its material and its point of view, it rather recalls Christopher Isherwood's *Goodbye to Berlin*, but it is more poetic in treatment and more general in implication. The little plaster leaning tower of Pisa which has been cherished by the Viennese landlady but gets broken by her

American tenant stands for something in the destruction of which not merely the Germans but also the Americans have somehow taken a criminal part (though the American is himself an artist, he finds that he can mean nothing to the Germans but the power of American money). So, in a fine earlier story, *Hacienda*, a Mexican peon is somehow destroyed—with no direct responsibility on the part of any of the elements concerned—by a combination of Soviet Russians intent on making a Communist movie, their American business manager and a family of Mexican landowners.

In both cases, we are left with the feeling that, caught in the meshes of interwoven forces, some important human value has been crushed. These stories especially, one gathers, are examples of what Miss Porter means when she says, in her foreword to *Flowering Judas* in the Modern Library edition, that most of her "energies of mind and spirit have been spent in the effort to grasp the meaning" of the threats of world catastrophe in her time, "to trace them to their sources and to understand the logic of this majestic and terrible failure of the life of man in the Western world."

But perhaps the most interesting section of Katherine Anne Porter's work is composed of her stories about women —particularly her heroine Miranda, who figured in two of the three novelettes that made up her previous volume, *Pale Horse, Pale Rider*. The first six pieces of *The Leaning Tower* deal with Miranda's childhood and her family background of Louisianians living in southern Texas. This is the setting in which Miss Porter is most at home, and one finds in it the origins of that spirit of which the starvation and violation elsewhere make the subjects of her other stories. One recognizes it in the firm little sketches that show the relations between Miranda's grandmother and her lifelong colored companion, the relations between the members of the family and the relations between the family and the Negro servants in general. Somewhere behind Miss Porter's stories there is a conception of a natural human spirit in

terms of their bearing on which all the other forces of
society are appraised. This spirit is never really idealized,
it is not even sentimentalized; it can be generous and loving
and charming, but it can also be indifferent and careless,
inconsequent, irresponsible and silly. If the meaning of
these stories is elusive, it is because this essential spirit is so
hard to isolate or pin down. It is peculiar to Louisianians in
Texas, yet one misses it in a boarding house in Berlin. It is
the special personality of a woman, yet it is involved with
international issues. It evades all the most admirable moralities, it escapes through the social net, and it resists the
tremendous oppressions of national bankruptcies and national wars. It is outlawed, driven underground, exiled; it
becomes rather unsure of itself and may be able, as in *Pale
Horse, Pale Rider*, to assert itself only in the delirium that
lights up at the edge of death to save Miranda from extinction by war flu. It suffers often from a guilty conscience,
knowing too well its moral weakness; but it can also rally
bravely if vaguely in vindication of some instinct of its
being which seems to point toward justice and truth.

But I said that this review would be clumsy. I am spoiling Miss Porter's stories by attempting to find a formula
for them when I ought simply to be telling you to read
them (and not merely the last volume but also its two
predecessors). She is absolutely a first-rate artist, and what
she wants other people to know she imparts to them by
creating an object, the self-developing organism of a work
of prose. The only general opinion on anything which, in
her books, she has put on record has been a statement about
her craft of prose fiction, and I may quote it—from the
foreword to which I have referred—as more to the purpose
than anything that the present critic could say. Here is the
manifesto of the builder of this solid little sanctuary, so
beautifully proportioned and finished, for the queer un-
controllable spirit that it seems to her important to save:

"In the face of such shape and weight of present misfor-
tune, the voice of the individual artist may seem perhaps

of no more consequence than the whirring of a cricket in the grass, but the arts do live continuously, and they live literally by faith; their names and their shapes and their uses and their basic meanings survive unchanged in all that matters through times of interruption, diminishment, neglect; they outlive governments and creeds and the societies, even the very civilizations that produced them. They cannot be destroyed altogether because they represent the substance of faith and the only reality. They are what we find again when the ruins are cleared away. And even the smallest and most incomplete offering at this time can be a proud act in defense of that faith."

September 30, 1944

A Picture to Hang in the Library: Brooks's Age of Irving

THE NEW VOLUME of Van Wyck Brooks's literary history of the United States, *The World of Washington Irving*, though the third in order of publication, is the first in chronological order. It covers the ground from 1800 to the early years of the forties, and treats at length Jefferson, Audubon, Cooper, Irving, Simms, Poe, Bryant and Willis. It treats also dozens of minor figures and deals not only with literature proper but with political oratory, the reports of explorers and naturalists, the folklore of Davy Crockett and Mike Fink, and ethnological and archeological study; and it contains so much information about painting, music, landscape-gardening, architecture, mechanical invention and social manners that it might almost be more appropriately described as a history of American culture.

These decades were enormously lively: the country was still uncommercialized; the Americans were still exhilarated by the success of the Revolution and the adventure of the new country; the great intellectual figures were many-sided in their interests and talents, and men of the great worlds of society, geography and nature. There was a splendor of the Renaissance about figures like Jefferson and Audubon; Joel Barlow, diplomat, promoter and poet; Samuel F. B. Morse, who was a painter as well as a mechanical genius; William Dunlap, who was a painter, a historian of painting, a dramatist and a theatrical producer; and even Cooper, sailor, landowner, novelist, historian and critic of society— though we remember only his Indian tales. Poe—whom we greatly slight by reading him mainly for his tales of horror —was also typical of the period in the variety of his curiosities and his virtuosity in literary form. It is a wonderful period to go back to, and Mr. Brooks has written about it what seems to me so far the most attractive volume of the series that began with *The Flowering of New England*. The book is quite free from the cloggedness and overpainting that sometimes appeared in the earlier volumes. He has mastered his method so completely that we never get the effect of labor: style, narrative and organization have been brought to a point of perfection seldom reached in our historical and critical writing. Yet he has had to assimilate vast masses of print, surveying the whole field afresh and reading all the books for himself, and he has accepted none of the conventional limits by which scholars simplify their tasks: his light overflows these limits and seems to penetrate every crevice, reveal every in-between phase, of the observing and imagining American mind of the early years of the Republic. For the reader who is curious about cultural phenomena, there is not a dull page or dull footnote in the book. Mr. Brooks has the answers to all the questions with which the academic historians of literature will not usually help you much. Why did the South—apart from the political writing that accompanied the Revolution—produce so little in the way of literature? Why did people set so much store by Bryant? Why did they devour Washington Irving? How and when did the piety and prudery which have so tended to stunt the national art and thought close down on the free-thinking plain-speaking tradition of the realistic and cosmopolitan minds that presided at the birth of the Republic? What was the effect of the actual experience of the putting into practice of social equality and of the career open to the talents on the classically educated men of property who had defended the democratic ideal against the political tradition of Europe? How did they meet the age of Andrew Jackson?

To explain and dramatize all these matters is what Mr. Brooks can do as no one else in the United States has done it. Rarely, in fact, outside France has the appetite for learning been united with intelligence and literary ability to the degree that we find it here. He has put on the whole picture a color, a finish, a glaze like those of the best paintings of the period: the portraits of the pupils of Benjamin West, the genre studies of Mount and Bingham, the landscapes of the Hudson River school. You can hang this new volume in your library uninhibited by any embarrassment such as you may have felt in connection with his New England portraits, over a sometimes too fulsome treatment and a sometimes too pink-and-blue palette. You may occasionally pull yourself up with the reflection that the ripe and harmonious picture must still, to some extent, represent an idealization; but, after all, what Mr. Brooks is engaged on is not a sociological report but a presentation of the early eighteen-hundreds through the eyes of imaginative writers who brought to it their own color and excitement, and an account of these writers from the point of view of how they looked and what they meant to their contemporaries. (It is curious to contrast this volume with the bleak surveys of American civilization in 1800 and 1817 of Henry Adams' history. Though Adams is telling the same story of the birth of a national character and culture, an American intellectual, in the trust-ridden eighties and nineties, was not able to believe in these with such certainty as a man of Mr. Brooks's generation, and could not, therefore, find in our past so much to be cheerful about.)

In this reliving of the visions of our fathers, the question of absolute values becomes, for Mr. Brooks's purpose, unimportant and almost irrelevant. But there is a common complaint against this series that, in neglecting to deal with such values, in failing to measure the American writers by the best that has been done in the world, Mr. Brooks has been shirking the true business of the critic. This complaint has less force in the present case than it had in connection with the previous volumes, because the author does not here overinflate the men of mediocre ability as he did in the earlier books. He does not mislead us by creating the impression that Cooper and Washington Irving, the two dominant writers of the era, were men of greater talent than they were. Yet the question has still to be dealt with. Between *The World of Washington Irving* and its immediate predecessor in the series, *New England: Indian Summer,* Mr. Brooks has published a more personal book, *Opinions of Oliver Allston,* in which he has stigmatized as "coterie-literature" the work of some of the greatest of his contemporaries, and revealed that his own standards of excellence are still more or less those of an enthusiastic young man in his twenties in the heyday of H. G. Wells, a young man for whom Tolstoy and Ibsen, on the one hand, and Victor Hugo and Browning, on the other, all inhabit the same empyrean of greatness. But the paradox of Brooks's career is that he has himself been able to develop into one of the first-rate American writers of his time without achieving any commensurate development of his appreciation of other writers save as material for cultural history. He has, in the present volume, one case of an artist —Poe—who takes his place in a company far higher than that of his literary companions in the book. One looked forward with interest to his handling of Poe as a test case of his literary judgment, and since Poe is a great favorite of mine, I watched Mr. Brooks like a hawk during the chapters in which he deals with this subject, so peculiarly fraught with pitfalls—moral, social, aesthetic and regional— which has probably given rise to more rubbishy and vulgar writing, both romantic and denunciatory, than any other

American career with the exception of Abraham Lincoln's. Now Mr. Brooks has walked right through all these pitfalls with perfect delicacy, coolness and sense, and he has brought to his presentation of Poe's pathological personality a touch of that psychological insight which, I believe, has not appeared in his work since *The Ordeal of Mark Twain.* Van Wyck Brooks's interest in Poe is not the interest of Baudelaire or of Walter de la Mare, but from his own entirely different point of view he can indicate correctly Poe's importance: "With Poe another age had opened," he says, "intenser, profounder than [Washington Irving's]"; and this makes us see Poe in his historical perspective as we may not have done before.

In his attempts to evaluate literature, Mr. Brooks is still likely to fall back on rather vague and conventional phrases. He says of Bryant's poem *To a Waterfowl* that it is "the most intense of all his poems, in which for a moment he entered the realm of magic." Well, I know that Mr. Yvor Winters admires this poem of Bryant's, but I doubt whether it would be possible to find many modern poets who would agree with Mr. Brooks. If the magic he means is the magic that Matthew Arnold introduced into literary criticism with a famous discussion of such passages as Shakespeare's "daffodils, That come before the swallow dares, and take The winds of March with beauty," then Bryant's poor old waterfowl that guides through the boundless air his certain flight and brings to the poet the conviction that God will lead his steps aright can scarcely deserve that description.

And here is a passage on the prose of Cooper: "With his marked feeling for the sublime, he rose moreover now and then to moments of the noblest and most eloquent prose. Such were the descriptions of the icefields in *The Sea Lions*—a tale of American sealers in antarctic waters— the vast mass of floating mountains, generally of a spectral white, through which the mariners moved in an unknown sea. The walls, like ridges of the Alps, bowed and rocked and ground one another, stirred by the restless ocean, with a rushing sound, and sometimes a prodigious plunge as of a planet falling tossed the water over the heaving ramparts. The cliffs, half a league in length, with their arches and pinnacles and towers and columns, suggested the streets of some fantastic city that was floating in the sunlight in the sea, black here and there in certain lights and orange on the summits, throwing out gleams and hues of emerald and gold." Now if someone were to speak to you suddenly of "the noblest and most eloquent prose," in connection with a work of fiction, you might think of Melville, you might think of Flaubert, you might think of D. H. Lawrence; but you would not be at all likely to think of anything you had ever read in Cooper, where an occasional poetry of atmosphere seems barely to manage to seep through the verbose and clumsy writing. If there is something in Cooper as good as Mr. Brooks seems here to suggest, then you feel that you ought to know about it. But when you look up the icebergs in *The Sea Lions,* you find that Van Wyck Brooks has not merely been reflecting the glory of something that is much better in the original: he has put together his very pretty passage out of more or less undistinguished bits scattered through a great number of pages: "Each time, however, the sun's rays soon came to undeceive him; and that which had so lately been black and frowning, was, as by the touch of magic, suddenly illuminated, and became bright and gorgeous, throwing out its emerald hues, or perhaps a virgin white, that filled the beholder with delight, even amid the terrors and dangers by which, in very truth, he was surrounded. The glorious Alps themselves, those wonders of the earth, could scarcely compete in scenery with the views that nature lavished, in that remote sea, on a seeming void. . . . The passages between the bergs, or what might be termed the streets and lanes of this mysterious-looking, fantastical, yet sublime city of the ocean, were numerous, and of every variety," etc., etc.

The creation is not Cooper's but Brooks's: he has sifted out the images from *The Sea Lions* and made out of them something quite new. With the work of a Thoreau or a

Hawthorne, this method does not succeed, because you cannot rewrite a good writer: you can only discolor and weaken. But with somebody like Cooper, Mr. Brooks has a field almost like that of the artist who deals directly with crude experience. And how many inferior or tedious writers he must have transmuted in this book! We cannot compare the art with the phenomena themselves so readily as we can in the novelist's case; but when we go to the trouble of doing so, we are amazed at the skill with which Brooks has been turning the old carriage springs, spectacle frames and pickaxes of 1800–1840 into a fine-beaten kind of white gold.

October 7, 1944

Why Do People Read Detective Stories?

FOR YEARS I have been hearing about detective stories. Almost everybody I know seems to read them, and they have long conversations about them in which I am unable to take part. I am always being reminded that the most serious public figures of our time, from Woodrow Wilson to W. B. Yeats, have been addicts of this form of fiction. Now, except for a few stories by Chesterton, for which I did not much care, I have not read any detective stories since one of the earliest, if not the earliest, of the imitators of Sherlock Holmes—a writer named Jacques Futrelle, now dead, who invented a character called the Thinking Machine and published his first volume of stories about him in 1907. Enchanted though I had been with Sherlock Holmes, I got bored with the Thinking Machine and dropped him, beginning to feel, at the age of twelve, that I was outgrowing that form of literature.

Since, however, I have recently been sampling the various types of popular merchandise, I have decided that I ought to take a look at some specimens of this kind of fiction, which has grown so tremendously popular and which is now being produced on such a scale that the book departments of magazines have had to employ special editors to cope with it. To be sure of getting something above the average, I waited for new novels by writers who are particularly esteemed by connoisseurs. I started in with the latest volume of Rex Stout's Nero Wolfe stories: *Not Quite Dead Enough*.

What I found rather surprised me and discouraged my curiosity. Here was simply the old Sherlock Holmes formula reproduced with a fidelity even more complete than it had been by Jacques Futrelle almost forty years ago. Here was the incomparable private detective, ironic and ceremonious, with a superior mind and eccentric habits, addicted to over-eating and orchid-raising, as Holmes had his enervated indulgence in his cocaine and his violin, yet always prepared to revive for prodigies of intellectual alertness; and here were the admiring stooge, adoring and slightly dense, and Inspector Lestrade of Scotland Yard, energetic but entirely at sea, under the new name of Inspector Cramer of Police Headquarters. Almost the only difference was that Nero Wolfe was fat and lethargic instead of lean and active like Holmes, and that he liked to make the villains commit suicide instead of handing them over to justice. But I rather enjoyed Wolfe himself, with his rich dinners and quiet evenings in his house in farthest West Thirty-fifth Street, where he savors an armchair sadism that is always accompanied by beer. The two stories that made up this new book—*Not Quite Dead Enough* and *Booby Trap*—I found rather disappointing; but, as they were both under the usual length and presented the great detective partly distracted from his regular profession by a rigorous course of training for the Army, I concluded that they might not be first-rate examples of what the author could do in this line and read also *The Nero Wolfe Omnibus*, which contains two earlier book-length stories: *The Red Box* and *The League of Frightened Men*. But neither did these supply the excitement I was hoping for. If the later stories

were sketchy and skimpy, these seemed to have been somewhat padded, for they were full of long episodes that led
nowhere and had no real business in the story. It was only
when I looked up Sherlock Holmes that I realized how
much Nero Wolfe was a dim and distant copy of an original.
The old stories of Conan Doyle had a wit and a fairy-tale
poetry of hansom cabs, gloomy London lodgings and lonely
country estates that Rex Stout could hardly duplicate with
his backgrounds of modern New York; and the surprises
were much more entertaining: you at least got a room
with a descending ceiling or a snake trained to climb down
the bellrope, whereas with Nero Wolfe—though *The League
of Frightened Men* makes use of a clever psychological
idea—the solution of the mystery was not usually either
fanciful or unexpected. I finally got to feel that I had to
unpack large crates by swallowing the excelsior in order to
find at the bottom a few bent and rusty nails, and I began
to nurse a rankling conviction that detective stories in
general are able to profit by an unfair advantage in the
code which forbids the reviewer to give away the secret to
the public—a custom which results in the concealment of
the pointlessness of a good deal of this fiction and affords
a protection to the authors which no other department of
writing enjoys. It is not difficult to create suspense by
making people await a revelation, but it does demand a
certain talent to come through with a criminal device which
is ingenious or picturesque or amusing enough to make
the reader feel that the waiting has been worth while. I
even began to mutter that the real secret that Author Rex
Stout had been screening by his false scents and interminable divagations was a meagerness of imagination of
which one only came to realize the full ghastliness when the
last chapter had left one blank.

I have been told by the experts, however, that this endless carrying on of the Doyle tradition does not represent
all or the best that has been done with the detective story
during the decades of its proliferation. There has been also
the puzzle mystery, and this, I was assured, had been

brought to a high pitch of ingenuity in the stories of
Agatha Christie. So I have read also the new Agatha
Christie, *Death Comes as the End,* and I confess that I
have been had by Mrs. Christie. I did not guess who the
murderer was, I was incited to keep on and find out, and
when I did finally find out, I was surprised. Yet I did not
care for Agatha Christie and I hope never to read another
of her books. I ought, perhaps, to discount the fact that
Death Comes as the End is supposed to take place in Egypt
two thousand years before Christ, so that the book has a
flavor of Lloyd C. Douglas not, I understand, quite typical
of the author. ("No more Khay in this world to sail on the
Nile and catch fish and laugh up into the sun whilst she,
stretched out in the boat with little Teti on her lap,
laughed back at him"); but her writing is of a mawkish-
ness and banality which seem to me literally impossible to
read. You cannot *read* such a book, you run through it to
see the problem worked out; and you cannot become interested in the characters, because they never can be
allowed an existence of their own even in a flat two dimensions but have always to be contrived so that they can seem
either reliable or sinister, depending on which quarter, at
the moment, is to be baited for the reader's suspicion. This
I had found also a source of annoyance in the case of Mr.
Stout, who, however, has created, after a fashion, Nero
Wolfe and Archie Goodwin and has made some attempt at
characterization of the people that figure in the crimes; but
Mrs. Christie, in proportion as she is more expert and concentrates more narrowly on the puzzle, has to eliminate
human interest completely, or, rather, fill in the picture
with what seems to me a distasteful parody of it. In this
new novel, she has to provide herself with puppets who
will be good for three stages of suspense: you must first
wonder who is going to be murdered, you must then wonder who is committing the murders, and you must finally
be unable to foresee which of two men the heroine will
marry. It is all like a sleight-of-hand trick, in which the
magician diverts your attention from the awkward or

irrelevant movements that conceal the manipulation of the cards, and it may mildly entertain and astonish you, as such a sleight-of-hand performance may. But in a performance like *Death Comes as the End*, the patter is a constant bore and the properties lack the elegance of playing cards.

Still fearing that I might be unjust to a department of literature that seemed to be found so absorbing by many, I went back and read *The Maltese Falcon*, which I assumed to be a classic in the field, since it had been called by Alexander Woollcott "the best detective story America has yet produced" and since, at the time of its publication, it had immediately caused Dashiell Hammett to become—in Jimmy Durante's phrase, referring to himself—"duh toast of duh intellectuals." But it was difficult for me to understand what they had thought—in 1930—they were toasting. Mr. Hammett did have the advantage of real experience as a Pinkerton detective, and he infused the old formula of Sherlock Holmes with a certain cold underworld brutality which gave readers a new shudder in the days when it was fashionable to be interested in gangsters; but, beyond this, he lacked the ability to bring the story to imaginative life. As a writer, he is surely almost as far below the rank of Rex Stout as Rex Stout is below that of James Cain. *The Maltese Falcon* today seems not much above those newspaper picture-strips in which you follow from day to day the ups and downs of a strong-jawed hero and a hardboiled but beautiful adventuress.

What, then, is the spell of the detective story that has been felt by T. S. Eliot and Paul Elmer More but which I seem incapable of feeling? As a department of imaginative writing, it looks to me completely dead. The spy story may perhaps only now be realizing its poetic possibilities, as the admirers of Graham Greene contend; and the murder story that exploits psychological horror is an entirely different matter. But the detective story proper had borne all its finest fruits by the end of the nineteenth century, having only declined from the point where Edgar Allan Poe had been able to communicate to M. Dupin something of his own ratiocinative intensity and where Dickens had invested his plots with a social and moral significance that made the final solution of the mystery a revelatory symbol of something that the author wanted seriously to say. Yet the detective story has kept its hold; had even, in the two decades between the great wars, become more popular than ever before; and there is, I believe, a deep reason for this. The world during those years was ridden by an all-pervasive feeling of guilt and by a fear of impending disaster which it seemed hopeless to try to avert because it never seemed conclusively possible to pin down the responsibility. Who had committed the original crime and who was going to commit the next one?—that second murder which always, in the novels, occurs at an unexpected moment when the investigation is well under way; which, as in one of the Nero Wolfe stories, may take place right in the great detective's office. Everybody is suspected in turn, and the streets are full of lurking agents whose allegiances we cannot know. Nobody seems guiltless, nobody seems safe; and then, suddenly, the murderer is spotted, and—relief!—he is not, after all, a person like you or me. He is a villain—known to the trade as George Gruesome—and he has been caught by an infallible Power, the supercilious and omniscient detective, who knows exactly where to fix the guilt.

October 14, 1944

Reëxamining Dr. Johnson

IT IS A PITY that Boswell's *Life of Johnson* should so largely have supplanted for the general reader the writings of Johnson himself. If we know nothing but Boswell and Macaulay's essay, which is read in so many schools, we are likely to have a picture of a great eccentric who was even a bit of a clown. Boswell, in spite of his great respect and of the filial role he assumed, could not help making Johnson a character in an eighteenth-century comedy of manners; Macaulay pointed him up as a monster, at once grotesque and banal, in a bright-colored Victorian novel. And lately the figure of Boswell has become even more prominent at Johnson's expense through the discovery of the Boswell papers and the work of Mr. Chauncey Tinker. That Johnson himself was really one of the best English writers of his time, that he deserved his great reputation, is a fact that we are likely to lose sight of.

Mr. Joseph Wood Krutch, in a new biography called *Samuel Johnson,* has at last provided a study that is designed to restore to Johnson his real literary interest and importance. With all the work that has been done on Johnson and his friends, there has, as he says, been no such biography. "The very intensity of this specialization," he explains in his introduction, "(as well, of course, as the tremendous reputation of Boswell's *Life*) has tended to discourage any attempt in recent times to produce a large inclusive book which would serve to give the general reader a running account of Johnson's life, character and work as they appear in the light of contemporary knowledge and contemporary judgment." Mr. Krutch follows this announcement with some entirely unnecessary apologies for having played down the figure of Boswell. The truth is that he has devoted quite enough attention and given a quite favorable enough account of Boswell, and his nervously apprehensive glances in the direction of the Boswell fans are simply a part of that continued tribute which one dislikes to see exacted to that point by the vain and pushing diarist.

Mr. Krutch, then, has taken on a job which very much needed to be done, and has acquitted himself with honor. This biography is by far the best book that I have ever read by Joseph Wood Krutch. His *Poe,* written back in the twenties, was a rather half-baked performance: incomplete, depending too much on a Freudian oversimplification, insufficiently sympathetic with its subject and somewhat distracted in its judgments by what one might call the despair-hysteria of the period. The *Johnson* is quite another affair. It is scrupulous and comprehensive, and it makes use of the insights of modern psychology in a careful and moderate way—in fact, perhaps leans a little too much over backward in the attempt not to press them too far (since Mr. Krutch has been through Boswell's diary, which is scandalous and has been printed only privately, and since he tells us that Boswell was "neurotic" and has evidently a theory about him, we regret that he has not let us know what this theory is). This new book also shows a capacity for steady and independent judgment, as well as a flexible intelligence, in the discussion both of Johnson's work and of the problems of his personality, that constitute a striking advance in Mr. Krutch's development as a critic.

The only serious general objection that can be brought against Mr. Krutch's treatment is that, in one sense, he does not seem especially close to his subject. Johnson was so solid a man, who saw the world in such concrete terms, and the give-and-take of his age was so lively, direct and brusque, that Mr. Krutch's presentation of them seems, by comparison, attenuated and pallid. His book a little bit lacks *impact*. But he compensates us for this and more or less leads us to forget it by the subtlety, lucidity and sureness of the analysis which he has made his method. And his style—though it has nothing in common with the stout-knotted texture of Johnson, the phrases, the sentences, the paragraphs, that one can feel between one's teeth, though it does sometimes run a little to repetition, to an old-fashioned Southern verbosity and the old-fashioned Southern eloquence of such phrases as "a devotee of Bacchus" —his style has become, on the whole, an admirable instrument for this kind of analysis. Except for an occasional balled-up sentence, the book reads easily and carries you rapidly; and, though it isolates to some extent from the immediate background of their period the principal actors of the Johnson legend, it surrounds them with an even luminosity which, though gentle, is always revealing.

The chapters on Johnson's chief works are not, as so often happens with the products of academic research, merely studies of their historical significance, though Mr. Krutch covers this, too, but—except in the case of Johnson's poems, which Mr. Krutch rather underrates—sound critical appreciations. One hopes that they will stimulate the reading of Johnson. The romantics and their successors have created, by exaggerating Johnson's limitations, an unfair prejudice against him as a critic. Actually, *The Lives of the Poets* and the preface and commentary on Shakespeare are among the most brilliant and the most acute documents in the whole range of English criticism, and the products of a mind which, so far from being parochially local and hopelessly cramped by the taste of its age, saw literature in a long perspective and could respond to the humanity of Shakespeare as well as to the wit of Pope.

One feature of Mr. Krutch's biography I feel moved to dwell upon here a little more than it perhaps deserves from its importance in the whole scale of his book.

There is a tendency in the scholarly writing done by professors and composers of theses that sometimes becomes rather exasperating to the reader outside the college world. This tendency may be briefly described as an impulse on the part of the professors to undermine their subjects or explain them away. An expert on Byron, say, will prove, on purely documentary grounds, that there is no reason to believe that Byron ever had anything to do with women; an authority on Whitman will attempt to show that Whitman had no originality, since everything to be found in his work was already to be found in someone else, and will thereby seem to try to create the impression that there is no real merit in Whitman's poetry. To the outsider, this sounds perverse; but, since these scholars are apparently not the men for perversity, he may be baffled for an explanation. In order to understand this peculiar phenomenon, which it seems to me has been growing more formidable, one must understand, first of all, the relation of the professor to his subjects. This relation is, nine times out of ten, a strained and embarrassing one. The professor would be made most uncomfortable if he had to meet Whitman or Byron; he would not like him—he does not, in fact, like him. But he has gone in for studying literature and he must try to do something to advance himself in that field. His demonstration of Byron's chastity or of the nullity of Whitman's achievement may have no relevance whatever to his author, may indeed amount to an effort to annihilate him, but it *does* constitute a tangible evidence of the scholar's assiduous reading, his checking of dates and texts, and his long hours getting something written out. It is also an act of self-assertion which may produce the illusion that a dent has been left in the author, though it may not add anything to our knowledge of him; and it does raise the status of the scholar in the hierarchy of the academic world.

But to the non-academic reader, this, as I say, can only seem rather stupid. Now, there are just a moment or two when Mr. Krutch, who has been teaching at Columbia, gives some evidence of being attainted with this tendency. He creates the impression that he is trying to show, in his discussion of Johnson's early years in London, that since there is no real documentary proof that Johnson ever missed many dinners, there is no genuine reason for believing that he was as poor as he has been thought to have been; and later, in appraising Johnson's two long poems, Mr. Krutch takes the disheartening line of arguing that the first of these fine pieces, *London,* is merely a monument to the bad old habit of stupidly imitating classical models, and the second, *The Vanity of Human Wishes,* mostly a conventional exercise which hardly rises above the level of commonplace eighteenth-century verse. Yet if anything is plain in Johnson's writings and in his attitude toward the destitute and helpless—as Mr. Krutch's own account clearly shows—it is some intimate and scarifying experience of hardship in these undocumented early years. This is one of the elements in the ground-tone, dolorous, steadfast and somber, that gives emotional depth to his work; and one feels it especially in these poems, which owe certain of their most effective passages to Johnson's first-hand acquaintance with all but the last of his melancholy catalogue of the miseries of a writer's life: "Toil, envy, want, the patron and the jail."

Mr. Krutch does not often depress us thus, but it is regrettable that he should do so at all. He has not been a professor for long and he should be wary of the dangers of the academic air. As a critic, he has been trained in the best tradition of contemporary literary journalism; but it may be that not only the symptoms just noted, but also a feeling one gets that Johnson has been presented in a vacuum, with no general implications, should be charged to the habitual blankness of the outlook of academic scholarship. When Mr. Krutch wrote *The Modern Temper,* he had a much more definite point of view as a critic of literature in relation to life and of life in relation to history.

November 18, 1944

Leonid Leonov:
The Sophistication of a Formula

Road to the Ocean is a long novel about Soviet Russia by a prominent Soviet novelist. It centers around "socialist construction": the operation of a Russian railroad; but the author, Leonid Leonov, has genuine literary gifts which do not lend themselves readily to propaganda, and he has tried to do something subtler, more complex and more humanly plausible than the ordinary Communist Sunday-school story. Leonov has a novelist's interest in the crude mixed materials of life and a literary sophistication very rare in Soviet fiction. His novel, which is extremely intricate, with a great multiplication of characters, involves elements of the landowning class dispossessed by the Revolution, of the bourgeois professional class trying to function in the new socialist economy, of the original generation of devoted and intrepid revolutionists who established the Soviet society and of the younger generation of the Komsomol who are helping to get it running in the spirit of Boy and Girl Scouts.

The presentation of all this is quite skilful: the interdependence of the various individuals is gradually brought out in a dramatic but usually not obvious way. Episode leads to episode by transitions apparently meaningless: a character who seems unimportant in one chapter will be shown at full length in the next; till, later a new nexus of relationships which gives the whole picture a new significance is unexpectedly established either by continuing the story in the present or by exploring its earlier phases in the past. For example, the discovery by a Communist historian of a set of old papers in a country house makes a number of the characters fall together into a Chekhovian drama of the old regime and connects them with the original flotation, seen as a typical capitalist swindle, of that railroad which is now the arena of the entirely different exploits of Soviet industrial effort; then the same house, now turned into a "rest home" for vacationing Soviet workers, is made to produce a new grouping of characters and exert a new kind of influence, when the railroad's Politbureau chief goes for a sojourn there. And there are even long-distance projections into the future of the Soviet world which, though sometimes a little tedious, are also handled in a novel way. Through old documents, through the memories of the characters, we have been shown the Russian past; what is the world that they are working for to be? Leonov is much too clever to bore us with a socialist utopia. He gives us the visions of Kurilov, the veteran Politbureau chief who is the central figure of the story, and these visions are conditioned by Kurilov's mood, and thus by his personal situation at the moment, just as the visions of Tsarist Russia are conditioned by the outlook of

the Communist historian who has found the old papers and
is making out a case against capitalist enterprise, or by the
failing and romantic memories of the survivors of the gentry
and the merchant class. Moreover, the efforts of Kurilov to
imagine the world that is coming—the great wars, the displacements of civilization, the navigation of interplanetary
space—are not in the nature of blueprints but merely imperfect, sometimes comic dreams which provide not so
much a prophecy as a picture of our own state of mind
when we try to prefigure the future.

What Leonov is attempting to do is, therefore, ambitious
and interesting, and he has been able to fill in his project
with so much lively observation of life, so much entertaining invention of incident, that he carries us quite through
his elaborate book. We are conscious from the beginning
that the characters are types, but we do not at first sight
take them for the conventional types of Soviet fiction.
They do not seem to be doing the regulation things or
striking the regulation attitudes: the bourgeois who has
buried his past is evidently working in all good faith at
his Soviet railroad job; the Komsomol engine crew make
a mess of their first difficult run. And the internal life
of these people is presented with as much circumstantiality
as the external detail of their homes and work, so that the
author half creates the illusion that he is on intimate terms
with his characters. We give him the benefit of the doubt:
we assume that he knows what he is doing and that he
has something astonishing and revealing in store. It is not
till we come to the end that we are definitely let down by
Leonov, but then we are badly let down. The *ci-devant*
bourgeois yardmaster, with whom we have been led rather
to sympathize, is shown as, after all, incapable of going
along with the new society: incurably egoistic and cold, he
is doomed to plot a dastardly crime against the noble Communist Kurilov, and he must be publicly denounced by his
brother, an upright and hardworking surgeon. The bad
actress and bitchy little wife is transfigured by her contact
with Kurilov and becomes not merely a worker for socialist

construction but also, apparently, an excellent artist. Looking back, we become aware that these people have never been real in the first place and that we have simply been distracted from minding it by the technical agility of the author, his succession of diverting anecdotes and his air of being up to something intelligent.

Leonov himself, we conclude, must be somewhat more intelligent than his book. He is extraordinarily resourceful and adroit in evading dangerous issues—either by simply omitting things from his picture or by treating them in an objective way which enables him to remain noncommittal. *Road to the Ocean* was published in 1936, and the story is supposed to take place somewhere around 1932. The class stratification of the Soviet society and the tyranny of Moscow officialdom through the agencies of the propaganda press and the terror of the G.P.U. were well under way by that time. But Leonov has contrived a story all in terms of old revolutionists, struggling intelligentsia and earnest young Komsomols. And, by unobtrusively causing his characters to say or think certain things, he manages to indicate an attitude which is distinctly humane and liberal. He says, for example, of Kurilov's sister, an austere saint of the heroic generation, that "it did not occur to her to take revenge on an enemy's offspring for the crimes of a whole political system." It is true that a few years in the middle thirties, the period when this book must have been written, saw a relative relaxation, in cultural and political matters, of the rigors of the Kremlin dictatorship. But after the murder of the liberal Kirov, in December, 1934, the aspiration behind this was rapidly stifled. The political terror began, and millions of men and women were shot or sent to prison. People who knew one another well were afraid to comment aloud on anything they read in the paper, because denunciations to the authorities like that of Leonov's villain by his brother had now become the order of the day; and tried party workers like Kurilov and his sister were vanishing overnight into the dungeons of the G.P.U., till there was hardly an old Bolshevik left.

It was so far from occurring to the rulers of Russia that one ought not to revenge oneself on the children for the political crimes of the fathers that the children of liquidated officials were left orphaned and without support, to be ostracized at school, avoided by their neighbors and sometimes driven to suicide. The forces that Leonov seems to deprecate, that have produced the distortions of his story itself, were the forces that were to dominate in Russia.

The net effect, therefore, of Leonov's book is a peculiarly depressing one. In reading a book by a Frenchman written under the Nazi oppression—such as the *Imaginary Interviews* of André Gide—we share his humiliation in being reduced to guarded statements and riddles. A Russian novel like *Road to the Ocean* embarrasses us in a similar way. I should not say, on the evidence of this book—though Gorky highly praised Leonov—that the author was a first-rate novelist; but, among Soviet writers, he is talented, he does have some serious idea of what literature ought to be, and it is painful to see him working to produce a real social novel that would stand up with Malraux or Dos Passos, only to have to surrender his project to the requirements of the Soviet formula.

It is curious to compare Leonov, almost an official Soviet writer, with another Russian novelist, Mark Aldanov, a non-fellow-travelling émigré. I do not know whether they have influenced one another or whether they have been influenced separately by some general literary tendency, but they are in some respects surprisingly similar. Both like to make their stories out of episodes in the careers of assorted characters whose orbits compose a larger pattern but who may barely intersect one another's; and both have taken for their principal figures old men bred in Tsarist Russia who have survived into the new society but who are now very close to death. Leonov has the great advantage over the author of *The Fifth Seal* that he himself has lived the new society: his material is all first-hand; whereas a weakness of Aldanov's novel is the vagueness, if not sometimes the blankness, of the Soviet backgrounds of the characters whom he sees so clearly in their context as visitors to Western Europe. Yet Aldanov has the advantage of freedom: he can write what he observes and feels; and if we want to see how important that advantage is, we may consider the two books side by side. To do so is to put to ourselves problems about which it is rather difficult to arrive at any definite conclusions. Is Aldanov "better" than Leonov because he is so much more satisfactory from this point of view—because he can choose his effect and achieve it? Would Leonov have been more like Aldanov, more impartial and independent, if he had written his book abroad? Or is Leonov "better" than Aldanov, both because of his more abundant material and because he has been able to associate himself with a great creative social purpose? Assuming that abilities are equal—something of which one can by no means be sure—I am afraid that it is Aldanov, the exile, who enjoys the more important advantage. The Leninist idealism which was stimulating in the Soviet literature of the twenties, which struck a kind of moral vitality into some even of the relatively crude melodramas of the earlier Soviet stage, is perceptibly flagging in *Road to the Ocean*. We are continually being shown the miracles wrought upon human nature by the magic of the revolutionary morality, but we no longer really feel its virtue. Instead, we feel the Soviet state, present not in its habit as it lives, as the old Tsarist officialdom was in Gogol, but in a much more powerful and damaging way: by the mold into which it has crushed the book.

December 9, 1944

Who Cares Who Killed Roger Ackroyd?

THREE MONTHS AGO I wrote an article on some recent detective stories. I had not read any fiction of this kind since the days of Sherlock Holmes, and, since I constantly heard animated discussions of the merits of the mystery writers, I was curious to see what they were like today. The specimens I tried I found disappointing, and I made some rather derogatory remarks in connection with my impressions of the genre in general. To my surprise, this brought me letters of protest in a volume and of a passionate earnestness which had hardly been elicited even by my occasional criticisms of the Soviet Union. Of the thirty-nine letters that have reached me, only seven approve my strictures. The writers of almost all the others seem deeply offended and shocked, and they all say almost exactly the same thing: that I had simply not read the right novels and that I would surely have a different opinion if I would only try this or that author recommended by the correspondent. In many of these letters there was a note of asperity, and one lady went so far as to declare that she would never read my articles again unless I were prepared to reconsider my position. In the meantime, furthermore, a number of other writers have published articles defending the detective story: Jacques Barzun, Joseph Wood Krutch, Raymond Chandler and Somerset Maugham have all had something to say on the subject—nor has the umbrageous Bernard De Voto failed to raise his voice.

Overwhelmed by so much insistence, I at last wrote my correspondents that I would try to correct any injustice by undertaking to read some of the authors that had received the most recommendations and taking the whole matter up again. The preferences of these readers, however, when I had a tabulation of them made, turned out to be extremely divergent. They ranged over fifty-two writers and sixty-seven books, most of which got only one or two votes each. The only writers who got as many as five or over were Dorothy L. Sayers, Margery Allingham, Ngaio Marsh, Michael Innes, Raymond Chandler and the author who writes under the names of Carter Dickson and John Dickson Carr.

The writer that my correspondents were most nearly

unanimous in putting at the top was Miss Dorothy L. Sayers, who was pressed upon me by eighteen people, and the book of hers that eight of them were sure I could not fail to enjoy was a story called *The Nine Tailors*. Well, I set out to read *The Nine Tailors* in the hope of tasting some novel excitement, and I declare that it seems to me one of the dullest books I have ever encountered in any field. The first part of it is all about bell-ringing as it is practised in English churches and contains a lot of information of the kind that you might expect to find in an encyclopedia article on campanology. I skipped a good deal of this, and found myself skipping, also, a large section of the conversations between conventional English village characters: "Oh, here's Hinkins with the aspidistras. People may say what they like about aspidistras, but they do go on all the year round and make a background," etc. There was also a dreadful stock English nobleman of the casual and debonair kind, with the embarrassing name of Lord Peter Wimsey, and, although he was the focal character in the novel, being Miss Dorothy Sayers's version of the inevitable Sherlock Holmes detective, I had to skip a good deal of him, too. In the meantime, I was losing the story, which had not got a firm grip on my attention, but I went back and picked it up and steadfastly pushed through to the end, and there I discovered that the whole point was that if a man was shut up in a belfry while a heavy peal of chimes was being rung, the vibrations of the bells might kill him. Not a bad idea for a murder, and Conan Doyle would have known how to dramatize it in an entertaining tale of thirty pages, but Miss Sayers had not hesitated to pad it out to a book of three hundred and thirty, contriving one of those hackneyed cock-and-bull stories about a woman who commits bigamy without knowing it, and larding the whole thing with details of church architecture, bits of quaint lore from books about bell-ringing and the awful whimsical patter of Lord Peter.

I had often heard people say that Dorothy Sayers wrote

well, and I felt that my correspondents had been playing her as their literary ace. But, really, she does not write very well: it is simply that she is more consciously literary than most of the other detective-story writers and that she thus attracts attention in a field which is mostly on a sub-literary level. In any serious department of fiction, her writing would not appear to have any distinction at all. Yet, commonplace in this respect though she is, she gives an impression of brilliant talent if we put her beside Miss Ngaio Marsh, whose *Overture to Death* was also suggested by several correspondents. Mr. De Voto has put himself on record as believing that Miss Marsh, as well as Miss Sayers and Miss Allingham, writes her novels in "excellent prose," and this throws for me a good deal of light on Mr. De Voto's opinions as a critic. I hadn't quite realized before, though I had noted his own rather messy style, to what degree he was insensitive to writing. I do not see how it is possible for anyone with a feeling for words to describe the unappetizing sawdust which Miss Marsh has poured into her pages as "excellent prose" or as prose at all except in the sense that distinguishes prose from verse. And here again the book is mostly padding. There is the notion that you could commit a murder by rigging up a gun in a piano in such a way that the victim will shoot himself when he presses down the pedal, but this is embedded in the dialogue and doings of a lot of faked-up English county people who are even more tedious than those of *The Nine Tailors*.

The enthusiastic reader of detective stories will indignantly object at this point that I am reading for the wrong things: that I ought not to be expecting good writing, characterization, human interest or even atmosphere. He is right, of course, though I was not fully aware of it till I attempted *Flowers for the Judge*, considered by connoisseurs one of the best books of one of the masters of this school, Miss Margery Allingham. This tale I found completely unreadable. The story and the writing both showed a surface so wooden and dead that I could not keep my mind on the page. How can you care who committed a murder which has never really been made to take place, because the writer hasn't any ability of even the most ordinary kind to persuade you to see it or feel it? How can you probe the possibilities of guilt among characters who all seem alike, because they are all simply names on the page? It was then that I understood that a true connoisseur of this fiction must be able to suspend the demands of his imagination and literary taste and take the thing as an intellectual problem. But how you arrive at that state of mind is what I do not understand.

In the light of this revelation, I feel that it is probably irrelevant to mention that I enjoyed *The Burning Court*, by John Dickson Carr, more than the novels of any of these ladies. There is a tinge of black magic that gives it a little of the interest of a horror story, and the author has a virtuosity at playing with alternative hypotheses that makes this trick of detective fiction more amusing than it usually is.

I want, however, to take up certain points made by the writers of the above-mentioned articles.

Mr. Barzun informs the non-expert that the detective novel is a kind of game in which the reader of a given story, in order to play properly his hand, should be familiar with all the devices that have already been used in other stories. These devices, it seems, are now barred: the reader must challenge the writer to solve his problem in some novel way, and the writer puts it up to the reader to guess the new solution. This may be true, but I shall never qualify. I would rather play Twenty Questions, which at least does not involve the consumption of hundreds of ill-written books.

A point made by three of these writers, Mr. Maugham, Mr. De Voto and Mr. Krutch, is that the novel has become so philosophical, so psychological and so symbolic that the public have had to take to the detective story as the only department of fiction where pure story-telling survives.

This seems to me to involve two fallacies. On the one hand, it is surely not true that "the serious novelists of today"—to quote Mr. Maugham's assertion—"have often," in contrast to the novelists of the past, "little or no story to tell," that "they have allowed themselves to be persuaded that to tell a story is a negligible form of art." It is true, of course, that Joyce and Proust—who, I suppose, must be accounted the heaviest going—have their various modern ways of boring and playing tricks on the reader. But how about the dreadful bogs and obstacles that one has to get over in Scott? the interpolated essays in Hugo? the leaking tap of Thackeray's reflections on life, in which the story is always trickling away? Is there anything in first-rate modern fiction quite so gratuitous as these *longueurs?* Even Proust and Joyce and Virginia Woolf do certainly have stories to tell, and they have organized their books with an intensity which has been relatively rare in the novel and which, to my mind, more than makes up for the occasional viscosity of their narrative.

On the other hand, it seems to me—for reasons suggested above—a fantastic misrepresentation to say that the average detective novel is an example of good story-telling. The gift for telling stories is uncommon, like other artistic gifts, and the only one of this group of writers—the writers my correspondents have praised—who seems to me to possess it to any degree is Mr. Raymond Chandler. His *Farewell, My Lovely* is the only one of these books that I have read all of and read with enjoyment. But Chandler, though in his recent article he seems to claim Hammett as his master, does not really belong to this school of the old-fashioned detective novel. What he writes is a novel of adventure which has less in common with Hammett than with Alfred Hitchcock and Graham Greene—the modern spy story which has substituted the jitters of the Gestapo and the G.P.U. for the luxury world of E. Phillips Oppenheim. It is not simply a question here of a puzzle which has been put together but of a malaise conveyed to the reader, the horror of a hidden conspiracy that is continually turning up in the most varied and unlikely forms. To write such a novel successfully you must be able to invent character and incident and to generate atmosphere, and all this Mr. Chandler can do, though he is a long way below Graham Greene. It was only when I got to the end that I felt my old crime-story depression descending upon me again—because here again, as is so often the case, the explanation of the mysteries, when it comes, is neither interesting nor plausible enough. It fails to justify the excitement produced by the elaborate build-up of picturesque and sinister happenings, and one cannot help feeling cheated.

My experience with this second batch of novels has, therefore, been even more disillusioning than my experience with the first, and my final conclusion is that the reading of detective stories is simply a kind of vice that, for silliness and minor harmfulness, ranks somewhere between smoking and crossword puzzles. This conclusion seems borne out by the violence of the letters I have been receiving. Detective-story readers feel guilty, they are habitually on the defensive, and all their talk about "well-written" mysteries is simply an excuse for their vice, like the reasons that the alcoholic can always produce for a drink. One of the letters I have had shows the addict in his frankest and most shameless phase. This lady begins by pretending, like the others, to guide me in my choice, but she breaks down and tells the whole dreadful truth. Though she has read, she says, hundreds of detective stories, "it is surprising," she finally confesses, "how few I would recommend to another. However, a poor detective story is better than none at all. Try again. With a little better luck, you'll find one you admire and enjoy. Then you, too, may be

A MYSTERY FIEND."

This letter has made my blood run cold: so the opium smoker tells the novice not to mind if the first pipe makes him sick; and I fall back for reassurance on the valiant little band of my readers who sympathize with my views on the subject. One of these tells me that I have under-

estimated both the badness of detective stories themselves
and the lax mental habits of those who enjoy them. The
worst of it is, he says, that the true addict, half the time,
never even finds out who has committed the murder. The
addict reads not to find anything out but merely to get
the mild stimulation of the succession of unexpected incidents and of the suspense itself of *looking forward* to learning a sensational secret. That this secret is nothing at all
and does not really account for the incidents does not matter to such a reader. He has learned from his long indulgence how to connive with the author in the swindle:
he does not pay any real attention when the disappointing
dénouement occurs, he does not think back and check the
events, he simply shuts the book and starts another.

To detective-story addicts, then, I say: Please do not
write me any more letters telling me that I have not read
the right books. And to the seven correspondents who
are with me and who in some cases have thanked me for
helping them to liberate themselves from a habit which
they recognized as wasteful of time and degrading to the
intellect but into which they had been bullied by convention and the portentously invoked examples of Woodrow Wilson and André Gide—to these staunch and pure
spirits I say: Friends, we represent a minority, but Literature is on our side. With so many fine books to be read,
so much to be studied and known, there is no need to bore
ourselves with this rubbish. And with the paper shortage
pressing on all publication and many first-rate writers
forced out of print, we shall do well to discourage the
squandering of this paper that might be put to better use.

January 20, 1945

"Mr. Holmes, They Were the Footprints of a Gigantic Hound!"

MY ARTICLE of four weeks ago on detective stories has called forth a burst of correspondence even more overwhelming than that provoked by my earlier piece—well over a hundred letters. But in this case the people who write me mostly agree with my adverse attitude. Among the few letters from those who do not, some, however, are excessively bitter. One lady adds a postscript in which she declares that she has never liked men named Edmund, and another asks me jeeringly how much I have been paid by "the non-detective fiction publishers." The furious reaction of these readers confirms me in my conclusion that detective stories are actually a habit-forming drug for which its addicts will fight like tigers—an opinion that is explicitly corroborated by many of the approving letters. The evangelical note at the end of my piece was intended to have a burlesque flavor, but some of my correspondents seem to have taken it more seriously than it was meant, and write to tell me that, though they have long been addicts, they have made a vow, since reading my article, never to touch another detective story. An old friend, a classical scholar and archeologist, has rather horrified me by writing to confess that he, too, has been a victim of this form of narcotic and that he had already had the intention of doing for it in literature what De Quincey has done for opium-eating.

I will now confess, in my turn, that, since my first looking into this subject last fall, I have myself become addicted, in spells, to reading myself to sleep with Sherlock Holmes, which I had gone back to, not having looked at it since childhood, in order to see how it compared with Conan Doyle's latest imitators. I propose, however, to justify my pleasure in rereading Sherlock Holmes on grounds entirely different from those on which the consumers of the current product ordinarily defend their taste. My contention is that Sherlock Holmes *is* literature on a humble but not ignoble level, whereas the mystery writers most in vogue now are not. The old stories are literature, not because of the conjuring tricks and the puzzles, not because of the lively melodrama, which they have in common with many other detective stories, but by virtue of imagination and style. These are fairy-tales, as Conan Doyle intimated in his preface to his last collection, and they are among the most amusing of fairy-tales and not among the least distinguished.

The Sherlock Holmes stories, almost as much as the Alice books or as Edward Lear's nonsense, were the casual products of a life the main purpose of which was something else, but creations that in some sense got detached from their author and flew away and had a life of their own. Conan Doyle, it seems, worked conscientiously to document his historical romances, which he considered his serious work, but he regarded Holmes and Watson as the paper dolls of rather ridiculous and undignified potboilers, and he paid so little attention to what he wrote about them that the stories are full of inconsistencies, which Doyle never bothered to correct. He forgot Watson's Christian name and later on gave him a new one; he shifted the location of his wound; he began by making an ignorance of literature an essential trait of Holmes's personality and then had him talk about Petrarch and Meredith; and he even, on one occasion, changed the season abruptly from July to September. (It is an odd evidence of Holmes's vitality that some of his admirers should have gone to the trouble of attempting to account for these discrepancies, as if Watson and Holmes had been real men, and that they should actually have published their conjectures in a volume called *Profile by Gaslight*.) Doyle had become so impatient with his hero by the end of the second series in the *Strand Magazine* that he got rid of him by killing him off, totally without preparation, in a manner that was little short of frivolous. But Sherlock Holmes was like a genie let out of a bottle; there was no way of getting him back and, once at large, he was always available to minister to his master's wants. Doyle eventually brought Holmes back to life and wrote five more volumes about him. For perhaps the only time in his life, he had hit upon a genuine spell.

Whence had he mustered this spell and what elements had been mixed to make it? Well, there was Poe, of course, and there was also unquestionably R. L. Stevenson's *New Arabian Nights*. *The Adventure of the Hansom Cab* and *The Adventure of the Superfluous Mansion* must have suggested both the Sherlock Holmes titles and the formula of taking people to unexpected places and having them witness mysterious happenings. But Doyle, though much less "literary" than Stevenson, somehow got solider results, which depended on quite different qualities from Stevenson's suave Oriental tone and the limpid iridescence of his fantasy. For one thing, Stevenson was weak on character, whereas Doyle had produced two real personalities. And, for another, Conan Doyle had created his own vein of fantasy, which was vivider, if rather less fine, than Stevenson's. You see the force of his imagination exemplified in a curious way in some of those stories in which the dénouement is inadequate or disappointing. A young woman goes to work in a country house where she will be extravagantly overpaid if she will consent to have her hair cut short, to wear a dress of electric blue, to sit in certain places at certain times and to allow herself to be made to laugh uproariously at a succession of funny stories told by the master of the house; a professional interpreter of Greek finds himself suddenly shanghaied in a cab and taken to a stuffy London house with velvet furniture, a high white marble mantelpiece and a suit of Japanese armor, where a man who wears glasses and has a giggling laugh compels him to put questions in Greek to a pale and emaciated captive, whose face is all crisscrossed with sticking plaster.

Neither of these stories—*The Copper Beeches* or *The Greek Interpreter*—quite lives up to its opening evocation. The way of accounting for the sticking plaster seems, indeed, entirely unsatisfactory, and since Watson tells us that this "singular case" is "still involved in some mystery," we are almost inclined to suspect that the affair concealed something else which the detective had failed to penetrate; but the images have exercised their power—a power that is partly due to their contrast with, their startling emergence from, the dull surface of Victorian London.

Here Doyle is exploiting a device quite remote from the suave story-spinning of Stevenson: he is working in the familiar tradition—in which the English art of fiction has excelled since the days of *Robinson Crusoe*—of the commonplace and common-sense narrative which arouses excitement and wonder. He can make us feel the presence of the "sinister"—to use one of his favorite words—even in a situation which does not include any fantastic ingredient. Take the story of *The Naval Treaty*, which follows *The Greek Interpreter* in Doyle's carefully varied program. A young man in the Foreign Office has been entrusted with an important document, which he has been copying at night in his office. He is alone and there is no entrance to the room save by a corridor that leads to the street. No one except the Foreign Minister knows that he has the treaty. At last he rings for the doorman to bring him some coffee, but an unknown woman answers the bell, large and coarse-faced and wearing an apron. She says that she is the doorman's wife and promises to send the coffee, but some time passes and the coffee does not come, and he goes downstairs to see what is the matter. He finds the doorman asleep, but the man is immediately awakened by a bell that rings loudly overhead.

"'I was boiling the kettle when I fell asleep, sir.' He looked at me and then up at the still quivering bell with an ever-growing astonishment upon his face.

"'If you was here, sir, then who rang the bell?' he asked.

" 'The bell!' I cried. 'What bell is it?'
" 'It's the bell of the room you were working in.' "

Both these incidents, so soberly told, the appearance of the woman and the ringing of the bell, give us shocks that reverberate. Of course there is no one upstairs in the room and the naval treaty has been taken.

The stories have also both form and style of a kind very much superior to what one finds in our padded novels, though sometimes, it seems to me, the requirements of length for short stories in the *Strand Magazine* compelled Doyle somewhat to skimp his endings. There is wit, not mere tricks, in the "deductions" of Holmes and wit in the dialogue, and not only in the interchanges between Watson and Holmes but even in some of the stagy lines which Doyle's very sure sense of point save from being merely absurd. Take, for example, the conclusion of *The Second Stain*:

" 'Come, sir,' said he. 'There is more in this than meets the eye. How came the letter back in the box?'

"Holmes turned away smiling from the keen scrutiny of those wonderful eyes.

" 'We also have our diplomatic secrets,' said he and, picking up his hat, he turned to the door."

The writing, of course, is full of clichés, but these clichés are dealt out with a ring which gives them a kind of value, while the author makes speed and saves space so effectively that we are rarely in danger of getting bogged down in anything boring. And the clichés of situation and character are somehow made to function, too, for the success of the general effect. This effect owes its real originality not only to the queer collocations of elements, such as those I have mentioned above, but also to the admirable settings: the somber overcarpeted interiors of the musty empty houses of London, the remote old or new country places, always with shrubbery along the drives; and the characters—the choleric big-game hunters and the high-spirited noble ladies—have been imbued with the atmosphere of the settings and charged with an energy sufficient—like the fierce puppets of a Punch-and-Judy show—to make an impression in their simple roles.

But over the whole epic there hangs an air of irresponsible comedy, like that of some father's rigmarole for children, like that of, say, Albert Bigelow Paine in his stories about the Coon, the Possum and the Old Black Crow who all lived together in a Hollow Tree. The story-teller can make anything happen that will entertain his nightly audience and that will admit some kind of break at bedtime. The invention of Professor Moriarty, that scientific master-mind of crime who was to checkmate the great scientific detective, is simply an improvisation to bring to an end an overlong story, and the duel in which each is straining to outthink and outtrick the other is exhilarating because totally impossible. I do not share the prejudice of some Holmes experts against the two latest series of stories. Inferior though these often are in plot, Doyle amuses himself here in a way which makes them extremely funny. I am delighted by *The Adventure of the Dying Detective*, in which Holmes feigns a tropical disease and refuses to let Watson treat him: "Facts are facts, Watson, and after all, you are only a general practitioner with very limited experience and mediocre qualifications. It is painful to have to say these things, but you leave me no choice." "I was bitterly hurt," says Watson. And it was a capital idea to have Watson himself sometimes undertake the inquiry and bungle it, or, conversely, in other cases, to have Holmes tell the stories instead of Watson, in an attempt to divest them of the fortuitous glamor which he insists that his friend has added. (I have discovered, by the way—though I see that it had already been hinted by Christopher Morley—that Rex Stout's great detective, Nero Wolfe, has the look of having been inspired by one of the most diverting of Doyle's variations: Sherlock's brother Mycroft, who is also a master-mind but who has grown so stout and inert that he is unable to work on a problem till all the data have been dug out and brought him.)

And it all takes place in the Hollow Tree—in that atmosphere of "cozy peril," to quote a phrase from, I think, Mr. Morley, who, in his prefaces to the Sherlock Holmes omnibus and an anthology called *Sherlock Holmes and Dr. Watson*, has written so well on this subject. They will, of course, get safely back to Baker Street, after their vigils and raids and arrests, to discuss the case comfortably in their rooms and have their landlady bring them breakfast the next morning. Law and Order have not tottered a moment; the British police are well in control: they are the stoutest, most faithful fellows in the world if they can only be properly directed by Intellect in the form of a romantic personality possessed by the scientific spirit. All the loose ends of every episode are tidily picked up and tucked in, and even Holmes, though once addicted to cocaine, has been reformed by the excellent Watson. In this world, one can count on the client to arrive at the very moment when his case has just been explained, and Holmes and Watson always find it possible to get anywhere they want to go without a moment's delay or confusion. Here is an incident from *The Greek Interpreter* which illustrates this unfailing punctuality. The interpreter, after his visit to the mysterious house, has been driven away and dropped.

"The carriage which had brought me was already out of sight. I stood gazing round and wondering where on earth I might be, when I saw someone coming towards me in the darkness. As he came up to me I made out that he was a railway porter.

" 'Can you tell me what place this is?' I asked.

" 'Wandsworth Common,' said he.

" 'Can I get a train into town?'

" 'If you walk on a mile or so to Clapham Junction,' said he, 'you'll just be in time for the last to Victoria.' "

So, no matter what those queer Greeks do in London, there will always be a British porter and he will always help you to get your train. In the newer kind of mystery novel, this porter would not have been a real porter; he would have had some unintelligible connection with the men in the upholstered house, and, far from helping the poor interpreter to catch the train, he would have involved him in endless further trouble—just as the man who wanted a young woman in an electric blue dress to cut her hair and laugh at his jokes would have turned out to be suffering from some form of derangement suggested by Krafft-Ebing or Freud. One rarely finds the word "sinister" even in mystery fiction today; it implies that a spy or a murder, a piece of treachery or an insane neurosis, is something of exceptional occurrence.

February 17, 1945

Splendors and Miseries of Evelyn Waugh

THE NEW NOVEL by Evelyn Waugh—*Brideshead Revisited* —has been a bitter blow to this critic. I have admired and praised Mr. Waugh, and when I began reading *Brideshead Revisited,* I was excited at finding that he had broken away from the comic vein for which he is famous and expanded into a new dimension. The new story—with its subtitle, *The Sacred and Profane Memories of Captain Charles Ryder*—is a "serious" novel, in the conventional sense, and the opening is invested with a poetry and staged with a dramatic effectiveness which seem to promise much. An English officer, bored with the Army, finds himself stationed near a great country house which has been turned into soldiers' quarters. It is a place that he once used to visit—his life, indeed, has been deeply involved with the Catholic family who lived there. The story reverts to 1923, at the time when Charles Ryder was at Oxford and first met the younger son of the Marchmains, who became his most intimate friend. This early section is all quite brilliant, partly in the manner of the Waugh we know, partly with a new kind of glamor that is closer to Scott Fitzgerald and

Compton Mackenzie. It is the period that these older writers celebrated, but seen now from the bleak shrivelled forties, so that everything—the freedom, the fun, the varied intoxications of youth—has taken on a remoteness and pathos. The introduction of the hero to the Catholic family and the gradual revelation of their queerness, their differences from Protestant England, is brought off with accomplished art, and through almost the whole of the first half of the book, the habitual reader of Waugh is likely to tell himself that his favorite has been fledged as a first-rank straight novelist.

But this enthusiasm is to be cruelly disappointed. What happens when Evelyn Waugh abandons his comic convention—as fundamental to his previous work as that of any Restoration dramatist—turns out to be more or less disastrous. The writer, in this more normal world, no longer knows his way: his deficiency in common sense here ceases to be an asset and gets him into some embarrassing situations, and his creative imagination, accustomed in his satirical fiction to work partly in two-dimensional caricature but now called upon for passions and motives, produces mere romantic fantasy. The hero is to have an affair with the married elder daughter of the house, and this is conducted on a plane of banality—the woman is quite unreal—reminiscent of the full-dress adulteries of the period in the early nineteen-hundreds when Galsworthy and other writers were making people throb and weep over such fiction as *The Dark Flower*. And as the author's taste thus fails him, his excellent style goes to seed. The writing—which, in the early chapters, is of Evelyn Waugh's best: felicitous, unobtrusive, exact—here runs to such dispiriting clichés as "Still the clouds gathered and did not break" and "So the year wore on and the secret of the engagement spread from Julia's confidantes and so, like ripples on the water, in ever widening circles." The stock characters—the worldly nobleman, the good old nurse—which have always been a feature of Waugh's fiction and which are all right in a harlequinade, here simply become implausible and tiresome. The last scenes are extravagantly absurd, with an absurdity that would be worthy of Waugh at his best if it were not—painful to say—meant quite seriously. The worldly Lord Marchmain, when he left his wife, repudiated his Catholic faith, and on his deathbed he sends the priest packing, but when the old man has sunk lower, the priest is recalled. The family all kneel, and Charles, who is present, kneels, too. Stoutly though he has defended his Protestantism, his resistance breaks down today. He prays that this time the dying man will not reject the final sacrament, and lo, Lord Marchmain makes the sign of the cross! The peer, as he has drifted toward death, has been soliloquizing at eloquent length: "We were knights then, barons since Agincourt, the larger honors came with the Georges," etc., etc., and the reader has an uncomfortable feeling that what has caused Mr. Waugh's hero to plump on his knees is not, perhaps, the sign of the cross but the prestige, in the person of Lord Marchmain, of one of the oldest families in England.

For Waugh's snobbery, hitherto held in check by his satirical point of view, has here emerged shameless and rampant. His admiration for the qualities of the older British families, as contrasted with modern upstarts, had its value in his earlier novels, where the standards of morals and taste are kept in the background and merely implied. But here the upstarts are rather crudely overdone and the aristocrats become terribly trashy, and his cult of the high nobility is allowed to become so rapturous and solemn that it finally gives the impression of being the only real religion in the book.

Yet the novel is a Catholic tract. The Marchmain family, in their various fashions, all yield, ultimately, to the promptings of their faith and bear witness to its enduring virtue; the skeptical hero, long hostile and mocking, eventually becomes converted; the old chapel is opened up and put at the disposition of the troops, and a "surprising lot use it, too." Now, this critic may perhaps be insensible to some value the book will have for other readers, since he is un-

sympathic by conviction with the point of view of the
Catholic convert, but he finds it impossible to feel that
the author has conveyed in all this any actual religious
experience. In the earlier novels of Waugh there was always a very important element of perverse, unregenerate
self-will that, giving rise to confusion and impudence, was
a great asset for a comic writer. In his new book, this theme
is sounded explicitly, with an unaccustomed portentousness
and rhetoric, at an early point in the story, when he speaks
of "the hot spring of anarchy" that "rose from deep furnaces
where was no solid earth, and burst into the sunlight—a
rainbow in its cooling vapors with a power the rocks could
not repress," and of course it is this hot spring of anarchy,
this reckless, unredeemed humanity, that is supposed to
be cooled and controlled by the discipline of the Catholic
faith. But, once he has come to see this force as sin, Evelyn
Waugh seems to be rather afraid of it: he does not allow
it really to raise its head—boldly, outrageously, hilariously
or horribly—as he has in his other books, and the result is
that we feel something lacking. We have come to count on
this Serpent; we are not used to seeing it handled so gin-
gerly; and, at the same time, the religion that is invoked
to subdue it seems more like an exorcistic rite than a force
of regeneration.

There is, however, another subject in *Brideshead Revisited*—a subject which is incompletely developed but
which has far more reality than the religious one: the
situation of Charles Ryder between the Brideshead family
on the one hand and his own family background on the
other. This young man has no mother and his only home
is with a scholarly and self-centered father, who reduces
life to something so dry, so withdrawn, so devoid of affection or color that the boy is driven to look for a home in
the family of his Oxford friend and to idealize their charm
and grace. What are interesting to a non-Catholic reader
are the origins and the evolution of the hero's beglamored
snobbery, and the amusing and chilling picture of Charles's

holidays at home with his father is one of the very good things in the book.

The comic parts of *Brideshead Revisited* are as funny as anything that the author has done, and the Catholic characters are sometimes good, when they are being observed as social types and get the same kind of relentless treatment as the characters in his satirical books. I do not mean to suggest, however, that Mr. Waugh should revert to his earlier vein. He has been steadily broadening his art, and when he next tries a serious novel, he may have learned how to avoid bathos.

In the meantime, I predict that *Brideshead Revisited* will prove to be the most successful, the only extremely successful, book that Evelyn Waugh has written, and that it will soon be up in the best-seller list somewhere between *The Black Rose* and *The Manatee*.

January 5, 1946

When Evelyn Waugh was converted to Catholicism by the Jesuit Father d'Arcy, he wrote, as a tribute to d'Arcy and in celebration of the rebuilding of Campion Hall, the Jesuit college at Oxford, a short biography of Edmund Campion, the Elizabethan Jesuit martyr. This book, which first appeared in 1935, has now been republished and given a new edition. The story is quite soberly and simply told —with no attempt to create historical atmosphere—and it is not uninteresting to read. Campion is very impressive in the utterances which Mr. Waugh quotes. A man of intellectual distinction, exalted religious vocation and great moral and physical courage, he was the victim, after the suppression of Catholicism in England, of one of those political frame-ups which, though not carried out on the same enormous scale or engineered with the same efficiency as those of our own day, were already a feature of the struggle between Catholicism and Protestantism.

Mr. Waugh's version of history, however, turns out, in its larger perspectives, to be more or less in the vein of *1066 and All That*. Catholicism was a Good Thing and

Protestantism was a Bad Thing, and that is all that needs to be said about it. The book is valuable mainly for providing a curious glimpse of the author's conception of modern England. The triumph of Protestantism under Elizabeth meant, he writes, that the country was "secure, independent, insular; the course of her history lay plain ahead: competitive nationalism, competitive industrialism, the looms and coal mines and counting houses, the joint stock companies and the cantonments; the power and the weakness of great possessions." For him, Protestantism is not merely one of the phases of the rise of the middle class; it is the cause of all the phenomena mentioned above. And, in recounting this incident of a period of general religious intolerance, he continually insists on the cruelties of the Protestant persecution of the Catholics but passes lightly over any instance—such as the St. Bartholomew Day's massacre—of the crimes committed by Catholics against Protestants. If we had no source but Mr. Waugh, we might assume that the Society of Jesus had always consisted solely of mild-spirited servants of God, who had never had anything to do with rigging racks or lighting fagots for their enemies.

July 13, 1946

Mr. Waugh has since published two books: *Scott-King's Modern Europe* and *The Loved One,* in which he returns to his earlier manner. Both are short stories rather than novels and both, in comparison with his other work, seem sketchy and incomplete. The first of these, rather like *Scoop,* deals with the misadventures of a teacher from an English public school in Communist-ridden post-war Europe; the second, much the better of the two, with a less ingenuous Englishman in Hollywood. *The Loved One* is extremely funny, but it suffers a little, for an American, from being full of familiar American jokes which Evelyn Waugh has just discovered. It recalls the Nathanael West of *Miss Lonelyhearts* as well as of *The Day of the Locust.* In connection with Mr. Waugh's Catholicism, it suggests one obvious criticism that nobody, I think, has made. *The Loved One* is a farcical satire on those de luxe California cemeteries that attempt to render death less unpleasant by exploiting all the resources of landscape-gardening and Hollywood mummery. To the non-religious reader, however, the patrons and proprietors of Whispering Glades seem more sensible and less absurd than the priest-guided Evelyn Waugh. What the former are trying to do is, after all, merely to gloss over physical death with smooth lawns and soothing rites; but, for the Catholic, the fact of death is not to be faced at all: he is solaced with the fantasy of another world in which everyone who has died in the flesh is somehow supposed to be still alive and in which it is supposed to be possible to help souls to advance themselves by buying candles to burn in churches. The trappings invented for this other world by imaginative believers in the Christian myth—since they need not meet the requirements of reality—beat anything concocted by Whispering Glades.

George Saintsbury's Centenary

THE CENTENARY of George Saintsbury's birth has been celebrated in England by a memorial volume of his uncollected essays. In this country, Mr. Huntington Cairns has edited a volume of Saintsbury's articles on French literature from the *Encyclopaedia Britannica: French Literature and Its Masters*. These essays are not of Saintsbury's best. He needed more room to do himself justice. The article on *French Literature from the Beginning to 1900* has to account for too many names to have a chance to say anything very interesting about them, but the pieces on single figures—especially the Voltaire—are wonderful feats of condensation that manage, in summarizing a lifetime, to include a maximum of detail and, in their briefly expressed comments, to hit all the nails on the head.

It is a good thing to have these essays in book-form, but what are really most needed now are reprints of Saintsbury's important works, which are out of print and very hard to get. Saintsbury, since his death, has come more and more to stand out as the sole English literary critic of the late-nineteenth early-twentieth centuries, the sole full-length professional critic, who is really of first-rate stature. He is perhaps the only English critic, with the possible exception of Leslie Stephen, whose work is comparable, for comprehensiveness and brilliance, to the great French critics of the nineteenth century. Unlike them, he has no interest in ideas. In religion he was Church of England and in politics an extreme Tory, but his prejudices were rarely allowed to interfere with his appetite for good literature, wherever and by whomever written. He was probably the greatest connoisseur of literature—in the same sense that he was a connoisseur of wines, about which he also wrote—that we have ever had in English. In this, he stood quite outside the academic tradition. Though he contributed to the *Encyclopaedia* and to *The Cambridge History of English Literature,* he has always more or less the air of a man who is showing a friend the sights of some well-studied and loved locality.

In his *History of English Prose Rhythm,* Saintsbury apologizes for his own prose style; but the truth is that his prose is excellent: the rhythm of his own writing never falters. He had, in fact, invented a style of much charm and a certain significance: a modern, conversational prose that carries off asides, jokes and gossip as well as all the essential data by a very strong personal rhythm, that drops its voice to interpolate footnotes without seriously retarding the current, and that, however facetious or garrulous, never fails to cover the ground and make the points. The extreme development of this style is to be seen in the *History of the French Novel* written in Saintsbury's later years and one of the most entertaining of books on literature. It is all a gigantic after-dinner talk with an old gentleman who, to his immense entertainment, has read through the whole of French fiction. The only other writer I know who has created a style similar to Saintsbury's is the late Ford Madox Ford. Both these men are worth attention as writers because they found out how to manage a fine and flexible English prose on the rhythms of informal speech rather than on those of literary convention.

The *History of the French Novel* could never have been written by a Frenchman, because the books and the writers it deals with have not been organized and grouped as would have been done by a French professor. The literature of France itself has always been so much guided and rationalized by a criticism that was an integral part of it that it falls naturally into a well-ordered historical picture. Saintsbury's critical method had been evolved in connection with English literature, which, with its relative indifference to movements and schools and its miscellany of remarkable individuals, does not lend itself to this sort of treatment. In consequence, he stops a good deal longer over somebody like Pigault-Lebrun or Restif de La Bretonne than the ordinary French historian would. He does not need to make them fit into a scheme; he simply likes to tell you about them; and, since you will probably never read them, you do not mind getting them thus at second hand. Now, with English writing, this leisurely method of merely showing a guest the sights succeeds where other methods are inadequate. It is inevitable for academic surveys, English as well as French, to attempt to systematize, and since the material with which the English ones deal has been produced with a minimum of system, a great deal that is important and valuable is invariably left out or slighted. English surveys are likely to be dull, where French surveys may be stimulating, and are nearly always readable. But Saintsbury is never dull, because he misses no point of interest. He is to be seen at his very best in his studies of the minor nineteenth-century writers in his *Collected Essays and Papers:* such people as

Peacock, Crabbe, George Borrow, Hogg, Praed and Barham of *The Ingoldsby Legends.* It is impossible to take
care of these writers by subsuming them under some bigger
name. Each is unlike anyone else, unique and fully developed; each has to be explored for his own sake. And
Saintsbury explored and appraised them as nobody else
has done. Though more searching essays than Saintsbury's
have been written on some of the greater nineteenth-century writers, it would be true in a sense to say that the
full history of English nineteenth-century literature has
never been written except by Saintsbury.

Nor did his relish for such lesser figures confuse his view
of the greater. He made a few rather queer evaluations,
as every good critic does—his almost unqualified enthusiasm
for Thackeray and his contempt for *Liaisons Dangereuses;*
and it is true, as has sometimes been said of him, that he
does not plumb the deepest literature deeply. But at least
he has arrived by himself at his reasons for the greatness
of the greatest. He never takes merits for granted. If the
relative amount of space assigned to the various subjects
may not always, in a given book of Saintsbury's, seem
proportionate to their importance, it is likely to be due to
the fact that he had, in his career as a journalist, to treat
some of the great figures so many times. If you feel, say,
that Shakespeare seems slighted in his *History of Elizabethan Literature,* you will find that he has done him
magnificently in *The Cambridge History of English Literature;* if Bulwer-Lytton, in some other work, seems to
command as much attention as Dickens, you will find
Dickens studied on a larger scale and in a more serious way
somewhere else.

He had for a long time had some prejudice against Dante
and did not read him till rather late in life, when the tastes
of many critics would have already formed a closed cosmos;
but when he did sit down at last to *La Commedia Divina,*
he conceded its greatness at once. It is curious to find this
confession cropping up in the history of the French novel,
and it is somehow characteristic of Saintsbury that he

should be comparing Dante with some novelist of the nineteenth century, and mention incidentally that he puts him at the top of imaginative fiction. For, except in treating books chronologically, as he might arrange wines in his cellar, he has little real interest in history, and social changes tend merely to annoy him because they distract from the enjoyment of literature. The books are on his shelves like bottles, and it is the most natural thing in the world for him to take down a good medieval vintage made from astringent Italian grapes along with a good dry vintage of French nineteenth-century realism.

February 2, 1946

Ambushing a Best-Seller

THIS MAGAZINE has not always shown foresight in recognizing future successes, and it has sometimes ignored or dismissed in a note novels that were destined to sell hundreds of thousands and to go on selling for years. I have, therefore, lately been watching the publishers' lists in the hope of catching one of these books before it started on its triumphant progress; and, difficult though it seems to be to distinguish the coming best-seller from other specimens of inferior fiction, I have decided—from the amount and kind of advertising that the book is being given by the publisher and from the appearance of a picture of the heroine on the cover of *Publishers' Weekly*—that *The Turquoise*, by Anya Seton, has a good chance of landing in the upper brackets. I may be wrong, but I am going to report on it on the assumption that it will be widely read.

The heroine of *The Turquoise*, then, is, as I hardly need to say, a Cinderella. The child of the younger son of a Scottish baronet and of the daughter of a Spanish hidalgo resident in the American Southwest, she is early left a penniless orphan and grows up among the illiterate natives, part Indian, part Spanish, of New Mexico. "Her mouth, always wide, lost its childish innocence, and the lips revealed a passionate curve. Her skin grew moister and more glowing; beneath the dirt and tan shone the velvety whiteness of her Castilian heritage. She was still a thin, ugly child, her gray eyes were still too big for the small face and gave her a goblin look, but she now sometimes showed the first indications of the sex magnetism which was later to give her an illusion of beauty more seductive than actual symmetry." Her natural high breeding and dignity also asserted themselves in the sordid milieux of her early years, so that people instinctively deferred to her quality.

She had been named Santa Fe, after the place where she was born, but her father had been shy of the name for its association with her mother's death. " 'Santa Fe—' said Andrew bitterly, and at the sound of his voice the baby suddenly smiled. 'Aye, 'tis a daft name for ye, small wonder ye smile.' He repeated the name, and this time the last syllable echoed in his mind with a peculiar relevance. 'Fey! There's a true Scottish word will fit you, for ye're fated—doomed to die as we all are, poor bairnie.' " She was doomed, yet she was also chosen, for she had inherited from a Scottish grandmother a gift of mind-reading and second sight, which enabled her not only, by a little concentration, accurately to predict the future but also to know what other people were thinking and to tell them what they had in their pockets. "You are born to great vision, little one," said an old Indian shaman in a "deep, singing tone." "For you they have made thin the curtain which hides the real. But there is danger. You must listen to the voice of the spirit, or your body and its passions will betray you." And he gave her a turquoise pendant, "the color of the Great Spirit's dwelling," in order that she should always remember that her power derives from the Spirit.

She ran away, at the age of seventeen, with a travelling Irish adventurer who had a one-man medicine show. She amazed him by divining at once the ingredients of the

"Elixir" he was selling. "There came the sensation of light and a swift impression which she translated into words. 'In this bottle, there is river water—' She paused, then amplified, 'Water from the Rio Grande where you filled it.' Terry made an exclamation and uncrossed his legs. Fey continued calmly, 'There is also whiskey, a little sugar and —chile powder. No more.' She put the bottle on the floor beside her stool, and raised her eyes." He was impressed by her possible usefulness as a feature for his medicine show, a dependable mind-reading act which required no confederate or code; and she, on her side, was attracted to him strongly. "He was twenty-three and of that dashing Irish type which rouses many a woman's imagination. . . . The chin was pugnacious, the mouth, warmly sensual, also showed humor, while the greenish eyes, ill-tempered now, as they often were, seldom produced that impression on women because of their romantic setting of thick dark lashes. He was vivid and very male. Fey, unaccustomed to height and breadth of shoulder, gazed at the ripple of muscles beneath his white silk shirt, and thought him miraculous."

They took to the road together, got married. But her gift, when she debased it, failed her: she could no longer tell prostitutes their original names or inventory the contents of pocketbooks. Dashing Terry—who sincerely admires her but who has to be got out of the way—is rather implausibly made to desert her in a cheap lodging-house in New York. She had been pregnant, though he had not known it, but for a time she was able to earn a living at the Arcadia Concert Saloon. "While she sang, wandering from table to table strumming her guitar and smiling, she diffused sex magnetism, and she titivated the goggling out-of-towners who comprised three-quarters of the Arcadia's patronage." (The proper meaning of "titivate"—here, as often, used for titillate—seems hopelessly to have suffered the fate of "jejune" and "disinterested.") Then she goes to have her baby in a hospital, where a Quaker woman doctor befriends her and tries to persuade her to study medicine. Here she is nursing her baby: "The girl was beautiful; she [the woman doctor] had never realized it before. Or if not exactly beautiful, something far more disturbing. She was alluring, every line of her body, partly unclothed as it now was, pointed to seductive allure."

But the hospital is repellent to Fey: "I loathe sick people and poor people," she tells herself. "I want nothing now of life but luxury and refinement." She has conceived an audacious design on a certain Simeon Tower, the son of a Jewish peddler, who has become one of New York's richest men by dint of his native shrewdness and by "throwing plums to Big Bill Tweed as he rose to power by means of the most corrupt politics ever known in New York." She goes straight to his office in Wall Street and forces her way into his presence. "I think we would like each other," she says. " 'That is a trifle crude,' he said coldly. 'Will you kindly state your business?' His blunt, well-manicured hand made a slight gesture, the prelude to dismissal." But he looks "at the full high outline of her breasts under the leaf-brown silk, at the wide coral-tinted mouth," and succumbs to her seductive allure. He soon gets her a divorce and marries her, and there begins one of those period pageants which, with the recent patriotic exploitation of the American historical legend, have become a cheap and routine feature of so many of our books, plays and films. There is an "at home" at Phoebe and Alice Cary's, at which the visitor is "drawn over to a red settee where Susan B. Anthony and Elizabeth Cady Stanton are discussing . . . the advent of the bustle." (Fey has of course recognized early the greatness of Walt Whitman. Opening *Leaves of Grass* in a book store, " 'This is for me,' she said" at once, "her eyes shining. 'This man understands.' Mr. Tibbins had flushed a dull red. 'That's not a proper book for a young woman to read!' 'Oh, but it is!' said Fey, hardly conscious of him. 'It's true and good. It makes me strong.' And her rapt eyes reread a page.") Simeon is shocked and alarmed by the fact that "on January sixth, Jim Fisk had been shot and killed by Josie Mansfield's paramour, Edward Stokes," and he has a life-or-death struggle with Jay Gould, as "the Mephisto of Wall Street sits like a small black spider silently enmeshing enterprise after enterprise." Simeon Tower has hitherto been excluded from the social Four Hundred, the custodian of which is Ward McAllister; but Fey, with her usual directness—which Simeon "dimly recognized as the product of generations of breeding"—goes to McAllister and asks to be taken in. "It is," he tells her, "my privilege to help guard the—may I say—inner sanctum from pollution"; but "I'll see what I can do," he ends, bowing.

At the first great ball that the Towers give, with Mrs. Astor present, Fey's rascally ex-husband turns up, having impudently crashed the gate. Fey yields again to his Irish charm and spends a night in a raffish hotel with him. But Terry has conceived the idea of blackmailing Simeon Tower and, "sunk in an amorous drowsiness," he murmurs, " 'The old boy's an easy mark.' 'Why do you say that?' She pulled the light chain and the gas flared up, while she contemplated Terry with steady narrowed eyes." "Listen then, Terry," she announces, when she has grasped the situation. "It is finished at last, and I feel for myself a loathing. I was always a—an incident to you, as I have been now. I knew this. I even told myself this over and over, but I— Oh, what's the use! Perhaps it was necessary that by yielding to my body I might become free of it and you."

Unfortunately, Fey's second sight was still in abeyance at this time, so she could not prepare herself for what was about to happen. With the connivance of a villainous secretary, Terry launches his campaign of blackmail, and one day, when he has thrown it in Simeon's teeth that Fey has been unfaithful to him, Simeon takes out a revolver and shoots him. Simeon is sent to the Tombs, and we are led to believe that Fey is going to marry a Scottish relation who has been sent over by her grandfather to find her. But, on a visit to her husband in prison, her power of clairvoyance dramatically comes back (though it is now, it seems, moral insight rather than mind-reading or knowledge of the future). The words of the old Indian return; the past reveals itself to her in a series of blinding flashbacks. She knows she has been to blame. Her consciousness is penetrated "with annihilating truth": *"You are responsible, you!"* She tells her suitor that she can never be his and makes him return to Scotland; she trains herself in hospital work; she goes on the stand at her husband's trial and, by confessing her infidelity, obtains the acquittal of Simeon. Then she takes him away to New Mexico, where they live for the rest of their years in a four-room adobe house, while she ministers to the natives, who "regard her with semi-superstitious reverence." "She had much medical knowledge and she had an almost miraculous intuition as to what ailed the sick bodies or souls which came to her." After her death, she was known as "La Santa."

The Turquoise thus follows a familiar line. It is a typical American novel written by a woman for women. The great thing about this kind of fiction is that the heroine must combine, in one lifetime, as many enjoyable kinds of role as possible: she must be sexually desirable and successful, yet a competent professional woman; she must pass through picaresque adventures, yet attain the highest social position; she must be able to break men's hearts, yet be capable of prodigies of fidelity; she must have every kind of worldly success, yet rise at moments to the self-sacrifice of the saint. She must, in fact, have every possible kind of cake and manage to eat it, too. A bait is laid for masculine readers, also, by periodically disrobing the heroine and writing emphatically of her sexual appetite. And the whole book is written in that tone and prose of the women's magazines which is now so much a standard commodity that it is probably possible for the novelist to pick it up at the corner drugstore with her deodorant and her cold cream.

Yet *The Turquoise* sticks below the level of the more compelling specimens of this fiction by reason of the lack in it of any real feeling of even the feminine day-dreaming kind that does sometimes enliven these books. There is not even a crude human motivation of either the woman or the men. The heroine, who is supposed to be intuitive, full of warm emotions and eager desires, is as incredible in her relations with her husbands as they are in their relations with her. She is made, for example, to lay siege to Simeon simply because she craves money and position, but the stigma of calculation is eliminated by showing her later as passionately in love with her husband—yet not so passionately, it appears still later, that she will not be tempted to slip with Terry. The whole thing is as synthetic, as arbitrary, as basically cold and dead, as a scenario for a film. And now the question presents itself: Will real men and women, in large numbers, as the publishers obviously hope, really buy and read this arid rubbish, which has not even the rankness of the juicier trash? Or have I been using up all this space merely to warn you against a dud? Watch the best-seller lists for the answer.

February 16, 1946

Several people who read this article imagined that it was a burlesque; they assumed, from the absurdity of the story, that I must have made the whole thing up. But *The Turquoise* was perfectly real, and it has justified my worst apprehensions by selling more than nine hundred thousand copies.

Oscar Wilde: "One Must Always Seek What Is Most Tragic"

THE VIKING PRESS has brought out in its Portable Library series a selection from the writings of Oscar Wilde, with a dozen unpublished letters and an introduction by Richard Aldington, and Harper is about to publish a new biography of Wilde by Hesketh Pearson: *Oscar Wilde: His Life and*

Wit. This last book is a journalistic job. Mr. Pearson is an actor turned writer, who has also done biographies of Erasmus Darwin, Sydney Smith, Hazlitt, Gilbert and Sullivan, Labouchère, Anna Seward, Tom Paine, Shakespeare, Bernard Shaw and Conan Doyle. His book makes interesting reading, for he has assembled from various sources an immense number of anecdotes and sayings, and he has managed to tell a straighter story than we usually get where Wilde is concerned. Oscar Wilde has hitherto been written about mostly by his personal friends, among whom the vituperative controversies seem with time to become more embittered. Mr. Pearson stands quite clear of all these disputes, and he writes with good sense and good temper. But his book is only another example of the current kind of popular biography that adds little to our knowledge of its subject: non-critical, non-analytic and, though dealing with literary matters, essentially non-literary.

Mr. Pearson does, however, tell Wilde's story with a new emphasis which is all to the good. The public disgrace of Wilde's trial has been allowed so much to blur the outline of the whole of his preceding career and to tarnish the brilliance of his abilities that it is a good thing to have him presented by someone, not afraid to admire him, who restores to him the pride and prestige of the days before his disaster. From Frank Harris's biography, for example, you get an almost completely grotesque picture of Oscar's parents, Sir William and Lady Wilde. Frank Harris, with gusto, makes the most of Sir William's bad reputation as an insatiable seducer of women, and there is little in his chapter on the Wilde family save an account of the scandalous lawsuit in which the elder Wilde became involved, when a more or less deranged young lady, who had come to him as a patient, accused him of having raped her while she was under an anesthetic. Nor does he tell us much more about Lady Wilde than that R. Y. Tyrrell considers her "a hifalutin, pretentious creature" with a "reputation founded on second-rate verse-making." Lord Alfred Douglas, in his ghost-written book *Oscar Wilde and Myself*, permitted his name to be signed to sneers that were quite unwarranted about the origins and standing of the Wildes. Mr. Pearson is, so far as I know, the first of Oscar Wilde's biographers to do his remarkable parents justice, and a new biography of the elder Wilde—*Victorian Doctor*, by T. G. Wilson—gives an even more complete account of the family background of Oscar. This latter book, the work of a Dublin doctor, is a variedly interesting chronicle of political and medical events and of antiquarian research in Ireland, and it confirms Mr. Pearson in establishing the importance of Lady Wilde in the first of these fields and the distinction of her husband in the others. William Wilde, who was knighted for his achievements, was, it seems, one of the greatest aurists and oculists of the English-speaking world of his time; Jane Francesca Elgee (the Elgees were Algiati of Florence, and Oscar's Italian blood should be taken into account in considering his theatrical instincts and his appetite for the ornate), though a somewhat worse than mediocre poet, had played in youth a conspicuous role as a champion of Irish nationalism and later translated from German and French and wrote books on social problems. Both were persons of wide cultivation and remarkable intellectual ability, and they shared also an independence of character and a personal eccentricity that sometimes got them disliked in Dublin.

Oscar was brought up in this tradition, and he followed it from his earliest years. Though he liked to appear off-hand and lazy, his assimilative powers were prodigious, and he seems to have been at Oxford the best Greek scholar of his day. Nor was he lacking in strength or courage. The notion of him as soft and wilting has been partly the result of his "aesthetic pose," parodied by Gilbert in *Patience*, partly an unjustified inference from his homosexual habits. On a trip through one of the wilder parts of Greece in his undergraduate days, he carried a gun, Mr. Pearson tells us, and seems to have stood up to the natives as boldly as Byron did, just as later, on his visit to the United States, he won the respect of the cowboys, the Colorado miners and the San Francisco Bohemian Club by the intrepid good humor with which he accepted the crudeness and the outlandishness of pioneer life and by his indomitable head for liquor (a virtue which Lord Alfred Douglas, even at his most vindictive, admits that Wilde retained till a short time before his death). Mr. Pearson, on the testimony of an Oxford Blue of Oscar Wilde's time at Magdalen, is able to explode the story of his having been held under the pump by a group of jeering students, who had also smashed his china. "So far from being a flabby aesthete," says this contemporary, Sir Frank Benson, "there was only one man in the college, and he rowed seven in the Varsity Eight, who had the ghost of a chance in a tussle with Wilde." When a mob that had set out to maul him sent four boys in their cups to his rooms, Wilde succeeded in throwing them out and, picking the last of them up like a baby, "carried him to his rooms, and, having ceremoniously buried him beneath a pile of his own luxurious furniture, invited the spectators, now pro-Oscar to a man, to sample the fellow's wines and spirits, an invitation that was accepted with peculiar pleasure on account of the owner's present plight and past stinginess." It was precisely this self-confidence and audacity that misled him into bringing his libel suit against the Marquess of Queensberry and that sustained him to face trial when the Crown brought its action against him. Mr. Pearson gives an exhilarating version—for which, of course, we can have only Wilde's word—of his reception of the Marquess and a pugilist bodyguard when Queensberry came to his house to insult him: "This is the Marquess of Queensberry," he told his seventeen-year-old footman, "the most infamous brute in London. You are never to allow him to enter my house again." There is thus much in Mr. Pearson's book to confirm W. B. Yeats's view, expressed in his autobiography, that Wilde was "essentially a man of action, that he was a writer by perversity and accident, and would have been more important as soldier or politician."

After the decades of bickering among Wilde's friends as to who was the cause of his downfall and as to who, in his years of exile, did or did not give him money, it is a relief to read an account that brings out the stronger side of Wilde's personality, as well as his natural generosity and kindness, of which Mr. Pearson gives many instances. But it is a weakness of Mr. Pearson as a biographer of Wilde that he tends to ignore, though he cannot exclude, his subject's fundamental perversity. Mr. Pearson's sole attempt to throw light on the complexities and conflicts of Wilde's nature is a theory that his intellect had developed while his emotions remained immature. But the perversity of Oscar Wilde—by which I do not mean merely his sexual inversion—was as much a part of his thought as it was of his emotional life. The whole force of his wit is derived from it. He regarded himself, as he wrote in *De Profundis*, as "one of those who are made for exceptions, not for laws." It was Wilde's special gift, in his writings, to find expression for this impulse in a form that charms at the same time that it startles, but this perversity was also the mainspring of the tragedy of Wilde's career which is somehow so much more impressive than anything he ever wrote, or, rather, which gives to his writings an impressiveness they might not otherwise have.

This drama has never as yet really been dealt with by any of his biographers. The homosexuality that grew on Wilde was merely among its elements. There was nothing inevitable, from the moral point of view, in his having been punished for this. It is absurd for Bernard Shaw to say, as he does in his preface to the new edition of Frank Harris's book on Wilde, that "Oscar's ruin was caused by his breach of the Criminal Law Amendment Act and by nothing else." His suit against the Marquess of Queensberry was a disinterested though an ill-advised action, prompted by his infatuation with Lord Alfred Douglas, who, childish and hysterical himself, wanted revenge against his rabid father, and who never for a second hesitated, in gratifying his selfish spite, to let Oscar run terrible risks. Lord Alfred, as he appears in the descriptions of him written by other people and in his own self-justificatory polemics, makes such an unpleasant impression that it is only by reading *Dorian Gray* and *The Portrait of Mr. W. H.*, in which Wilde, writing before he met Douglas, describes his romantic ideal, that we can see how Lord Alfred represented it, and it is only by reading Douglas' sonnet on Wilde, written after the latter's death, that we can see that Wilde's admiration was not entirely misplaced. But it was certainly, on Wilde's side, this idealization of Douglas, and, on Douglas' side, his adoption of Wilde as a kind of substitute father, who, as he thought, could stand up to his real father, that set the machinery of disaster in motion.

The next question, however, is why Oscar, after losing his suit against Queensberry, insisted on remaining in England to face the second of the criminal trials—the jury having disagreed in the first—in which he was prosecuted by the public authorities on charges arising from the evidence presented by Queensberry in the original suit, when he could perfectly well have escaped to the Continent. The explanations usually given are Wilde's pugnacious Irish pride, stimulated by that of his mother, who had told him that if he ran away she would never speak to him again, and his desire to vindicate his character in the interests of his wife and children. But by that time he already knew what the evidence against him was and he should have foreseen his defeat, as, in fact, he should have had the foresight not to take the legal offensive against Queensberry (Bernard Shaw says he was drunk when he did this). I want to point out that a sense of damnation, a foreboding of tragic failure, is to be found in the writing of Wilde from a time long before he was caught in the particular noose that landed him in Reading Jail. It is the theme of the sonnet *Hélas!* as it is of *Dorian Gray*: it is sounded, as Mr. Pearson notes, even in *An Ideal Husband*. And the conflict that is to end in collapse is reflected by his continual antithesis of what he regarded as his "pagan" side to what he regarded as his "Christian" instincts, by which literary phrases he really referred to his appetites and his moral sense. For an "aesthete" like Wilde's master, Pater, it was possible to savor both points of view in a state of serene contemplation; but, though Wilde could see "beauty" alike in the sensuous pleasures of the one and in the suffering implied by the other, he could not help, behind his smiling boldness, being troubled and torn between them. The impulse of perversity in him was constantly working both ways: it impelled him not only to disconcert the expectations of the conventional world by shocking paradoxes and scandalous behavior, it caused him also to betray his pagan creed by indulgence in Christian compunction. There are moments when we get the impression not merely that he apprehended catastrophe but that he even in some sense invited it; when we feel that, having flouted the respectable world by making an immense amount of money and a conspicuous social success through mockery of its codes and standards, he turned against his own arrogance and kicked wealth and success downstairs.

It throws some light on this psychological procedure of Wilde's to refer to Yeats's portrait of him in *The Trembling of the Veil*. Yeats describes the Wilde family in Ireland as "very imaginative and learned," "dirty, untidy" and "daring," and speaks of Wilde's "half-civilized blood," which did not allow him to "endure the sedentary toil of creative art." It is certainly true of Wilde that, with much sensitivity and nobility, he had also a certain coarseness, and his pursuit of the "pagan" ideal always had a tendency to lead him into vulgar ostentation and self-indulgence. The trouble is that, when, fed up with luxury, he turns away in disgust, it is usually not in the direction of the "sedentary toil of creative art" but in the direction of a version of the Christian ideal of humility and abnegation—some of his fairy-stories illustrate this appallingly—that is itself ostentatious and vulgar. Yet one finds in him, also, at moments, a sense of guilt and a bitter chagrin at having fallen very far short of the best that he could imagine. There is, of course, in *De Profundis,* a certain amount of maudlin Christian emotion, but there is also the other thing. "While I see," he says soberly enough, "that there is nothing wrong in what one does, I see that there is something wrong in what one becomes." One of his principal reproaches against Lord Alfred Douglas, whether the latter deserved it or not, is that Douglas interfered with his work, and it is his consciousness of sin for the neglect of this work rather than grief at having injured his family which seems to make him feel, in prison, that it is just for him to expiate his debaucheries. Even here, to be sure, he is acting, and there is testimony, as Mr. Pearson indicates (he might have added that of Ford Madox Ford), that Oscar sometimes overacted the poverty and misery of his final years. But the fact that he is always acting does not deprive his performance of value. This performance is not merely literary. In his writing, his imagination often dresses itself floridly and trashily; it is only at his most intellectual—that is, when we get his wit at its purest and its least arty—that he arrives at an excellent style. One has to combine his writing, the records of his conversation and the sequence of events in his life in order to appreciate Wilde and to see that, though one cannot describe him as precisely a first-rate writer, he did somehow put on a first-rate show.

There is as yet no biography of Wilde which goes at all behind the scenes of this drama, and the only descriptions of him which show any real psychological insight are those of Yeats and Gide. It seems to have been to Gide, always conscious of moral problems, that Wilde, always sensitive to his audience, made the most vivid revelation of his own conception of his role in the successive scenes of the play. "My duty to myself," he told Gide when he saw him in Algeria in January, 1895, at the time when the Marquess of Queensberry had already begun to bait him, "is to amuse myself terrifically . . . no happiness— only pleasure. One must always seek what is most tragic.*

* *"Pas le bonheur! Surtout pas le bonheur. Le plaisir! Il faut vouloir toujours le plus tragique."* These quotations are from

. . . My friends are extraordinary; they advise me to be prudent. But prudence!—is that possible for me? It would be to return on my tracks. I must push things as far as possible. I cannot go any further, and something will have to happen—something different." And later, when he had come out of prison and Gide had gone to see him in France: "One must never take up again the same existence one has had before. My life is like a work of art: an artist never repeats the same work—or if he does, it is only for the reason that he did not succeed the first time. My life before I went to prison was the greatest success possible. Now it is a completed thing."

As for the clinical aspect of Oscar Wilde's case, there has been no careful study of it—though he deserves the same kind of attention that has been given to Maupassant and Swift. Mr. Pearson, Dr. Wilson and Frank Harris have pointed out the striking parallel between the last years of Oscar's life and the last years of Sir William Wilde's. Both were dragged down, at the height of their fame, by sexual scandals that brought them into court, and the father withdrew afterward from Dublin and almost completely abandoned his profession, just as the son fled to France and ceased to write. Did the father's example here exert a compulsive influence or was some pathological principle operating in both cases? Bernard Shaw suggested, in his memoir in the first edition of Harris's life, that both Oscar and his mother had the physical signs of a derangement of the pituitary gland, and Dr. Wilson has discussed this idea on the basis of more recent researches into the various glandular types. But there is apparently another factor in the pathology of Oscar Wilde—a factor which, so far as I know, has never been emphasized save in the writings of Wilde's quixotic and non-homosexual friend, Robert Harborough Sherard. We are usually told in the books about

---

Gide's little book on Wilde. He adds: "*Je n'ai rien inventé, rien arrangé, dans les derniers propos que je cite. Les paroles de Wilde sont présentes à mon esprit, et j'allais dire à mon oreille.*"

Wilde, as if it were something of merely casual interest, that he probably died of syphilis. But if he was really a victim of syphilis, it is surely important to know how this malady had been acquired and how long and how severely he had been suffering from it. We learn now from Dr. Wilson's book that he is supposed to have contracted it at Oxford, but he does not pursue the subject. It would help to explain Wilde if it were proved that he was haunted through his adult life by an uncured syphilitic infection, and his illness—made rapidly worse, it is said, by the drinking of his last years—should certainly be taken into account in considering the demoralization into which he finally sank. In the cases of Baudelaire and Maupassant, it seems obvious that the morose disaffection of the one and the desperate pessimism of the other were the shadows of the syphilitic's doom in the days when the disease was incurable. In Wilde's case, the man is so bland, the work so bright-hued and amusing, that his biographers—having already to deal with the problem of his homosexuality— seem reluctant to come to grips with another distasteful factor; but, in shirking it, I believe, they slight also both the interest of Oscar Wilde's work and the tragedy of his life. Read *The Picture of Dorian Gray*, or even the best of his fairy tales, *The Birthday of the Infanta*, with the *Spirochaeta pallida* in mind. In such stories, the tragic heroes are shown in the peculiar position of suffering from organic maladies—in the one case, a moral corruption which grows; in the other, a permanent repulsiveness—without, up to a point, being forced to experience the evils entailed by them. Dorian Gray conceals his vices and is able to evade their consequences; the Dwarf in *The Birthday of the Infanta* is not saddened or embittered by his ugliness because he does not know how he looks. But in the end, in both cases, the horror breaks out: the afflicted one must recognize himself and be recognized by other people as the odious creature he is, and his disease or disability will kill him. This theme of impending collapse is a recurrent one with Oscar Wilde, and it must have some very close connection with his conception of his own nature and its destiny. One can account for it purely in terms of Wilde's sexual and moral life, without supposing him to have been doomed by syphilis; yet it is hard to believe that a nature so elastic and so insouciant could have been broken so completely and so quickly without some shattering physical cause.

June 29, 1946

Since the above was written, a volume called *The Trials of Oscar Wilde* in the *Notable British Trials* series has supplied the clinical facts that the biographies of Wilde lack. I quote from Appendix E by the editor, H. Montgomery Hyde: "Certain it is that Wilde betrayed no signs of abnormality in adolescence and early manhood. On the contrary, his inclinations seem to have been decidedly heterosexual. While an undergraduate at Oxford, he contracted syphilis as the result of a casual connexion, probably with a prostitute. In those days the recognized treatment for this disease was with mercury. In Wilde's case this treatment undoubtedly produced the discolouration and decay of his teeth, which remained a permanent feature of his appearance for the remainder of his life and added to the general impression of physical overgrowth and ugliness which his person presented on acquaintance. Nor, it may be added, was there the slightest suggestion of effeminacy about him, either at Oxford or at any subsequent period. . . . We know, too, that he was deeply in love with his wife at the time of their marriage, and that they experienced normal sexual intercourse. Indeed, two sons were born of the union before the rift between them took place. . . . Before proposing to his wife, Wilde had been to consult a doctor in London, who had assured him that he was completely cured of his youthful malady. On the strength of his assurance he got married. About two years later he discovered to his dismay that all traces of syphilis had not been eradicated from his system, and it was this unpleasant discovery which obliged him to discontinue physical relations with his wife. In the result, *inter alia*, he turned toward homosexuality." The doctor who attended him in prison reported that Wilde's disease was then in an advanced stage. No wonder he soon ceased to function when he finally got away to the Continent.

Books of Etiquette and Emily Post

PROFESSOR ARTHUR M. SCHLESINGER, the Harvard historian, has written an entertaining little treatise called *Learning How to Behave: A Historical Study of American Etiquette Books.* It is curious and rather instructive to look at the development of the United States from the point of view of the literature of etiquette. The first manuals derived from Europe and emphasized deference to rank to the point of, in one case, admonishing the young: "If thy superior be relating a story, say not, 'I have heard it before.' . . . If he tell it not right, snigger not"; but after the Revolution, and especially after the advent of Jackson, the object became not to define class differences but to provide a set of prescriptions which would show anyone how to become a gentleman. The Southerners had, however, based their practice on seventeenth-century guides which helped the planter "to model his life on that of the English landed gentry" and "provided a fairly consistent chart of behavior . . . in emulation of the ancient ideals of Christian chivalry"; and they continued to follow this code. In the period after the Civil War, when the big fortunes were being made, a fresh crop of volumes appeared which had the purpose of orienting the newly rich among the refinements and complications of calling cards and formal dinners. There was an average of five such a year, and this continued through to 1945.

The two greatest publishing successes in the department

of etiquette date from the beginning of the nineteen-twenties. At this time, a Miss Lillian Eichler, an advertising copywriter, then eighteen and just out of high school, sold thousands of copies of an *Encyclopedia of Etiquette* by means of a series of advertisements with the caption "What's Wrong with This Picture?" But the book—which had been written in 1901—was by that time, it seems, obsolete (Mr. Schlesinger does not tell us in what respect), for it was returned by "droves of dissatisfied customers." The publisher then proposed to Miss Eichler that she should herself do an up-to-date book, and the result was *The Book of Etiquette*, which between 1921 and 1945 sold over a million copies. In 1922, Emily Post brought out her *Etiquette*, which by 1945 had sold more than two-thirds of a million.

An examination of these two manuals reveals fundamental differences between them and suggests that they have been appealing to two rather different publics. Miss Eichler is practical and comfortable (her book is now frankly called *Today's Etiquette*). She tells you how to teach the children table manners and how to give a dinner without servants. She makes rough tabulations of vintage wines and supplies reliable recipes for half-a-dozen well-known cocktails; she recommends, in a chapter on *The Nature and Meaning of Culture*, that one "read more than one kind of literature: not mystery stories alone, nor light fiction alone," and she lists "nine painters of undisputed glory, with whose work every person of culture should be at least familiar." The precepts are mostly appropriate for anyone of moderate income, and the whole tone is non-invidious. She makes social life sound easy and jolly. But Mrs. Post is another affair. I had had no conception of her extraordinary book till I looked into it recently, fell under its spell and read it almost through. Mrs. Post is not merely the author of a comprehensive textbook on manners: she is a considerable imaginative writer, and her book has some of the excitement of a novel. It has also the snob-appeal which is evidently an important factor in the success of a Marquand or a Galsworthy. (I should explain that the edition I read was the third printing, of 1922.)

Mrs. Post has produced a world which has its characters, its atmosphere, its drama. I was reminded, after reading *Etiquette*, of the late Scott Fitzgerald's once telling me that he had looked into Emily Post and been inspired with the idea of a play in which all the motivations should consist of trying to do the right thing. The element of dramatic conflict would be produced by setting people at cross-purposes through stalemates of good form, from which the only possible rescue would be through the intervention of some bounder as *deus ex machina* to put an end to the sufferings of the gentlefolk who had been paralyzed by Mrs. Post's principles. (There are actually novels by Howells, and even by Henry James, which very nearly fulfill this formula.) For it is true that Mrs. Post has supplied all the materials for such a drama. Her ideal gentleman-clubman and her ideal feminine house guest—described in little essays like the "characters" of La Bruyère or the *Spectator*—are models which can never deviate, and thoroughly priggish figures which would lend themselves to satirical comedy. The "considerate guest," in particular, who is always perfectly sweet to everyone and always wants to do what the others are doing, who pretends to like children and dogs and lets them "climb over her" though she loathes them, could easily be shown as a menace from whom the party would have to be saved by Mrs. Post's hideous villain: "The Guest No One Invites Again."

But Mrs. Post, in providing illustrations, has also invented types that have names, personalities and histories, and that are threaded, like the characters of Proust, in and out all through her book. These figures were originally intended merely as convenient dummies to stand in the places of hosts and guests when she was showing how the right kind of entertaining might be done on various scales by people on different income levels; but they have taken such a hold on the author that they have gratuitously been developed to exemplify, like the groups in Proust, a variety of social milieux. They do, however, all belong to Society, and the author, unlike Miss Eichler, always assumes that the reader wants to belong to Society, too.

At the top of Mrs. Post's structure, from the point of view of a wealth which is combined with "social credentials," stand the Worldlys of Great Estates (run by their butler Hastings) and the Gildings of Golden Hall. The Worldlys are a little difficult, they are constrained by the expensive habits and the inflated self-importance of the rich; but the Gildings are more human and always fun. Of Golden Hall, Mrs. Post writes: "The house is a palace, the grounds are a park. There is not only a long wing of magnificent guest rooms in the house, occupied by young girls or important older people, but there is also a guest annex, a separate building designed and run like the most luxurious country club. . . . Perfectly equipped Turkish and Russian baths in charge of the best Swedish masseur and masseuse procurable . . . a glass-roofed and enclosed riding ring—not big enough for games of polo, but big enough to practise in winter," etc. It was after a party at Golden Hall that Mrs. Toplofty, Bobo Gilding's great-aunt, exclaimed, "How are any of us ever going to amuse any one after *this?* I feel like doing my guest rooms up in moth balls." Bobo Gilding (whose nickname is incidentally explained in a section intended to discourage what Mrs. Post calls conversational "door-slammers": "As for the name 'Bobo,' it's asinine." "Oh, it's just one of those children's names that stick sometimes for life." "Perfect rot. Ought to be called by his name.")—Bobo Gilding, on his side, does not care for his aunt's rather pompous parties, since "entering a drawing-room [for Bobo] was more suggestive of the daily afternoon tea ordeal of his early nursery days than a voluntary act of pleasure." And Mrs. Gilding (who was Lucy Wellborn) "did not care much to go either if none of her particular men friends were to be there. Little she cared to dance the cotillion with old Colonel Bluffington or to go to supper with that odious Hector Newman." Yet old Mrs. Toplofty is by no means dull, for, finding herself once at dinner "next to a man she quite openly despised, [she] said to him with apparent placidity, 'I shall not talk to you—because I don't care to. But for the sake of the hostess I shall say my multiplication tables. Twice one are two, twice two are four—' and she continued on through the tables, making him alternate them with her. As soon as she politely could, she turned to her other companion."

Lucy Gilding "smokes like a furnace and is miserable unless she can play bridge for high stakes." At her wedding, the bridesmaids were dressed "in deep shades of burnt orange and yellow, wood-colored slippers and stockings, skirts that shaded from brown through orange to yellow; yellow leghorn hats trimmed with jonquils, and jonquil bouquets"; and the affair was a great success for everybody except a "distinguished uncle," with whom Mrs. Post frankly sympathizes, who declared: "I did not think it was lovely at all. Every one of the bridesmaids was so powdered and painted that there was not a sweet or fresh face among them."

The Gildings' especial friends are rich young people like the Lovejoys and the Gailys, rich bachelors like Jim Smartlington and Clubwin Doe (the former of whom was elected "with little difficulty" to Clubwin Doe's club, at the same time that young Breezy was kept out by two men who "disliked his 'manner'"). But there are also, in the higher brackets, Mr. and Mrs. Kindhart. Mrs. Kindhart, unlike Mrs. Worldly, "talks to everyone, everywhere and always." Her "position is as good as Mrs. Worldly's every bit, but perhaps she can be more relaxed." It is the Kindharts who try to be helpful at the catastrophic "bungled dinner" which is given by "you," the reader—the evening when the fire smokes and Mrs. Toplofty issues orders that the logs are to be thrown out into the yard; when the Swedish maid says "Dinner's all ready!" instead of "Dinner is served" and deals the plates out like cards and then stacks them; when the clear soup turns out a "greasy-looking brown" and the hollandaise sauce "a curdled yellow mess"

—the evening after which Mrs. Toplofty, Clubwin Doe and the Worldlys and the Gildings, all of whom you invited together, will, as you well know, be telling their friends: "Whatever you do, don't dine with the Newweds unless you eat your dinner before you go, and wear black glasses so no sight can offend you." On that occasion, Mr. Kindhart is the only guest who tries to eat the soup, and Mrs. Kindhart says to you gently: "Cheer up, little girl, it doesn't really matter"—making you know for the first time "to the full how terrible the situation is." (The other guests, on this unfortunate occasion, seem to have fallen a little short of the qualities of delicacy and grace which the author has elsewhere ascribed to the truly well bred.) It was the Kindharts who gave the houseparty at informal Mountain Summit Camp which inspires Mrs. Post to one of her most memorable chapters—that party at which Mr. Kindhart points out after lunch to the guests "a dozen guides who are waiting at the boat-house" and "a small swimming pool which can be warmed artificially" for those who find the lake too cold, but at which the Worldlys strike a false note, for Mr. Worldly insists on bringing his valet, though he well knows that this was not expected, and Mrs. Worldly, at the long pine lunch-table, "looks at her napkin ring as though it were an insect"—till Mrs. Kindhart smiles and says: "I'm sorry, but I told you 'it was roughing it.'"

And then there are the Littlehouses (Mrs. Littlehouse was Sally Titherington), who, when you visit them, may "press you into service as auxiliary nurse, gardener or chauffeur," but whose "personality" is "such that there is scarcely a day in the week when the motors of the most popular of the younger set are not parked at the Littlehouse door." And, on the fringes, such occasional guests as Grace Smalltalk, who *did* write to Mrs. Norman an admirable bread-and-butter letter, and the boring Professor Bugge, who was rather a social problem till he was seated by a clever hostess next to Mrs. Entomoid. In a somewhat different category, not frowned on but not included in the Eastern set, are Mr. and Mrs. Spendeasy Western and Mr.

and Mrs. Jameson Greatlake, of 24 Michigan Avenue, Chicago.

But Mrs. Post's real hero and heroine are Mr. and Mrs. Oldname. Mrs. Oldname is *"une dame élégante"*—because, as Mrs. Post tells us, there is no English word to "express the individuality of beautiful taste combined with personal dignity and grace which gives to a perfect costume an inimitable air of distinction." Her tact is unfailing and consummate: to a lady going in to dinner, she will say quietly: "Mr. Traveler, who is sitting next to you at the table, has just come back from two years alone with the cannibals." And "how does Mrs. Oldname walk? One might answer by describing how Pavlowa dances. Her body is perfectly balanced, she holds herself straight, and yet nothing suggests a ramrod. She takes steps of medium length, and, like all people who move and dance well, walks from the hip, not the knee. On no account does she swing her arms, nor does she rest a hand on her hip! Nor, when walking, does she wave her hands about in gesticulation." One of the most telling of the little episodes with which Mrs. Post's commentary is interspersed is her account of a visit to the Oldnames, which has the title *The Small House of Perfection.* "A great friend of the Oldnames, but not a man who went at all into society, or considered whether people had position or not, was invited with his new wife—a woman from another State and of much wealth and discernment—to stay over a weekend at Brook Meadows." She asks her husband what sort of clothes to take, and he tells her that he has never seen Mrs. Oldname "dressed up a bit." The wife wonders whether to pack her cerise satin. The husband thinks it "much too handsome," but the wife decides to put it in. They drive up to a low, white shingled house, and the visitor notices that the flowers bordering the old-fashioned brick walk are "all of one color, all in perfect bloom." "She knew no inexperienced gardener produced that apparently simple approach to a door that has been chosen as frontispiece in more than one book on Colonial architecture. The door was opened by a maid in a silver gray taffeta dress, with organdie collar, cuffs and apron, white stockings and silver buckles on black slippers, and the guest saw a quaint hall and vista of rooms that at first sight might easily be thought 'simple' by an inexpert appraiser." Mrs. Oldname herself was electrifying to the visitor of wealth from another State. To describe her as "simple," exclaims Mrs. Post, "is about as apt as to call a pearl 'simple' because it doesn't dazzle; nor was there an article in the apparently simple living-room that would be refused if it were offered to a museum." The furniture, the appointments, the other guests are filled in with glowing rapture. "That night the bride wore her cerise dress to one of the smartest dinners she ever went down to"; and when later she is alone with her husband she bursts out: "Why in the name of goodness didn't you tell me the truth about these people?" The husband misunder-stands: "I told you it was a little house—it was you who insisted on bringing that red dress. I told you it was much too handsome!" "Handsome!" she cries in tears. "I don't own anything half good enough to compare with the least article in this house. That 'simple' little woman, as you call her, would, I think, almost make a queen seem provincial! And as for her clothes, they are priceless—just as everything is in this little gem of a house. Why, the window curtains are as fine as the best things in my trousseau."

There is only one instance on record of anybody's scor-ing off the Oldnames. Mrs. Oldname had hanging in her dining-room a portrait of a Colonial officer, to which she was rather attached. One day, however, "an art critic, whose knowledge was better than his manners, blurted out, 'Will you please tell me why you have that dreadful thing in this otherwise perfect room?' Mrs. Oldname, some-what taken aback, answered rather wonderingly: 'Is it dreadful?—Really? I have a feeling of affection for him and his dog!' The critic was merciless. 'If you call a cotton-flannel effigy a dog! And as for the figure, it is equally false and lifeless! It is amazing how anyone with your taste can bear looking at it!' In spite of his rudeness, Mrs. Old-

name saw that what he said was quite true, but not until
the fact had been pointed out to her. Gradually she grew
to dislike the poor officer so much that he was finally rele-
gated to the attic." It will be noted that, though the art
critic carried his point, he was still guilty of a grave breach
of manners.

The latest edition of Emily Post omits, as she says on
the jacket, "certain non-essential customs and old-fashioned
ideas," and aims to accommodate itself to the habits of
later decades—including even those of the war and post-
war young people—when formalities have been going by
the board. The chapter, for example, which in the 1922
edition is called *The Chaperon and Other Conventions* is
now headed *The Vanished Chaperon and Other Lost Conventions*. But the book is still dominated by the prestige of
the Oldnames and the Gildings. Their prestige for Mrs.
Post may finally have the effect of making some of her
readers sympathetic toward the characters who are awful
examples: the Upstarts, Mr. and Mrs. Unsuitable and that
touching Mr. Richan Vulgar, who crossed the Atlantic four
times a year in order to meet the smart people on shipboard
and who, by capturing an innocent celebrity, attracted for
a time to his table the Smartlys, the Wellborns and the
Lovejoys, only to lose them every one when they found out
what he was really like and took to eating their meals on
deck. (The story of Mr. Richan Vulgar has been dropped
from the new edition, as have also, the Unsuitables and the
Upstarts, but a pathetic Miss Nobackground has appeared.)
One feels, in fact, something like sadism in the whole approach of Mrs. Post. She likes to humiliate. She cannot
tell us how charming Miss Wellborn is or how perfect is
Mrs. Oldname's taste without putting in a little incident to
show us this polish or grace making somebody else uncomfortable. Mrs. Post's popularity, I think, is partly due
to precisely this.

It is obvious that the Gildings and the Oldnames do
not themselves need Mrs. Post's book of etiquette; and

that the ordinary amiable American, to whom Miss Eichler addresses herself, does not necessarily need to hear about either Great Estates or the Small House of Perfection. But there are people who want to believe in the existence of a social Olympus and who find here the satisfaction that is somehow derived at once from imagining the enjoyment of glamor and power and from immolating oneself before them—since the reader is let in on the lives of the dwellers in these privileged places but is constantly being reminded how desperately he should have to watch his step if he were ever admitted among them.

What you get in Emily Post, for all her concessions to the age's vulgarization, is a crude version of the social ideal to which the mass of Americans aspired after the Civil War: an ideal that was costly and glossy, smart, self-conscious and a little disgusting in a period when even Mrs. Oldname reflected the lavish Gildings in stimulating her visitors to realize that the clothes she wore were "priceless" and her tableware and furniture museum pieces. Today this ideal must be fading with the money that kept it up, but, such as it is, a great many people must still enjoy reading about it. The publishers of Mrs. Post's *Etiquette* have announced that it has sold fifty thousand copies since the beginning of this year: its biggest sale in a decade.

July 19, 1947

A Dissenting Opinion on Kafka

FRANZ KAFKA has been looming on the literary world like the meteorological phenomenon called the Brocken specter: a human shadow thrown on the mist in such a way that it seems monstrous and remote when it may really be quite close at hand, and with a rainbow halo around it. Since the publication in English of *The Trial* in 1937 (*The Castle* came out in 1930 but did not attract much attention), Kafka's reputation and influence have been growing till his figure has been projected on the consciousness of our literary reviews on a scale which gives the illusion that he is a writer of towering stature. New translations of him are constantly appearing, an endless discussion of his writing goes on, and a new collected edition in German is being brought out in New York. This edition, under the imprint of Schocken Books, is in part a reprinting of the old German edition which the war made unavailable, but, when complete, it will include ten or eleven volumes instead of the original six, with two volumes of Kafka's diaries, two of his letters and one or two of his miscellaneous fragments, of all of which only selections were given in a single volume before. We may be proud that this admirably produced and authoritatively edited version of a modern German classic, which was begun in Berlin under Hitler and only finished in Prague on the eve of the German occupation of Czechoslovakia, should thus have been salvaged from the ruins of Central European culture and brought out in the United States. Schocken has also published, both in German and English, *Franz Kafka: A Biography,* by Max Brod, and a selection, in English translation, from Kafka's "stories and reflections" under the title *The Great Wall of China;* and it has announced some further translations. In the meantime, a translation of *Metamorphosis,* one of the most important of Kafka's short stories, has recently been brought out by the Vanguard Press; and *A Franz Kafka Miscellany,* which contains translated scraps of Kafka as well as essays on his work, has been published by the Twice A Year Press. A compilation of essays and memoirs called *The Kafka Problem* has been published by New Directions; and *Kafka's Prayer,* an interpretation by Paul Goodman, has just been brought out by Vanguard.

These last two volumes, in the first of which the editor, Mr. Angel Flores, has assembled no less than forty-one pieces by writers of all nationalities, oversaturate and stupefy the reader and finally give rise to the suspicion that Kafka is being wildly overdone. One realizes that it is not merely a question of appreciating Kafka as a poet who gives expression for the intellectuals to their emotions of helplessness and self-contempt but of building him up as a theologian and saint who can somehow also justify for them—or help them to accept without justification—the ways of a banal, bureaucratic and incomprehensible God to sensitive and anxious men. Now, it may make a good deal of difference whether one was born, like the present writer, before the end of the nineteenth century, when stability and progress were taken for granted, instead of in a period when upheaval and backsliding seemed the normal conditions of life; but, with much admiration for Kafka, I find it impossible to take him seriously as a major writer and have never ceased to be amazed at the number of people who can. Some of his short stories are absolutely first-rate, comparable to Gogol's and Poe's. Like them, they are realistic nightmares that embody in concrete imagery the manias of neurotic states. And Kafka's novels have exploited a vein of the comedy and pathos of futile effort which is likely to make "Kafka-esque" a permanent word. But the two of these novels, *The Trial* and *The Castle*, which have become for the cultists of Kafka something like sacred writings, are after all rather ragged performances—never finished and never really worked out. Their themes, as far as Kafka had got, had been developed with so little rigor that Max Brod, when he came to edit them, found mere loose collections of episodes, which he had to piece together as best he could so as to give them a consistent progression, though he was not always able to tell in precisely what order they should come. To compare Kafka, as some of the writers in *The Kafka Problem* do, with Joyce and Proust and even with Dante, great naturalists of personality, great organizers of human experience, is obviously quite absurd. As for the religious implications of these books, they seem to me to be practically nil. I agree with Mr. D. S. Savage, who contributes to *The Kafka Problem* one of its most sensible essays, that the trouble with Kafka was that he could never let go of the world—

of his family, of his job, of his yearning for bourgeois happiness—in the interest of divine revelation, and that you cannot have a first-rate saint or prophet without a faith of a very much higher potential than is ever to be felt in Kafka.

All that insulated and eventually nullified the spiritual charge that he carried is indicated in Max Brod's biography. Franz Kafka was the delicate son of a self-made Jewish merchant in the wholesale-women's-wear business in Prague, a vigorous and practical man, who inspired him with fear and respect, and gave him a lifelong inferiority complex. The son was a pure intellectual, who derived from the rabbinical tradition of the mother's side of the family; but he yielded to the insistence of the father and, though at times reduced to thoughts of suicide, he took his place in the drygoods warehouse. His real interest had always been writing, which represented for him not merely an art but also somehow a pursuit of righteousness —he said he regarded it as a form of prayer—and he finally got himself a job in a workers' accident-insurance office, which left him his afternoons free. He wanted, or thought he ought to want, to get married, but his relationship with his father seems to have deprived him of sexual self-confidence. He became engaged to a girl whom he described as "wholesome, merry, natural, robust"; and, after five years of gruelling hesitation, developed tuberculosis, on purpose, in his own opinion, to make it impossible for him to marry. He was by this time, one supposes, too much at home in his isolation to be able to bring himself to the point of taking the risk of trying to get out of it; and he now, at the age of thirty-six, addressed to his father an enormous letter (never yet printed in full), an apologia for his own life, in which he seems to have blamed his failure on him. Later he did get away to Berlin. He had found an intellectual girl who studied Hebrew with him and whom he seems really to have wanted to marry. Her orthodox Chassidic father was forbidden by the rabbi to allow it when Franz confessed that he was not a practising Jew; but the girl, in revolt against her family tradition, set up housekeeping with him and took care of him. Though he was eager now to work and to live, his disease had left him little time, and, after less than a year of this life, he was dead at forty-one.

The connection of all this with what Kafka wrote is made plain by his friend Max Brod in a book full of understanding. Herr Brod—whom the more metaphysical Kafkians tend to accuse of Philistinism—has, it seems to me, precisely the merit of looking in Kafka's work less for divine than for human meanings. That Kafka was weak-willed, that he was psychologically crippled, Max Brod is quite ready to admit, since he had made it his task during Kafka's life to keep his friend's morale up and make him work. He did stimulate Kafka to write and to have a few of his stories published, but he was very much less successful in his efforts to get him to break with his family. Other people escape from their parents, protests Herr Brod in astonishment and sorrow, so why on earth couldn't Kafka? Why *should* he have allowed his father so to crush and maim his abilities? Why, the reader may second Max Brod, remembering one of Kafka's most effective stories, should this artist have gone on past boyhood accepting the role of cockroach for which, like the hero of *Metamorphosis,* he had been cast by the bourgeois businessman? Well, the cards were stacked against poor Kafka in an overpowering way. His impotence was that of a man constitutionally lacking in vitality and walled in by a whole series of prisons that fitted one into the other like Chinese eggs. There was, first, the strangling father relationship; then the pressure of the tight little group of the Jewish orthodox family; then the constraints of the Jewish community incompletely emerged from the ghetto (Brod points out that the problems of Kafka's heroes are often those of the Jew among semi-alien neighbors—that the wanderer of *The Castle,* for example, is always trying to get himself accepted; he might have added that Joseph K., in *The Trial,* is constantly pursued for some crime which he is not aware of having committed); then the boredom and the spiritual starvation of the writer tied down to business hours—with the impression of hopelessness made on him by the workers who came to his office in the attempt to collect their insurance and who were met by all sorts of evasions and subjected to endless delays ("How modest these men are," he once said to Max Brod. "They come to us and beg, instead of storming the institute and smashing it to little bits."); then the deep-seated inhibitions which seem to have made his love affairs difficult; then the position of the Czechs in the Austrian Empire as an oppressed and somewhat scorned minority; then the privations of a defeated Central Europe, blighted, among other plagues, by the tuberculosis that undermined Kafka. This bewildered and darkened captivity, which may have seemed at the time rather special, was later to become, in Europe, more or less the common lot, and Kafka's fantasies were to gain a validity which could hardly have been foreseen—when, under the rule of the Nazis and the Soviets, men were to find themselves arrested and condemned on charges that had no relation to any accepted code of morals or law, or were driven from place to place to labor or to fight by first one then another inhuman unpetitionable government, which they hadn't the force to defy or the intellect to grasp and disintegrate.

But must we really, as his admirers pretend, accept the plights of Kafka's abject heroes as parables of the human condition? We can hardly feel toward Kafka's father, whose aspect Kafka's God always wears, the same childish awe that Kafka did—especially when the truth is that Kafka himself cannot help satirizing this Father-God as well as his own pusillanimity in remaining in bondage to him. A good deal has been made of the influence on Kafka of the Danish theologian Kierkegaard; but we learn from Max Brod that Kafka was at least equally influenced by Flaubert, and his work is full of a Flaubertian irony which the critics have tended to disregard. There is a story of Kafka's, for example, called *Investigations of a Dog* (included in *The Great Wall of China*), in which a dog is supposed to be inquiring into certain rather puzzling phenomena that are basic to the dog world. Where, he asks, does the food for dogs come from? The conventional explanation—which all right-minded dogs have been taught —is that this food comes out of the earth and is elicited by watering the earth and by singing incantatory hymns and performing ritual dances. Yet, as the scientist-dog has observed, the dogs, when they are invoking food, look not down toward the ground but up. Why *do* they look up, and is this essential? Then there are other unsolved problems: the dogs that roll over in unison and walk on their hind legs to the sound of mysterious music, and the small dandified dogs that seem to float through the air. The point is, of course, that the dogs have had their own reasons for pretending that human beings do not exist. Now, if you read the interpretations of this story which have recently been appearing, you will gather that it is simply an allegory of the relation of man to God—though the analogy does not hold, in view of the fact that the dogs *can* perfectly well see their masters, as man cannot do God, and are dependent on them in a practical way. Kafka remarked of this story, started—and never finished—not long before he died, that it was his *Bouvard et Pécuchet,* by which he must certainly have meant, not merely, as he said, that he thought it was a late work rather lacking in vitality, but also that it had something in common with Flaubert's most contemptuous indictment of the pettiness and ineptitude of the modern world. The sting of Kafka's story resides in the reluctance of the dogs to admit that they are in servitude to men—so that they have all entered into a conspiracy to conceal this fact from themselves, and even their boldest thinker cannot allow himself to find out the secret because it would rob him of his own self-respect. This is much less like an edifying allegory of the relations between God and man than like a Marxist-Flaubertian satire on the parasites of the bourgeoisie.

I do not deny that the enslaver, the master, is often given, in Kafka's stories, a serious theological meaning;

but this side is never developed in anything like equal proportion to the ironical self-mocking side. Is the man condemned to death in *The Trial*, and finally convinced of his guilt for some crime which is never named, really either adapted or intended to illustrate Original Sin?— or is Kafka not rather satirizing the absurdities of his own bad conscience? In *The Castle*, there is also self-irony, but, besides this, a genuine wistfulness in K.'s longing to settle down and find a modest place in life for himself. But neither—unless one takes them as parodies of the Calvinist doctrine of Grace—seems to me to possess much interest as the expression of a religious point of view. The Christian of *Pilgrim's Progress* had obstacles to overcome and required moral fortitude to meet them; but all the struggling, such as it is, that is done by Kafka's K. is against an omnipotent and omniscient authority whose power and lights he can never share but to whose will he is doomed to succumb. And Dante, whose religious vision is all an exercise in control and direction, makes even his pagan Ulysses urge his men not to sleep before evening and tells them they were not made "to live like brutes but to follow virile courage and knowledge"; whereas Kafka is at his most characteristic when he is assimilating men to beasts—dogs, insects, mice and apes—which can neither dare nor know. On the other hand, for me, these stories too often forfeit their effectiveness as satires through Kafka's rather meaching compliance, his little-boylike respect and fear in the presence of the things he would satirize: the boring diligence of commercial activity, the stuffiness of middle-class family life, the arid reasonings and tyrannous rigidities of Orthodox Judaism (which have a good deal in common with those of our old-fashioned Puritan Protestantism).

If, however, one puts Kafka beside writers with whom he may properly be compared, he still seems rather unsatisfactory. Gogol and Poe were equally neurotic, in their destinies they were equally unhappy; and if it is true, as Mr. Savage says, that there is present in Kafka's world neither personality nor love, there is no love in either Gogol or Poe, and though there are plenty of personalities in Gogol, the actors of Poe, as a rule, are even less characterized than Kafka's. But, though the symbols that these writers generate are just as unpleasant as Kafka's, though, like his, they represent mostly the intense and painful realization of emotional culs-de-sac, yet they have both certain advantages over Kafka—for Gogol was nourished and fortified by his heroic conception of Russia, and Poe, for all his Tory views, is post-Revolutionary American in his challenging, defiant temper, his alert and curious mind. In their ways, they are both tonic. But the denationalized, discouraged, disaffected, disabled Kafka, though for the moment he may frighten or amuse us, can in the end only let us down. He is quite true to his time and place, but it is surely a time and place in which few of us will want to linger—whether as stunned and hypnotized helots of totalitarian states or as citizens of freer societies, who have relapsed into taking Kafka's stories as evidence that God's law and man's purpose are conceived in terms so different that we may as well give up hope of ever identifying the one with the other.

"One must not cheat anybody," says Kafka, in an aphorism which has been much applauded, "not even the world of its triumph." But what are we writers here for if it is not to cheat the world of its triumph? In Kafka's case, it was he who was cheated and never lived to get his own back. What he has left us is the half-expressed gasp of a self-doubting soul trampled under. I do not see how one can possibly take him for either a great artist or a moral guide.

July 26, 1947

Jean-Paul Sartre: The Novelist
and the Existentialist

The Age of Reason is the first novel of Jean-Paul Sartre's
to be translated into English. It is the first instalment of
a trilogy under the general title *The Roads to Freedom*,
of which the second instalment in translation has been
announced for the fall. *The Age of Reason* deals with a
group of young people in Paris—*lycée* teachers and students, Bohemians and night-club entertainers—in the summer of 1938. The second novel, *The Reprieve*, which has
already appeared in French, carries the same characters
along but works them into a more populous picture of
what was going on in France during the days of the Munich
Conference. The third volume, *The Last Chance*,* has not
yet been published in French, so it is impossible at the
present time to judge the work as a whole or even to know
precisely what the author is aiming at.

The Age of Reason, however, stands by itself as a
story. Sartre displays here the same skill at creating suspense and at manipulating the interactions of characters that we have already seen in his plays. His main
theme is simply the odyssey of an ill-paid *lycée* teacher
who does not want to marry his pregnant mistress and
who is trying to raise the relatively large fee required
for a competent abortion; but though the author makes
this provide a long narrative, in which we follow the
hero's every move and in which every conversation is reported in its banal entirety, he stimulates considerable excitement, holds our attention from beginning to end and
engineers an unexpected dénouement which has both moral
point and dramatic effectiveness. The incidents are mostly

* There are now to be four volumes instead of three. The third,
La Mort dans L'Âme, has appeared in French. 1950.

sordid, but, if you don't mind this, entertaining. The characters are well observed and conscientiously and intelligently studied, so that the book makes an interesting document on the quality and morale of the French just before their great capitulation. An American reader is struck by the close similarity of these young people, with their irresponsible love affairs, their half-hearted intellectual allegiances and their long drinking conversations, to the same kind of men and girls at the same period in the United States—just as the novel has itself much in common with certain novels that these young people produced. I do not believe, however, that this is the result of imitation by Sartre of the contemporary American novelists whom he is known to admire so much. It is rather that such young people everywhere have come to be more alike, so that the originals for Sartre's Parisians must have been far less specifically Parisian than the Parisians of Balzac or Flaubert or Anatole France or Proust.

It is true, besides, that the writing of the book shows few of the traditional traits that we have been used to in French fiction. It tells the story with a "functional" efficiency, but it is colorless, relaxed, rather flat. It loses little in the English translation, not merely because the translator knows his business, but also because Sartre's style does not put upon him any very severe strain. The conversation is mainly conducted in a monotonous colloquialism of catch-words, where some expression like "*C'est marrant*" does duty for as many emotions as our own ever-recurring "terrific"; and for this Mr. Eric Sutton has been able to find a ready equivalent in a jargon basically British with a liberal admixture of Americanisms.

Of Sartre's imaginative work, I have read, besides this novel, only his plays and a few of his short stories. On this showing, I get the impression of a talent rather like that of John Steinbeck. Like Steinbeck, Sartre is a writer of undeniably exceptional gifts: on the one hand, a fluent inventor, who can always make something interesting happen, and, on the other, a serious student of life, with a good deal of public spirit. Yet he somehow does not seem quite first-rate. A play of Sartre's, for example, such as his recent *Morts sans Sépulture*—which is, I suppose, his best drama so far—affects me rather like *Grapes of Wrath*. Here he has exploited with both cleverness and conviction the ordeal of the French Resistance, as Steinbeck has done that of the sharecroppers; but what you get are a virtuosity of realism and a rhetoric of moral passion which make you feel not merely that the fiction is a dramatic heightening of life but that the literary fantasy takes place on a plane that does not have any real connection with the actual human experience which it is pretending to represent.

I have approached *The Age of Reason* purposely from the point of view of its merits as a novel without reference to the Existentialist philosophy of which Sartre is one of the principal exponents and which the story is supposed to embody. But, with the publication, also, of a translation of a lecture of Sartre's called *Existentialism* and a pamphlet called *What Is Existentialism?* by William Barrett, this demands consideration, too. It should, however, be said that neither of these discussions of the subject provides for the ordinary person the best possible key to Sartre's ideas. The Barrett essay, though very able, is mainly an exposition of the ideas of Martin Heidegger, a contemporary German philosopher, from whom Sartre took some of his prime assumptions, and it presupposes on the part of the reader a certain familiarity with the technical language of philosophy. The lecture by Sartre himself has the special object of defending Existentialism against charges which have been brought against it by the Communists, so that it emphasizes certain aspects of the theory without attempting to state its fundamental principles. It would have been well if the publisher had included a translation of the article called *Présentation*, in which Sartre explained his position in the first number of his magazine, *Les Temps Modernes*

(October 1, 1945), and which gives the best popular account I have seen of what this literary school is up to. I can also recommend especially a short summary of the history of Existentialist thought and of its political and social implications—*Existentialism: A New Trend in Philosophy*—contributed by Paul Kecskemeti, a former U.P. foreign correspondent who is also a trained philosopher, to the March, 1947, issue of a magazine called *Modern Review* (published in New York by the American Labor Conference on International Affairs). This study has the unusual merit of not getting so deeply enmeshed in the metaphysical background of Existentialism that it fails to focus clearly on the picture of mankind on the earth which is the most important thing to grasp in a doctrine that is nothing if not realistic.

What is this picture, then? In Sartre's version—to skip altogether the structure of philosophical reasoning on which it is made to rest and which Sartre has set forth at length in a book called *L'Être et le Néant*—it places man in a world without God (though not all Existentialists are atheists), in which all the moral values are developed by man himself. Human nature is not permanent and invariable: it is whatever man himself makes it, and it changes from age to age. Man is free, beyond certain limits, to choose what he is to be and do. His life has significance solely in its relation to the lives of others—in his actions or refrainings from action: to use a favorite phrase of Sartre's, the individual must "engage himself."

Now, this conception of man's situation may appear to the non-religious reader, if he has also the "historical" point of view, precisely what he has always assumed, and may cause him to conclude with surprise that he was already an Existentialist without knowing it. To a Marxist, when he has further discovered that Sartre assigns human beings to the categories of the social classes almost as relentlessly as Marx, it will be evident that Sartre has borrowed from Marxism, and he may ask in what way Existentialism is an improvement over Marxism. In a debate between Sartre and a Marxist, a record of which follows the printed lecture, the Marxist actually scores rather heavily. The one advantage, it seems to me, that the doctrine of Sartre has is that it does away with Dialectical Materialism and its disguised theological content. There is for Sartre no dialectical process which will carry you straight to salvation if you get on the proletarian train. He sides with the proletariat, but intellectual or proletarian has to put up his own battle, with the odds looking rather against him. Yet Sartre does insist like a Marxist that every member of modern society belongs to a social class, and that "every one of his feelings, as well as every other form of his psychological life, is revelatory of his social situation." This molding of the individual by class—and Sartre allows also for the effects of "origin," "milieu," nationality and sexual constitution—produces the limitation on freedom which I mentioned in passing above. One finds oneself in a situation which one did not make for oneself, but, given that situation, one can choose various ways of behaving in it. The bourgeois—with whom Sartre is particularly concerned—can either go along with his class or rebel against it and try to get away from it. The Marxist may inquire how this differs from the classical Marxist formulation that "men make their own history, but . . . do not choose the circumstances for themselves," and how Sartre's practical doctrine of man realizing himself through action differs from Marx's conception of testing our ideas through action. To the writer, the conception of a wholly free will seems as naïve as the contrary conception of a wholly mechanistic determinism, and it is surely hardly less naïve to declare, as Sartre appears to do, that we are determined up to a certain point, but that beyond that we can exercise choice. If Marx and Engels, in exploring these problems, are somewhat less schoolmasterishly clear than Sartre, they seem to me, in their tentative way, to give a more recognizable picture than he does of what happens when what we take for the will tries to act on what we take for the world, and of the relation between man and his environment.

But the Existentialist philosophy of Sartre is the reflection of a different age from that which stimulated the activist materialism of Marx, and it has the immense advantages of sincerity and human sympathy over the very peculiar version of Marxism, totalitarian and imperialistic, now exported by the Soviet Union. Let us see it in its historical setting. Mr. Kecskemeti has shown in his essay how the neo-Kantian idealism of the pre-1914 period in Germany, which "admirably expressed the average German's awe in the presence of every kind of expert and official," had to give way, after the first German defeat, which shook this faith in specialized authority, to an effort to find principles of morality in the study of human conduct itself. So, eventually, the Germans got Heidegger. In the same way, Kecskemeti says, the defeat of the French in 1940 deprived them of all they had leaned on: they had at one stroke lost both their great traditions—the tradition of the French Revolution, which collapsed with the Third Republic, and the monarchist-Catholic tradition, which, through Pétain, had sold them out to the invaders. It is characteristic of the French that the destruction of French institutions should have seemed to them a catastrophe as complete as the Flood and caused them to evolve a philosophy which assumes that the predicament of the patriotic Frenchmen oppressed by the German occupation represented the condition of all mankind. They felt imperatively the duty to resist, with no certainty of proving effective, and they had, as Albert Camus has said, to formulate for themselves a doctrine which would "reconcile negative thought and the possibility of affirmative action." Hence the emphasis on the individual—since the Resistance was always an effort of scattered men and women—so different from the emphasis of Marx on the importance of collective action at a time when a great working-class movement was looming and gathering strength. Hence, also, the suffocating atmosphere of corruption,

degradation and depression which is a feature of Sartre'
work and for which the French Communists, hopped up
by the Kremlin to the cocksureness of propaganda, are in
the habit of showering him with scorn. But such reproaches
have no real validity, either artistic or moral: this atmos
phere is Sartre's subject, and he has not allowed it to drug
his intelligence or his conscience. It is the climate of the
Occupation, and the chief literary achievement of Sartre
is to have dramatized the moral poisoning of a France
humiliated and helpless, in which people, brooding guilt
ily or blaming someone else, squabbled horribly, betrayed
one another or performed acts of desperate heroism. For
says Sartre, though you cannot appeal to God, you have
always a margin of freedom: you can submit, you can
kill yourself or you can sell your life dear by resisting
Where this freedom is now to lead Frenchmen since the
Germans have been driven out, I do not think that Sartre
has yet made clear. Though anti-bourgeois and pro
working-class, he is evidently not an orthodox Communist
of the kind who takes his directives from Moscow. One
has a little the feeling about him that his basic point o
view has been forged, as his material has been supplied
so completely under pressure of the pain and constraint o
the collapse and the Occupation that he may never readap
himself to the temper of any new period.

And now how does *The Age of Reason* point the moral
of Existentialist principles? Well, if you already know
something of the subject, you will recognize some of it
concepts turning up in the reflections of the hero as he
drearily walks through the Paris streets. And the conflic
of classes is there: a seceder from the bourgeoisie, we se
this hero, Mathieu, revolving in a lonely orbit but exper
encing gravitational pulls from a successful lawyer brother
who represents the bourgeoisie, an old friend who ha
become a Communist and represents the proletariat, an
a young girl of Russian émigré parents who represents th
old nobility. It is not, however, this central character, so fa

as this volume takes him, who "engages himself" by a choice: his choices are all of the negative kind. It is the sexual invert Daniel, a neurotic and disconcerting personality, who, exercising free will, resists his suicidal impulses and performs, unexpectedly and for devious reasons, a responsible and morally positive act. Here the difficult "situation" is a matter not of social class but of biological dislocation; and the triumph of Daniel's decision is to be measured by the gravity of his handicap.

Yet it is difficult to see how *The Age of Reason* can have been very profoundly affected by Sartre's Existentialist theory. In such a production of his as his play *Les Mouches,* the dramatist turns academic and rather destroys the illusion by making the characters argue his doctrine; but this novel might perfectly have been written if Sartre had never worked up Existentialism. It does differ from the picture of life presented by the embittered French naturalists after the French defeat of 1871, whose characters were invariably seen as caught in traps of heredity and circumstance, and rarely allowed to escape —though Sartre's mood, as in his play *À Huis Clos (No Exit)*, is sometimes quite close to theirs. But this book does not essentially differ from the novels of other post-naturalistic writers, such as Malraux, Dos Passos and Hemingway, for whom the international socialist movement has opened a door to hope and provided a stimulus to action that were unknown to such a Frenchman as Maupassant or to the Americans who paralleled his pessimism. In Sartre, as in these other writers, you have a study of the mixture in man's nature of moral strength and weakness, and a conviction that, although the individual may not win the stakes he is playing for, his effort will not be lost.

Since *Partisan Review* has published, in the same series as Mr. Barrett's pamphlet, a translation of one of Sartre's long articles, *Portrait of the Anti-Semite*, one should say something about his activity as a journalist. These essays that he contributes to his *Temps Modernes* seem to me among the most interesting work of their kind that has appeared during the current slump in serious periodical writing. In this field, Sartre can be compared only with George Orwell in England; we have nobody so good over here. Mr. Barrett, in an article on Sartre, has complained that he ignores, in his *Portrait*, the Freudian springs of anti-Semitism. It is true that Sartre makes no attempt to explain this phenomenon historically in its political and social connections; but he does pursue with merciless insight at least one of the psychological factors involved: the need of small frustrated people to fake up some inalienable warrant for considering themselves superior to somebody. Sartre's whole essay, in fact, pretends to be nothing else than an elaborate development of this theme. It is no scientific inquiry but an exercise in classical irony, which might almost have been written, we reflect, by one of the more mordant eighteenth-century Encyclopedists. *The Age of Reason* of Sartre's novel is the intellectual maturity of the hero, but the phrase recalls also a period with which Sartre has a good deal in common. In penetrating these enormous editorials that mix comment on current affairs with a philosophy which, whatever its deficiencies, is always clearly and firmly expressed, we are surprised and reassured to find ourselves chewing on something which we might have feared the French had lost. For it is Sartre's great strength in his time that he has managed to remain quite uninfected by the Cocteau-esque Parisian chichi of the interval between the wars. If Existentialism has become, like surrealism, something of a *mouvement à exporter*, no one has probed so shrewdly as Sartre, in one of his articles in *Les Temps Modernes*, the recent attempts of the French to distract the attention of the world from their political and military discredit by exploiting the glory of their writers, or pointed out so boldly the abuses to which this practice may lead. If he sometimes has the air of pontificating, it is probably almost impossible for a French literary man whose influence is being felt to refrain from playing the role of *chef d'école*. And Sartre, bourgeois and provincial, has succeeded in preserving for the French qualities which they very much need and which it is cheering to see still flourish: an industry, an outspokenness and a common sense which are the virtues of a prosaic intelligence and a canny and practical character. This does not, perhaps, necessarily make Sartre a top-flight writer, but, in these articles of *Les Temps Modernes*, it does provide some very good reading.

August 2, 1947

The Musical Glasses of Peacock

AN OMNIBUS of Thomas Love Peacock, under the title *The Pleasures of Peacock*, has been brought out by a New York publisher. It is a good thing to have these novels reprinted, and Mr. Ben Ray Redman, who has edited the volume, contributes a well-informed introduction that touches briefly on almost every side of Peacock. But this book has what seems to me the serious defect of being mainly a collection of excerpts. Only two novels are given complete: *Nightmare Abbey* and *Crotchet Castle*. The other five appear merely in selections. Now, it is true that from one point of view Peacock lends himself easily to anthologizing: his plots are not usually important, and his narrative is a loose series of episodes. Yet each of his books as a whole shows the same delicate sense of form as each of the episodes and each of the sentences, and it is a pity to take them to pieces—especially since they are all so short that it was possible, in a thin-paper edition published some years ago, to include the complete novels in one pocket-size volume. It is also rather unfair, it seems to me, to shear off, as Mr. Redman has done, all the quotations that head Peacock's chapters, and to trim away a part of his learned notes. The main text can stand without them, but they do represent the soil out of which that text has grown and help to situate Peacock's mood in an early-nineteenth-century library, where the Greek and Latin classics are mingled with Italian light comedies and the wild folk ballads of Wales. Surely anyone who can care for Peacock would prefer to have him intact.

The Pleasures of Peacock, however, serve to remind us, in any case, of a very fine writer and to offer a pretext for talking about him. We have already seen one revival of Peacock—during the twenties, when J. B. Priestley did a book about him and when Aldous Huxley gave him some vogue by deliberately imitating him. The element that Huxley exploited was the characteristic Peacock symposium: the conversation in a country house, with much passing of port and claret, among highly intellectual guests, each of whom appears as the exponent of some current tendency or doctrine reduced to its simplest terms and carried to its most absurd lengths. This is the critical side of Peacock, for which he is now perhaps most famous because Huxley has seized upon it, injected into it moral earnestness and transposed it into a peevish key. But it is by no means the whole of Peacock, as one can see by comparing him and Huxley. With the later as with the earlier writer, the opinions of the various philosophers more or less cancel one another out; but for Huxley this leads to bitterness and a demand for religious certainties, whereas in Peacock it leads to a final drink and a song in which everyone joins. And this fencing by Peacock's cranks with rigid contradictory ideas—excellent sometimes, of course, but not always remarkably clever—is hardly enough to have preserved him so long. What is it, then, that makes Peacock live? Why is it that Mr. Redman believes that we can still enjoy reading his novels?

Another critic, Mr. Ronald Mason, asked this question three years ago in the English review *Horizon,* and, after discounting almost every source of interest that one may expect to find in a novel, came to the conclusion that Peacock's strength lay mainly in his firmness as a nipper of extremes and in his admirable prose style. Both these merits Peacock certainly had. It was a godsend that in the early nineteenth century, with its seraphic utopianisms, its attitudinizing anti-social romanticisms and its cannibalistic materialisms, one man who had the intelligence to understand and the aesthetic sensibility to appreciate the new movements and the new techniques that were going to people's heads, should have been able to apply to their extravagances a kind of classical common sense; and Peacock's value, as Mr. Mason suggests, should by no means be less today, at a time when extreme ideas are being violently put into practice. As for his style: to the mature reader, whom mere sonority and movement and color do not intoxicate as they did in youth, it seems one of the best in English. Light, lucid, neat and dry, it is as far from the prose of his own period, mossily clogged or grassily luxuriating, as from the showy upholstery of the later age. It redeems him from insipidity at the moments when he is running thinnest; it gives charm to his most telling jokes by slipping them in with a minimum of emphasis. "Nothing superfluous and nothing wanting" was the comment of India House on the papers that won Peacock his job there. If one compares him, particularly, with Thackeray, who liked his work and who is sometimes praised for qualities similar to his, one is struck by the relative coarseness of the texture of the Victorian's writing, with its dilutions and its repetitions, and by the relative commonplaceness of his mind, with its worldly preoccupations and its embarrassing exhibitions of benevolence. When we come to Peacock from this, we are aware of his restraint and distinction, of the spareness and sureness of the pencil which he uses for his prose line-drawings.

This brings us to an aspect of Peacock which Mr. Mason leaves out of account. The fact that Peacock's *imagination* is not vigorous, varied or rich has, I believe, rather kept people from realizing how exquisite his effects sometimes are. It is usual to treat him as a satirist whose power is more or less weakened by his scoring off both sides of every question; but the truth is that Peacock is an artist the aim of whose art is to achieve not merely a weaving of ideas but also an atmosphere—an aroma, a flavor, a harmony. You get closer to what Peacock is trying to do by approaching him through his admiration for Mozart—"There is," he wrote, "nothing perfect in this world except Mozart's music" —than by assimilating him to Lucian or Voltaire. His books are more like light operas than novels (it was quite natural that *Maid Marian* should have been made into one) and the elements of fantasy with which they play—the civilized orangutan of *Melincourt*, who is chivalrous with the ladies, the seven lovely maidens of *Gryll Grange* who keep house for the young man in the tower—as well as the landscapes of mountain streams, the drives and rides in the New Forest, the boating and skating parties, are as important as the conversations. It all makes a delicious music, at the same time sober and gay, in which the words fall like notes from a flute, like progressions on an old-fashioned pianoforte, lighted by slim white candles. In *Gryll Grange*, when we come to the snowstorm, we almost have the illusion that these pale and sifted words of Peacock's are dropping on the page like snowflakes and that they melt away as we read. Even the openings of Peacock's unfinished novels— so sure is his touch on the keyboard to convey us at once to his realm—may be enjoyed as little works in themselves, like the "preludes" of Debussy or Chopin.

It seems to me, too, that the nonchalance of Peacock in dealing with political and moral systems has been given a wrong meaning by his critics—for he is always, in some way, on the *human* side, and he shared the generous ideas of the romantic and utopian generation to an extent that his conservative encomiasts are sometimes reluctant to recognize. I have a suspicion that the relative indifference of the typical Peacockian to *Melincourt* may be partly due to the fact that the hero of this early novel gives expression to such ideas with an eloquence which can almost be called glowing and which suggests real conviction on Peacock's part. The book does go on a little too long, for Peacock has not yet quite found his form; but it is certainly one of his best—with its gentleman anthropoid, its beautiful blue-stocking oread, its forthright and very funny satire on rotten-borough politics and the publishing business, and its admirable discussion, at the end, under the title *The Hopes of the World*, of the future of civilization. Mr. Redman could not have remembered *Melincourt* when he wrote in his introduction in such a way as to give the impression that Peacock's friendship with Shelley is only to be explained on the ground of the attraction of opposites. The creator of the Rousseauist Mr. Forester had no difficulty in sympathizing with the poet's utopian yearnings toward a happier and freer society. It was only that he could not help kidding his friend in the skit of *Nightmare Abbey*—the dry diagnosis of which is a corrective to more impassioned portraits—for the self-delusions of Shelley in his childish relations with women; and that the cool human sympathy I have spoken of compelled him to defend Harriet—in his *Memoirs of Percy Bysshe Shelley*—against the slanders of the Shelley-worshippers.

The mountain-loving Anthelia of *Melincourt* is one of Peacock's most attractive versions of his ideal young Englishwoman—always a strongly positive element in his stories. These girls of his—frank, independent, brave, intelligent and rather intellectual—stand somewhere between the heroines of Shelley and the heroines of Jane Austen. I find them a great deal more attractive, as well as a great deal more convincing, than the women of Victorian fiction. That these latter could not have been found particularly sympathetic by Peacock may be concluded from the unfinished *Cotswold Chace*, in which he is careful to explain that his heroine "wears no crinoline, and, if I might venture to divine, no stays." It is obvious that Peacock's young girls—witty, athletic and fresh—are the mothers of the anti-Victorian goddesses of his son-in-law George Meredith's novels.

The later Peacock was less interested in reformers, less "progressive" and less optimistic. But it is true, as Mr.

Redman reminds us, that he had already in the sixties lived long enough to see a great many reforms accomplished but life rendered rather less agreeable than it had been in the early years of the century, and to foresee the mechanical developments—prophesied in *Gryll Grange*—which were to increase men's productive powers and at the same time to reduce them to bondage. When he had retired from his job at India House, he took his family to live in the country, where he spent most of his time with books—though he liked to go to visit Lord Broughton, who, as John Hobhouse, had been Byron's friend and who could give Peacock the good entertainment and the free-ranging conversation with which he had filled his novels. Thackeray met Peacock once in 1850 and called him "a white-headed jolly old worldling"; but he was never really a Thackeray character. He was not worldly in Thackeray's sense. The world he loved was the world of his library—to which he fled when, at the age of eighty, he was warned that the house was on fire, declaring, when they tried to get him out: "By the immortal gods, I will not move!" He was upset when his favorite daughter, who had been educated, on the model of his heroines, both in literature and in outdoor sports and who is said to have been both brilliant and beautiful, married the young George Meredith. Meredith wore a beard, which Peacock could not abide; and, though the young man respected his father-in-law and was influenced in his own work by Peacock's, his ardors, energetic and uneasy, annoyed the old man and made him nervous. It was quite a different thing from Shelley.

Nor did Meredith and his bride get along together. They were both sharp-tongued and self-willed, and they had very little money to live on. They tormented one another unbearably. Mary Meredith, at the end of nine years, ran away to Capri with another man, but soon came back to die in England. Peacock, then seventy-nine, did not go to her funeral, but he composed for her an epitaph in Latin and Greek, which was never inscribed on her grave. Meredith published soon after, as a commentary on his tragic marriage, the great sequence of sonnets called *Modern Love*, full of self-probings and passionate frustrations of a kind that must have been inconceivable to Peacock; and when one glances back on this mid-century Peacock from the point of view of *Modern Love*, one seems to see an old man in a bottle, whose unshakable poise and calm depend on his not coming out.

For when we look back on Peacock from Meredith's time instead of seeing him in the dawn of the century, he seems to us less mobile and cooler. Peacock's father was a dealer in glassware, and there is sometimes a glint of glassware in the clear, sound and smooth work of Peacock. The editors of the Halliford Edition of Peacock have included in his last novel, *Gryll Grange*, a peculiarly appropriate frontispiece which shows a spun-glass bust of Homer that Peacock had hung in his library. It makes us reflect that the classics in Peacock's hands do a little take on the aspect of having been deftly spun into glass; and his own work may look to us at moments like a fine antique sideboard display, with rows of graceful flower-calyxed goblets all ready for the very best wine—which you will have to buy from somebody else: somebody like Meredith or Shelley. In the meantime, however, Peacock can elicit from them a very pretty music by delicately moistening the rims and rubbing them with the tips of his fingers.

August 23, 1947

The Original of Tolstoy's Natasha

THE PRINCIPAL MODEL for Natasha in Tolstoy's *War and Peace* was his sister-in-law, Tatyana Andreyvna Behrs. She was sixteen when Tolstoy married, a gay, attractive and spirited girl, who was already a great favorite with him. She lived much in the Tolstoy household at Yasnaya Polyana in the country, and her brother-in-law used to tell her that she was paying her way by sitting as a model for him. Later, when she married a young magistrate, she continued to visit the Tolstoys, bringing her family to stay with them in the summer. Her husband died in 1917, and she went to Yasnaya Polyana to live with Tolstoy's daughter Alexandra, on a small pension from the Soviet government. Here, at seventy-five, she set out to write her memoirs, but did not live to bring her story much beyond her marriage in 1867, at the age of twenty-one.

This chronicle has just been translated and brought out for the first time in English under the title *Tolstoy as I Knew Him* and signed with the author's married name, Tatyana A. Kuzminskaya. The original Russian title, here retained as subtitle, *My Life at Home and at Yasnaya Polyana*, describes the contents better, for the book is by no means all about the Tolstoys; it is an autobiography of Tatyana. As such, it is a rewarding document, though not infrequently a boring book. Tatyana-Natasha was writing as a very old lady, on the basis of diaries and letters that date from her remote girlhood. Most of her comments on the literary figures whom she saw at close quarters in her youth—Ostrovsky, Turgenev, Fet and her brother-in-law Leo himself—show no respect for famous names. They are simply the reactions of a woman to various men she has met. At one point, after taking poison over a love affair that was going wrong, she quickly changed her mind about dying when another of her suitors called—received him politely and, going to her mother, begged to be given an antidote. Exercising no sense of selection, she merely writes down all the things that moved her at the moment of their occurrence, in the terms in which they interested her then. None of them seems to have acquired—it is perhaps what one would expect of Natasha—any sort of new significance in the light of her later experience. It is as if the child's passionate "crushes," her vanity in being admired, had been simply relived in memory. Though almost all Tatyana tells you fits perfectly the character created by Tolstoy and though the book is full of other people's test

mony to her vivacity and her beauty, the excitement of
Natasha is not there. What Tatyana had was evidently
overflowing life, not literary ability. She was unable to
dramatize herself and what she gives you is a long and
slow record of sisters and brothers and parents, uncles and
aunts and cousins, nurses and maids and coachmen, protracted visits to country houses and social calls in Moscow
(where her father was Court Physician and the Behrses
lived in a house at the Kremlin). All the incidents, the
most serious and crucial, as well as the most trivial and
frivolous, are noted down in the same casual proportions
that they had for the young girl at the time. The marriage
of a servant, the remodelling of a house, an accident on a
dangerous road, a saddle that comes loose at a hunt, a
cat that jumps out of the arms of one of the actors in amateur theatricals, are presented on about the same level as
the volatile flirtations and engagements, the continual birth
of children (in those days people had one a year), and the
long illnesses and premature deaths that even the best city
doctors could not seem to do much to prevent.

But the most important episode of Tatyana's youth affords a significant insight, much more so than she is aware,
into the society to which she belonged and which her
brother-in-law so brilliantly depicted. It is an episode
typical of their world and yet one for which Tolstoy presents no equivalent in *War and Peace*—a drama that raises
a problem which he was only much later to treat. The
Natasha of real life had her Anatole Kuragin, as in *War
and Peace*—his real name was even Anatole; and her
eventual marriage with Kuzminsky seems to have had
something in common with Natasha's final acceptance of
Pierre. But, in between, had occurred the most serious love
affair of her life: her tragically frustrated engagement to
Leo Tolstoy's older brother Sergei.

Sergei Tolstoy had been living for years with a gypsy
woman named Marya Mikhailovna, by whom he had two
children. He had inherited an estate, which he farmed, not

far from Yasnaya Polyana, and he lived there with his uncultivated mistress, shutting himself off from social intercourse with the neighbors of his own class. He fell in love with Tatyana and she with him, and he thought he could manage to marry her without telling Marya Mikhailovna. But the news of what was afoot soon reached her, and when her gypsy parents were told, they threatened to sue Sergei and create a public scandal. She was having another baby, which made things very difficult for him. And there was also another difficulty. Two brothers, in Tsarist Russia, were forbidden to marry two sisters unless both ceremonies were performed at the same time—since as soon as one of the marriages had taken place, the in-laws of both the bride and the groom became technically their blood relations. This in itself made the match between Sergei Tolstoy and Tatyana rather a shady transaction: a compliant priest had to be found. (This point is not explained by the editors, with the result that the situation is partly unintelligible to the non-Russian reader.) Sergei began to stay away from Yasnaya Polyana, and when Tatyana grasped the situation, she broke the engagement off, though her disappointment was bitter and the shock had a serious effect on her health. The rest of Sergei's story is not told by Tatyana, but one can find it in *The Tragedy of Tolstoy*, by Tolstoy's daughter Alexandra. Sergei married Marya Mikhailovna and became more and more unsocial. His wife and daughters did all the housework and lived in terror of him. He made it impossible for one of these daughters to see a young man of the local gentry who was in love with her and wanted to marry her, on the ground that he was not well enough educated; and presently another of the daughters, "homely, small, almost a dwarf," ran away with a good-looking cook, who opened a shop with her money, treated her brutally and finally deserted her, leaving her with several children. She died during the Revolution, "alone and unhappy in a faraway village." The third daughter eloped with a Bashkir, who had been brought from the steppes to make kumiss, a fermentation of mare's milk which had been prescribed for her health. She returned the next year, with an under-grown little boy, who had yellow Oriental skin and slanting Oriental eyes. Her father let her live in the house, in a back room as far as possible from his study, but would not see the child. They and Marya Mikhailovna, left alone by Sergei's death, died miserably after the Revolution, when their house, from which they had fled, was burned down and the estate sacked. After the elopement of the second daughter, Sergei had made haste to agree to the marriage of his only remaining child to her insufficiently educated nobleman.

Now, Tatyana could hardly have known at the time that her brother-in-law Leo, who had first accepted her match with Sergei, then applauded her breaking it off, had himself had a serf-girl for a mistress not long before he married her sister. His diaries show how much he had cared for this girl: "I am in love," he declares in one entry, "as I never was before in my life. I have no other thought. I suffer." He has moments of indifference, of revulsion even, but his affection for her seems steadily to grow stronger, "It is getting to be even frightening," he later writes, "how close to me she is. . . . It is not merely the feeling now of a rutting stag, but that of a husband and a wife." He had a son by her, who afterward became coachman for one of his legitimate sons. And in the meantime, by one of those gestures of what he liked to regard as uncompromising honesty that were often so admirably calculated to give pain to other people, he had shown his young wife this diary at a time when his former mistress still sometimes came to the house—with the result that the poor Countess, already of a jealous disposition, was visited by homicidal impulses when she found the woman scrubbing the floors, and even took to disguising herself as a peasant and way-laying her husband about the estate to see whether he were still susceptible to the blandishments of pretty serf-girls. Twenty-seven years after his marriage, Tolstoy tried to write about this love affair, combining it with the story of a similar complication, in which a neighbor, after marrying a jealous wife, had shot his peasant mistress. Tolstoy, in one of his versions of this story, follows the real tragedy; in another, he has the landowner shoot himself. He could not bring himself to publish the piece—to which he gave the title *The Devil*—presumably because, when he showed it to his wife as late as 1909, she was upset by it and made a scene; and it did not appear until after his death.

This situation was evidently a common one. Tolstoy's father, at the age of sixteen, had had an affair with a peasant girl, an affair arranged by his parents themselves; and a son, who was the product of this union, had turned up from time to time to plague the legitimate children. Tolstoy tells of his "strange feeling of consternation when in after years this brother of mine, fallen into destitution and bearing a greater resemblance to my father than any of us, used to beg help of us and was thankful for the ten or fifteen rubles we used to give him." The memory of his own illegitimate family recurred to torment Leo. "I looked at my bare feet," he wrote in his diary of 1909, "and remembered Aksinya [his mistress]—that she is still alive and that they say Ermil is my son, and that I do not beg her forgiveness, have never done penitence, do not repent every hour, and dare to judge others."

D. S. Mirsky, in his *History of Russian Literature*, has truly described *War and Peace* as an "heroic idyll of the Russian nobility," and pointed out that, in spite of the horrors of war and the ineptitudes of civilization, "the general message . . . is one of beauty and satisfaction that the world should be so beautiful." He suggests, I believe correctly, that Tolstoy's penchant for the idyllic is "the opposite pole to his unceasing moral uneasiness." Certainly *War and Peace* is one of the greatest of novels as it is one of the most enchanting. If it is not, as I do not think it is, quite one of the very summits of literature, it is because this idyllic tendency does here get the better of the author at the expense of the conditions of life as he actually knew and lived it. There is in the book, for all its realism,

a certain element of the idealization in which we are all
disposed to indulge in imagining the lives of our ancestors.
In the case of Tolstoy, who had hardly known either his
grandparents or his parents, this temptation must have been
very strong. In the novel, Prince André and Pierre have
their struggles with the problem of the peasantry, but the
main problem is expelling the invader, and neither Natasha
nor any of the men has to face any human relationship as
painful as those in which the real Tatyana and the real
Sergei and Leo Tolstoy found themselves involved. The
Levin of *Anna Karenina*, which followed *War and Peace*,
has to deal in a more direct and drastic way with his
relation to the estate he has inherited and with the humans
who are part of the estate, as Tolstoy did with Yasnaya
Polyana; and immediately after *Anna Karenina*, Tolstoy
himself appears in the character of Levin, writing the eloquent *Confession* in which he declares the insufficiency,
for the moral life of a man, of property, social position and
a comfortable family life, as well as of philosophy and
science and the enjoyment and practice of literature. And
he later tries to satisfy his moral needs by bringing himself
closer to the peasants, on whose work he has always lived
and who have given him the leisure to write—eating the
same food as they and wearing the same clothes, working
the same hours in the fields and mastering their manual
skills. It was disturbing, no doubt, to a sensitive man, even
after the liberation of the serfs in 1861—which Tatyana, by
the way, hardly mentions, so little was it evidently notice-
able in the relations of her people with their laborers and
servants—to feel that one owed one's education and one's
chance to pursue serious interests, as well as one's luxuries
and pleasures, to the maintenance of a breed of inferior
beings. But to know that one's own blood was mixed with
the blood of this breed and to have to watch, in one form
or another, the humiliation of one's own children must
have been even harder to bear, a constant source of helpless
anguish. (A gypsy singer, of course, might represent a
higher stratum than that of a simple serf, but the con-

sequences of marrying one, in Sergei's case, turned out to be just about as disastrous as if she had been a serf. When his daughter who eloped with the cook went to her Uncle Leo and asked him to approve this union, on the ground that she was following his doctrine by trying to put herself on a plane with the peasant, he lectured the girl severely, telling her that "no marriage could be happy between people who stood on different levels of development and had no interests in common.")

The emotional effects of this dilemma are not anywhere presented directly either in *War and Peace* or in *Anna Karenina,* though the situation appears in both. In the former, it is idyllic, like everything else. The uncle at whose house the Rostovs spend the night after the hunt has a housekeeper who is also his mistress, but the whole thing is most amiable and comfortable, and when Natasha has done her peasant dance—Tatyana tells us that this incident was derived from a performance of her own—the rosy and plump and good-looking woman sheds a tear or two through her laughter as she perceives that "this slim graceful countess, brought up in velvet and silk, this being so alien to her . . . was able to understand everything about Anisya and Anisya's father and her aunt and her mother, and every Russian in the world." In *Anna Karenina,* a similar situation is presented in a more embarrassing light. When Levin goes with his wife to visit his dying brother, he winces at having her meet the latter's ex-prostitute mistress, with whom he has been living in misery, and he notes, for a fleeting moment, her "expression of eager curiosity" at encountering "that dreadful woman, so incomprehensible to her." It is only later, with *Resurrection,* begun in 1889 and not finished and published till 1899, that Tolstoy comes to grips with this situation. In his youth, he had had an affair with one of his aunt's maids, who had been dismissed for this reason and had come later to a bad end. In the novel, Prince Nekhlyudov finds himself sitting on a jury which has to pass judgment on a girl whom he recognizes as a maid of his aunt's whom he has seduced under similar circumstances and deserted when she was pregnant. She has since become a prostitute and is now implicated in a sordid murder, of which she is completely innocent. At the trial, there is a miscarriage of justice, due partly to the carelessness of the Court but partly to Nekhlyudov's own cowardice, and the girl is condemned to Siberia. Nekhlyudov now brings all his influence to have the decision reversed and makes a vow to expiate his guilt by following her into exile and marrying her. He does get her sentence commuted, and he accompanies the convicts on their journey; but Maslova spares him the final test, for, understanding the undesirability of his spending the rest of his life with her, she marries one of her fellow-prisoners. Nekhlyudov, on the very last pages, happens to pick up a copy of the *New Testament* which has been given him by a travelling evangelist, and is converted to a creed like Tolstoy's own. From that day, for Nekhlyudov, says the author, a new life begins, and "what the new period will come to, time alone will show."

So we never know what happened to Nekhlyudov. It is impossible, from what we have been told of him, to imagine him turning saint or even finding employment that would satisfy his hunger for righteousness. Yet *Resurrection*, though it ends in the air, is not unworthy of its predecessors, and certainly does not deserve the disparagement that it usually gets. It is the novel in which Tolstoy comes closest to the problems of his own life, the only one in which he really grapples with the tragedies of a class-society, as he had seen them at first hand, as he had helped to produce them himself—the only one that gets out into the open such episodes as Tatyana had locked away in her diary. We do know what happened to Tolstoy when he tried to lead a new life: his fanaticisms and his worldly relapses, his absurdities and his desperate death. The story he himself had been living could no more come out satisfactorily than Nekhlyudov's story could. After the period of his first gratification at re-creating his lost parents and in restoring at Yasnaya Polyana the patriarchal family life of which in the preceding generation the continuity had been broken, a malaise which had survived these distractions inescapably asserted itself and came to ache through the whole of his work.

We have seen a somewhat similar preoccupation in the literature of our own South, from the days when George W. Cable was forced to come to live in the North for his boldness in describing the half-colored branches of the prominent white families of New Orleans to the days when the continued anguish of Negro and white relations has inspired those stories of Faulkner's in which neither reader nor author is ever allowed a moment's relief or repose, because the subject admits of no resolution. In Russia, the black-and-white issue was not present to deepen the class distinctions, and it was possible for the landowners in Tolstoy's fiction to contemplate marrying their mistresses, as it was possible for Sergei Tolstoy to remain in serious doubt as to whether it was right for him to put away his gypsy and marry Tatyana. But the strains and the mutilations incurred through these social differences periodically made themselves felt among all those gay parties in country houses, all those balls in St. Petersburg and Moscow, all those jolly affectionate family scenes, all those gallantries of handsome cousins.

August 28, 1948

William Faulkner's Reply to the Civil-Rights Program

WILLIAM FAULKNER'S NEW NOVEL, *Intruder in the Dust*, is the story of a Negro with white blood who refuses to behave with the submissiveness demanded of his color in the South and has developed so rigid a pride that, even when wrongfully charged with the murder of a white man, he can hardly bring himself to stoop to defend himself against the enemy of his race. The narrative deals with the adventures of the handful of people in the community (the Jefferson, Mississippi, which is the locale of most of Faulkner's fiction) who, having come to respect Lucas' independence, interest themselves in his case and exert themselves to save him from lynching. These champions include a boy of sixteen, who had once been rescued by Lucas when he had fallen through the ice; the boy's uncle, a local lawyer, who has lived abroad and has, to some degree, been able to surmount provincial prejudices; and an old lady of the best local quality, who had grown up with the accused man's dead wife in the relation of mistress and maid. All the happenings are presented from the point of view of the boy. It is his loyalty to the old Negro that leads to the discovery of evidence that the crime has been committed by someone else; and his emergence, under the stimulus of events, out of boyhood into comparative maturity is as much the subject of the book as the predicament of the Negro. The real theme is the relation between the two.

The novel has the suspense and excitement that Faulkner can nearly always create and the disturbing emotional power that he can generate at his best. The earlier Faulkner of *Sanctuary* was often accused of misanthropy and despair, but the truth is that, from *Pylon* on, at any rate, one of the most striking features of his work, and one that sets it off from that of many of his American contemporaries, has been a kind of romantic morality that allows you the thrills of melodrama without making you ashamed, as a rule, of the values which have been invoked to produce them. I do not sympathize with the line of criticism which deplores Faulkner's obstinate persistence in submerging himself in the mentality of the community where he was born, for his chivalry, which constitutes his morality, is a part of his Southern heritage, and it appears in Faulkner's work as a force more humane and more positive than almost anything one can find in the work of even those writers of our more mechanized societies who have set out to defend human rights. *Intruder in the Dust* is one of the most ardent demonstrations of this reconditioned Southern chivalry; and the question that arises in connection with it is not whether it paints too hopeless a picture but, on the contrary, whether it is not too positive, too optimistic—whether the author has not yielded too much to the temptations of the novelist's power to summon for innocence in difficulties the equivalent of the United States Marines.

I shall return to this aspect of *Intruder in the Dust*. In the meantime, it ought to be said that, from the point of view of the writing, this is one of the more snarled-up of Faulkner's books. It is not so bad as *The Bear*, which has pages that are almost opaque. But in his attempt to record the perceptions—the instinctive sensations and the half-formed thoughts—of his adolescent boy, in aiming at prisms of prose which will concentrate the infra-red as well as the ultra-violet, he leaves these rays sometimes still invisible, and only tosses into our hands some rather clumsy and badly cut polygons. It would require a good deal of very diligent work and very nice calculation always to turn out the combinations of words that would do what Faulkner wants them to do. His energy, his image-making genius get him where he wants to go about seventy per cent of the time, but when he misses it, he lands in a mess. One cannot object in principle to any of Faulkner's practices: to his shifting his syntax in the middle of a sentence, to his stringing long sequences of clauses together with practically no syntax at all, to his inserting in parenthesis in the middle of a scene (in one case, in the middle of a sentence) a long episode that took place at some other time, to his invention of the punctuation (( )) to indicate a parenthesis within a parenthesis or to his creation of non-dictionary words. He has, at one time or another, justified all these devices. But what is the excuse for writing "the old grunt and groan with some long familiar minor stiffness so used and accustomed as to be no longer even an ache and which if they were ever actually cured of it, they would be bereft and lost"?—a mismanagement of relatives quite common in

the Faulkner of the latest books. One is willing to give the
benefit of the doubt to "regurg," "abnegant," "dismatch-
ment," "divinant," "perspicuant," until one runs into a
dictionary word used out of its real meaning, as in "it's
only men who burk at facts"—when one realizes that
Faulkner is not merely coining but groping. It is true that
his new way of writing has enabled him to render impressions more accurately than he did before: but the passages
that become unintelligible on account of a confusion of
pronouns or that have to be read twice for lack of proper
punctuation are not really the results of an effort to express
the hardly expressible but the casualties of an indolent taste
and a negligent workmanship that did not appear to the
same degree in the prose—for the most part so steady and
clear as well as so tense and telling—of such a novel as *Light
in August.*

One finds here both the vigor of a tradition and the signs
of its current decay. For the writing of Faulkner, too, has
a noble and ancient lineage. Though he echoed, in his
earlier novels, Hemingway and Sherwood Anderson, he
belongs, really, not to their school but to the full-dress
post-Flaubert group of Conrad, Joyce and Proust, whom
he has sometimes echoed since. To their kind of highly
complex fiction he has brought the rich and lively resources,
reappearing with amazing freshness, of English lyric verse
and romantic prose (as distinguished from what we now
call American). This is an advantage that the Southern
writers sometimes have—a contact with the language of
Shakespeare which, if they sidestep the oratorical Southern
verbiage, they may get through their old-fashioned education. And Faulkner, it must be said, often succeeds as
Shakespeare does—by plunging into the dramatic scene
and flinging down the words and images that flow to the
ends of his fingers. This book, like all his books, is full of
passages that could not have been written if he had sat
down and contemplated the object—as Flaubert is said to
have done the cabbage garden by moonlight—instead of
allowing himself to be possessed by it. Minor but admirable

examples in *Intruder in the Dust* are the renderings of the impression on the white boy of the smell of a Negro cabin, with all its social implications, and of the effect of a little frame church that, though lacking a steeple and shabbily patched, speaks to him with the spirit of the Calvinism to which its Scotch-Irish congregation have erected a degenerate shrine. Though he sometimes loses his grasp of language, he has described so many things so well—got out of them so much human meaning! No other of our contemporary novelists, perhaps, can compete with him in this department—for most of the best of them were bred in a world that is based on abstract assumptions, and they cannot help sharing these; whereas, for Faulkner the Mississippian, everything that a man has made wears the aspect of the human agent, and its impact is that of a human meeting.

To be thus out of date, as a Southerner, in feeling and in language and in human relations, may prove, for a novelist, a source of strength. But the weaknesses of Faulkner, also, have their origin in the antiquated community he inhabits, for they result from his not having mastered—I speak of the design of his books as wholes as well as of that of his sentences and paragraphs—the discipline of the Joyces, Prousts and Conrads (though Proust had his solecisms and what the ancients called anacolutha). If you are going to do embroidery, you have to watch every stitch; if you are going to construct a machine, you have to test every part. The technique of the modern novel, with its ideal of technical efficiency, its specialization of means for ends, has grown up in the industrial age, and it has, after all, a good deal in common with the other manifestations of that age. In practising it so far from such cities as produced the Flauberts, Joyces and Jameses, Faulkner's provinciality, stubbornly cherished and turned into an asset, inevitably tempts him to be slipshod and has apparently made it impossible for him to acquire complete expertness in an art that demands of the artist the closest attention and care.

But *Intruder in the Dust* does not come to us merely as a novel: it also involves a tract. The story is evidently supposed to take place sometime this year or last, and it seems to have been partly inspired by the crisis at the time of the recent war in the relations between whites and Negroes and by the recently proposed legislation for guaranteeing Negro rights. The book contains a kind of counter-blast to the anti-lynching bill and to the civil-rights plank in the Democratic platform. The author's ideas on this subject are apparently conveyed, in their explicit form, by the intellectual uncle, who, more and more as the story goes on, gives vent to long disquisitions that seem to become so "editorial" in character that it is difficult to regard them merely as a part of the presentation of the furniture of the uncle's personality. The series may be pieced together as something in the nature of a public message delivered by the author himself. This message, however, suffers from the handicap of being very obscurely expressed. Faulkner, who has shown himself a master at making every possible type of Mississippian talk in his natural idiom, has chosen to couch the uncle's conversations with the boy in a literary prose like his own at its most complicated and non-colloquial—so that it is difficult to reduce what is said to definite propositions. I shall, however, make an attempt to do so.

The point of view, then, seems to be as follows (interpolated comment by the critic):

"The people named Sambo" [the uncle's way of designating the Negroes] have survived the ordeal of slavery and they may survive the ordeal of dictatorship. The capacity for endurance of the Negro is a recurrent theme of Faulkner's, and his respect for their humble persistence is unconsciously but strikingly contrasted here with his attitude toward "the coastal spew of Europe, which this country quarantined unrootable into the rootless ephemeral cities" [as if the Italians, Greeks, Hungarians, Poles, and Czechs had not shown as much tenacity as the Negroes, and as if the Southern Negroes had not been kept alive—

that is, encouraged to persist—by the people who had an interest in employing them, just as the immigrants from Europe were].

The Southerners in the United States are the only "homogeneous people." (The New Englander, in his pure and respectable form, crowded back by the coastal spew of Europe, is no longer of real importance.) "We are defending not actually our politics or beliefs or even our way of life, but simply our homogeneity, from a federal government to which, in simple desperation, the rest of this country has had to surrender voluntarily more and more of its personal and private liberty in order to continue to afford the United States." The Negro is homogeneous, too, "except that part of him which is trying to escape not even into the best of the white race but into the second best." The saving remnant of Southerners, such as the characters in the story who rescue old Lucas Beauchamp, should combine with the non-second-rate Negro—the second-rate variety being, by the author's definition, the Negro who demands "not an automobile nor flash clothes nor his picture in the paper, but a little of music (his own), a hearth, not his child but any child [back to Uncle Tom and Uncle Remus!], a God, a heaven which a man may avail himself a little of at any time without having to wait to die [oh, dem golden slippers!], a little earth for his own sweat to fall on among his own green shoots and plants [no large-scale agriculture for Sambo!]." Let the white man give the Negro his rights, and the Negro teach the white man his endurance, and "together we would dominate the United States; we would present a front not only impregnable but not even to be threatened by a mass of people who no longer have anything in common save a frantic greed for money and a basic fear of a failure of national character which they hide from one another behind a loud lipservice to a flag." [The Mississippian may have hold of something here.]

Lucas-Sambo must be defended "from the North and East and West—the outlanders who will fling him decades back not merely into injustice but into grief and agony, and violence, too, by forcing on us laws based on the idea that man's injustice to man can be abolished overnight by police." Any other course of conduct toward the Negro will risk dividing the country. Attempts on the part of the people in other sections of the United States to strengthen the hand of the Negro amount to nothing more than "a paper alliance of theorists and fanatics and private and personal avengers plus a number of others" [including a good many Negroes] against "a concorded [i.e., solid] South," which is now full of "ignorant people" from other parts of the country, "who fear the color of any skin or shape of nose save their own." Such action will force the many Southerners "who do begrieve Lucas' shameful condition and would improve it" and will eventually abolish it, to ally themselves with all those objectionable elements "with whom we have no kinship whatever, in defense of a principle [the inalienable right to keep the Negro down] which we ourselves begrieve and abhor." They will thus be forced into "the position of the German after 1933, who had no other alternative between being either a Nazi or a Jew, or the present Russian (European, too, for that matter), who hasn't even that, but must be either a Communist or dead." So the Southerners must be allowed, on their own initiative, in their own way, with no intervention by others, to grant the Negro his citizenship. Otherwise—

Otherwise, what? I have been able, I think, up to now, to make Faulkner's argument clear by quoting or paraphrasing his own words, with the addition of a little punctuation; but here I must present you with a chunk of his text without any elucidation, for I cannot be sure what it means: Otherwise "Lucas' equality" cannot "be anything more than its own prisoner inside an impregnable barricade of the direct heirs of the victory of 1861–1865 which probably did more than even John Brown to stalemate Lucas' freedom which still seems to be in check going on a hundred years after Lee surrendered." But, the other side may object: The South will never get around to doing anything for the Negro. Your policy, the South retorts, is dangerous, in any case: it will give rise to "a people divided [Faulkner thus seems to take it for granted that if Washington tries to back the Negroes, it will arouse the whole South to resistance] at a time when history is still showing us that the anteroom to dissolution is division."

But is pressure from outside worth nothing? Has it had no moral effect on the South? It seems to me that this book itself, which rejects outside interference, is a conspicuous sign that it has. The champions of Lucas Beauchamp are shown as rather reluctant, as even, at moments, resentful, in recognizing his rectitude and his dignity, but they do rally to get him cleared. It is true that you have had already, in the title story of *Go Down, Moses,* the same liberal lawyer and decent old maid working together to do the Beauchamps a kindness when their grandson has been executed for murder; but in this new book these white folks of the best old stock come to the rescue of the Negro with a zeal that I do not remember to have seen displayed by the inhabitants of Yoknapatawpha County in any other of Faulkner's books. Young Charles and his young Negro pal are transformed into Boy Scouts. Miss Habersham proves herself a dear gallant old thoroughbred. The uncle is as ironic and delightful as the uncle of the boy next door in E. Nesbit's books about the Bastable children. When this wonderful posse is on the march, they have hairbreadth escapes but get all the breaks. And, in the end, the vulgar upstarts who wanted to see Lucas lynched get into their vulgar cars and turn tail and run away. There has been nothing so exhilarating in its way since the triumphs of the Communist-led workers in the early Soviet films; one is thrilled by the same kind of emotion that one got from some of the better dramatizations of the career of Abraham Lincoln.

This is a new note to come from the South; and it may really represent something more than Faulkner's own courageous and generous spirit, some new stirring of public conscience. In the meantime, in harping on this message, I do not want to divert attention from the genius that produced the book, which sustains, like its predecessors, the polymorphous polychromatic vitality, the poetic truth to experience, of Faulkner's Balzacian chronicle of Yoknapatawpha County. Old Lucas and certain other characters have, as I say, appeared in *Go Down, Moses,* to which *Intruder in the Dust* is, indeed, more or less of a sequel, and the later adventures of Lucas are more interesting if you know his past history as recounted in the earlier volume, and understand his role in the tangle of black-and-white relationships which Faulkner has presented there. This subject of the complicated consequences of the mixture of white with Negro blood has been explored by Faulkner with remarkable intelligence and subtlety and variety of dramatic imagination; and Lucas himself, the black man who embarrasses a set of white relatives by having inherited the strongest traits of a white ancestor common to them all, is one of the author's most impressive creations. Even when the prose goes to pieces, the man and his milieu live.

October 23, 1948

INDEX

Adams, Franklin Pierce, 55
Adams, Henry, 169, 319
Adams, Léonie, 89
Ade, George, 40
Adventure, An, 288
Adventure of the Dying Detective, The, 351
Adventure of the Hansom Cab, The, 348
Adventure of the Superfluous Mansion, The, 348
Aeneid, 108, 297
After Many a Summer Dies the Swan, 237, 241–42
Age of Innocence, The, 91
Age of Reason, The, 398–400, 404–5, 406
A Huis Clos, 405
Aiken, Conrad, 86
Airways, Inc., 128–31, 132
A la Recherche du Temps Perdu, 103
Aldanov, Mark, 337–38
Aldington, Richard, 369
Allingham, Margery, 339, 341
All Summer in a Day, 102
Alpine Idyl, An, 98
American Language, The, 82, 94
American Tragedy, An, 218
America's Coming of Age, 56
Anderson, Sherwood, 38, 45, 80, 81, 82, 91, 222, 223, 425
Andrewes, Lancelot, 133, 135–36
Andria, 138
Angels and Earthly Creatures, 109
Angel That Troubled the Waters, The, 140
Anna Karenina, 419, 420
Anthony, Katherine, 84
Apollonius Rhodius, 156
Apparition of Mrs. Veal, 288
Appearance and Reality, 107
Appointment in Samarra, 220, 221, 222
Aquinas, Thomas, 135, 136
Arabian Nights, 137
Aristocracy and Justice, 150
Aristotle, 95, 147, 150, 152
Arnold, Matthew, 148, 152, 321
Arnold, Thomas, 167
Arsenic and Old Lace, 288
Arvin, Newton, 189

Ash Tree, The, 289
Atalanta in Calydon, 16
At the End of the Passage, 291
Audubon, John James, 317, 318
Austen, Jane, 287, 302–9, 411
Babbitt, 39, 78, 96
Babbitt, Irving, 9, 16, 90, 123, 133, 134, 146–53, 155, 159
Bach, Johann Sebastian, 95
Bacon, Roger, 95
Balzac, Honoré de, 78, 106, 301, 399
Barbusse, Henri, 101
Barham, Richard H., 362
Barlow, Joel, 318
Barrett, William, 400, 405, 406
Barrie, James M., 226
Barrymore, Ethel, 261–62, 263
Barrymore, John, 259–65
Barrymore, Lionel, 261, 262
Barrymore, Maurice, 262
Bartleby the Scrivener, 291
Barzun, Jacques, 339, 342
Baudelaire, Pierre Charles, 16, 69, 73, 133, 155, 321, 378
Bear, The, 424
Beautiful and Damned, The, 33, 34–37
Beebe, William, 85
Beer, Thomas, 84
Beerbohm, Max, 35, 78
Beethoven, Ludwig van, 95
Bell, Clive, 162, 163
Benchley, Robert, 55, 56
Benét, William Rose, 109
Ben-Hur, 310, 311
Benito Cereno, 291
Bennett, Arnold, 39
Benson, E. F., 289
Benson, Frank, 372
Bentley, Richard, 147
Berle, Milton, 61
Berlin, Irving, 52, 57
Bernice Bobs Her Hair, 33
Best Ghost Stories of M. R. James, 287, 289
Best Short Stories of 1923, 43
Better Things of Life, The, 242
Beyond Life, 78
Bibliography of the Works of Ernest Hemingway, 44

Bierce, Ambrose, 241
Big Money, The, 248
Bikle, Lucy Leffingwell Cable, 123
Birthday of the Infanta, The, 378
Birth of a Nation, 44
Bishop, John Peale, 19
Black Mischief, 267, 269
Black Rose, The, 357
Blackwood, Algernon, 293, 294
Bleak House, 251
Blumfeld, an Elderly Bachelor, 294
Boccaccio, Giovanni, 18
Bodenheim, Maxwell, 87
Bogan, Louise, 89
Booby Trap, 324
Bookman's Daybook, A, 41
Book of Etiquette, The, 381
Book of Prefaces, A, 56, 94
Borrow, George, 362
Boswell, James, 328–29, 330
Bottom Dogs, 141–42
Boule de Suif, 100
Boy Meets Girl, 241
Bradley, Francis Herbert, 133
Brahms, Johannes, 162
Bramhall, John, 133
Brideshead Revisited, 353–57
Bridge of San Luis Rey, The, 103, 104–5, 106, 107
Broch, Hermann, 29
Brod, Max, 390, 391, 392–94
Bromfield, Louis, 271–78
Brontë, Emily, 287
Brooks, Van Wyck, 56, 68, 83, 84, 91, 120, 188, 317–23
Brothers Karamazov, The, 178
Brownell, William Crary, 90
Browning, Robert, 17–18, 320
Bryan, 85
Bryant, William Cullen, 317, 318, 321
Buddha, 152
Bulwer-Lytton, Edward George Earle Lytton, 311, 362
Burning Court, The, 342
Butler, Samuel, 81
Butterfield 8, 212, 220, 222
Byron, George Gordon, Lord, 18, 20, 21, 69, 100, 173, 255, 331–32, 371, 412

Cabala, The, 103–4, 107, 108, 136, 141
Cabell, James Branch, 78, 81, 106
Cable, George Washington, 90, 123–28, 422
Cain, James M., 216–19, 242n., 243, 327
Cairns, Huntington, 359

Callot, Jacques, 63
Cambridge History of English Literature, The, 360, 362
Campbell, Joseph, 295–302
Campion, Edward, 357
Camus, Albert, 403
Candide, 245, 266
Cane, 79
Carlyle, Thomas, 152
Carr, John Dickson, 339, 342
Carroll, Lewis, 55, 56, 297
Case, Charles, 54–55
Case of M. Valdemar, 72
Castle, The, 389, 391, 393, 396
Caterpillars, 289
Cather, Willa, 78, 80
Catullus, 89
Cervantes, Miguel de, 95
Champion, 40
Chandler, Raymond, 339, 343–44
Chants de Maldoror, Les, 213
Chaplin, Charlie, 47, 51, 52, 57, 63, 208, 210
Chapman, John Jay, 123, 279
Chateaubriand, François René, Vicomte de, 69
Chaucer, Geoffrey, 17
Chénier, André, 14
Chevalier, Haakon, 189
Chiang Kai-shek, 177
Chivers, Thomas Holley, 66, 74
Christie, Agatha, 326
Chrysanthemums, The, 232
Cinquains, 89
Clay-Shuttered Doors, 289
Clemm, Virginia, 71
Cobb, Irvin S., 37, 40
Cocteau, Jean, 55, 57
Cohen, Morris, 84
Cohn, Louis Henry, 44
Colby, Frank Moore, 64
Coleridge, Samuel Taylor, 69, 74, 302
Collected Essays and Papers, 361–62
Colum, Mary, 43, 44
Colum, Padraic, 75
Condition Humaine, La, 172, 173–78
Confessions, 15
Confucius, 149, 152
Conquérants, Les, 172, 174, 176, 178
Conrad, Joseph, 174, 291, 425
Constrained Attitudes, 64
Contemplations, Les, 12
Cook, Joe, 54, 55, 56, 57
Cool Million, A, 245
Copper Beeches, The, 349
Costello, Dolores, 265

Cotswold Chace, 411
Count Ten, 228–29, 230, 240–41
Crabbe, George, 362
Crane, Frank, 227
Crane, Stephen, 90, 123, 230, 264
Crapsey, Adelaide, 89
Crashaw, Richard, 133
Creeps by Night, 287
Creighton, Mandell, 169
Crime de Sylvestre Bonnard, Le, 21
Crotchet Castle, 407
Crowninshield, Frank, 109
Cummings, E. E., 43, 87
Cymbeline, 207, 279

Dahlberg, Edward, 141–42, 145
Dante Alighieri, 12, 14, 18, 19, 20, 24, 26, 152, 278, 296, 297, 362–63, 391, 396
Daring Young Man on the Flying Trapeze, 224
Dark Flower, The, 354
Darwin, Charles, 160
Darwin, Erasmus, 370
David Copperfield, 251
Davies, Joseph E., 254–59
Day at the Races, A, 209, 210
Day of the Locust, The, 241, 245–48, 358
Death Comes as the End, 326–27
Death in the Afternoon, 199
Decline and Fall, 265, 266, 267, 270
Decline of the West, The, 21
Deffand, Marie Anne, Marquise du, 168
Defoe, Daniel, 213, 288, 294
De Kruif, Paul, 85
de la Mare, Walter, 294, 321
Dell, Floyd, 77
Demon of the Absolute, The, 157
Dennis, Nigel, 270
De Profundis, 373, 376
De Quincey, Thomas, 69, 81, 297, 346
Descent into the Maelström, 72
Deutsch, Babette, 89
Devil and the Deep Sea, The, 229
De Voto, Bernard, 339, 341, 342
Dewey, John, 28, 84
Diamond as Big as the Ritz, The, 36
Diary of Dostoevsky's Wife, The, 117
Dickens, Charles, 251, 268, 302, 328, 362
Dickinson, Lowes, 85
Diderot, Denis, 15
Dietrich, Marlene, 209

Disney, Walt, 63, 210
Divine Comedy, The, 20, 297, 362–63
Doctor Jekyll and Mr. Hyde, 70
Doctor's Son, The, 221
Dodd, Lee Wilson, 97, 98, 99, 101
Doolittle, Hilda, 86–87
Dorsey, George Amos, 85
Dos Passos, John, 79, 81, 101, 128–33, 136–37, 142–45, 157–58, 222, 248, 337, 405
Dostoevsky, Anna Grigorevna, 117–19
Dostoevsky, F. M., 78, 117–22, 202, 278, 297
Douglas, Alfred, 370–71, 372, 373–74, 376
Douglas, Lloyd C., 309–13, 326
Douglas, Norman, 161–66
Doyle, Arthur Conan, 75, 292–93, 325, 340, 346–52, 370
Dream Life of Balso Snell, The, 245
Dreiser, Theodore, 69, 78, 92
Drew, John, 262
Dunlap, William, 318
Dunsany, Lord (Edward John Moreton Drax Plunkett), 81, 106
Durante, Jimmy, 63, 327

Edgar Allan Poe: A Study in Genius, 66
Edgar Allan Poe, the Man, 66
Edgar Poe et les Premiers Symbolistes Français, 73
Egg, The, 38
Eichler, Lillian, 381, 383, 389
Einstein, Albert, 156, 160
Eleanora, 72
Elinor Wylie: The Portrait of an Unknown Lady, 109
Eliot, Charles W., 28
Eliot, T. S., 89–90, 92, 133–38, 169, 268, 296, 327
Elizabeth, Queen, 168, 169
Elizabeth and Essex, 168
Emerson, Ralph Waldo, 68, 90, 92, 152
Eminent Victorians, 166–67, 170–71
Emma, 304, 306–8, 309
Encyclopedia of Etiquette, 381
Enemy of the People, An, 263
Engels, Friedrich, 21
Enormous Room, The, 43
Ethan Frome, 276
Etiquette, 381–89
Evgeni Onegin, 256
Eureka, 93

Euripides, 56, 95
Evelina, 306
Existentialism, 400
Existentialism: A New Trend in Philosophy, 401

Facts, The, 37
Fall of the House of Usher, The, 290
Farewell, My Lovely, 343
Farewell to Arms, A, 200
Faulkner, William, 222, 230, 422–31
Fielding, Henry, 296
Fifth Seal, The, 337
Files on Parade, 221–22
Finnegans Wake, 295–302
Fishbein, Morris, 85
Fite, Warner, 85
Fitzgerald, F. Scott, 19, 30–37, 79, 96, 132, 222, 245, 248–49, 266, 285–86, 353, 382
Flaubert, Gustave, 16, 19, 20, 100, 155, 169, 296, 297, 322, 394, 395, 399, 425
Fletcher, John Gould, 86
Fleurs du Mal, Les, 73
Flight, 232
Flores, Angel, 390
Flowering Judas, 315
Flowering of New England, The, 318
Flowers for the Judge, 341–42
Ford, Ford Madox, 47, 361, 376
Ford, Henry, 22
For Lancelot Andrewes, 133–34
Forster, E. M., 174, 302
Fortune Hunter, The, 264
Fortunes of Falstaff, The, 279
42nd Parallel, The, 143–45
For Whom the Bell Tolls, 242n.
Fowler, Gene, 259–65
France, Anatole, 21, 52, 53, 140, 169, 399
Frank, Tenney, 84
Frank, Waldo, 68, 79
Franz Kafka: A Biography, 390
Franz Kafka Miscellany, A, 390
Fraser, Phyllis, 287
French Literature and Its Masters, 359
French Literature from the Beginning to 1900, 359–60
Freud, Sigmund, 108, 295
Frost, Robert, 86
Furness, Horace Howard, 109
Futrelle, Jacques, 323

Galantière, Lewis, 41, 42
Gale, Zona, 79

Galsworthy, John, 264, 354, 382
Garbo, Greta, 208
Garnett, David, 231
Garrod, Heathcote William, 85
Gauss, Christian, 9–29
Gauss, Karl Friedrich, 20, 156
Gentlemen Prefer Blondes, 306
George, Henry, 244
George W. Cable: His Life and Letters, 123
Gide, André, 171, 337, 345, 376, 377, 377n.
Gilbert, W. S., 370, 371
Gilder, Richard Watson, 123
Go Down, Moses, 430, 431
Goethe, Johann Wolfgang von, 152–53, 278
Gogol, Nikolai V., 195, 290, 291, 294, 295, 338, 391, 397
Gold, Michael, 132
Golden Bough, The, 108
Golden Day, The, 68
Golden Honeymoon, The, 38, 51
Goldwyn, Samuel, 206–8, 209, 210, 211
Gone With the Wind, 306
Goodbye to Berlin, 314
Good-bye to Western Culture: Some Footnotes on East and West, 161–66
Goodman, Paul, 390
Good Night, Sweet Prince, 259–65
Gorky, Maxim, 263, 337
Gottschalk, Laura, 89
Goya, Francisco, 46
Grandissimes, The, 125–27
Grapes of Wrath, The, 227, 231, 233, 236, 237, 242n., 400
Great Audience, The, 58–63
Great Gatsby, The, 19, 79, 266
Great God Pan, The, 293
Great Goldwyn, The, 206–8
Great Tales of Terror and the Supernatural, 287
Great Wall of China, The, 390, 394
Greek Interpreter, The, 349, 352
Green Bay Tree, The, 271
Greene, Graham, 327, 343, 344
Green Hills of Africa, 196–200, 204
Gryll Grange, 410, 412, 413
Guérin, Maurice de, 69
Guest, Eddie, 227
Guitry, Sacha, 53
Guizot, François, 169

Hacienda, 315
Hackett, Francis, 77

Hallas, Richard, 216, 217, 218, 242
Hamlet, 67, 263, 264, 279, 282, 283, 306
Hammett, Dashiell, 216, 287, 327, 343
Handful of Dust, A, 267–68
Harbor, The, 32
Hardy, Thomas, 35, 100, 274
Harrington, John, 169
Harris, Frank, 370, 373, 377
Harte, Bret, 241
Hartley, Marsden, 42
Hauptmann, Gerhart, 81, 263
Hawthorne, Nathaniel, 90, 290, 323
Hazlitt, William, 370
Heard, Gerald, 242
Hearn, Lafcadio, 125
Heart of Darkness, 291
Heaven's My Destination, 187
Hecht, Ben, 77, 79
Heidegger, Martin, 400, 403
Heine, Heinrich, 241
Hélas!, 374
Hemingway, Ernest, 41–49, 80, 81, 96–101, 132, 145, 186, 190, 196–206, 212, 216, 217, 219, 222, 223, 227, 242n., 266, 405, 425
Henry IV, 279–84
Henry V, 280, 281, 282
Henry, O., 40, 260
Hepburn, Katharine, 208
Hergesheimer, Joseph, 78, 81
Herriman, George, 52, 53
Hichens, Robert, 289
Hicks, Granville, 189, 204
Hippocrates, 95
History of Elizabethan Literature, 362
History of English Prose Rhythm, 360
History of Russian Literature, 418
History of the French Novel, 360–61
Hitchcock, Alfred, 343
Hogg, James, 362
Holiday, 79
Holmes, Oliver Wendell, 307
Homer, 95, 152, 156
Hope of Heaven, 220, 221, 222, 243, 243n.
Hopes of the World, 411
Horace, 152
Horseshoes, 40
Housman, A. E., 85, 284
How about Europe?, 161
Howells, William Dean, 22, 90, 126, 382

How Love Came to Professor Guildea, 289
How to Abolish the Slums, 165
How to Write Short Stories, 37
Hoyt, Nancy, 109
Huckleberry Finn, 39, 40, 81, 145
Hueffer, Ford Madox, see Ford, Ford Madox
Hugo, Victor, 12, 13, 20, 320, 343
Hull, Helen R., 289
Humanism: An Essay at Definition, 146–53
Humanism and America, 146
Hume, David, 169
Humility of Common Sense, The, 153–60
Huneker, James, 66, 83
Huston, Walter, 254, 255
Huxley, Aldous, 172, 237–38, 241–42, 408
Huysmans, Joris-Karl, 73, 116
Hyde, H. Montgomery, 379

Ibsen, Henrik, 263, 320
Ideal Husband, An, 374
Iliad, 149
I'm a Fool, 38
Imaginary Interviews, 337
In Dubious Battle, 230, 231, 234–35, 238
Ingoldsby Legends, The, 362
In His Steps, 311
Innes, Michael, 339
In Our Time, 41n., 43, 44, 45–48, 80, 97, 99, 100, 198
International, The, 131
Intruder in the Dust, 422–24, 426–27, 431
Investigations of a Dog, 394–95
Irving, Washington, 317, 318, 320, 321
Isherwood, Christopher, 314
I Should Have Stayed Home, 217, 243

Jabberwocky, 298
Jacobs, W. W., 293
James, Henry, 22, 77, 90, 91, 92, 219, 292, 293, 306, 382
James, M. R., 293, 294
James, William, 84
James Lee's Wife, 18
Jannings, Emil, 208
Jebb, Richard C., 146
Jeffers, Robinson, 243
Jefferson, Thomas, 317, 318
Jennifer Lorn, 88, 109, 111
Johnny Bear, 236
Johnson, Samuel, 51, 282, 328–33

Johnston, Alva, 206–8, 210, 211
Jolly Corner, The, 292
Jolson, Al, 57
Jonson, Ben, 302
Jowett, Benjamin, 146, 268
Joyce, James, 20, 52, 56, 77, 79, 116, 117, 156–57, 193, 295–302, 343, 391, 425
Julius Caesar, 282
Jurgen, 78
Justice, 264

Kafka, Franz, 294, 295, 389–97
Kafka Problem, The, 390, 391
Kafka's Prayer, 390
Karloff, Boris, 287
Kashkin, I., 198, 199, 200–1, 202, 203
Kaufman, George S., 210, 248, 253
Kaye-Smith, Sheila, 303–9
Keats, John, 31, 69
Kecskemeti, Paul, 401, 403
Keynes, John Maynard, 21
Kierkegaard, Sören, 394
King John, 283
Kings Row, 277
Kipling, Rudyard, 226, 229, 232, 251, 291–92, 293, 302
Knight, Eric, see Hallas, Richard
Kovalevsky, Sonia, 117
Krazy Kat, 51, 52, 56, 57, 63
Kreymborg, Alfred, 87
Krutch, Joseph Wood, 66–68, 71, 72, 97, 99, 329–33, 339, 342
Kubla Khan, 74, 106
Kukla, Fran, and Ollie, 61
Kuzminskaya, Tatyana A., 413–22

Labouchère, Henry du Pré, 370
Lady Chatterley's Lover, 113–17, 215
Lardner, Ring, 37–40, 48, 51, 52, 53, 56, 57, 77, 80, 81, 143, 222, 223, 284
Last Chance, The, 398
Last Days of Pompeii, The, 310
Last Tycoon, The, 248n.
Lathrop, George Parsons, 126
Laughton, Charles, 209
Lautréamont, le Comte de, 245
Lawrence, D. H., 113–17, 142, 231, 232, 322
Lawson, John Howard, 81, 128, 130, 131
Leacock, Stephen, 40
Leader of the People, The, 236
League of Frightened Men, The, 324, 325

Leaning Tower and Other Stories, The, 313–15
Lear, Edward, 55, 56
Learning How to Behave: A Historical Study of American Etiquette Books, 380
Leaves of Grass, 93, 366
Leavis, Queenie, 304
Lenin, Nikolai, 196
Leonov, Leonid, 333–38
Leopardi, Giacomo, 18
L'Etre et le Néant, 401
Levi-Civita, Tullio, 156
Levy, Oscar, 162
Lewis, Sinclair, 34, 38, 39, 40, 65, 69, 78, 79, 80, 96, 254
Lieven, Dariya Khristoforovna, de, 169
Life of Samuel Johnson, The, 328, 329
Ligeia, 71, 72
Light in August, 425
Li'l Abner, 63
Lindsay, Vachel, 85
Little Flowers of Saint Francis, 232
Lives of the Poets, The, 331
Living and the Dead, The, 225
London, 332
London, Jack, 243
Longfellow, Henry Wadsworth, 68
Long Valley, The, 230, 232
Loos, Anita, 143, 242
Lorentz, Pare, 242n.
Losses, 19
Lost Hearts, 289
Lost Lady, A, 276
Loved One, The, 358–59
Lovely Leave, The, 286
Love's Old Sweet Song, 227
Lowell, Amy, 86, 88
Lowell, James Russell, 68, 152
Lower Depths, The, 263
Loy, Mina, 42
Lubitsch, Ernest, 209
Lucian, 410

McAlmon, Robert, 42
McCoy, Horace, 216, 217, 218
McPherson, Aimee S., 247
McTeague, 243n.
Macaulay, Thomas, 302, 328–29
Machen, Arthur, 293
Machiavelli, Niccolò, 29, 108, 133
Mackail, J. W., 85
Mackenzie, Compton, 30–31, 34, 354
Madame Butterfly, 172
Made in U.S.A., 227, 229, 230
Maeterlinck, Maurice, 206

Maid Marian, 410
Main Street, 39, 40, 78, 96
Malesherbes, C. G. de, 15
Mallarmé, Stéphane, 73
Malraux, André, 171–78, 186, 337, 405
Maltese Falcon, The, 327
Manatee, The, 357
Manhattan Transfer, 129, 143, 157–58
Manning, Henry, 167
Man's Fate, 186–87
Mansfield Park, 304, 305–6
Man Who Came to Dinner, The, 252–53, 254
Many Marriages, 38
Mariés de la Tour Eiffel, Les, 56
Maritime History of Massachusetts, 85
Marius the Epicurean, 140
Mark Twain, 84
Marquand, John P., 382
Marsh, Ngaio, 339, 341
Marx, Karl, 21, 196, 401–4
Marx Brothers, 209, 210
Mason, Ronald, 408–9
Masters, Edgar Lee, 85
Maugham, W. Somerset, 339, 342, 343
Maupassant, Guy de, 100, 377, 378, 405
Mayakovsky, V. V., 194, 196
Medea, 56
Medina, Harold R., 23–25
Melincourt, 410, 411
Melville, Herman, 290, 291, 322
Memoirs of Percy Bysshe Shelley, 411
Mencken, H. L., 34, 39, 44, 49, 52, 56, 65, 68, 77, 81–82, 83, 88, 91, 92–96, 133, 136, 137, 162, 163, 180, 188, 255, 313
Mendel, Gregor, 156
Mendiant, Le, 12
Men without Women, 97
Merchant of Venice, The, 283
Meredith, George, 347, 411, 412, 413
Merry Wives of Windsor, The, 281
Metamorphosis, 294, 390, 393
Michelet, Jules, 168
Middleton, Thomas, 133
Millay, Edna St. Vincent, 30n., 88–89, 91, 190, 284
Miller, Henry, 211–16
Milne, A. A., 50
Milton, John, 152, 296, 297
Mirbeau, Octave, 116
Mirsky, D. S., 418

Mission to Moscow, 254–59
Miss Lonelyhearts, 245, 246, 247, 248, 358
Moby Dick, 92
Modern Love, 413
Modern Temper, The, 333
Molière, 53, 303
Monkey's Paw, The, 293
Montaigne, Michel de, 108
Moody, William Vaughn, 86
Moore, George, 106, 302, 308
Moore, Marianne, 86
Moral Philosophy, 85
More, Paul Elmer, 16, 22, 84, 90, 123, 146, 149, 150, 153–60, 327
Morella, 71
Morison, Samuel E., 85
Morley, Christopher, 51, 351, 352
Morse, Samuel F. B., 318
Mort dans L'Ame, La, 398n.
Morton, James J., 54–55
Morts sans Sépulture, Les, 400
Mother India, 161
Mouches, Les, 405
Mozart, Wolfgang Amadeus, 410
Mrs. Bathurst, 292
Mumford, Lewis, 68, 83
Murray, Gilbert, 85
My Old Man, 42
My Roomy, 38

Nathan, George Jean, 83, 180, 211, 226
Naval Treaty, The, 349
Nero Wolfe Omnibus, The, 324
Nerval, Gérard de, 106
Nesbit, Edith, 430
New Arabian Nights, 348
New England: Indian Summer, 320
Newton, Isaac, 95
Nicolson, Harold, 270
Nietzsche, Friedrich Wilhelm, 92
Nightingale, Florence, 167, 168
Nightmare Abbey, 407, 411
Nine Tailors, The, 340, 341
Norris, Frank, 243, 243n., 244n.
Northanger Abbey, 304
Nose, The, 294
No-Siree, The, 50
Notes on Democracy, 92–96
Not Quite Dead Enough, 324
Nouvelle Revue Française, La, 172

O'Brien, Edward, 43
Of Mice and Men, 230, 232, 233, 243n.
O'Hara, John, 212, 216, 219–22, 243, 243n.

Once in a Lifetime, 210
O'Neill, Eugene, 81, 148, 190
One of Ours, 43
Opinions of Oliver Allston, The, 320
Oppenheim, E. Phillips, 343
Opper, F., 53
Ordeal of Mark Twain, The, 321
Origines du Christianisme, Histoire des, 140
Orwell, George, 406
Oscar Wilde: His Life and Wit, 369
Oscar Wilde and Myself, 370–71
Ostrovsky, A. N., 414
Outline of Royalism, The, 134
Out of Nowhere into Nothing, 38
Out of the Deep, 294
Overture to Death, 341

Paine, Albert Bigelow, 351
Paine, Thomas, 370
Pale Horse, Pale Rider, 315, 316
Pal Joey, 222
Paradis Artificiels, Les, 16
Parker, Dorothy, 89, 284–87
Passage to India, A, 174
Pastures of Heaven, The, 231
Pater, Walter, 16, 81, 140
Patience, 371
Paul, 152
Peacock, Thomas Love, 362, 407–13
Pearson, Hesketh, 369–73, 374, 376, 377
Pericles, 207
Persuasion, 304–5, 308–9
Petrarch, 347
Phantom Rickshaw, The, 291
Phelps, William Lyon, 85, 227
Phidias, 152
Phillips, Mary E., 66
Picasso, Pablo, 52
Pickwick Papers, 251
Picture of Dorian Gray, The, 374, 378
Pigault-Lebrun, Charles Antoine, 361
Pilgrimage of Henry James, The, 120–21
Pilgrim's Progress, 396
Pippa Passes, 17
Pity the Tyrant, 227, 229–30
Plato, 95, 146, 150, 152, 159
Playing with Fire, 293
Pleasures of Peacock, The, 407–8
Plutarch, 213
Pocket Book of Mystery Stories, The, 287, 294

Pocket Mystery Reader, The, 287
Poe, 329
Poe, Edgar Allan, 65–76, 92, 93, 264, 290, 294, 295, 317, 318, 320, 321, 327, 348, 391, 397
Pollock, Frederick, 307
Poole, Ernest, 32
Pope, Alexander, 331
Porter, Katherine Anne, 313–17
Portrait of Mr. W. H., The, 374
Portrait of the Anti-Semite, 405, 406
Portraits in Miniature, 169–70
Post, Emily, 381–89
Postman Always Rings Twice, The, 216, 219
Potomok, Le, 55
Pound, Ezra, 16, 86, 137
Praed, Winthrop M., 362
Premature Burial, 75
Présentation, 400
Price's Always Open, 220
Pride and Prejudice, 303, 304, 308
Priestley, J. B., 408
Primer for Tomorrow, A, 21
Prince, The, 29
Principles of Modern Heresy, The, 134
Problems of the Chinese Revolution, 172
Profile by Gaslight, 347
Proust, Marcel, 20, 77, 102–5, 108, 202–3, 205, 343, 382, 383, 391, 399, 425, 426
Pursuit Race, A, 98
Pushkin, A. S., 255–56, 278
Putnam, Phelps, 87
Put Out More Flags, 269, 270, 271
Pylon, 423

Queensberry, Marquess of (John Sholto Douglas), 372, 373–74, 376
Queen Victoria, 170
Quintanilla, Luis, 200
Quo Vadis?, 310

Rabelais, François, 12
Racine, 169
Raphael, 95
Rascoe, Burton, 41, 42, 43, 44, 83, 189
Red Box, The, 324
Redman, Ben Ray, 407–8, 411–12
Red Pony, The, 233
Reed, Myrtle, 124
Reese, Lizette Woodworth, 88
Renaissance, The, 16
Renan, Ernest, 140

Reprieve, The, 398
Resurrection, 19, 420
Ricci, C. G., 156
Richard III, 264
Rimbaud, Arthur, 73, 245
Rise of Silas Lapham, The, 22
Roads to Freedom, The, 398
Road to the Ocean, 333–38
Roar, China!, 194
Robe, The, 309–13
Robertson, J. W., 66
Robinson, Edwin Arlington, 89–90, 91
Robinson, Henry Morton, 295–302
Robinson Crusoe, 349
Romains, Jules, 172
Rose Bernd, 263
Rosenfeld, Paul, 82–83
Ross, Mary, 277
Rousseau, Jean-Jacques, 14–15, 20, 147, 151
Rubens, Peter Paul, 95
Russell, Bertrand, 85

Sacco, Nicola, and Vanzetti, Bartolomeo, 122, 129, 150n.
Sacred Wood, The, 134
Sainte-Beuve,   Charles-Augustin, 170, 188
Saint Joan, 312
Saint Katy the Virgin, 232
Saintsbury, George, 15, 106, 359–63
Samuel Johnson, 329
Sanctuary, 423
Sandburg, Carl, 85–86, 87
Santayana, George, 28
Saroyan, William, 190, 216, 222–27, 243
Sartre, Jean-Paul, 398–407
Savage, D. S., 391
Sayers, Dorothy L., 339, 340, 341
Schlesinger, Arthur M., 380–82
School of Donne, The, 134
Schulberg, B. P., 211, 248
Science and the Modern World, 12, 160
Scoop, 268, 358
Scott, Walter, 302, 343
Scott-King's Modern Europe, 358
Sea Lions, The, 321–22
Seaton's Aunt, 294
Second Stain, The, 350
Seldes, Gilbert, 49–65, 83
Selections from the Works of Jean-Jacques Rousseau, 14
Sense and Sensibility, 304, 308
Serenade, 216, 218, 219, 243
Seton, Anya, 363–69
Seven Lively Arts, The, 49–58

70,000 Assyrians, 225
Seward, Anna, 370
Seylaz, Louis, 73, 76
Shakespeare, William, 12, 18, 19, 25, 81, 97, 152, 170, 207, 237, 255, 260, 278–84, 302, 306, 321, 331, 362, 370, 425
Shaw, George Bernard, 33, 34, 94, 266, 312, 370, 373, 374, 377
Shelley, Percy Bysshe, 19, 74, 100, 111, 411, 413
Sherard, Robert Harborough, 377
Sheridan, Ann, 277
Sherlock Holmes and Dr. Watson, 352
Sherman, Stuart P., 77, 188, 189
Ship That Found Herself, The, 229
Shorey, Paul, 84
Short View of Gamalielese, A, 255
Silence, 85
Simms, William Gilmore, 317
Simple Inquiry, A, 98
Sinclair, Upton, 124, 132, 155, 156, 229, 243
Sinister Street, 30–31
Sister Carrie, 78
Sitwell, Edith, 57, 87
Sitwell, Sacheverell, 102
Skeleton Key to Finnegans Wake, A, 295
Slosson, Edwin, 85
Smith, Sydney, 370
Snake, The, 231, 232
Socrates, 150
Sombart, Werner, 21
Some Like Them Cold, 39
Song of the Shirt, The, 286
Sophocles, 146, 147, 148, 149
Southey, Robert, 302
Speaking of Jane Austen, 303–9
Speaking of Operations, 37
Spengler, Oswald, 21, 108
Spoon River Anthology, The, 85
Stalin, Joseph, 211, 258
Statue and the Bust, The, 17
Stein, Gertrude, 41, 44, 45, 80, 197
Steinbeck, John, 216, 227, 230–39, 242n., 243, 243n., 244, 244n., 399–400
Sten, Anna, 209
Stendhal, Henri Beyle, 10
Stephen, Leslie, 360
Stern, G. B., 303–9
Stevens, Wallace, 87
Stevenson, Robert Louis, 70, 291
Stewart, Donald Ogden, 48
Storm, Hans Otto, 216, 227–30, 243, 243n., 244

Story, William Wetmore, 125
Story of Bras-Coupé, The, 126–27
Stout, Rex, 324–25, 327, 351
Strachey, Giles Lytton, 84, 105, 166–71
Strange Case of Miss Annie Spragg, The, 271
Strange True Stories of Louisiana, 127
Stratton-Porter, Gene, 313
Stravinsky, Igor, 52, 57
Sullivan, Arthur S., 370
Sun Also Rises, The, 97, 99, 100, 101, 114, 266
Sur la Pierre Blanche, 140
Sutton, Eric, 399
Swift, Jonathan, 81, 94, 96, 108, 294, 377
Swinburne, Algernon Charles, 16, 19

Taggard, Genevieve, 89
Taine, Hippolyte-Adolphe, 12, 196
Tales of Terror, 287
Tate, Allen, 87
Tchaikovsky, Peter I., 256
Teasdale, Sara, 88
Tempest, The, 279
1066 and All That, 357
Tentation de Saint Antoine, La, 16, 297
Terence, 138, 141
Thackeray, William Makepeace, 343, 362, 409, 412
Théorie de l'Intelligence, 196
They All Made Peace—What Is Peace?, 41n., 44n.
They Shoot Horses, Don't They?, 217
This Side of Paradise, 19, 30–33, 34, 36
Thoreau, Henry David, 22, 322
Those Not Elect, 89
Thousand and One Nights, 217
Three Lives, 45, 80
Three Stories and Ten Poems, 41, 44
Three Times Three, 225
Time of Your Life, The, 223
Tinker, Chauncey, 329
To a God Unknown, 232, 237, 239
To a Waterfowl, 321
Today's Etiquette, 381
To Have and Have Not, 212
Tolstoy, Alexandra, 416
Tolstoy, Leo N., 19, 97, 320, 413–22
Tolstoy as I Knew Him, 414
Toomer, Jean, 79
Torrents of Spring, The, 196

Tortilla Flat, 230, 231, 236, 239, 243
Toulouse-Lautrec, Henri de, 57, 63
Tragedy of Tolstoy, The, 416
Trembling of the Veil, The, 375
Tretyakov, Sergei, 194–96
Trial, The, 389, 391, 393, 396
Trials of Oscar Wilde, The, 379
Troilus and Cressida, 207
Trollope, Anthony, 301
Tropic of Cancer, The, 211–16
Trotsky, Leon, 172–74, 177
Trouble with Tigers, The, 224, 225
Turgenev, I. S., 118–19, 195, 196, 414
Turn of the Screw, The, 288, 292
Turquoise, The, 363–69
Twain, Mark, 39, 40, 81, 143
Twenty-four Hours, 271

Ulysses, 52, 108, 116, 117, 157, 193, 215, 295, 296, 297, 302
Uncle Tom's Cabin, 127
Undefeated, The, 97, 201
Uninvited, The, 289
Untermeyer, Louis, 77, 87
Up in Michigan, 46

Valéry, Paul, 73
Van Doren, Carl, 77
Vanity of Human Wishes, The, 332
Van Vechten, Carl, 79, 106
Vathek, 107
Vegetable, The, 36
Venetian Glass Nephew, The, 109
Verlaine, Paul, 19, 73, 89
Verrall, A. W., 280
Vesalius, Andreas, 95
Victoria, Queen, 167–68
Victorian Doctor, 371
Vidor, King, 209
Vigny, Alfred de, 10
Vile Bodies, 265, 266
Villiers de l'Isle-Adam, Philippe Auguste Mathias de, 73
Virgil, 95, 108, 152, 156, 296
Viy, 290, 292
Voltaire, 169, 266, 359, 410

Walden, 92
Walkley, A. B., 83
War and Peace, 194, 271, 413, 415, 418, 419, 420
War of the Worlds, The, 62
Waugh, Evelyn, 265–71, 353–59
Weber, Joseph, and Fields, Lew, 54
Welles, Orson, 62

Wells, H. G., 135, 320
Werner, M. R., 84
West, Benjamin, 319
West, Herbert, 215
West, Mae, 209
West, Nathanael, 241, 242n., 245–48, 249, 358
Wharton, Edith, 91
What Became of Anna Bolton, 271–77
What Is Existentialism?, 400
What Maisie Knew, 306
What Makes Sammy Run, 248
What Price Glory?, 49
Whitehead, A. N., 12, 85, 149, 158–60
White Quail, The, 232
Whitman, Walt, 22, 63, 92, 331–32, 366
Whittier, John Greenleaf, 68
Who Killed the War-Veterans in Florida?, 204n.
Wilde, Jane, 370–71
Wilde, Oscar, 16, 17, 27, 369–80
Wilde, William, 370–71, 377
Wilder, Thornton, 102–8, 132, 138–41, 145, 187, 190, 222
Williams, William Carlos, 42, 87
William Wilson, 70–71

Willis, Nathaniel Parker, 317
Wilson, J. Dover, 278–84
Wilson, T. G., 371, 377, 378
Winner Take Nothing, 200, 203
Winters, Yvor, 321
Winter's Tale, The, 279
Wise, Herbert A., 287
Woman of Andros, The, 138–41
Woolf, Virginia, 302, 343
Woollcott, Alexander, 249–54, 260, 327
World of Washington Irving, The, 317–23
Wright, Harold Bell, 313
Wright, Lee, 289
Wright, Willard Huntington, 83
Wuthering Heights, 178, 306
Wylie, Elinor, 88, 109–13
Wynn, Ed, 55, 58

Yeats, William Butler, 372, 375, 376
Young, Stark, 302
You Play the Black and the Red Comes Up, 217, 240, 242

Ziegfeld, Florenz, 57
Zola, Emile, 116